The Dialectics of Exile

Comparative Cultural Studies
Steven Tötösy de Zepetnek, Series Editor

Comparative Cultural Studies is a contextual approach in the study of culture in all of its products and processes. The framework is built on tenets of the discipline of comparative literature and cultural studies and on notions borrowed from a range of thought including literary and culture theories, constructivism, communication theories, and systems theories. In comparative cultural studies focus is on theory and method as well as on application. In comparative cultural studies metaphorical argumentation and description are discouraged. Colleagues interested in publishing in the series are invited to contact the editor, Steven Tötösy, at <clcweb@purdue.edu>.

Volumes in the series to date are:

Comparative Central European Culture. Ed. Steven Tötösy de Zepetnek. West Lafayette: Purdue UP, 2002. 190 pages, bibliography, index. ISBN 1-55753-240-0

Comparative Literature and Comparative Cultural Studies. Ed. Steven Tötösy de Zepetnek. West Lafayette: Purdue UP, 2003. 356 pages, bibliography, index. ISBN 1-55753-288-5 (ebook), ISBN 1-55753-290-7 (pbk)

Sophia A. McClennen, *The Dialectics of Exile: Nation, Time, Language, and Space in Hispanic Literatures.* West Lafayette: Purdue UP, 2004. 252 pages, bibliography, index. ISBN 1-55753-315-6

Sophia A. McClennen

The Dialectics of Exile

Nation, Time, Language, and Space in Hispanic Literatures

Purdue University Press
West Lafayette, Indiana

Copyright 2004 by Purdue University. All rights reserved.

Printed in the United States of America

Library of Congress Cataloging-in-Publication Data
McClennen, Sophia A.
 The dialectics of exile : nation, time, language, and space in Hispanic literatures / Sophia A. McClennen.
   p. cm. -- (Comparative cultural studies)
  ISBN 1-55753-315-6 (pbk. : alk. paper)
  1. Spanish American literature--20th century--History and criticism. 2. Spanish literature--20th century--History and criticism. 3. Exiles' writings, Spanish American--History and criticism. 4. Exiles' writings, Spanish--History and criticism. 5. Goytisolo, Juan--Political and social views. 6. Dorfman, Ariel--Political and social views. 7. Peri Rossi, Cristina, 1941– --Political and social views. 8. Nationalism and literature--Latin America. 9. Nationalism and literature--Spain. I. Title. II. Series.
  PQ7081.M3724 2002
  860.9'98'0904--dc21
                                                   2003012531

In memory of my grandfather, Henry R. Hope, who gave me the inspiration to follow my dreams, and for my mother, who gave me the courage to persevere.

Contents

Acknowledgments	ix
A Note on Citations and Translations	xi

Chapter One
Introduction ... 1
   Cultural Context and the Comparative Framework ... 5
   Keywords of Exile ... 14

Chapter Two
The Dialectics of Exile: Towards a Theory of Exile Writing ... 29

Chapter Three
Alien Nation ... 35
   The Politics of Nationalism ... 41
   The Theory and Practice of Exile and Nationalism ... 46

Chapter Four
Exile's Time ... 58
   Myths of Exile versus Myths of Fascism ... 74
   Crossing Time Zones ... 113

Chapter Five
To Be Is Not to Be:
Exile and the Crisis of Linguistic Representation ... 119
   Who Is the Author(ity)? ... 130
   What's in a Name? ... 150
   Postmodernism and the Crisis of Language: Politics or Play? ... 157

Chapter Six
Lost in Space: The Geography of Exile ... 163
   There's No Place Like Home:
   The Tension between Utopia and Dystopia ... 191

Chapter Seven
Culture Shock ... 204

Conclusion ... 222
Works Cited ... 225
Index ... 237

Acknowledgments

Two early events helped to shape the direction of this book and led me to study exile literature as a challenge to contemporary theories about cultural identity. The first experience took place while I was a graduate student at Duke. Jean Baudrillard came to lecture and he spoke about the Bosnian war. He lectured to a packed auditorium full of faculty and students, fascinated, yet bewildered, by his statements about the end of history and the flat, superficial culture of contemporary society. As I sat taking notes, Ariel Dorfman was in the adjacent seat, rubbing his eyes and fidgeting. When Baudrillard spoke about the farcical media coverage of events in Eastern Europe, Dorfman leaned over, grabbed my pen and wrote "PAIN" on the top of my notebook. Baudrillard could not account for the pain. His view of the world was unable to explain the reality of human suffering and the many ways that artists try to express such pain in their work. I knew then that I wanted to confront the playful way that exiles had been appropriated by theory and stripped of their tragic edge.

The second crucial experience took place over dinner with my father, Mohammad Sami. My father is Afghan and grew up in the desert, northwest of Kabul, before coming to the United States to pursue his studies. His life has been a painful example of the difficulties of living across two cultures. Yet, he is a proud man, proud of his heritage, despite the overwhelming prejudices people from his country face in the United States. I asked him during dinner about the nomads in Afghanistan. Did they really have an existence that was unbound by geography? He looked at me with surprise, shocked at the suggestion. His description of their life, as he had observed it, gave me an important insight into the way that the nomad, just like the exile, had been co-opted by postmodern theories as representative of a life free of pain and confining boundaries. Careful understanding of the conditions of the exile or the nomad leads to a practical denial of theoretical claims that represent these experiences as utopic.

These two experiences have helped to frame my interests in this book, but without the help, encouragement, and insights of friends, colleagues, and family I would never have been able to turn my interests into what you are reading today. When I began this project I was interested in exploring my combined interests in history, literature, and philosophy as they relate to the case of exile. As a student of philosophy and Hispanic culture at Harvard, I have to thank my professors Stanley Cavell, Carlos Fuentes, and Luis Fernandez-Cifuentes for teaching me that the interactions between these fields were not only fascinating, but were also an inescapable part of my intellectual curiosity.

As a graduate student at Duke in the Department of Romance Studies I was provided with a supportive environment that encouraged me to continue to work on these issues. Many thanks to Fred Jameson, Walter Mignolo, Alberto Moreiras, and Stephanie Sieburth, who all read earlier versions of this book and gave me valuable comments. I still reap the benefits of the intellectual exchange I was able to forge with my fellow students, Alex Fitts and Christina Tourino, who gave me patient and detailed comments on this manuscript. I am especially grateful for the continued commitment of Christina to this project. Her unwavering faith in me has been crucial. I would also like to thank Natalie Hartman and Sharon Mújica, of the Duke-UNC Program in Latin American Studies, for the many ways in which they helped me.

Neil Larsen has been especially supportive and his enthusiasm after reading early pieces of my argument helped to support me through this process. Thanks also to Vassos Argyrou, who read and carefully commented on the manuscript.

While conducting research in Spain and the Southern Cone many writers and critics, especially Carlos Franz, shared their thoughts and personal experiences with me and for that I am extremely grateful. I was also fortunate to receive funding for this book from the Tinker Foundation, The Program in International Studies and the Department of Romance Studies at Duke University, The Duke-UNC Program in Latin American Studies, Illinois State University, and the National Endowment for the Humanities.

Portions of this book relating to Ariel Dorfman have been previously published in the *Review of Contemporary Fiction*. I would like to thank them for permission to reprint those sections here.

While teaching at Illinois State University I was fortunate to have the support and guidance of a number of colleagues. Valentine Moghadam, Maria Pao, Ronald Strickland, and James Van der Laan all helped to create a lively and engaged intellectual environment for my work. Diane F. Urey has been an exceptionally supportive mentor and friend. Her enthusiastic readings and incisive comments helped shape this manuscript. Our scholarly collaboration and intellectual exchange have been one of the most satisfying experiences of my academic life.

Ariel Dorfman's commitment, guidance, and friendship have been a never-ending source of inspiration and strength. Early in the process, he patiently helped me to clarify my thoughts. He has been extremely dedicated to seeing this book take its final form and has been a careful and exacting reader.

Later in the process, I had the good fortune to meet Steven Tötösy, who has been a wonderful mentor, editor, and friend. His dynamic and passionate commitment to forging the field of comparative cultural studies led to this series, Comparative Cultural Studies, with Purdue and I am grateful for his vision and dedication, without which this book might not have found such an excellent home.

There have been many students who have helped me to refine and rethink my research. Many of my students have also been invaluable reminders of why I began a career in academia and they have helped me to continue to balance theory with practice. A number of students, though, have been an especially encouraging source of energy and inspiration. Among them I would like to mention Bridget Fahrner, Carrie Koberiecki, Deanna Kohrs, Stephanie Nabor, Ericka Parra, Pablo de la Rosa, and Tasha Walston.

While working on this, I have had the support of my family, especially my mother and my brother and I am thankful for the ways that they helped me to balance my life and keep things in perspective. My husband, Henry, has been an extraordinary gift. He is supportive in every way. His dedication to reading chapters late at night, his unending enthusiasm, and his sense of humor kept reminding me of his love and support when I needed it most.

A Note on Citations and Translations

At the first mention of each literary work, I give the Spanish title, followed by the title in English, in italics (or quotation marks) if a translation is available, in roman type (without quotation marks) if it is not. Subsequent references to the text only use the Spanish title of the work, except in the case of Ariel Dorfman's *The Last Song of Manuel Sendero*, since I have chosen to use the English version as my primary source. Page references are given in the text for all citations. When a page number follows the English translation, it refers to the published translation. When the translation into English does not have a page reference, the translation into English is mine.

CHAPTER ONE
Introduction

My research on exile began in the late 1990s and coincided with an increased scholarly interest in the exile as a metaphor for a new phase of social alienation. We heard of the theorist as exile, of inner exile, cultural migrancy, nomadism, dislocation, etc. The exile floated through texts by Gilles Deleuze and Félix Guattari, Jacques Derrida, Edward Said, and Homi Bhabha, spilling onto the pages of many analyses of particular literary works. Much in the same way that the term "diaspora" has come to refer to people without national ties, the exile was, and often still is, described as being free of the repressive state of national identity.

There are two flaws to this line of thinking. First, even if it were possible to experience a purely transnational existence, most of us recognize that globalization does not lead to a power-free, liberated, multicultural state of being. Second, the exile's material existence in a world that requires visas, passports, and so on, in a world, that is, where the exile is forbidden to cross particular geographical boundaries, cannot be understood as existence free of the repressive nature of nationalism. I found that in many scholarly works the term "exile," having lost its reference to a painful state of being, was empty of history and an association with material reality.

Consequently, this book is dedicated, in part, to reconciling the exile of theoretical discourse with concrete cases of exile from repressive authoritarian regimes. Amy Kaminsky, in *After Exile*, echoes my concern that the "exile" of recent theory has tended to disregard the condition's necessary association with anguish and loss (xi). Angelika Bammer also calls attention to the need to reinsert historical particularity into discussions of displacement and she hopes to "refocus attention on that which too abstracted and metaphorized a notion of displacement has displaced, if not repressed, and that is history" (xiii). Emphasizing the need to read theory through context, this book illustrates how the work of exiles in the latter part of the twentieth century indicates the empirical limits of many abstract claims (such as those of a free-floating, anti-historical, incommunicable, untraceable, relativistic identity) found in certain postmodern theories that associate writing and cultural identity with exile. Through a detailed examination of the work of exiled writers who were chosen precisely for their dense, complex, and conflicted literature, this book highlights the extent to which such literature resists many critical categories. Due to their challenge of certain theories of cultural identity, the texts I analyze test the boundaries created by contemporary criticism and call for their rearticulation and remapping. *The Dialectics of Exile* explores the ways in which these writers depict cultural identity as caught between abstract theories of boundary-free identity, the politics and problematics of representation, and the painful realities of exile, authoritarianism, and social marginalization.

While my starting point for this book sprang forth from the conviction that exile writing challenges certain conclusions central to contemporary cultural theories, my research of exile criticism led me to further recognize the need for a theory of exile writing that could account for its complexity and inherent contradictions. The history of exile literature is as old as the history of writing itself. Despite this vast and varied literary tradition, criticism of exile writing has tended to analyze these works according to a binary logic, where exile either produces creative freedom or it traps the writer in restrictive nostalgia. Either scholars suggest that exile is a creative and liberating state, which enables the writer to function freely of the limitations of the local or the national, or they argue that exile literature is profoundly nostalgic and yearns for the lost nation (see Guillén; Seidel). Exile either causes creative freedom and reflects a global aesthetic or it results in heightened provincialism and literary regionalism. Exile writing is either global or it is national. In "On the Literature of Exile and Counter Exile" Claudio Guillén describes two categories of exile writing: exile (nostalgic) and counter exile (creative). Even though he suggests that many texts may fall along a spectrum between these two positions, his theory does not account for texts that might hold these concepts in tension. Later in *Múltiples moradas*, Guillén further elaborates on this theory and suggests that exiled writers can be described as solar (referring to Plutarch) if they tend to look up towards the sun and the stars, or they can look within (like Ovid) and focus on loss (29–30). While Guillén does not draw this connection between his two tendencies, we might describe his categories as the difference between the exile who looks up at the sky and sees that he shares the same sun as the rest of the world, or the exile who looks down and sees that he no longer stands on the same ground. Once again, the literature of exile is characterized as either universal or local.

Reading a number of texts from Spain and Latin America by exiled writers, I found that rather than favor one side of a binary, many texts actually presented both sides of these dialectics in irresolvable tension. I ultimately chose to focus on three exemplary writers: Juan Goytisolo (Spain), Ariel Dorfman (Chile), and Cristina Peri Rossi (Uruguay). I use these cases to argue for a theory of exile writing that reflects these tensions and refuses to overemphasize only one facet of the exile's complex cultural condition. My overall argument is that the literature of exiles contains a series of dialectic tensions revolving around central components of the exile's cultural identity: nation, time, language, and space. Understanding the exile's experience of nation as dialectical allows us to account for the tensions between nationalism, transnationalism, globalization, counternationalism, and anti-nationalism present in exile texts. Regarding time, writing about the exile experience reflects the fact that the exile has been cast out of the present of his or her nation's historical time. This causes a series of dialectic tensions between different versions of linear/progressive/historical time and the experience that exile is a suspension of linear time. This suspension of linear time includes a sense that time is cyclical and primordial (linking exiles across the ages) and a sense that time is relative and fractured (casting the exile outside of meaningful/monumental time). Exiles tend to recognize that they are in exile due to specific historical events and yet, once outcast from that history, they begin to question the legitimacy of historical time. Furthermore, writers in exile typically are forced to leave their countries precisely because of their relationship to, and use of, language. Consequently, they see language as both a source of power and a source of pain. They appreciate language's ability to fuel the imagination just as they realize that dictatorships manipulate language (through censorship and propaganda) in order to quell independent thought. The dialectics of language for the exile relate to contradictory depictions of language as regional or universal, meaningful or meaningless, powerful or useless, authoritarian or liberating, communicative or misleading, and so on. The fourth dialectic tension I analyze relates to space. Exiles describe the spaces in which they live as liberating and also confining. Their depictions of "imagined communities" either are comforting and capable of solidarity or threaten to repress difference and destroy the individual (see Anderson). It is noteworthy that the dual gestures of narrating utopic and dystopic spaces are common in exile writing. Consequently, spatial dialectics in exile writing relate to many factors regarding both real and imagined territories of existence. I have dedicated a chapter to analyzing the dialectics of exile as they relate to each of these four key categories of identity, followed by a chapter that applies these concepts to the cultural identity of the exile.

While these categories of analysis are central to any investigation of the experience of exile regardless of historical moment or regional origin, they obtain to each particular case of exile in specific ways. One of the key dialectics in exile studies is the tension between the universal, transhistorical, and shared elements of exile writing and those elements that are historical, regional, and personal. Even though I hope that the theory I propose will be useful to future studies of exile culture, such an application will require that significant attention be paid to the specificities of each case of exile studied. For the purposes of this book, I have narrowed my historical moment to the latter part of the twentieth century and I have chosen to focus on the three writers mentioned above: Juan Goytisolo, Ariel Dorfman, and Cristina Peri Rossi. The following analysis does not exhaust the interpretive potential of the field of contemporary exile: it serves, rather, as a springboard to future work. As Bammer suggests, "the separation of people from their native culture through physical dislocation... is one of the most formative experiences of [the twentieth] century" (xi). The task of analyzing, understanding, and remembering the experiences of these displaced peoples has only just begun.

Even though the following analysis centers on three writers, their shared characteristics illuminate certain issues that are common to other exiled writers from the same time period. The dialectics of exile in the latter part of the twentieth century reflect two intertwined and inseparable historical transformations. First, the concept of the nation has been radically altered as a consequence of the increasing globalization of capital and the corresponding reduction in national sovereignty. Michael Hardt and Antonio Negri claim, "in step with the processes of globalization, the sovereignty of nation-states, while still effective, has progressively declined" (xi). Exiles after 1960 are thrust from the nation and must become global citizens at a time when nationalism is undergoing significant revision. They are also exiled from dictatorships that came to power not through purely national political developments, but rather as a consequence of international interventions and covert operations. The unmasking of the lost sovereignty of the nation-state leads them to recognize the ways that global pressures have often determined local power structures. (For instance, Cristina Peri Rossi's writing is greatly influenced by Michel Foucault's theories of power and social control.) Second, exiles after 1960 were separated from their home, language, and cultural centers in the same historical moment that theories of cultural identity were being recast in light of postmodernism. The skepticism of certain strands of postmodern thought, the fractured language of poststructuralism, and the questioning of all master narratives of cultural identity converge on this generation of exiles and influence their writing. If the exile represents cultural identity as fragmented, does that indicate an affinity with postmodern theory? Alternatively, does narrative fragmentation represent an effort to reconstitute the multicultural national experience endangered by forced cultural unification under authoritarianism? Or, does narrative fragmentation reflect the exile's sense of loss and cultural separation? To what do we attribute the fragmentation of narrative in these exile texts? Perhaps the answer is that each of these issues plays a role. The following analysis will demonstrate how all of these factors intersect and intertwine, dialectically, in the narrative of these writers.

The selection of these three particular writers allows for a comparative study of certain shared features of exile, not the least of which is the common bond of Hispanic culture and the long legacy of Hispanic exile. It has been suggested that the history of Hispanic literature is a history of exile. Beginning with the famous epic poem of *The Cid*, each literary movement throughout the history of Spain and Latin America has been marked by exile. Gloria da Cunha-Giabbai suggests that exile has been one of the strongest links among Hispanic authors across all ages (27). In the twentieth century, many Hispanic writers have been forced into exile by their nations' regimes. The dictatorships of Francisco Franco (1939–75) in Spain, Augusto Pinochet (1973–89) in Chile, and the military government of Uruguay (1973–85) represent only a portion of the authoritarian regimes from which many exiles fled. Even though the nation-state had long been formed, the twentieth-century exiles were often expelled from countries that were difficult to define. The political struggles of the twentieth century in Spain and Latin America were often specifically tied to efforts to redefine the nation, and we find a consistent tension between conservative efforts to homogenize national culture and progressive efforts to pluralize it. Consequently, the cultural background of these authors was not fixed, unified, or homogenous. Noting fragmentation or a plurality of discursive voices in their narratives, then, does not imply that they are rejecting ties to their nations' past. Because the work of these authors resists conventional forms of literary and critical categorization, they best depict the crisis of cultural identity produced through contemporary exile. Moreover, the writers chosen for analysis represent a highly varied exile experience. Differences of national origin, gender, sexuality, political involvement prior to exile, and literary concerns among these writers allow me to claim that their suggestion of an alternative theory of cultural identity is highly significant. Through comparative analysis of how the dialectics of exile represent a crisis of cultural identity in the work of Goytisolo, Dorfman, and Peri Rossi, this book seeks to generate a theory of exile that moves beyond the current theories of exile offered by both cultural studies and exile studies.

CULTURAL CONTEXT AND THE COMPARATIVE FRAMEWORK

> *Innumerables, los desterrados. Repetida, reiniciada un sinfín de veces, interminable, la experiencia del exilio a lo largo de los siglos. Sin embargo, ésta cambia. Se modifican las consecuencias, sus dimensiones, sus acentuaciones y desequilibrios. No cabe poner en duda la importancia de los condicionamientos históricos que modelaron en su día una experiencia tan específica, tan inextricablemente unida al devenir político y social de los pueblos.*
>
> *Innumerable, the exiles [desterrados]. Repeated, reinitiated endless times, interminable, the experience of exile throughout the centuries. Nevertheless, the experience changes. The consequences, dimensions, accentuations, and imbalances are modified. There is no doubt of the importance of the historical conditions that shaped in their day an experience so specific, so inextricably linked to the political and to the social evolution of nations.*

With these words, Guillén opens his analysis of exile writing in *Múltiples moradas* (29). He explains that a comparative study of exile must strike a careful balance between historical specificity and repetitive structures found in narratives of the exile experience. In each chapter to come, I will point to elements of the exile experience particular to the cases studied, just as I will draw lines of comparative connection. For those readers unfamiliar with the history of Spain, Chile, or Uruguay, or with the background of Goytisolo, Dorfman, or Peri Rossi, the following section explains relevant aspects of these writers' cultural context.

Comparative studies between Spanish and Latin American authors have never been common practice. Despite shared connections of culture, historical development, religion, and language, the legacy of colonialism has hindered the development of comparative studies in two significant ways. One major obstacle to comparisons between Spanish and Latin American culture is a consequence of postcolonial theories that argue for the incommensurability of postcolonial and post-imperial culture. Theories of the postcolonial have been a dominant voice in contemporary arguments about the separation of cultural production between the First and Third World. (Aijaz

Ahmad's *In Theory* is an excellent survey of this debate as well as a critique of it.) As a result, among Latin American countries comparison is common, even though such comparisons have often been marginalized by traditional comparative literature because the works analyzed are typically in the same language (see McClennen, "Comparative Literature and Latin American Studies"). The difference between cultural production from a Caribbean country like the Dominican Republic and a South American nation like Argentina can be as significant as the difference between Spanish and Latin American culture. The comparison between the two Latin American countries, because of the commonality of postcolonial experiences, is generally considered more viable. Certainly, the imperial history of Spain separates it, on one level, from the colonial experience of Latin America. Yet both regions share cultural hybridity, uneven historical development, religion, and language, to name only some of the most obvious links.

A second challenge to Spanish and Latin American comparison relates to scholarly formation. Academic study of Hispanic literature in the United States was dominated in the 1940s by texts from Spain. The valorization of Spanish literature over Latin American began to shift later as a direct consequence of the exile of Latin American intellectuals who came to the United States and worked as professors. The Spanish Civil War exiles that had taken refuge in U.S. universities after 1939 were slowly replaced by a new generation of exiles from Latin America, beginning with the Cuban diaspora of 1960 (Kaminsky xvii–xviii). According to Emily Apter, comparative literature "is unthinkable without the historical circumstances of exile" (86). Certainly, the condition of exile has had a direct impact on U.S. study of Hispanic literature, since shifts in objects of study were initiated by new waves of Hispanic exiles. Nevertheless, comparative approaches to Hispanic texts are not as common as one might expect. Even though scholars are attentive to Spanish influences on Latin America and vice versa, we rarely engage in transatlantic comparative study. This trend, though, has begun to shift, especially as a consequence of increasing attention to Transatlantic Studies, which seek to understand cultural interaction between the Americas and Europe (see Ortega).

As is the case with any comparative study, one must be careful not to erase significant differences. Exiled writers from Latin America invariably respond to the legacy of colonialism and its concomitant structures of social power that left their imprint throughout the region. In the cases of Goytisolo, Dorfman, and Peri Rossi we find that all three writers have a complex connection to a European and Latin American heritage. In the mid-nineteenth century Goytisolo's great-grandfather traveled to Cuba from the Basque region, while the island was still a Spanish colony, in order to seek his fortune. A slave owner, he became wealthy in the sugar cane industry and he eventually established his family in Barcelona. Goytisolo learns about this aspect of his family's past shortly after the end of the Spanish Civil War (1939), as his family begins the process of recuperating their home from the Republicans, who had taken it over to use as a residence for orphaned children. Goytisolo recounts this tale in the introduction to *Pueblo en marcha* (A Country on the Move), which narrates his experiences traveling in Cuba shortly after the Revolution of 1959. The inheritance of family ties to colonization and slave ownership marks Goytisolo deeply and arouses an early social conscience. According to Randolph Pope, "Great-grandfather Augustine's creation of the Goytisolo family fortune by exploiting black labor in the paradisiacal island of Cuba in the mid-nineteenth century is Juan Goytisolo's original sin, an inborn inheritance he has felt the need to redeem through a life of searching and discipline" (*Understanding* 1–2). Goytisolo's impression of Cuba changes from romantic idealization as a boy to mature political interest as a university student. As he revisits photographs and letters associated with the plantation he increasingly feels disgusted by his legacy. Goytisolo recounts this transformation: "Bruscamente, mi respetabilidad burguesa me horrorizó. El simple nombre de Cuba constituía un reproche, y la conciencia de mi culpa y de la culpa de mi estirpe y de mi clase y de mi raza, me abochornaron" (723–24) ["Suddenly, my bourgeois respectability horrified me. The simple name of Cuba constituted a reproach, and the consciousness of my guilt and of the guilt of my lineage and of my class and of my race, embarrassed me"]. Consequently, Goytisolo is acutely and critically aware of Spain's colonial past. Arguably he takes a postcolonial position in his writing; he repeatedly narrates alternative histories that challenge the glory of Spain's imperial past.

Ariel Dorfman's connections to Europe and Latin America are especially multifarious. Dorfman's parents were both Jewish immigrants to Argentina, although the circumstances of their arrival were quite different. Dorfman's mother, Fanny Zelicovich Vaisman, was born in 1909 in Kishinev, which belonged at the time to Greater Russia. After her maternal grandfather was murdered in the pogrom of 1903, most of the family began the process of immigrating to Argentina. Fanny was three months old when the family embarked on a ship from Hamburg to Argentina. Dorfman's father, Adolfo, was born in 1907 in Odessa, then part of Greater Russia, now part of the Ukraine. When Dorfman's grandfather's business went bankrupt, the family fled to Argentina to escape creditors. Later in 1914, Adolfo and his mother went back to Russia for a visit, where they were caught up in the Russian Revolution, causing them to stay. They later actively participated in the process of the revolution. But, as the violence and hardship worsened, they found it necessary to leave Odessa again in 1920 to return to Argentina. Dorfman's parents met each other in Buenos Aires and Dorfman was born in 1942. By then, Dorfman's father was a professor of Industrial Engineering in Buenos Aires. After a pro-Axis coup in 1943 took over in Argentina and stripped Marxist Adolfo Dorfman of his position as a professor, Dorfman's family moved to the United States, where Adolfo had received a Guggenheim Fellowship. They lived in the United States until 1954, at which point the political onslaught of McCarthyism reached the Dorfman house and Adolfo Dorfman found himself the subject, again, of political persecution. Adolfo fled to Chile and the family established itself in Santiago in 1954 (this information comes from Dorfman's memoir, *Heading South, Looking North*). These multiple migrations cause Ariel Dorfman to understand global power relations beyond a reductive colonial/postcolonial rubric. His family has been exiled (or compelled to emigrate) due to religious persecution, economic hardship, and political affiliation. Before Dorfman's exile from Chile, his family had moved from Europe to Latin America to Europe to Latin America to the United States and back to

Latin America. The United States provided a safe haven for the family in 1943 only to become hostile towards them in the 1950s. Dorfman's family was well aware of the irony of seeking refuge in the United States (a pattern that would repeat itself when Dorfman sought refuge from Pinochet in Washington years later, as the recipient of a fellowship at the Wilson Center): "My anti-imperialist father fled in December of 1943, to the United States, the most powerful capitalist country in the world, protected by a foundation built with money that had come from one of the world's largest consortiums" (24). These experiences affect Dorfman's sense that identity is marked by political, religious, economic, and cultural affiliations, in addition to national origin.

Cristina Peri Rossi tells Parizad Tamara Dejbord in an interview that she always felt closer to her mother's side of the family than her father's (218). Her mother's side is Italian, from Genoa, and according to Peri Rossi: "eran italianos típicos: el clan, la mafia, siempre todos reunidos, católicos, muy tradicional, de origen humilde y campesino" (218) ["they were typical Italians: the clan, the mafia, always together, catholic, very traditional, from humble, peasant origins"]. Peri Rossi's grandmother was conceived on a ship while the family was heading from Genoa to Montevideo. On her father's side, Peri Rossi's heritage is Basque and from the Canary Islands. While Peri Rossi does not explain the motives for her ancestors' decision to come to Uruguay, we can assume that they were part of the large tradition of Italians and Spaniards who came to the Southern Cone in the late nineteenth and early twentieth centuries to seek better economic opportunities. Uruguay had four or five major waves of European (principally Italian and Spanish) immigrants during the nineteenth century and the census from 1860 indicated that 35 percent of the population was foreign (Barran n.p.). Dejbord explains that Peri Rossi's family as members of the proletariat was very class conscious and that Peri Rossi was raised in an atmosphere attuned to issues of social exploitation: "Su padre fue un obrero textil que 'conoció los sinsabores de la explotación, del desempleo, la angustia económica continua, y la injusticia'"(53) ["Her father was a textile worker who 'knew the pain of exploitation, unemployment, continuous economic anguish, and injustice'"]. Similar to Goytisolo and Dorfman, Peri Rossi's family history leads her to recognize the intricate ways that identity is shaped by national and transnational affiliations.

When discussing the crisis of cultural identity caused by exile, a consideration of the connections between both national and international experiences is vital. Are exiles only influenced by a crisis in national identity? Or are they also affected by internationalism? How can cultural identity be both international and national? Many nations have been greatly affected by international events, suggesting that cultural identity cannot be understood as strictly a national construct. In particular, international developments have played a significant role in the development of cultural identity in Spain, Chile, and Uruguay. Not only do the personal family histories of Goytisolo, Dorfman, and Peri Rossi complicate an easy affiliation with national origin, but the nations from which they were exiled were also historically tied to international developments.

The international developments which give a certain commonality of experience to the exiles of the twentieth century fleeing authoritarian, corporativist governments are directly related to the conflicting ideologies of capitalism, socialism, and communism. Although capitalism masked itself as a primarily nationalist movement, it occurred on an international scale. In Marxism, descriptions of alienation, for instance, applied to the conditions of all workers and nationality was irrelevant. Spain's Second Republic (1931–36) suffered devastating division due to competing leftist positions affiliated with communism, socialism, and anarchism. The result was a bloody civil war leading to a Fascist-influenced dictatorship headed by Francisco Franco from 1939–75. In many ways, the Spanish Civil War reflected international conflicts that took place within a single nation's borders. Both the Germans and the Italians, in what many considered to be a rehearsal for World War II, actively supported the Nationalist side. The Republicans received aid from the Russians and thousands of men and women from across the globe joined in the Republican International Brigades. After his assumption of power, Franco's opposition to Stalin and his repeated attacks on the "communist threat" helped Spain avoid invasion by the Allies at the end of World War II (Ellwood 138). Speaking against the division of the globe into three worlds, Ahmad argues that at this same period all nations "witnessed the historically unprecedented growth, unification and technological power of capitalism itself" (20). The "capitalist zones of Europe" were made safe and, in Spain, Franco's government ensured that the threat of socialism was "contained" (22).

The international battle between capitalism and socialism occurred not only in Spain, but also in Latin America, where the threat of socialism greatly increased in the 1950s. Two decades after the end of the Spanish Civil War, the success of the Cuban Revolution in 1959 had an enormous impact on the hopes of Marxists across Latin America. In Uruguay the Tupamaro Guerrilla movement, named after an Inca warrior who had fought the Spanish conquistadors, rose in the 1960s and challenged the hegemony of capitalism. The Tupamaros were also influenced by the Chilean Socialists and, later, by the success of Salvador Allende, who was elected president of Chile in 1970. Both the Tupamaros and the Unidad Popular, Chile's Socialist party, challenged the capitalist structure of private property and the foreign ownership of national resources. In both countries, the security of the middle class and of capitalist economics was threatened and, consequently, socialism was eradicated by military regimes receiving foreign aid from the United States: Augusto Pinochet was dictator of Chile from 1973–89 and Uruguay was ruled by a military government from 1973–85. The connection to events in Spain is, again, notable. Exiles fleeing these countries left dictatorships that had risen to power as a consequence of foreign intervention. Moreover, the ideological foundations for these authoritarian regimes had ties to fascism, yet another international phenomenon. William Pfaff points out that, although fascism is considered ultra-nationalist, fascism and its authoritarian variations were also an international phenomenon.

The authoritarian attempts at cultural homogenization in Spain, Chile, and Uruguay led Goytisolo, Dorfman, and Peri Rossi to react by creating literary images that were fragmented and that transcended the merely national. Based on these observations, the comparative analysis of Juan Goytisolo, Ariel Dorfman, and Cristina Peri Rossi allows for an investigation into literary responses to anti-leftist politics. Moreover, similarities in narrative strategy, despite temporal and spatial shifts, sexual orientation, and gender difference, suggest that the literature of these exiles represents a much broader cultural phenomenon. Just as Franco's dictatorship was affected by international events, the U.S. government, especially through the actions of the CIA, enabled Augusto Pinochet's coup and the military regime in Uruguay. The exiles from each of these three authoritarian governments represented substantial portions of their nation's population and they were well aware of the international interventions that forced them to flee their nations.

The most massive wave of exiles from Spain left directly after the end of the Civil War. Those who remained in Spain had to endure the hardships of dictatorship. For writers, this translated into a complex and pervasive system of censorship. Goytisolo was a child during Spain's Civil War but became actively involved in a Socialist underground in his 20s. Because this generation of Spanish writers inherited the consequences of the Civil War and felt powerless to overthrow Franco, they are particularly sensitive to the notions of historical agency and an active subject. Referring to his generation, Goytisolo writes, "para los hombres y mujeres de dos generaciones sucesivas, más o menos dotados de sensibilidad social y moral, y para quienes la libertad de medrar o enriquecerse de forma más o menos honesta no podía satisfacer en modo alguno sus aspiraciones de equidad y justicia, las consecuencias del sistema han sido de un efecto devastador: un verdadero genocidio moral" (*España* 206) ["For the men and women of two successive generations, generally endowed with social and moral sensibility, whose hopes for equity and justice could never be satisfied by the freedom to thrive or enrich themselves more or less honestly, the consequences of the system have had a devastating effect: a true moral genocide"]. Goytisolo first leaves Spain for Paris in 1953 out of frustration and despair that he was unable to write and study in the oppressive Franco state. From 1953 to 1960 his relationship with Spain became increasingly strained. After his brother, Luis, was detained in 1960 and after the scandalous release of his documentary on the South of Spain, *Campos de Níjar* (The Countryside of Níjar), which depicted the extreme poverty of the region, he began the transition from expatriate to exile. In *Understanding Juan Goytisolo*, Pope details the impact of censorship on Goytisolo's decision to formally exile (25–31). Goytisolo also writes about the ways that censorship manipulated his writing in his autobiography *En los reinos de Taifa* (*Realms of Strife*). Like many writers he self-censored, anticipating the desires of the official regime: "such an exercise involved the writer in a painful self-mutilation, the devastating effects of which would be later revealed" (21). In order to be liberated from this system, Goytisolo decides on exile; yet his freedom comes at a cost: "they would ban everything I wrote in Spain up to the death of the dictator" (21).

After Goytisolo's exile from Spain in 1960, most critics recognize a transformation in his narrative style. (For a summary of the different periodizations of Goytisolo's narrative prior to exile, see Santos Sanz.) This shift is based on his desire to find a "new language" in order to challenge the social and economic structures of Spain. Goytisolo distanced himself from the literary production of politically committed writers still residing in Spain at a round table discussion in the 1970s at the University of Wisconsin: "En España, todavía hoy, la mayor parte de los escritores comprometidos que atacan la clase social que ocupa el poder (esta casta que controla los mecanismos del poder) emplean, sin darse cuenta, el mismo lenguaje que ella. Una misma retórica, aunque de signo opuesto" (qtd. in Sanz 88–89) ["In Spain, even today, the majority of politically committed writers that attack the social class in power (that caste that controls the mechanisms of power) uses, without realizing it, the same language. The same rhetoric, even though it signifies the opposite"]. Once in exile, Goytisolo sought a new narrative voice to critique the political situation in his country and this critique became less local. The critical analysis of the bourgeoisie seen in his pre-exile work *Para vivir aquí* (To Live Here) (1960) became multi-focal. Santos Sanz explains that "con *Señas de identidad* [his first novel published in exile] se intenta abarcar el conjunto nacional (obreros, clases medias, profesiones liberales; superestructura política, cultural, religiosa)" (95) ["with *Marks of Identity* [his first novel published in exile] he attempts to cover the entire nation (workers, middle classes, liberal professions; political, cultural, religious superstructure)"].

The experience of exile causes Dorfman, Peri Rossi, and Goytisolo to expand the object of their narrative in order to politically challenge local experience. Yet, while there are many similarities in the strategies of representation in Goytisolo, Dorfman, and Peri Rossi's work, it is important to recall that Goytisolo's exile occurs some ten years before that of Dorfman and Peri Rossi. By examining Goytisolo's "trilogy of exile," *Señas de identidad* (*Marks of Identity*) (1966), *Reivindicación del conde don Julián* (*Count Julian*) (1970), and *Juan sin tierra* (*Juan the Landless*) (1975), all novels which precede the exile literature of Dorfman and Peri Rossi, Goytisolo's work will be shown to be distinct because it more directly confronts the transition from modernism to postmodernism. Furthermore, the effects of childhood under Franco, the loss of his mother to the war, the sense of historical apathy common to his generation, and his critique of heterosexuality and consumerism are all features of his writing that set his work apart.

The success of Salvador Allende, elected Socialist President of Chile from 1970–73, had a profound effect on Dorfman's experience of exile. As a child, Dorfman's family had lived in Argentina and the United States and he arrived as a teenager in Chile. Because of his family's experiences with anti-Semitism and their itinerant lifestyle, the desire to belong is strong in Dorfman's work. It is precisely because he felt that he did belong to the Unidad Popular, Allende's party, that exile, for Dorfman, is particularly difficult. As he recounts in *Heading South, Looking North*, the decision to go into exile is especially painful. He cannot help but continue to imagine that he should have died with his comrades in Chile. Grinberg and Grinberg explain that exiles often suffer intense feelings of guilt and anxiety (156–65).

A series of events led Dorfman to formally seek asylum at the Argentine embassy. First, he witnesses the burning of his book *How to Read Donald Duck* on television; next, when he tries to visit a friend to seek his advice, he finds that the police have abducted him. Dorfman is still stubborn and procrastinates, hiding out within an underground network until he is explicitly told that he is worth more to the party abroad than in Chile (*Heading* 139–49). As he waits to gain entrance to the Argentine embassy, hiding out in the home of the Israeli ambassador, he watches through the window as his wife, Angélica, is picked up and questioned by two secret police after visiting him. It is the experience of seeing Angélica in such a perilous situation that causes Dorfman to realize that he has to get his family out of Chile. After that day he becomes reconciled to exile (175–77).

The utopian years of Allende made those working with the Unidad Popular experience a strong sense of historical agency, in contrast with the experience of Goytisolo. Nevertheless, exile forces Dorfman to rethink Marxist strategy for achieving economic and social change and it also calls into question the notion of historical agency. Once in exile, it becomes increasingly clear to Dorfman that the Unidad Popular was doomed by the requirements of transnational capitalism. National sovereignty was a myth. Alice Nelson, who interviewed Dorfman, explains: "After his exile, Dorfman experienced a tremendous difficulty in writing, as all of the structures used to describe reality before the coup seemed to fall along with the Utopian impulse of the Allende years" (n.10). By studying Dorfman's three novels written in exile, *Viudas (Widows)* (1981), *The Last Song of Manuel Sendero* (1986), and *Máscaras (Mascara)* (1988), in addition to poetry from his collection *Pastel de choclo (Last Waltz in Santiago)* (1986) the effects of exile on his literary aesthetics will become clear. Since his vision of utopia forms part of his memory of the past, of the one time when he felt that he truly belonged within a cultural community and was an active participant in history, his work is always marked by a deep sense of loss. On the other hand, unlike Goytisolo and Peri Rossi, Dorfman never loses hope. Even when faced with a seemingly ubiquitous capitalism, his novels tell stories of successful, although minor, resistance to official history.

Cristina Peri Rossi's collection of stories *Indicios pánicos (Panic Signs)* (1970) foreshadowed the repressive state that was to govern her country and force her into exile. The government in Uruguay was threatened by a rise in socialist sentiment while its economy continued to decline in the early 1970s. Consequently, the government moved progressively toward the repressive military state, which officially took power in 1973. Peri Rossi saw the connections between bourgeois values and authoritarianism in her country. Yet merely narrating these connections did not help her country to avoid full-scale dictatorship; it only caused her to flee into exile. Like Dorfman, Peri Rossi was reluctant to leave her home. Her early work was openly political and her notoriety as a political writer would have been enough to lead to her exile. Nevertheless, it is only after personal loss that Peri Rossi decides to flee her country. In March of 1972 Peri Rossi gave refuge to a young student, Ana Luisa Valdés, who was being pursued by the secret police. On the one day that Ana decided to venture out of the house she was picked up and never heard from again. It was then that Peri Rossi began to realize the extent of her dangerous situation and she made plans to leave Uruguay, arriving by boat in Barcelona in October of 1972. (For a detailed account of these events see Dejbord.) Her work, once she was in exile, continued to include a critique of bourgeois values, and like Dorfman's and Goytisolo's, this critique was changed formally. Graciela Mántaras Loedel explains that "el primer cambio que se advierte en la narrativa correspondiente al exilio se atañe al estilo" (5) ["The first noteworthy change in the narrative of exile is concerning style"]. As in the case of Dorfman and Goytisolo, her narrative shows signs of displacement and distanciation. Yet these changes also include a certain continuity. Like Goytisolo and Dorfman, Peri Rossi saw a need to expand the basis of her critique and to find a language that could challenge the authoritarian structures in her country. She explains: "Escribo contra la realidad. Empecé a hacerlo porque la realidad que veía a mi alrededor—en mi casa primero; luego en mi país—no me gustaba. Y sigo escribiendo, me parece, por la misma razón.... En ese sentido poco importa cuál sea la realidad geográfica" (qtd. in Basualdo 48) ["I write against reality. I began to do it because I didn't like the reality that I saw around me—first in my house; later in my country. And it seems to me that I continue writing for the same reason.... In this sense, geographical reality is not very important"]. What begins at home moves to the national level and later is applied to a transnational realm. The connection between identity, exile, and geographic space is problematized after these authors recognize that their national problems are global in scale. Struggle at the national level could not be successful because of the global reach of economic imperialism and its corresponding social ideology.

Exile provides a distinct perspective that causes these writers to alter their strategies of critique. While straightforward, totalizing critiques of their nations' political situations seem no longer viable, these writers do not respond by poststructural pessimism nor do they celebrate their alienation. Mabel Moraña explains in an article on Peri Rossi's first novel in exile, *La nave de los locos* (*The Ship of Fools*), that "Ante el espectáculo de la vida nacional escindida y la realidad del exilio propio, la alienación de la vida moderna, la problemática de la mujer y la sexualidad, la ficción de Peri Rossi abre una brecha en el intento por instaurar una nueva lógica comunicativa" (213) ["Before the spectacle of a divided nation and the reality of exile, the alienation of modern life, the problematic of women and sexuality, the fiction of Peri Rossi breaks through in its effort to establish a new communicative logic"]. Peri Rossi still seeks narrative communication after exile but she recognizes that such communication must be fragmented in order to address not only the oppression of a society based on capitalist ideology but also its ties to patriarchy and compulsory heterosexuality. By studying short stories from her collections *La tarde del dinosaurio* (The Afternoon of the Dinosaur) (1977) and *El museo de los esfuerzos inútiles* (*The Museum of Useless Efforts*) (1983), poems from her collections *Descripción de un naufragio* (Description of a Shipwreck) (1975), *Lingüistica General* (General Linguistics) (1979), and *Europa después de la lluvia* (Europe After the Rain) (1987) in conjunction with the novel *La nave de los locos* (*The Ship of Fools*) (1984), the influence of psychoanalysis on her writing will be clear. In her work, Peri Rossi combines the trauma of political exile with explorations into female subjectivity and sexuality. For her, exile is an experience registered differently from that of Dorfman and Goytisolo. As a lesbian and a feminist, Peri Rossi investigates the connections between patriarchy, heterosexuality, Catholicism, and the myth of male-biased historical agency from the perspective of deconstructive feminism.

These writers, unlike the exiled writers who preceded them, witnessed a crisis of representation due to the effects of postmodernism as well as authoritarianism. For instance, the Spanish Civil War exiles primarily attempted to represent their version of the Civil War through autobiographical narratives, like Rosa Chacel's *Desde el amanecer* (Since the Dawn), Ramón Sender's *Crónica del alba* (*Chronicle of Dawn*), and Arturo Barea's *La forja de un rebelde* (*The Forging of a Rebel*). In general, these narratives employed a realist/social realist style. Goytisolo's writing confronts these literary reactions to the dictatorship of Franco by attempting to create a new language and a new literary form. His work represents the crisis of culture in Spain, which persisted even after his literary predecessors' narrative efforts.

As in the case of Spain, exile literature is by no means a new form of cultural production to Latin America. Lucía Guerra Cunningham explains that "En el espacio no sagrado de la historia latinoamericana, el exilio originado por la represión política, la marginalización social y la alienación cultural es, sin lugar a dudas, la marca esencial de toda su producción literaria" (63) ["In the non-sacred space of Latin American history, exile caused by political repression, social marginalization and cultural alienation is, without a doubt, the essential brand of all of its literary production"]. Nevertheless, the exiles that follow the period of the master narratives of the boom faced the challenge not only of narrating the condition of exile, but also of finding their own distinct aesthetics: these writers were no longer interested in the construction of totalizing narratives. Elia Kantaris points out the differences between exile writing from the boom and the post-boom: "The mass expulsion of thousands of intellectuals from Chile, Argentina, Uruguay, and Paraguay, coupled with the rigorous, centralizing control exercised by the military in all areas of public communication, created the hostile conditions in which a new 'politicized' literature of exile nevertheless began to take root" (248). These three writers share the common bond of facing a political crisis and a simultaneous crisis of representation. The common narrative desire to find a new language with which to narrate their histories must be considered, in part, as a reaction to what they perceive as the failure of previous texts to create a narrative voice capable of threatening authoritarian rhetoric.

KEYWORDS OF EXILE

The terms used to discuss the exile's cultural identity are difficult to define. For purposes of clarity, I would like to outline the way in which the writing of exiles establishes real limits to the elasticity of terms often used in cultural theory. The following section elaborates on the complexity of these terms, relates them to the specific case of the exile, and explains the ways in which these terms will be used throughout this book.

Exile originates from the Latin "exilium," where the prefix "ex" means "out" and the root "solum" refers to "ground, land, or soil." The Latin "exilium" is also thought to relate to the Latin verb "salire," "to leap or spring." Already within the Latin etymology of the term we find the contradictory notions of exile as a movement forward and also a forceful separation. Paul Tabori's *The Anatomy of Exile* is dedicated to the historical and semantic variations of the condition and his analysis is a crucial starting place in understanding the term.

"Exile" contrasts with the notion of the *expatriate;* which is a term that also comes from the Latin "ex" but is combined instead with "patria" ("fatherland" or "native land"). Even though these words share a similar etymology, "exile" typically refers to one who has been forced to leave one's country, whereas "expatriate" suggests that the separation is voluntary. These two concepts are not always epiphenomenal, as in the case of the Argentine Julio Cortázar, who began his life in Paris as an expatriate and then became an official exile during the Argentine military regime. What is more, dictionary definitions of "exile" often include voluntary absence from the homeland. When "expatriate" is used as a verb, as in "to expatriate someone," it also suggests the forcible removal of a citizen from his or her country. Nevertheless, Tabori suggests that expatriate, when it is used as a noun, "emphasizes its voluntary character" (23).

Tabori points out that these terms are political and ethical, but not legal. Legally, the exile will be referred to as a *refugee*, originating in the Latin "refugiare" and meaning "to flee, run away, escape." The status of the refugee as a legal category is a relatively new phenomenon. "Refugee" refers to a necessary territorial displacement and consequently relates to the term *diaspora*. The etymology of "diaspora" comes from the Greek "diaspeirein," "to spread about," where "dia" means "apart" and "speirein" means "to sow or scatter." The term is often associated with the Diaspora of the Jewish people outside of Israel in the sixth century B.C. when they were exiled to Babylonia. About fifty years later, the Jews were offered return to their homeland, but many chose not to move. "Diaspora" was used to describe the spread of the Jewish people after the end of their official exile. These ancient roots of the term have been expanded in current usage to signify beyond the Jewish community. For instance, "diaspora" is used by Amy Kaminsky in *After Exile* to refer to the state of the exile after the end of the dictatorship. At present the term often describes the dispersion of an originally unified entity and is applied to cultural markers, like language and social practices, that were at one time geographically concentrated and are now deterritorialized.

"Exile," "diaspora," and "refugee" are generally considered to be terms related to forced dislocations, whereas *immigrant* and *emigrant* describe a person who *migrates, immigrates,* or *emigrates* by choice. All of these words have their roots in the Latin "migrare" ("to transport, move, depart, remove"), and *emigrate*'s prefix originates in the Latin "ex" meaning "out." Etymologically these words are not associated with choice, but rather with movement. A further noteworthy distinction is that "immigrant," "emigrant," "migrate," etc. are terms that are not linked with the land, in contrast to "exile," "diaspora," and "refugee." Even though immigrations are often considered to be voluntary acts, it seems that a more accurate distinction between the exile and the immigrant is between political or economic expatriation. These conditions overlap and the literature of immigrants can be interestingly compared with the literature of exiles. According to Leon and Rebeca Grinberg in *Psychoanalytic Perspectives on Migration and Exile,* migration and exile create similar problems for the transplanted individual, but the case of exile is "unique" because the exile's condition is involuntary and return is impossible (2).

As we turn to the ways in which these terms function in the Spanish language we find even greater variation and linguistic intricacy. Guillermo Cabrera Infante, a Cuban exile, writes of the absence of the word "exile" from the dictionary of the *Real Academia Española* (Royal Spanish Academy), an institution Cabrera Infante describes as the "Big Brother" of the Spanish language (36). Even though common usage Spanish included the words "exilio" (exile, referring to the condition) and "exiliado" (as a noun meaning "exiled person" or as an adjective), the *Diccionario de la Real Academia* did not include the word "exilio" until 1956, and then the definition only referred to the condition of exile and not to an exiled person (37). Cabrera Infante explains that under Franco, "Exiles simply didn't exist" (37). Consequently, it is not surprising that official dictionaries were reticent to record the many definitions of exile.

Today's version of the Royal Academy's dictionary does include all of the variations of the term "exilio" and also "expatriar" (to expatriate) and "expatriado" (the noun, expatriate). Cabrera Infante neglects to mention another keyword in Spanish to signal the state of exile: "destierro." The word "destierro" appears in the first section, "Cantar del destierro" (Song of Exile), of the famous epic poem *El Cantar de Mío Cid* (*Poem of the Cid*), whose first complete appearance dates roughly to 1140. As observed in this classic Spanish text, the Spanish lexicon has clearly favored "destierro" as the word of choice to describe forceful banishment and exile, with the word "exilio" appearing later and with more frequency in the twentieth century. "Destierro" has its root in the verb "desterrar," which is typically translated as "to banish" or "to exile" and comes from the prefix "des" (from Latin "dis," meaning "apart" or "asunder") and "tierra" (from Latin "terra," meaning "earth"). Guillén also highlights his predilection for the term "destierro" and its variations in the title of his chapter on literature and exile: "El sol de los desterrados" (The Sun of the Exiles) (29).

The variations of the word "desterrar" also relate to another common Spanish word, "desarraigar" (from Latin "dis" and "radicare," meaning "to take root" or "grow roots"), used to describe the state of exile; both words are defined in the dictionary of the *Real Academia* as the act of forcibly banishing someone from his or her native land and they both are represented by nouns that describe someone who has been cut off from his or her land and roots. Unfortunately neither "destierro" nor "desarraigado" is easily translated into English and the words typically appear in translation as "exile" for "destierro" and "banished" or "uprooted" for "desarriagado." The difficulty of translating these Spanish subtleties is especially interesting when we consider that Deleuze and Guattari's commonly used term "deterritorial" is a closer approximation, etymologically, to "desterrado" than "exiled." Of course, the way in which Deleuze and Guattari's "deterritorial" often signifies landless, rootless, or nomadic—in a celebratory fashion—separates its current use from the painful banishment inherent in the Spanish "destierro."

The experience of exile, banishment, and expatriation in its long and complex history has generated a vast lexicon in both Spanish and English. It is noteworthy that all of these terms are etymologically coded through their Latin and Greek prefixes as negatives or forceful separations—*ex-, dis-, dia-*. Their roots often refer to the land or to growth—*solum, patria, speirein, terra,* and *radicare.* These etymologies point to the forceful nature of the exile experience and the physical separation of an individual from home, land, culture, and/or roots. Even when the exile seems to have faced a choice between staying in his or her homeland and leaving, the actual departure from the nation represents a painful separation. Kaminsky writes that "exile" as she uses the term is "always coerced" and she considers the term "voluntary exile" to be an "oxymoron that masks the cruelly limited choices imposed on the subject" (9). Nevertheless, it is clear that certain exiles are considered to be more authentic than others and that each dictatorship or repressive regime produces "representative" exiles. For instance Juan Goytisolo is often considered to be a self-exile, since he was not forcefully thrown out of Spain, and some critics question whether his exile is "real." Furthermore, Cabrera Infante notes that Cuban exiles have repeatedly been absent from the mention of Latin American exiles and he refers to his status as "invisible exile" (34). I would counter such a limited and confined notion of the meaning of exile with the following query: If the state of exile is a result of the individual's perceived threat to the status quo, why should we expect the condition of exile to carry its own status quo? In my analysis I will not question whether the exile is authentic according to some rigid and authoritarian criteria. If exiled writers use "exile," or some variation of the word, to describe their condition, and if their writing attempts to represent the experience of exile, then these writers produce exile literature.

Postmodernism and *poststructuralism* are loaded terms that have been employed in a variety of ways. If all of the diverse uses of these terms could be said to hold one common element it would be heterogeneity and instability of meaning, making any definition of these terms extremely difficult. There are a number of excellent scholarly studies dedicated to analyzing the meaning of these terms and a detailed presentation of their intricacies is well beyond the scope of this present project (for introductory study see Connor; Eagleton; Best and Kellner; Jameson; Hutcheon; Harvey). That said, given that these concepts hold particular importance for the following study, I would like to sketch out a couple of key defining factors, especially since, as mentioned above, these theories have repeatedly relied on exile as an illustrative metaphor.

Poststructuralism is commonly understood as a critique of structuralism. The poststructuralists (such as Derrida; Barthes; Lyotard) challenged the systematic and scientific claims of structuralism and instead argued that signifying systems were endlessly variable. Steven Best and Douglas Kellner explain that "the poststructuralists gave primacy to the signifier over the signified, and thereby signaled the dynamic productivity of language, the instability of meaning, and a break with conventional schemes of meaning" (21). The poststructuralists focus on the way that the subject is formed through signifying systems, which themselves are in constant flux. Toril Moi summarizes Derrida's theory of language: "There is no final statement, no fundamental unit, no transcendental signified that is meaningful in itself and thus escapes the ceaseless interplay of deferral and difference" (*Sexual* 9). Consequently, poststructuralism, through its focus on the signifier, is concerned principally with representations, and meaning is forsaken in favor of mediation and imperceptibility.

Such a limitation of the term "poststructuralism" allows Best and Kellner to consider it as a "subset of a broader range of theoretical, cultural and social tendencies which constitute postmodern discourses" (25). Nevertheless, such lines of difference between poststructuralism and postmodernism are not so easily drawn. Earl E. Fitz explains that critics of poststructuralism, like Alex Callinicos, often divide it into subsets, such as "textualism" and "worldly post-structuralism" (3). For the purposes of this study, "poststructuralism" is used to refer to practices, like "textualism," that focus on the instability of signification; those theoretical approaches which take a broader view of sociopolitical issues are referred to as "postmodernism."

Postmodernism is often understood as a critique of modernism, similar to the way that poststructuralism is a critique of structuralism. Nevertheless, as David Harvey has discussed, postmodernism can be characterized as a rupture, a continuation/elaboration, or a commercialization/domestication of modernism (42). One of the key common components of postmodern critique is the questioning of meta-narratives, truth systems, social/signifying hierarchies, and the foundations of knowledge. These common categories are implied in the ways that the term is used throughout this book.

Postmodern and poststructural theory, *per se*, do not appear in Latin America until somewhat after their debut in Europe and the United States, but that should not lead us to believe that the ideas associated with these theories were not present well before their "official" arrival. The attempt to mark the appearance of poststructuralism and postmodernism in these regions is further complicated by Spain and Latin America's history of uneven modernity (see Sieburth; Ramos). Nestor García Canclini and Fernando Calderón have discussed the ways cultural practice and critical theory are present in Latin America according to hybrid temporalities, which means that we find pre-modern, modern, and postmodern culture existing together, complicating the ease with which postmodern culture is identified. Fitz, in his study of the work of Clarice Lispector, discusses the relationship between poststructuralism and Latin American (particularly Brazilian) writing, and he points out that the poststructural elements of Lispector's writing clearly pre-date the formulation of poststructural theory (2). He discusses the fact that Hélène Cixous considers Lispector to be the finest example of her theory of *l'écriture féminine* since she developed her theory *after* reading Lispector (22). Raymond L. Williams points out a similar pattern with the work of Jorge Luis Borges, who "became a seminal figure for both many European theorists and Latin American postmodern novelists in the 1960s and 1970s, even though the now-classic Borges fiction they were reading dated back to the 1940s" (13).

Regarding Spain, postmodern theory takes hold, according to Jo Labanyi, after Franco's death (1975) and a postmodern sense of the "end of history" is associated with the "desencanto" (disenchanted) years from 1979–82 ("Postmodernism" 396). Prior to Franco's death, Labanyi states, there was no development of postmodern theory in Spain, but there was "a body of postmodern writing before the term became current, with the *novísimos* and the New Novelists' pastiche of mass cultural forms and conversion of world culture into a museum, blurring the boundary between 'high' and 'low' culture" (398). Randolph Pope also suggests that postmodernism does not fully enter Spain until the death of Franco (*Understanding* 35). Nevertheless, many Spanish authors writing during the dictatorship, like Goytisolo, were often influenced by literary developments in Europe and Latin America. For instance, Pope speaks about Goytisolo's friendship with Carlos Fuentes and its effects on his writing (94). Goytisolo was also close with Severo Sarduy, the Cuban writer who was a member of *Tel Quel,* the literary magazine credited with launching poststructural theory. Goytisolo writes about his contact with French intellectuals, like Roland Barthes, in his memoir, *Realms of Strife.* Placing the advent of postmodernism within a certain time period in these areas is extremely tricky, but it is clear that writers in Spain and Latin America had been exposed to European and U.S. theories of postmodernism by the 1970s. (For postmodernism in Latin American writing see Colás; Lindstrom; Shaw; Williams; for Spain see Labanyi; Balibrea.)

A key division between theories of the postmodern, and one which holds particular significance for the following analysis, can be found within what might be called ludic postmodernism versus resistance or political postmodernism. Mas'ud Zavarzadeh discusses these two trends in postmodern theory in *Seeing Films Politically.* It now seems clear that there are two different camps of postmodern theory, even though they are not always patently distinct. Best and Kellner, in the conclusion of their study of postmodern theory, state: "we have stressed the differences between various postmodern theories and have pointed to an important distinction between an extreme wing of postmodern theory that declares a radical break with modernity and modern theory in contrast to another reconstructive wing that uses postmodern insights to reconstruct critical social theory and radical politics" (257). *Ludic* postmodernism stays at the level of play and does not mourn the loss of some of the ideals associated with modern theory, like democracy, enfranchisement, social agency, and collective government (see Ebert; Larsen). *Resistance* or *political* postmodernism is skeptical of some of the tactics associated with modern theory and questions modernist examples of revolution and political action, but has not renounced the need to seek theories and engage in politics that can lead to social change. Another crucial distinction between the ludic and the political forms of postmodernism is their understanding of the world beyond the text. Adherents to ludic postmodernism are principally interested in representations and do not seek to understand the ties between the text and its material context. In contrast, political postmodernism sees the connections between text and material context as central, where neither makes sense without the other.

This distinction is especially important when considering the work of authors from Spain and Latin America, since it is political or resistance postmodernism that is most often found in cultural and theoretical applications/appearances of postmodernism in exile writing. Raymond L. Williams reveals that, while in North America postmodernism has been divided between politically neutral or politically active camps, "Latin American postmodernism is resolutely historical and inescapably political" (17). He goes on to suggest that the political charge of postmodern writing in the region relates to the fact that the historical and the political have been central components in the development of the Latin American novel (17). Santiago Colás explains that those Latin American authors who critique meta-narratives might seem to be simply following Lyotard's lead, but such a conclusion would be mistaken, since these authors "produce various, different but fundamentally related, alternative analyses and strategies for the reworking of modernity's egalitarian goals on the concrete terrain of contemporary Latin America" (14–15). Postmodern cultural practice and theory in Spain, in contrast to Latin America, are far more ambivalent and Labanyi suggests that both ludic and resistance postmodernism can be found in the contemporary cultural scene (399). Nevertheless, the writing of exiles and other marginalized groups, in Spain and Latin America, tends toward resistance postmodernism, seeking new methods for challenging social structures.

A number of key elements of postmodern theory are particularly compelling for exiled writers. For instance, postmodernism's critique of master-narratives relates to the exile's critique of authoritarian discourse. The privileging of the margins over the center, absence over presence, anarchy over hierarchy, open form over closed, difference over sameness, etc. found in postmodern theory's critique of modernity holds special meaning for the writer who has been forced into exile. These concepts go beyond metaphor and retain particularly painful weight for exiled writers. Even though a critique of cultural unification is common in exile writing, exiles from Spain and Latin America who had been exposed to postmodern theory were especially sensitive to the forced homogeneity of national culture common in dictatorship. We find, then, that exiled writers reflect many of the critical concerns associated with postmodern theory. Their historical condition as exiles from repressive dictatorships, though, marks this association as one driven by specific political needs and historical circumstances. Postmodern theories often blur difference into a normalizing condition; since displacement is so prevalent, it ceases to hold particular meaning. Bammer argues that "differences, thus universalized, disappear" (xii). So, while theories of the postmodern resonate with exiles, their experience of displacement, decentering and disempowerment is grounded in the particularities of their experience and cannot be categorized as merely symbolic of the condition of outsider or as representative of linguistic *différance*. For these reasons, the affinities between postmodernism, poststructuralism, and exile writing require that we consider the tensions and complicities between postmodern theory and politically charged, historically grounded, anti-authoritarian discourse.

Nationalism is a political position which argues for either the construction or the maintenance of a particular nation-state. The nation-state refers to the physical borders of a country as well as those formal institutions responsible for its existence, i.e., the government, army, public institutions, etc. Nationalism as a concept has been used to construct nations, as in the case of wars of independence or in revolutionary rhetoric, and has been used to maintain nations, as in the case of fascist ideology, which argues that its version of the nation constitutes a return to the nation's original essences. Ernest Gellner defines nationalism as "a theory of political legitimacy, which requires that ethnic boundaries should not cut across political ones" (1). Generally, some form of nationalism exists in any nation because, at the simplest level, nationalism is the notion that a particular group belongs in a particular place. The argument that certain people have a claim to a territory is the basis of nationalism.

Nationalism requires a sense of national identity. National identity is the description of those characteristics that constitute the cultural link between a group and its land. They are common traits that are distinctive of a particular territory. The most important facet of national identity is the description of a common national history that all occupants of the nation share. Obviously, the description of what exactly constitutes national identity is also political. Different versions of national history compete by claiming to be the most valid rendition of national identity. Therefore, the argument for the existence of a national identity is the first step in an argument for nationalism: the crucial difference is that nationalism is more openly a call to action or to defense. Nevertheless, the two concepts are very difficult to separate.

For the exile, a sense of both nationalism and national identity are necessary. Without the belief that there is a connection between an individual and a place, exile has no meaning. Yet, the exile's nationalism is usually contrary to the versions of nationalism and national identity fostered within the nation's borders. Gellner explains that nationalism tends to be an artificial construct generated by those who hold power in the nation-state: "nationalism is, essentially, the general imposition of a high culture on society, where previously low cultures had taken up the lives of the majority, and in some cases of the totality, of the population" (57). The exile commonly provides an alternative to these official positions. Because exiles are forcefully cast out of the nation, their concept of nationalism argues that the connections between people and land should be constructed differently from their current state under authoritarianism. So the exile's nationalism is constructive of an alternative: it is active. Alternatively, official nationalism is defensive of the nation as it has been constructed by the existing regime. It is important to see that a particular nation-state can provoke contradictory nationalisms that have in common the argument that a certain people belong to a certain land because of a common national culture.

Cultural nationalism is a political position very closely linked to nationalism. It is the argument that a nation has a common culture and that this culture has unique qualities that should be maintained. Cultural nationalism is often used to defend nationalism by arguing that, because a people have a special cultural connection, they should be able to have the right to maintain national autonomy, as in Basque cultural nationalism. It is used also to describe the notion that a nation's culture is necessarily connected to geography and its people's history. This type of cultural essentialism posits that culture is inherited. For instance, a Spaniard must have certain traits because he was born in Spain. Cultural identity, then, is in one's blood and inevitable. The twentieth-century Spanish essayist Angel Ganivet, for instance, continued the tradition of defining Spanish cultural identity by focusing on blood ties (see his *Idearium Español*). The arguments of intellectuals like Ganivet have been representative of a long history of Spanish cultural essentialism: All Jewish and Islamic occupants of the nation where forced to leave the country or convert to Catholicism in 1492, followed by the brutal acts of the Inquisition, which repeatedly attacked "Jewish converts," who, even though they had converted to Catholicism, were nevertheless considered to not have "pure" Catholic blood.

According to this view of cultural nationalism, the individual has no free will or ability to alter a cultural context that is necessarily inherited. The obvious contradiction is that, if one inherits culture, then, why are there conflicting versions? Should we not all peacefully agree as to what constitutes national culture? Because of this contradiction, arguments for cultural nationalism encounter the dilemma of arguing that their version of national culture is firmly rooted in a nation's common heritage and usually blood ties, yet, for some reason, not everyone is able to recognize this fact. Typically, fascist versions of cultural nationalism depend on such essentialist rhetoric. They claim that their regime will return the nation to its cultural origins. For instance, both Hitler and Franco used such tactics. Neil Larsen explains that such a notion of cultural nationalism depends on "the *fallacy of essentialism,* that is, the false idea that the nation or its 'tradition,' etc. is a fixed, free standing, and pre-existing content or 'essence' and that as such an essence, the nation bears a mechanical, transparently symbolic, or allegorical relation to its literary forms of expression" (*Determinations* 84). Cultural nationalists will select those elements of national culture that are "authentic" and all other cultural products will be considered deviant and antipatriotic (see Anderson).

Leftist variations on cultural nationalism do not rely on a mythical return to origins but are more concerned with returning the nation to the control of its inhabitants. Their rhetoric of cultural nationalism is based on revalorizing culture so that the culture of the disenfranchised will have more power in society and will not remain in the margins. Such a project can be seen in the work of the Cuban, José Martí, who argued that Latin Americans were not second cousins to North Americans, but were, in fact, a source of a valuable and important cultural identity. For him, cultural nationalism is the basis of his essay "Nuestra América" (Our America), which argues that power relations should be altered in favor of the cultural autonomy of Latin American nations. Roberto Fernández Retamar makes a similar argument about Cuban identity years later in *Caliban*. Arguments from revolutionaries, like that of Martí or Fernández Retamar, for a "return" to cultural nationalism are not conservative and do not explain national culture as a natural consequence of birth on national soil but, rather, as a historical and political construct. The nation should "return" to the forgotten aspects of its culture, which have been eliminated from official discourse or, as in the case of Cuba, obscured by imperialism.

In both cases, it becomes crucial to fight for the superiority of one's belief, and corresponding ideologies of nationalism demonstrate the force of these conflicts. Consequently, there will always be conflicting versions of what constitutes the cultural identity found in a given nation. All arguments for cultural nationalism share the conviction that there is a common culture that connects a nation's people even if such culture does not include all of the people in the nation. In fact, many versions of cultural nationalism imply an important contradiction: all members of the nation share national ties but some of the nation's members do not belong to the group. Because cultural nationalism is a political position, those who are from a different class, race, ethnicity, gender, or sexual orientation may not always be part of what some consider as the nation's cultural makeup. For example, the Basques and Catalonians were not part of Franco's Spain, which tried to eradicate all regional cultures and impose Castilian culture. In addition, in Chile, the Mapuche Indians were disregarded under Pinochet, whereas under Allende they were treated as valuable contributors to national culture.

Another battleground for cultural nationalism is the national hero, whose cultural importance is often reappropriated to signify differently according to political ideologies. A good example might be the figure of José Martí, who is integral to the argument for cultural nationalism for Castro's Cuba as well as for Cuban exiles. Both groups see Martí, the Liberator of Cuba, as a national hero, yet each group has a different version of Martí's dreams for Cuba and each group is exclusionary. Benedict Anderson argues that cultural forms are essential to the formation of nationalism: the "attachment" that people feel for their nations, which leads them to consider dying for a national cause, requires cultural products of nationalism (such as prose, poetry, music, and plastic arts) that represent the bond between the self and the nation (141). Cultural products, like heroes, anthems, flags, as well as literature, media, and the arts, are the foundation for the development and maintenance of cultural nationalism.

Cultural nationalism plays an important role for the cultural production of exiled intellectuals. Insofar as exiles are challenging the official culture of their nation, they must argue for an alternative cultural nationalism. This position typically maintains that there is a story that is being suppressed by official versions of cultural identity, which the exile must tell. The narrative of exiles attempting to counter official versions of their nation's culture includes stories that are no longer told within their countries and which the exiles hope will reach their compatriots. Michael Seidel writes that when exile is political or ideological "its victim claims to possess the values of his native place, as it were, in proxy—he is the truer version of the place from which he is barred" (9). The problem of censorship becomes central to these narratives, because the exile wants to challenge official culture at an international and a national level. The argument that there is a cultural tale that is integral to national identity that is being censored shapes cultural nationalism for exiles.

Generally, there are two important ways in which exiles challenge official versions of national culture: they provide an alternative/counter national culture, and/or they critique the concept of national culture. The second strategy attempts to deconstruct the hold on identity that cultural nationalism has forged in their countries, and elsewhere, by exposing the repressive connections between the self and the state. Such a position sees that the construction of any national culture is highly problematic and always involves a restriction of identity. Exiles seek the means of liberating the bonds that are constricting their national culture, and they often conclude that the notion of national culture must be abolished for true cultural freedom to be experienced.

As is the case with the authors studied in this project, exiles tend, to some degree or another, to incorporate both seemingly contradictory strategies. They attempt to re-map cultural identity, while simultaneously breaking down the externally imposed borders of cultural identity which correspond to a concept of the nation. One main reason for this is that, as these narratives attempt to construct counter-identities, they also attempt to undermine the influence of their nations' governments by destroying the image of the nation. For instance, in nations where gender has been shaped in a particular way, the exile may attempt to destroy those pre-established modes of controlling gendered identity. At the same time, though, the exile's narrative might recuperate a national narrative that has been silenced by the official regime, or may retell a story in such a way as to challenge the biases of the official version, and such a story may rely on traditional gendered stereotypes. For example, Marta Traba's *Conversación al sur* (*Mothers and Shadows*) depicts the struggle of the Madres de la Plaza de Mayo. In her text, as in the movement, motherhood functions in a traditional way. Yet the relationship between the two female protagonists challenges patriarchal stereotypes and demonstrates female identity as independent of male relationships.

Countering the notion of nationalism, *transnationalism* is a concept that relates to post-nationalism and to globalization. Motivated by the increasing presence of transnational corporations, scholars of cultural identity predicted that the borders defining national entities would increasingly erode. In the same way that modernism required the construction of the modern nation-state for industrialization and the creation of national markets, postmodernism is caused by a significant change in capitalist strategies that no longer attach to national space (see Jameson, "On 'Cultural Studies'"). Hardt and Negri observe: "As the world market today is realized ever more completely, it tends to deconstruct the boundaries of the nation-state. In a previous period, nation-states were the primary actors in the modern imperialist organization of global production and exchange, but to the world market they increasingly appear as mere obstacles" (150). Transnationalism renders the borders of a nation insignificant. People, goods, and culture flow across borders, which become merely geographic and no longer culturally meaningful. There are no "Others" or "Aliens" and culture, goods, and people are absent of national attachments.

There are two issues at work here. One is the observation that the scope and nature of capitalism has changed and that this has affected how we define cultural identity as it relates to the nation. The effects of these transitions must be accounted for in any description of cultural identity. The second issue is the prescriptive, forward-looking vision of what transnational capitalism may cause at its extreme, that is, the loss of any attachment to nation. While some may have experienced this type of change, it is highly dubious that all individuals have been affected by these changes in economic modes of production to the same degree. At the same time that we have witnessed a reduction in certain forms of nationalism we have also noted heightened ethnic nationalisms, such as that in Eastern Europe. It is also problematic to posit the end of the nation, when it appears that transnationalism actually refers to an even more pervasive spread of Western-based culture. Transnational corporations are the messengers of Western culture and its mode of production. Would transnationalism not imply a transfer and flux of cultures over and across borders? Why is the United States less affected by Latin American culture than the reverse, if the relationship is an unbiased transferal of culture?

The notion of a transnational cultural identity as a celebratory state of being has been greatly influenced by theories of poststructuralism and the ludic postmodern. Poststructuralism argues for the end of oppressive forms of existence through the destruction of all limiting and controlling facets of identity (which in the end becomes all forms of describing identity). Insofar as national identity is oppressive, transnational identity is liberating because it is unrestricted and unconnected to anything. People have no common traits; they are different, endlessly different (see Derrida). While such a position has been highly seductive for critics who no longer feel that leftist politics could lead to liberation, it is an argument full of contradictions. Larsen cautions that we should be suspicious of the "'ludic' post-nationalism that has recently dominated the 'growth sector' in much literary and cultural studies" (*Determinations* 55). While ludic poststructuralism seeks to rejoice in the splintered self, it runs into difficulty when a subject is posited who supposedly benefits from this position. Because poststructuralist theory opposes such modern concepts as free will, it cannot attribute any ability to control identity to the individual. Yet the position is not merely descriptive: it also argues that society should continuously move in a direction which "deconstructs" the self and the systems that attempt to control it. An argument of this nature requires that someone listen and act. Yet, according to the poststructuralists, we are incapable of such behavior and there is no reality beyond the text. Consequently, any celebration of transnationalism as a liberating force must be reconsidered. Inasmuch as nationalism is founded on the belief that there is an integral connection between a land and its people, transnationalism posits an alternative way of describing cultural identity that is less geographically restrictive. In this sense, transnationalism implies a weakening of nationalism's coercive nature. On the other hand, transnationalism, as it is tied to Empire and global capitalism, may be an even greater source of social oppression (see Hardt and Negri).

Transnationalism is very important for the study of the cultural production of exiles. Exiles exemplify the ways in which the physical borders of a nation do not always have ultimate significance. In fact, as exiles encounter new national spaces, they grapple with the issues of national identity in a critical way. For them borders are both more and less important. They are more important because they now acutely define "inside" and "outside," "native" and "alien." They are less important because culture is experienced as something displaced from territorial space.

Transnationalism is also significant because it is a useful way to describe the bond that exiles feel with other outsiders and/or intellectuals. When exiles must look beyond the boundaries of national identity for a community, they find that others who are from different nations share their fears and concerns. For this reason, exile narratives often seek other lines along which to draw identity that are not merely national—such as gender, race, class, or sexuality. This is not to say that such practices are nonexistent in the work of non-exiles: yet, because of their isolation, exiles are in a situation that calls their attention to commonalities that transcend the national and link them to others regardless of nationality, or even historical synchronicity. The emphasis on synchronic associations is reevaluated by the condition of exiles: they find cultural connections, which are both synchronic and diachronic, to be important in their identity. Exiles recognize that their plight is timeless and universal (there have always been exiles and outcasts) and that their condition is closely connected to their particular historical moment (they are exiled because of a set of historical events). This causes their sense of cultural identity to be general and local, transnational and national, historical and atemporal.

Transculturation is a concept that originated in the work of the Cuban Fernando Ortiz in 1940 (*Contrapunteo del tabaco cubano*) (*Cuban Counterpoint: Tobacco and Sugar*). Transculturation describes the impact on cultural identity of contact with another culture. By contrast with the term "acculturation," which would assume assimilation of new elements into a national culture, transculturation describes the importation of new cultural elements through a local, cultural filter. Ortiz fought for a Cuban culture that could withstand the influx of foreign culture without being eradicated. Consequently, it was incumbent upon him to describe such cultural contact as transforming, but not as replacing, already existing features of Cuban culture.

This concept later appeared in the work of the Uruguayan Angel Rama, *Transculturación narrativa en América Latina* (Transculturation in Latin American Narrative). He describes transculturation as the partial loss of the local and the partial gain of foreign elements. What is most significant about Rama's position is that he posits cultural producers capable of affecting these transitions and also of ensuring that foreign culture is unable to obfuscate local culture. Ortiz, on the other hand, simply describes the process that he sees as inevitable where contact with another culture produces neo-culture. Neo-culture retains vestiges of the original, local culture and acquires, through local codification, new elements as well. In contrast with Ortiz, Rama's notion of transculturation requires the participation of artists and authors in the creation of a culture capable of resisting outside domination.

Mary Louise Pratt uses these concepts in her notion of contact zones—spaces, like the liminal, where disparate cultures meet and confront each other (4). Contact zones are sites of transculturation because they are the areas that witness cultural transformation through contact with foreign elements. These are border areas much like the ones described by Victor Turner (*The Ritual Process*). It is important to note that Ortiz, Rama, and Pratt locate these issues primarily at the level of society and not of the individual. Nevertheless, their arguments have been used to maintain that this cultural process of transformation, visible on the broad scale of society, is also recognizable on an individual basis.

Interestingly, this concept has been significantly transformed in much critical writing today to be akin to transnationalism, where the borders that contain cultural identity are no longer significant and all culture is endlessly mixed and untraceable to any regional origin. This practice redefines the original meaning of the term "transculturation," which described the crisis facing non-Western societies that endeavored to preserve a minor culture threatened with destruction by dominant Western culture. Transculturation (as some use it now), like multiculturalism, describes a pastiche of cultural elements, where none enjoy a privileged position and all coexist in a state of flux. This radical version of transculturation takes the concept of cultural transformation to its extreme, where ultimately culture loses any connection to place or heritage, be it social, religious, gendered, economic, ethnic, or racial.

The work of Homi Bhabha is an example of such an extreme position. He argues for a radical deconstruction of cultural hierarchies. Yet, he also privileges postcolonial culture over First World culture all the while basing his theoretical analysis on First World, poststructuralist theories ("DissemiNation"). This practice places his work in a theoretical quandary. In contrast, the work of Nestor García Canclini, who argues for understanding Latin American culture as a cultural hybrid, is based on the premise that culture in Latin America is, by definition, affected by Western culture. Nevertheless, such a relationship does not result in the destruction of an autochthonous culture. Instead, the fusion of Western culture with Latin American culture, where Western culture is appropriated and altered by its Latin American versions, produces a cultural hybrid (*Culturas híbridas*) (*Hybrid Cultures*). In *Determinations* Neil Larsen also argues, against Bhabha, for the need to be wary of the destruction of all cultural categories, for this leads to the destruction of all ground for action, critique, and politics: "The error is to suppose that with the possible historical crisis of the nation as a cultural form, the question of *culture as historically determinate*, as a historically possible and necessary form of emancipation . . . is likewise superseded" (85–86).

One important difference between transculturation and cultural nationalism is the distinction between the creation of culture and the inheritance of it. Under cultural nationalism, there are elements of culture that cannot be modified and that are deterministically linked to a nation either due to history or to original essences. The possibility of self-control for the cultural receptor is highly tenuous. Transculturation is the notion that culture is constantly recreated even if certain elements remain tied to national cultural history. Here the question of self-control is also tenuous. Culture is not received because it is linked to one's history but rather because contact with another culture always involves a certain degree of transformation of the individual's cultural identity. The problem lies in defining what changes and what remains. As many critics have followed this theory to its extreme, they argue that there is no permanent cultural fixity which, in a state of transnationalism, would reduce all cultural associations to a superficial level void of any historical meaning.

Transculturation, like transnationalism, is crucial to the description of the cultural production of exiles from the latter part of the twentieth century. Like their attraction to transnationalism and the need to see their condition as transcending national borders, exiles find the concept of transculturation useful for explaining the influence of foreign culture on their writing. Obviously, transculturation is a process that affects all cultures, but the culture of exiles itself is an excellent example of the limits of this state. While the cultural condition of exiles demonstrates transculturation, the exile does not lose all ties to the national culture responsible for their condition of exile. Even those exiles who reject their nation and embrace transnational culture cannot escape defining themselves culturally in relation to their past, which in their case was very deeply affected by national history.

◆ ◆

The following chapters of this book analyze the ways in which these writers deal with a crisis of cultural identity comparatively by drawing on the methods of "comparative cultural studies" as proposed by Steven Tötösy de Zepetnek (1998, 1999, 2003). "The Dialectics of Exile: Towards a Theory of Exile Writing," maps out the theory that exile literature is best understood as a series of dialectic tensions, as opposed to a series of mutually exclusive binaries. Focusing on the dialectics surrounding nationalism and exile writing, "Alien Nation" demonstrates how the literary production of these writers produces significant challenges to the fundamental premises of much contemporary critical theory, in particular theories of nationalism and cultural identity. The goal in this chapter is to illuminate the cultural dilemmas that arose out of the specific problems these three writers encountered when they responded to different national and historical experiences. "Alien Nation" lays out central issues relating to the question of nationalism in exile writing, but, given the way that the exile's relationship to the nation is such a central concern, each of the subsequent chapters returns to the nation question as well. Next, "Exile's Time" addresses the complex relationship exile literature has to notions of time. Specifically, the work of these writers incorporates the purportedly contradictory views of time as circular/primordial (i.e., pre-modern), historical/linear (i.e., modern), and meaningless/absent (i.e., postmodern). Their theory of time challenges the notion that such visions of the individual's temporal reality are incommensurable by revealing these multiple perspectives as interpenetrating dialectics. The next chapter, "To Be Is Not to Be," focuses on the problems of language for the exiled writer caught between poststructuralist theories of language and a need for faith in politically effective discourse. The sixth chapter, "Lost in Space," outlines these writers' complicated visions of the geography of cultural community and its ties to spatial relations. The chapter analyzes each writer's metaphorical construction of an alternative nation and then evaluates the ways each writer represents cultural identity as both utopic and dystopic. The last chapter, "Culture Shock," argues that the literature of these writers has an intricate relationship with many of the terms commonly applied to questions of cultural identity, which allows for insight into some of the most pressing issues concerning cultural politics. For instance, the work of these writers tests the binary divisions of assimilation versus dissimilation, identity politics versus multiculturalism, and cultural essentialism versus cultural agency. This book reveals the ways in which the exile literature of Goytisolo, Dorfman, and Peri Rossi questions the concepts of the nation, history, linguistic representation, and cultural identity and exposes the limitations of many theories dedicated to these issues that tend to emphasize only one side of a multifaceted dialectic. The following chapters argue that, rather than favor one side of these dialectics, scholarship of exile literature should investigate how and why these tensions persist. Ultimately, the analysis of Goytisolo, Dorfman, and Peri Rossi illustrates the complex ways that the literature of exiles provides an alternative discourse of cultural identity by challenging the official versions of national identity imposed by authoritarian regimes.

CHAPTER TWO

The Dialectics of Exile: Towards a Theory of Exile Writing

The history of the dialectic and dialectical thinking is as long as the history of exile. We find early examples of dialectics in the ancient philosophy of the Greeks, especially in the work of Aristotle and Heraclitus, who taught, "everything is in flux," and the Chinese, whose conceptions of *yin* and *yang* describe life as interpenetrating dualisms ("Definitions of Dialectics"). Dialectic's etymology from Greek "dialego," meaning to discuss or debate, highlights the ways the term was used to describe a process of analysis that assessed problems from many perspectives, taking into account opposing and contradictory points of view, in order to arrive at the truth. Unlike the concept of exile, though, which has been invoked by contemporary critics as a metaphor for many states of marginalization or isolation, the dialectic has been considered by some to be rigid and formulaic—a symbol of an intransigent system of analysis. This dismissal of the dialectic applies most specifically to a simplified version where two opposing theses are unified in a "higher" synthesis, i.e., the dialectical triad. Others eschew the dialectic, associating it with a deterministic view of society and a totalizing Marxist worldview. Damir Mirkovic, in his survey of dialectical thinking, argues that such reductive notions have led scholars to avoid engaging with the concept: "The dialectic seems to have fallen into disrepute, with the rise of positivism in the social sciences, and with the parallel dogmatic interpretations of dialectic.... Indeed, one generally hesitates to mention dialectic for fear of provoking suspicion among the dullards from the right, that one might be one of the dullards from the left" (v). As Mirkovic argues, though, the dialectical method is "far more complex" than most recognize. Even though the dialectic has come under critical suspicion, scholars like Marcial González have argued for a return to dialectical thinking and José David Saldívar's *The Dialectics of Our America* studies cultural identity as a form of dialectic.

An analysis of the many varied and often oppositional interpretations of the dialectic is well beyond the scope of this project. In the following section I will outline the key components of the dialectical method that are especially useful for analyzing exile writing and I will relate this theory to other scholarly accounts of exile writing. I hope to show that the dialectic provides a fluid and open-ended critical framework for understanding cultural production created in exile. Moreover, I will demonstrate ways that many scholars have suggested, perhaps unconsciously, perhaps subtly, that the many contradictory and contrapuntal elements of exile writing are not indicative of mutually exclusive binaries, but rather of the dialectics of exile.

The dialectic is about change, process, and flux. Frederick Engels explains dialectic in "The Science of Dialectics": "the whole world, natural, historical, intellectual, is represented as a process—i.e., as in constant motion, change, transformation, development; and the attempt is made to trace out the internal connection that makes a continuous whole of all this movement and development" (n.p.). Consequently any theory that rests on the dialectic should be fluid and malleable to the concrete, material cases it addresses. Understanding exile writing as dialectical provides a common theoretical explanation for the tensions and anxieties inherent in exile writing that is sufficiently loose as to be pertinent to a broad range of applications.

The Hegelian dialectic is perhaps the best known, or renown. Hegel described the world as a process and he outlined three key elements of his dialectic logic, which were adapted in later Marxist revisions of his theory: 1) the interpenetration (unity) of opposites, 2) the transition of quantity into quality, 3) and the negation of the negation. All three concepts apply to exile, but it is the first category of the dialectic that provides the richest resource for analyzing exile writing. Some of the more common unities of opposites that have been analyzed by Hegel, Engels, Marx, and Lenin are: finite and infinite, form and content, identity and difference, abstract and concrete, cause and effect, means and ends, subject and object, and positive and negative. (See G. W. F. Hegel's *Science of Logic*, Frederick Engels's *Socialism: Utopian and Scientific* and *Anti-Dühring*, Karl Marx's *Capital* and *Grundrisse*, and Vladimir Lenin's "Summary of Dialectics" and "On the Question of Dialectics" in volume 38 of the *Collected Works*. Almost all of these texts are available online at <http://www.marxists.org/>.) The interpenetration of opposites explains the ways that exile texts include conflicts and oppositions. For example, exile writing often contains the following unity of opposites: the condition of exile is depicted as physical and mental; exile is a state that both liberates and confines the writer; writing is both the cause of exile and the way to supersede it; exile is both spiritual/abstract and material; exile is personal/individual and political/collective; exile writing recuperates the past and re-imagines it; exiles write about the past and also about the future; the experience of exile is both unique and universal; exile improves and also restricts the writer's work; exile heightens both regionalism and cosmopolitanism, both nationalism and globalization. These interpenetrating oppositions are only a few of the most salient dialectical tensions found in exile writing. These tensions track in a variety of different ways in each particular case, but these tensions are a common feature of exile writing.

Few have ventured to propose explicit theories of exile writing. In fact, Michael Ugarte suggests that exile literature provides challenges to any theoretical project that would describe it: "The very phrase, 'theory of exile literature,' sounds strange, as if one could devise a theory of a particular type of literature solely according to political circumstance" (*Shifting* 17). Most scholars suggest that their analysis rests on the interpretation of a series of cases of exiled writers, focusing on a specific cohort. Or Ugarte suggests that his analysis attempts to understand how "an experience of exile might be linked to the unfolding of any creative process" (18). And yet, all of these scholarly efforts to analyze exile writing are guided by implicit theoretical frameworks. Certain scholars pay particular attention to the material (metaphysical, empirical) realities of exile and others focus on the abstract. Dialectics opposes a predefined notion of exile, meaning that abstract, idealist versions of the condition are inadequate. Focusing on the concrete (i.e., metaphysical), dialectics considers the material as a constantly changing process; the metaphysical is only part of the critical process, since the dialectician seeks to understand the intersections between forces in tension. Exile is not an abstract idea, nor is it an essence that can be predetermined, nor is it merely a series of material facts: a dialectical critique of exile culture understands texts produced in this condition as a complex combination of concrete elements that are in tension, in the process of change, and interconnected.

The state of exile creates a series of oppositions, antinomies, and contradictions. For instance, exile culture is both national and global. Binary logic would argue that the exile must be either local or global, but not both. Dialectic thinking argues that exile holds these contradictory positions in an ever-changing unity of opposites. In the Introduction to the *Anti-Dühring* (1877), Engels points out the limitations of binary, metaphysical thinking: "To the metaphysician, things and their mental reflexes, ideas, are isolated, are to be considered one after the other and apart from each other, are objects of investigation fixed, rigid, given once for all. He thinks in absolutely irreconcilable antitheses.... For him a thing either exists or does not exist; a thing cannot at the same time be itself and something else. Positive and negative absolutely exclude one another, cause and effect stand in a rigid antithesis one to the other" (34). Such binary thinking, when applied to the cultural production of exiles, is unable to account for the ways that contradictory concepts coexist in tension within the same work. In fact, the following analysis will show that the key tensions in exile writing are not merely two-fold (as in nationalism versus globalization), but are multiple (as in nationalism, counter-nationalism, alternative nationalism, anti-nationalism, and transnationalism). The focus on binaries tends to limit the categories of meaning that one looks for in a text. Dialectical thinking would encourage, instead, that one look for all angles or perspectives represented in a text.

Although few scholars have offered theories of exile writing in comparison with the vast body of exile writing and the extensive scholarly studies of these texts, certain key examples illuminate the predominance of binary thinking in relation to exile writing. The most well known example is the binary between the literary categories of "exile" and "counter-exile," proposed by Claudio Guillén. In the "literature of exile" as defined by Guillén "exile becomes its own subject matter" and such writing can be exemplified by the writings of Ovid and the "direct expression of sorrow" (272). In contrast, in the case of "literature of counter-exile," authors "incorporate the separation from place, class, language or native community, insofar as they triumph over the separation and thus offer wide dimensions of meaning and transcend the earlier attachments to place or native origin" (272). Such an approach, according to Guillén, would be exemplified by the theme of Ulysses. The "literature of exile" is also linked to "modern feelings of nationalism" (275), whereas in the "literature of counter-exile," Guillén argues, "no great writer can remain a merely local mind, unwilling to question the relevance of the particular place from which he writes" (280). It is clear that Guillén favors the pole of "counter-exile," where language acquires a sufficient level of allegory and metaphor and the local is transcended.

Guillén notes that literature may fall anywhere on the spectrum between exile and counter-exile. Nevertheless, if the literature of counter-exile exemplifies the complete transcendence of place or native origin, then such literature would have to be empty of history, of its material reality. Regardless of whether one believes that all literature is necessarily a product of its historical circumstance, the historical conditions of exile make complete transcendence from time and space impossible. Simply put, the condition of exile is directly a result of the social and political climate occupied by the author, making ahistorical exile literature a contradiction in terms. For the exiled writer, questions of language, problems with publication and audience, and the social context of the exile as outsider and outcast make transcendence unattainable. In this sense, the binary proposed by Guillén is unable to adequately describe the complexity of the concept. Instead of considering the literature of exile in binary terms, it is more productive to consider the writing of exile as a dialectic between the expression of the painful realities of the exile experience and the "imaginative representation of relatively fictional themes" (272).

Although Guillén's argument proposes two tendencies of writing that are oppositional, he points out that most work is neither wholly an example of "exile" nor "counter-exile." He also hints at the value of using the dialectic to describe the cultural tensions in exile texts when he describes the stages of "counter-exile" writing: "it might be reasonable to assume some form of movement away from the original situation as an effective manner of conveying the *dialectics* of counter-exile and the process whereby the initial separation is transcended" (my emphasis, 279). He then describes "counter-exile" literature as a process that moves beyond the polarities of absence and presence. In a later work, the previously mentioned *Múltiples moradas*, Guillén also hints at the dialectics of exile writing when he proposes another dichotomy: "arranco de una polaridad. Me propongo destacar dos valoraciones fundamentales. La primera es la imagen solar.... Esta actitud parte de la contemplación del sol y de los astros, continúa y se desarrolla rumbo a dimensiones universales.... La segunda reacción valoritiva, o bien asociada a la primera o bien opuesta, denuncia una pérdida, un empobrecimiento" (30) ["I start from a polarity. I would like to emphasize two fundamental value systems. The first is the solar image.... This attitude springs from the contemplation of the sun and the stars, it continues and develops towards universal dimensions.... The second valuable reaction, perhaps associated with the first or its opposite, denounces a loss, an impoverishment"]. The solar response to exile corresponds to Guillén's category of "counter-exile" writing. While Guillén does not name the second tendency this way, we might consider it to be terrestrial, where the terrestrial exiled writer corresponds to the literature of "exile" described above. Guillén also posits the possibility that these poles might be related. In a sense, Guillén is hinting subtly at a dialectical theory of exile writing where the exile can either look up towards the sun for inspiration, recognizing his shared humanity, or gaze down at the ground, contemplating his material existence far from his native land. Yet, despite what the writer chooses to emphasize, he or she is always between the land and the sun; exile identity is the unity of these opposite tendencies. Consequently, by suggesting that we understand exile writing as a dialectic instead of as a binary, I propose to make explicit what is subtly implicit in Guillén's interpenetrating dualities.

In addition to Guillén, Michael Seidel is one of the few scholars to propose an advanced theory of exile writing. His *Exile and the Narrative Imagination* considers the condition of exile as "an enabling fiction" that allows him to "address the larger strategies of narrative representation" (xii). While not as rigid as Guillén's dualisms, Seidel also suggests that the condition of exile may result in a flourishing of the literary imagination, making an "artistic virtue of exilic necessity" (5). Similar to Guillén's favored category of "counter-exile" or solar exile, Seidel focuses on writers who "have gained imaginative sustenance from exile" (x). Yet, also similar to Guillén, Seidel's theory of exile writing hints at its dialectical nature. When he describes "exile as an enabling fiction" he points out the tension between imagination and the devastating reality that drives exile narrative. Later, he explains that the exile is both a wanderer and a homebody (10). While Seidel does not mention this tension as dialectic, his analysis suggests that exile literature holds a number of key concepts in interconnected flux: exile narrative wavers between rupture and connection, depicting "separation as desire, perspective as witness" (x).

Edward Said describes exile writing as contrapuntal: the literature of exile provides a plurality of vision and demonstrates the author's awareness of simultaneous dimensions (366). The notion of the counterpoint is very similar to that of the dialectic. To be contrapuntal is to have two or more independent, but harmonically related, melodic parts sounding together. Like the dialectic, where opposing concepts are held in tension within a unified whole, the counterpoint suggests a similar dynamic between seemingly contradictory forces. It is noteworthy that Said selects the counterpoint to describe the writing of exiles instead of the dialectic. Perhaps, as noted in the quotation by Mirkovic above, the counterpoint is a less loaded term.

In a study of Hispanic exile writing, Gloria da Cunha-Giabbai suggests that exile literature tracks according to binaries and dualisms. She describes exile writing as either focused on the past or on the present and yet she also acknowledges that certain writers construct parallel realities (53). As a further example, Amy Kaminsky's study of Latin America, *After Exile*, also implies that exile writing is dialectic without specifically naming it. For instance, Kaminsky argues that exile writing narrates the nation as both physical/geographic and symbolic/political (23). She also points to a linguistic dialectic between literal, territorial exile and the linguistic representation of it (40).

All of these texts share a common latent theory that exile writing is fundamentally dialectical in nature. Critics who propose binaries of exile writing often refer to the tensions between these poles without specifically considering these literary characteristics as exemplary of the dialectic of interpenetrating opposites. Suggesting that exile writing is best understood as dialectical does not overshadow the theories of Guillén, Seidel, Said, da Cunha-Giabbai, or Kaminsky, but rather enhances them by pointing to a critical approach to exile writing that their work implies but never openly analyzes.

It is interesting to note the preponderance of binaries and oppositions in scholarly accounts of exile writing. Surely this pattern suggests that exile writing presents the reader with contrasting literary strategies. Also, as the previous analysis of exile theories has demonstrated, scholars often subtly hint that the literature of exile is dialectical. Understanding exile writing as dialectical accounts for the ways that these oppositions, binaries, and contradictions can exist simultaneously with the same text. To suggest that a productive theoretical approach to exile writing should be organized by a dialectical approach, moreover, allows for a theory of exile literature that is flexible and fluid, since the particular dialectical aspects of any text will be determined by its specific historical circumstances and narrative components. In the chapters that follow, the writing of Goytisolo, Dorfman, and Peri Rossi will be shown to reflect a series of dialectic tensions. In each case these tensions are not merely two-fold, as in the case of the dialectic triad where two opposing forces lead to a synthesis; these texts represent multiple forces in tension. The exile, for instance, does not simply alter between representing identity as local or global; identity is also regional, gendered, sexual, political, temporal, linguistic, social, etc. The condition of exile is not static. Rather, it is a condition that is constantly unstable and in flux.

As mentioned above, one of the central unities of opposites in exile writing is between form and content, and this tension is also central in the analysis of Goytisolo, Dorfman, and Peri Rossi. Exile writers tend to respond in formal ways to their state, either through experimentation or its obvious lack. And the content of their writing also relates to their state, either through its self-reflexive exploration or its denial or both. In Hegel's description of the dialectic of form and content from *The Logic* he writes: "Real works of art are those where content and form exhibit a thorough identity. The content of the *Iliad*, it may be said, is the Trojan War, and especially the wrath of Achilles. In that we have everything, and yet very little after all; for the *Iliad* is made an *Iliad* by the poetic form, in which that content is moulded" (Section 2, Chapter 2, n.p.). According to Hegel, the brutality of the *Iliad*'s content is reflected in the form, just as the brutality of exile is reflected in the formal structure of exile literature, and we will find this to be especially so in the fragmented and disjointed narratives of Goytisolo, Dorfman, and Peri Rossi.

In the literary cases analyzed in this book, a further central tension is between the experience of exile and its representation. These three writers display great distrust at their ability to convey through words the intensity of the exile experience. Exiled writers often find themselves trying to write what they have been physically barred from doing; they attempt to narrate aspects of their national history that are being silenced and censored by dictatorial regimes. The need to imagine and represent through language what one cannot experience through physical presence creates conflict in exile literature. As Ovid reminds us, exiled writers are expelled from their nations precisely because they write and yet the experience often does not silence the writer, but leads them to resort more fervently to literature as a way to maintain their identity and their social vision. The urgency of their writing lies in the way that literature serves as a memory of the past and an imaginative version of alternative realities, both of which provide creative sustenance and hope in an otherwise dire circumstance.

CHAPTER THREE
Alien Nation

They have landed and now they are among us.
—Alien Nation, 1988

Graham Baker's film *Alien Nation* leaves the viewer with a central dilemma: why is the movie a horror film? In fact, given the absurd characterization of the "newcomers," the film leans toward humor. Apart from the final scenes, the film is not scary. Or is it? Perhaps the fear is of the *alien nation:* the film suggests that many of the pivotal issues relating to exile, nationalism, and cultural identity are inseparable from *mass* cultural fear. Yet how can the nation be alien or of aliens? Do aliens bring their nation with them and threaten their host, making home look different and "alien"? Despite the doomsday treatment of the effects of an alien presence on national integrity, this film helps to emphasize an undeniable connection between migration, immigration, exile, and nation formation.

Similar to the alteration of filmic horror in *Alien Nation*, the following chapter suggests that the exile's experience of nation undergoes a physical and conceptual transformation in the latter part of the twentieth century as a consequence of transnationalism and postmodernism. The weakening of the nation-state associated with transnationalism combined with the fragmentation of the subject and language associated with postmodernism create an unprecedented situation for the political exile. The experience of these particular exiles, then, bears the marks of their historical context and puts pressure on the binary thinking of nationalism versus globalization. Their understanding of nation is governed by two fundamental conditions: first, the nation is not a free-floating, de-territorialized space for exiles that flee right-wing dictators; second, exiles reject idealistic patriotism for a nation ruled by authoritarianism. Holding nationalism and transnationalism in persistent dialectic, the exile writing of Juan Goytisolo, Ariel Dorfman, and Cristina Peri Rossi exemplifies an alternative way of defining cultural identity. These writers combine at least four separate attitudes about nationalism in their writing: first, they reject the authoritarian nationalism of their former countries; second, they promote a counter version of their nation; third, they oppose the negative effects of global politics and economic policies, since these are often directly or indirectly responsible for authoritarian nationalism; and fourth, they also suggest that transnationalism or post-nationalism may be liberating to the subject because nationalism always implies the repression of difference. It is my argument that the exile's competing and conflicting views on nationalism and globalization constitute the notion of *alien nation*.

Whether from space or from Spain and Latin America, the role of aliens arriving in cosmopolitan centers significantly shifts in the latter part of the twentieth century. While modern national identity reflects earlier mass migrations, the movement of people after the nineteenth century generally presents a threat to an already established national identity. Historians consistently observe a rise in nationalism in response to mass immigration and migration. In fact, Eric Hobsbawn, a seminal theorist of nationalism, "writes the history of the modern Western nation from the perspective of the nation's margin and the migrants' exile," leading Homi Bhabha to conclude that "the emergence of the later phase of the modern nation, from the mid-nineteenth century, is also one of the most sustained periods of mass migration within the West, and colonial expansion in the East" (*Location of Culture* 139). In the twentieth century immigrants move to nations that have already defined their borders and carved a national image. Hence, the horror of the film *Alien Nation*. After the establishment of national borders, it is culturally terrifying for a country to be threatened by the presence of a new culture that could potentially redefine national identity. So, the immigrants, refugees, and exiles of the twentieth century are faced with metropolitan centers that see them as outsiders. Unlike the European immigrants to Uruguay, Chile, and the United States in the nineteenth century, for example, who were accepted as part of the process of nation-building, immigrants today are seen as threats to national integrity. A banner in Graham Baker's film reads "Teach English to the Universe": the cultural paranoia is evident.

The place of the immigrant or the refugee is certainly not equivalent to that of the exiled intellectual. Nevertheless, the literature produced by exiles offers a narrative account of the crisis of cultural identity experienced by individuals who must live in a foreign country. (Grinberg and Grinberg point to many connections between the experience of migration and of exile.) Furthermore, as national identity has been increasingly threatened by transnational experiences of capitalism and technological advancement, the literature of exiles from the latter part of the twentieth century describes the role of nationalism and transnationalism in cultural identity. Intellectuals have always emigrated and been exiled. The question, then, is to determine how the exiles of the late-twentieth century represent a distinct version of this experience and how they relate to a concept of the nation.

These recent generations of exiles and immigrants typically arrive in nations that are hostile and unwelcoming. This antagonism is further exacerbated by the fact that many exiled intellectuals have found themselves in the "Belly of the Beast," José Martí's term for the metropolitan city. In the specific cases of Goytisolo, Dorfman, and Peri Rossi, they flee from authoritarian, corporativist governments in Spain, Chile, and Uruguay and arrive in Paris, Washington, D.C., and Barcelona, respectively. The beast for them is not only a metropolitan city but also a source of economic and cultural imperialism. While this analysis focuses on the literary work of Goytisolo, Dorfman, and Peri Rossi, these writers represent a larger group of exiles that confront national expulsion after the end of World War II, when most contemporary national borders were established. Some of the common traits these cases share shed light on a broader phenomenon of exiles that experienced their homeless condition as historical circumstances brought capitalism to an increasingly transnational scale. The nations to which these exiles fled were often supportive in varying degrees of the installation of authoritarian rule in their homelands. This bizarre situation, where exiles flee their homeland only to take up residence in a country that supported the dictatorship that caused their exile, has a profound impact on the exiles' sense of nationalism and globalization. Their former nation has been radically altered as a consequence of global politics. For these exiles nationalism and globalization no longer make sense as discrete concepts. The sick irony of the exile's condition is that the enemy also signifies "home," and the alien is now "nation."

Yet, what of the homeland, the lost nation? Exiles have been denied their rights to citizenship—to express their ideas freely, to participate in government, and to enter native borders. Their home has become alien as well. For these exiles the concept of the *alien nation* is a double-edged sword: the native country has expelled them and their new location is not only foreign but an accomplice to authoritarianism in their native lands. In this way the connection between the literature of exiles and a concept of nation can only be alien and strange.

These complications do not preclude the ability to discern a sense of nationalism in the cultural identity narrated in such literature. Nevertheless, it is commonly assumed that nationalism and transnationalism represent two opposing poles. Nationalism, or the belief that one's nation is distinct and constitutive of a community to which one belongs and from which one's cultural identity has been formed, is challenged by the theory of transnationalism which argues that such affiliations have been "rendered obsolete by the international realities of multinational corporations and the telecommunications industry" (Brennan 45). The exile is identified as precisely someone who has lost national ties, a transnational. Yet, the condition is a direct consequence of national developments (that prohibit existence at home) and international developments (that pressured these nations to join the international market and intervened in national politics). The effects of transnationalism and homelessness, then, influence the nationalism narrated by these exiles. The problem is that many critics argue that cultural identity must either be national or transnational, positing the two positions as philosophically incompatible and contradictory. It is the task of this study to show how the work of Goytisolo, Dorfman, and Peri Rossi challenges such assumptions. What seems at first to be a contradiction is better understood as a dialectic between many opposing positions.

Describing the role of the "nation" in the texts studied as that of an *alien nation* also connects, obviously, to the exile's condition of alienation. In many ways, it is the multiple alienations of the exile that make the concept of an *alien nation* clearer. The exiles I studied experience many layers of alienation, some historically specific and others transhistorical. Transhistorically, the figure of the exile is the quintessential "alien," solitary and melancholy, out of place. Paul Ilie, writing on pan-Hispanic exile literature, refers to the universal alienation of exiles: "across the centuries in different countries, the literatures of exiles originate in different national experiences and nevertheless converge in the common loneliness of physical or psychological displacement" ("Exolalia" 227). Ilie privileges this common bond and further states that this shared experience "reaches beyond nationality and time itself" (227). While Ilie is justified in highlighting the existence of alienation in the exile experience regardless of nationality or historical moment, this should not overshadow a critical assessment of alienation's historical particularities. Alienation, while universal, only makes sense when relating to a distinct, local space from which one has been expelled.

These exiles also suffer alienation in a Marxist sense. Expanding on Marx's theory, the alienation of the exile serves to magnify the four levels of alienation that the individual suffers in capitalist society. Marx argued that under capitalism the working class individual becomes alien to 1) the results of his labor, 2) the nature in which he lives, 3) other human beings and, finally, 4) himself. (See Karl Marx, "Economic and Philosophic Manuscripts of 1844" 72–74.) It is interesting to note that Marx was exiled from Germany in 1843 and wrote "Economic and Philosophical Manuscripts of 1844" in Paris. His experience of exile and estrangement coincides with his development of a theory of the alienation of the laborer under capitalism and his idealized description of the freedom of individual expression provided under the collective production of communism. In the case of the exile from capitalist society these alienations intensify: by being banished from his country the exile has lost his job, his land, his compatriots, and is further isolated and estranged from that society. Moreover, many of these exiled intellectuals find themselves in this position precisely because they advocated Marxist critiques of a class-based society. Both before and after exile, Goytisolo, Dorfman, and Peri Rossi leveled harsh criticisms at bourgeois values and capitalism (Goytisolo's *Para vivir aquí*, Dorfman's *Moros en la costa,* and Cristina Peri Rossi's *Indicios pánicos,* all written prior to exile, are texts critical of bourgeois values). Despite the bourgeois origins of Goytisolo and Dorfman, all three writers have a tenuous and complicated class identity, which only serves to exacerbate their experience of alienation. Consequently, Marx's universal condition of alienation under capitalism obtains to these exiles in a particular way. Moreover, these exiles' experience of Marxist alienation becomes intertwined with the transhistorical treatment of the exile as alien.

Thus far I have described two central layers to the complex alienation of these writers: they are alienated because they are outcasts and they are outcasts because they are critics of capitalism and its alienating effects on society. Andrew Gurr generalizes that alienation from a culture or a physical home has a radical effect on the writer's mind (15). The effects on the mind mentioned by Gurr must be further qualified in the case of writers who find themselves in exile after 1960. Here the narrative treatment of the exile's estrangement shows signs of the shift from modern to postmodern notions of estrangement. Alienation, as found in the writing of the high modernist period, is a condition that affects the artist as he confronts the rise of the metropolitan city. Aijaz Ahmad points to the work of the cubists, Joyce's *Ulysses,* and Eliot's *Waste Land* as artistic representations of the impact of the modern city on individual identity. He argues that "[i]n none of the major modernists, however, was the idea of a fragmented self, or the accompanying sense of unbelonging, ever a source of great comfort; it came usually, with a sense of recoiling, even some terror" (129). Despite its relentless nature, the modern desire to combat social isolation is never satisfied. In fact many modern writers who never were exiled have been described as "exiles in the homeland" or inner exiles, where one's exile is nationally internal. For instance, in the United States, the literature of the "lost generation" (Gertrude Stein's term for the generation of writers in the 1920s) refers to a group of writers who felt alienated from their national culture. This feeling of internal exile, described by Malcolm Cowley in *Exile's Return*, caused some of these writers to travel abroad to Europe. Moreover, the writers of the early 1900s, who witnessed the commercialization of culture preceding the Depression, felt a "sense of difference" and isolation, which became a constant theme in their writing (Cowley 7). In modernism, alienation is an unpleasant and painful experience. Much cultural production during modernism, then, demonstrates the self's alienation from the rise of the city and from the increasing entrenchment of modern society.

The 1960s witnessed the influence of poststructuralist theory, and the center for these changes in critical theory was Paris, a common way station for exiles and itinerant intellectuals. Structuralism was purported to be a science of signs. The structuralists believed that the sign, not the subject, was the key to meaning. By diminishing the importance of the subject and focusing on the sign, the structuralist movement radically altered modern theory. The humanism, phenomenology, and existentialism commonly practiced by modern thinkers and responsible for an emphasis on the human subject were shown to be problematic, because, as the structuralists argued, the subject was merely a linguistic construct. Later, after May 1968, Vietnam, and the Algerian War, the possibilities for "revolutionary thinking" were put into question. The poststructuralists transformed the systematic thinking of structuralism in favor of a view of the world as arbitrary and unconventional. Due to their disappointment with politics and history, "The poststructuralists attacked the scientific pretensions of structuralism which strove for the modern goals of foundation, truth, objectivity, certainty, and system" (Best and Kellner 20). Whereas structuralism was not primarily concerned with the dilemmas of the subject because it focused on the sign, under poststructuralism we find that there is an emphasis on the fragmented sign and consequently the fragmented self. Some suggested that a fragmented identity was no longer a source of anguish, as under modernism, but necessary and positive. Fragmentation challenged the unified subject posited by Enlightenment thought and rejected the systematic desires of the structuralists. The bourgeois obsession with representing the anxiety of the alienated self under modernism was abandoned in favor of a radical rearticulation of the self as endlessly splintered and different. The existential quests of modernism were discarded as useless efforts at uncovering a centered and knowable self. Ahmad explains the move from alienation as anguish to alienation as celebration: "The terrors of High Modernism at the prospect of inner fragmentation and social disconnection have now been stripped, in Derridean strands of postmodernism, of their tragic edge, pushing that experience of loss, instead, in a celebratory direction; the idea of belonging is itself seen now as bad faith, a mere 'myth of origins'" (129). According to poststructuralism, alienation has lost its Marxist resonance as a call toward revolution and the exile lives alienation positively as "new being" (Seidel x).

Alienation in the poststructuralist account of it has also lost any reference to geographical place. It no longer motivates one to act and it no longer has a connection to a political struggle in a particular location. The link between the exile's alienation and nationalism is no longer desirable because the individual's allegiance to a nation is considered to be oppressive. The broken ties between the exile and the nation are no longer problematic. If the goals of nationalism are "creating an administrative economy, a repressive apparatus capable of waging war, and a sense of belonging that glosses over class conflicts" then such repressive thinking must be destroyed (Brennan 45). Aijaz Ahmad explains that literary theory exalted "cultural nationalism as the determinate ideological form of resistance against the dominant imperial culture throughout the 1970s; but then in the 1980s [owing to the rise, in particular, of deconstruction and, in general, of poststructuralism], nationalism itself, in all its forms, came to be discarded as an oppressive, coercive mechanism" (37). The poststructuralists argue that the exile should enjoy the absence of national ties and abandon the quest for home. The exile is heralded as the postmodern hero, a role model for the fragmented self. (The obvious contradiction of proclaiming any figure as a "hero" of postmodernism seems clear and is also interesting when one notes that Deleuze and Guattari call the nomad a postmodern hero as well.)

The problem with this shift in meaning is that the cultural production of exiles in the latter part of the twentieth century is rarely, if ever, void of any connection to geography, history, and the subject's pain of alienation. Even pop culture renditions of this experience, like that of the film *Alien Nation,* show that the incurable fragmentation of the self produces horror—for both the "newcomers" and their "hosts." Like modernist writing, the literature of exiles in the era of postmodernism also displays great fear at the splintered self. While alienation in the work of Goytisolo, Dorfman, and Peri Rossi is different from that found in the work of Joyce, Unamuno, or Martí, to cite a sample of various modernist writers in exile, it is hardly something to celebrate. Because the writers in this study witnessed failed challenges to capitalism, they lack faith in the possibility of a successful Marxist revolution. This produces a crisis for these writers: they question whether culture can potentially be subversive. The trend after 1970 was to argue for local resistance and the abandonment of global or universal strategies. Yet, exile literature wavers between seeking subversion locally and globally. The local only makes sense within the global. Dorfman writes in the introduction to *Viudas* (1981), his first novel written in exile, that in an effort to avoid censorship in Chile and gain access for his text in his native country he had to use a distant language. Writing about the case of the *disappeared* (political prisoners who were abducted and never accounted for) his allegorical language transforms the story to a level which is "menos local y más universal" (8–9) ["less local and more universal"]. As an exile, narrating only the local is not sufficient. Dorfman must narrate his nation's horror from a new perspective—one that recognizes that similar atrocities happen all over the globe: "Esa tragedia podía ocurrir en todas partes y en cualquier momento y a cualquier persona" (9) ["This tragedy could occur anywhere, at any time, to anyone"].

THE POLITICS OF NATIONALISM

What issues complicate exiled nationalism? The central issue revolves around the tension between describing the connection between the self and the state as either fragmented or unified. This basic dichotomy represents a significant friction between modernism and postmodernism. During the Enlightenment the emphasis on rationalism favored a faith in the self's unity. This notion was challenged by modernism when rationalism seemed incapable of describing the conflicts between the self and industrialization. Hence, we note the anguish of the modern subject who is conscious of fragmentation and nostalgic for unification.

The connection between the subject and the state undergoes substantial historical shifts. According to pre-modern thought, the subject should give allegiance to the Crown or its equivalent source of political power. The subject's dedication to the Crown was akin to religious faith. Later, during modernization, the modern subject was the key to nation-building. The nation was its citizens and the citizen was responsible for upholding the values of the state. Significantly, the stress on unification between the self and its home was central to both pre-modern and modern political theory. What is important to consider, however, is that although "unification" (either social or individual) was desired in pre-modern and modern theory, these desires were not so easily realized. In fact, societies and subjects continued to undermine the cultural homogenization officially sought by both monarchies and modern nations. The inception of nationalism was central to the formation of modern nations because it described the inalienable ties between the subject and the state. Nevertheless, while nationalism projected a unified national body as part of its ideological persuasion, such unification rarely, if ever, existed.

In particular, if the countries of Latin America are primarily comprised of cultural heterogeneity, what has the role of nationalism been? According to William Rowe and Teresa Whitfield, "There have been three main moments of unification: conquest, liberation from direct colonialism, and incorporation into international capitalist culture" (232). Cultural nationalism, of the sort used to maintain government power, then, has been repeatedly associated with oppressive politics. Both Chile and Uruguay were on the threshold of this last phase of unification when their economies challenged the strength of international capitalism. For Dorfman, the Allende years represent an effort to overturn economic imperialism by nationalizing all foreign-owned business. This leads to an interesting twist on the nationalism issue, because national unification was necessary for the success of a leftist politics intent on liberating the populace. Later, under the dictatorial rule of Augusto Pinochet, the self-proclaimed "Father of the Nation," the doors opened for international business investment and the cultural climate stagnated under extreme repression and censorship. Therefore, Dorfman's problems with nationalism reflect his experience of "positive" leftist nationalism, reactionary "negative" nationalism, and Western economic imperialism at a transnational level.

Peri Rossi also witnessed the actions of the Tupamaro guerrillas, a nationalist movement that dominated Uruguayan political life in the late 1960s. The Tupamaros fought for national liberation and sought to regain political control of Uruguay. The military crushed the guerrilla movement in 1972 and 20 percent of the country fled into exile for either political or economic reasons (Rowe and Whitfield 230). The attempts of the Tupamaros to reunite the Uruguayan populace with their land were crushed. Under the military regime citizens were forcefully linked to the state and were stripped of any sense of power: it was even necessary to have a political permit in order to celebrate a birthday (Rowe and Whitfield 230). Thus, the forms of cultural nationalism imposed on Chile and Uruguay after the coups were something neither writer could advocate.

So, if these writers criticize cultural nationalism, do they necessarily promote its opposite? The opposite of cultural nationalism has been characterized by the notion of transnationalism where cultural identity has no connection to any "myth of origins." Because these writers do not abandon the political and continue to produce texts critical of society, their work does not directly translate into the category of transnational literature. However, they do transform their formal approach to narrative and they do become influenced by an international community of intellectuals. Perhaps it is worthwhile here to draw a distinction between national-cultural identity and cultural nationalism. The first is simply a description of one's experiences: it is one's lived history through language and other social relations like class, gender, and sexuality, as they constitute one's cultural background. The second is more clearly articulated as a political position, which seeks to claim an autonomous cultural territory. It implies that cultural difference can be distinguished and should be preserved and fostered. That literature has connections to either of these notions is contested by poststructuralism, but the difference is important. In particular, the work of these writers has exile as a clear marker of national-cultural identity. Moreover, they also have a complicated connection to cultural nationalism: in addition to their responses to authoritarian-capitalist nationalism, they have a personal stake in the future of their countries and its cultural production. The stories they narrate are caught in a struggle, still, to change the fate of their countries. Such desires, by definition, are nationalist.

Many of the writers exiled from Spain and the Southern Cone were responding to the negative nationalism and ultra-nationalism fostered by authoritarian political ideologies in place in their native lands. If nationalism in Latin America had commonly been considered a move of resistance toward Western imperialism, the authoritarian nationalisms found in Chile and Uruguay after 1973 needed to be reassessed. As Ahmad explains, the ideology of cultural nationalism in the "Third World" implies that "each 'nation' . . . has a 'culture' and a 'tradition,' and that to speak from within that culture and that tradition is itself an anti-imperialist act" (9). Latin America has historically been plagued with the dilemma of defining what actually constitutes autochthonous culture. Arturo Uslar Pietri indicates:

> La identidad del hombre latinoamericano ha sido conflictiva desde sus orígenes históricos. . . . ¿Cuál cultura española vino, qué culturas indígenas di-

> ferentes predominaron en distintos puntos de la vasta geografía, qué variedad de culturas africanas entró en la pedagogía de las ayas esclavas, cuáles combinaciones y grados de mezcla se dieron en el inmenso escenario terrestre y humano? (15)
>
> The identity of Latin Americans has been conflictive since its historical origins. . . . Which Spanish culture came, what different indigenous cultures predominated at distinct points in its vast geography, what variety of African cultures entered in the teachings of slave wet nurses, which combinations and degrees of mixing took place on its immense human and terrestrial stage?

At the very least, as Rosalba Campra argues, in Latin America, national essence is a cultural hybrid (46). The three founding cultures of Latin American identity—European, indigenous, African—have always complicated attempts at containing a unified national image. Nevertheless, the need to combat cultural domination by the West has led many Latin American intellectuals to seek a means for empowering their national identity.

Since independence there have been opposing positions taken on the question of cultural integrity in Latin America. Representative thinkers from the nineteenth and early twentieth centuries are Domingo Faustino Sarmiento, José Martí, and José Enrique Rodó, all of whom were concerned with the concept of Western civilization and its impact on Latin American nation-building and cultural identity. In the twentieth century Roberto Fernández Retamar, Angel Rama, and Fernando Ortiz also represent Latin American intellectuals concerned with the influence of the West on Latin American identity. The most marked difference between intellectuals from these two periods is that by the middle of the twentieth century the hegemony of Western ideals was more pervasive and was considered more insidious throughout Latin America. Consequently intellectuals from the period were intent on arguing for strategies that would foster cultural autonomy in the region.

In many ways, the cultural production of the Latin American literary boom of the 1960s can be described as just such an effort. The boom refers to the literary production of writers, mostly novelists, from Latin America who worked in the 1960s. These writers achieved international fame and are often considered to represent a decisive moment in the literary development of Latin America, because of the value accorded their work by Western intellectuals. Some of these writers include Gabriel García Márquez, Julio Cortázar, Mario Vargas Llosa, and José Donoso. Interestingly Juan Goytisolo was also greatly influenced by these writers, which points to the fact that the connection between Spanish literature and Latin American literature increased during this period of history due, at least in part, to the communication between exiles from dictatorships in both regions. During the boom writers sought to narrate their cultural identity by finding an autochthonous narrative voice, which also inscribed the influences of Western literary figures such as Faulkner and Proust.

The aesthetics of the boom are often associated with that of western modernism (see González Echevarría). During this period of time, coincidental with the success of the Cuban Revolution, narrative still sought an aesthetic of change that no longer seemed plausible to the generation that followed—a generation including the work of Ariel Dorfman and Cristina Peri Rossi. While the boom has often been considered a period of totalizing meta-narratives, those writers who followed tended to leave their texts open in order to allow their readers to draw their own conclusions. Opened narrative, fragmented text, and lack of closure caused the work of authors like Dorfman and Peri Rossi to be described as post-boom—a movement often associated with postmodernism (other post-boom writers include Antonio Skármeta, Severo Sarduy, Reinaldo Arenas, Ricardo Piglia, etc.; see Donald Shaw; González Echeverría). Yet, in the case of Dorfman and Peri Rossi, they avoid authoritarian discourse in their narratives as both a consequence of the dictatorships in their countries and the influence of new narrative techniques associated with postmodernism. Abandoning the desire to make a text overtly political does not in these cases result in celebrated fragmentation. According to Slavoj Žižek resistance to totality must be understood in the context of the totalitarian realities from which they arise. By questioning totality, these writers are not advocating nihilism, they are responding to the military's efforts to forcefully unify the heterogeneous cultural landscape of their countries. Dorfman explains in response to a question about the narrative style of *The Last Song of Manuel Sendero*, his second novel in exile: "Even though there is a constant mixing of different languages and dimensions of reality, the fairy-tale, the 'realistic', the scholarly footnotes, the mass media expressions, *this should not be understood as a postmodernist gliding over surfaces all of which have identical value*" (Boyers 156, my emphasis).

Nationalism also poses a problem in Spain, and much about the case of Dorfman and Peri Rossi applies to Goytisolo. Spanish cultural nationalism in the nineteenth and twentieth centuries had historically been used to combat cultural dominance by French and British neighbors and to combine Spain into one unified culture: Spanish nationalism under Franco was an extreme example. Franco imposed the use of the Castilian language in all regions of Spain, attempting to take away a cultural heterogeneity that had been characteristic of Spanish identity since the Middle Ages, when there existed a hybrid of Christian, Jewish, and Arabic culture. Spanish cultural unification reached its heyday in 1492 with the final expulsion of the Moors and the Jews and the encounter with Latin America. After 1492 Spanish culture remained heterogeneous: different regions spoke different languages (Basques, Galician, and Catalan) and even though the Inquisition attempted to impose Catholicism on all citizens of Spain, many continued to secretly practice Judaism or Islam. Spanish cultural unification was mythical and ideological, as in the case of Latin America. Individuals residing in Spain before 1939, the year Franco assumed power, would typically identify themselves as Catalan or Basque before Spanish. After 1939 such cultural associations continued, but were kept in the closet.

Américo Castro counters the unified national image artificially imposed on Spain under Franco by stating that Spain is a cultural colony (4). In this sense neither Spain nor Latin America, as is the case in many parts of the globe, can boast of a single identifiable national culture. Such a lack of straightforward national identity complicates the ability to make connections between literary production and cultural nationalism. Also like Chile and Uruguay, Spanish culture was far from powerful on a global scale in the twentieth century. Similar to Latin America, Spanish intellectuals historically grappled with the question of cultural nationalism. Parallel to the case of Latin America, Spain has a long history of intellectual debate about Spanish cultural integrity. In the nineteenth century, Benito Pérez Galdós wrote essays and literature aimed at illuminating the crisis of cultural identity for Spaniards. In the early twentieth century Miguel de Unamuno and José Ortega y Gasset dedicated essays to the need for Spain to retain its unique cultural heritage. In contrast with Latin America, though, Spanish cultural nationalism was typically connected to conservative politics and was not as readily accepted as a move to resist imperial cultural domination. As in much of Europe, nationalism in the twentieth century came to embody a notion of tyranny and no longer represented freedom from it (Brennan 57). In Spain, nationalist movements were usually conservative, Catholic, and supportive of the monarchy.

Another link between the case of Spain and that of Chile and Uruguay, then, is the rise of nationalism under authoritarian military regimes. In some cases, historians have argued that Franco's system of rule was exported to Latin America (see Hernán Vidal). The figure of the Caudillo, the paternal leader, existed in both the Southern Cone and Spain. Authoritarian rhetoric in these countries linked the family with nation, the dictator with father, and the people with children. In response to the link between dictatorship and patriarchy, Goytisolo, Peri Rossi, and Dorfman narrate worlds where family structure ruptures. Peri Rossi's story "La influencia de Edgar Allen Poe en la poesía de Raimundo Arias," Dorfman's *Viudas,* and Goytisolo's *Señas de identidad* question the structure of family as it has been constructed in an authoritarian state.

Goytisolo went into exile approximately ten years before Dorfman and Peri Rossi and was part of a second wave of Spanish exiles that fled in the 1950s (Max Aub, Ramón Sender, and Francisco Ayala are some of the well-known Civil War exiles who create a narrative style that greatly departs from that of the exiles of 1950; see Ferres and Ortega for other writers). Goytisolo's experience and his work differ from that of the exiles that left Spain in 1939. The writings of the Spanish exiles immediately following the Civil War were often autobiographical narratives that belied a deep nostalgia and mourning for the losses of the war. As Michael Ugarte explains: "The plentiful books of memoirs by Spanish exiles of 1939 serve to illustrate a need for recovery and compensation" (*Shifting* 69). The work of the exiles of 1950, because of its inheritance of the consequences of the Civil War, does not reflect a sense of loss similar to the work of the Civil War exiles. In fact, Goytisolo's narrative abandons totality and demonstrates an uneasy relationship with nostalgia. The twenty years since the Republic's loss of the Civil War had demonstrated that the political struggle fought on Spanish soil was not merely national. By 1955 Spain had a seat in the United Nations and was an official member of the international economic community. The ideals of the Republicans who had fought in the Civil War seemed a distant memory. Narratives of national politics needed a new language of representation. Paul Ilie states that language for Goytisolo fails "to represent a coherent reality [and imposes] an unexpected instability of perception" ("Exolalia" 243). Like Dorfman and Peri Rossi,

Goytisolo's connections to cultural nationalism are complex and untraditional: all three respond to authoritarian nationalism by rejecting totality and their work suggests a conviction that identity is also affected by global developments.

THE THEORY AND PRACTICE OF EXILE AND NATIONALISM

Goytisolo, Dorfman, and Peri Rossi come from literary traditions that are constantly suffering the lack of an empowered national culture and/or attempting to dislodge oppressive forms of national culture. While they resist authoritarian forms of nationalism, they also need to resist cultural death by the homogenizing power of cultural imperialism from the First World. All three writers will re-tell their nations' history according to criteria that are radically different from those being maintained in the authoritarian regimes in power at home. As Timothy Brennan argues: "In one strain of Third World writing the contradictory topoi of exile and nation are fused in a lament for the necessary and regrettable insistence of nation-forming, in which the writer proclaims his identity with a country whose artificiality and exclusiveness have driven him into a kind of exile—a simultaneous recognition of nationhood and an alienation from it" (63). The combined gestures of resisting the image of the nation under dictatorship and of insisting that the nation, and at times the world, be reformed is the basis of the concept of *alien nation*. The writing of these exiles, like that of the "wandering peoples" described by Homi Bhabha in *Location of Culture,* "will not be contained within the *Heim* of the national culture and its unisonant discourse, but are themselves the marks of a shifting boundary that alienates the frontiers of the modern nation" (164). The argument that those outside of the nation are also constitutive of national identity is an important point. Especially when culture within the nation's borders has been radically restrained, those artists working outside cannot be discounted. Their connection is different from that of those producing inside the nation's territory, but their place outside does not deterritorialize them. Dictatorships appropriate nationalism to repress and contain national identity, and these authors' work provides an alternative view of nationalist culture. That they also produce culture that participates in an international cultural context does not strip them of any connection to geographical space.

What may appear to be the same formal trappings of poststructural cultural production in the work of these authors must be qualified as postmodern, but not poststructural. Making a distinction between these positions is difficult, but I would argue that the work of these writers provides support for this distinction. What all theories of the postmodern have in common is a challenging of the typical boundaries of various disciplines. But, as I draw the distinction, poststructuralist positions are fundamentally skeptical, relativist, and unsystematic, which leads them to a state of hopelessness— the same state of hopelessness that has been the fate of skeptics across time. Poststructuralism focuses on the disintegration of signification and it adheres to the nihilistic, ludic, and hollow aspects of postmodern theory. Postmodern positions, in some cases, retain the hope of political agency even if that agency has been shown to be extraordinarily fragile. Postmodernists, like poststructuralists, question the validity of totalizing systematic theories, the main difference being that postmodern theory retains a commitment to socio-historical analysis. The bases for such analysis are often altered versions of systematic epistemes like those found in Marxism and psychoanalysis. The problematic separation of the two types of thought is due, at least in part, to the way in which the two positions intersect and overlap. Best and Kellner explain: "Poststructuralism forms part of the matrix of postmodern theory, and while the theoretical breaks described as postmodern are directly related to poststructuralist critiques, we shall interpret poststructuralism as a subset of a broader range of theoretical, cultural, and social tendencies which constitute postmodern discourses" (25). For the purposes of this project a significant indication of postmodern theory will be the recognition that there are many possible bases for hermeneutic study, such as gender, sexuality, race, and class. For instance, Marxist critiques alone do not adequately address problems with patriarchy, and gender studies do not lead to a change in economic modes of production. Certain strains of postmodern theory, though, are political and differ from ludic, textualist postmodernism (for more on these terms see my definitions in chapter one, "Keywords of Exile").

The murky connections between theory and literature complicate a clear-cut separation between postmodern culture and postmodern theory. In fact, it is often the resistance on the part of the texts under analysis that calls for a revamping of the theories used to critique them. The narratives of Goytisolo, Dorfman, and Peri Rossi reveal postmodern notions of history, the subject, and of the nation. In their work these concepts have been refigured: while they reject Enlightenment versions of the knowable self, for instance, and disdain bourgeois obsessions with existential angst, they narrate a notion of the self that is neither stable nor entirely knowable, but that avoids complete oblivion. Once again it is their place in history which leads them to such narrative junctures: their narrative style is characteristic of a cultural crisis that these writers observed from a position which was both marginal, that of exile, and central, that of belonging to an international community of intellectuals. What must be made clear is that these elements of the work of Dorfman, Goytisolo, and Peri Rossi are not only modernist. Significant formal and thematic changes differentiate their work from that of the generation of writers that preceded them. Yet their historical circumstance caused them to continue to narrate for change. It is their resistance to the standard categories proposed by critical theory that demands that such theory be reassessed.

Alienation in the work of these authors is general and local, Marxist and psychoanalytic, modern and postmodern. While alienation is a universal experience it only makes sense when referring to a particular system (or set of systems) that has left the exile outcast. The theoretical implications of the fact that these texts communicate at both a global and local level have been largely overlooked by criticism of their writing. Instead, most theories either argue that exile literature is nostalgic and mourns the loss of the nation, or is celebratory and loses all ties to national experience. As explained earlier, these theories about the role of cultural nationalism in exile literature can best be summed up by Claudio Guillén's categories of exile and counter-exile literature (see chapter two, "The Dialectics of Exile"). Exile literature is nostalgic and national, whereas the literature of counter-exile transcends the national and resonates transnationally.

The literature of "counter-exile" described by Guillén relates to Deleuze and Guattari's concept of deterritorialization. If a text has transcended connections to place or native origin, then it has become deterritorialized. For Deleuze and Guattari deterritorialization opposes territorialization, where the first is the "unchaining of both material production and desire from socially restricting forces" and the latter is "the process of repressing desire by taming and confining its productive energies" (Best and Kellner 88; for a more detailed account see their text *Anti-Oedipus*). Deleuze and Guattari use the concept of deterritorialization as an ideal state that counters the repression of capitalism. They link capitalist repression to fascist forms of society and seek release from it by reconsidering psychoanalytic impulses, in particular the bourgeois privileging of the oedipal. "Capitalism re-channels desire and needs into inhibiting psychic and social spaces that control them far more effectively than savage or despotic societies" (89). The condition of the exile as outcast from authoritarian, capitalist systems highlights the relevance of Deleuze and Guattari's theory, inasmuch as they are directly involved in a critique of authoritarian forms of society.

Another link between their theory and criticism of exile literature is found in their postulation of the nomad as a "post-modern hero." According to them the notion of the self should be associated with that of a "nomad"—someone who roams deterritorialized space and resists state power. In Deleuze and Guattari's text *Nomadology: The War Machine,* they explain: "If the nomad can be called the Deterritorialized *par excellence*, it is precisely because there is no reterritorialization *afterwards* as with the migrant. . . . With the nomad, on the contrary, it is deterritorialization that constitutes the relation to the earth" (52). The appropriation of the nomad for these purposes seems to be an example of Orientalism. In fact, the nomad represents one of the most static and predictable forms of pre-modern life. Nomads do not wander deterritorialized spaces: they cover the same territory according to the seasons. While the boundaries of the spaces they traverse are elastic, they are still very clearly defined, and are largely controlled by the weather—hardly the basis for a decentered and free-floating identity.

What is important to note from this analysis is that the notion of the nomad and of deterritorialization has influenced much theory that has come to celebrate the condition of exile. In particular, Emily Hicks's *Border Writing: The Multidimensional Text* covers the writings of various Latin American writers, most of whom have been exiled. In her words, "one could argue that the nineteenth-century European notion of the subject is replaced in the work of the border writer by fragmentation in cultural, linguistic and political deterritorialization" (xxiv). The subject, then, in "border writing" is just multiple fragmentation. She later states that "border writing is deterritorialized, political, and collective" (xxxi). The problem becomes the degree to which such writing could possibly be political or collective if it is so totally fragmented. Neil Larsen, in the Foreword to *Border Writing*, critiques Hicks's combination of a poststructural critical framework within a so-called political literary analysis. If language has become "deterritorialized" and is free of socially repressive systems, then it seems to be wholly disconnected from political discourse aiming at change. As Larsen explains, "to suppose that by merely having 'access to new images' and effecting changes 'at the level of signifiers,' etc., events such as Argentina's 'dirty war' might be avoided—is this not to finally reduce the 'dirty war' itself to some sort of symbol, to question its very existence as something 'real'?" (xix). A corollary example to the one above would be the use of Derrida in Michael Ugarte's *Shifting Ground: Spanish Civil War Exile Literature*. In his book Ugarte has a chapter on Goytisolo, "Exile as Nomad."

The common usage of the terms "deterritorialization," "cultural migrancy," "nomadism," and "liminality," as intoned by many poststructuralist critics, may seem to slip easily into descriptions of exile literature. The exile, or nomad, has become the role model for poststructural existence. However, without history and politics, exile is a condition that has no meaning. To strip the exile of history and celebrate displacement is to glorify the experience. Ahmad argues that poststructuralist non-attachment advocates the image of the theorist as "traveler" (36). The vision of the theorist as "traveler" is the result, at least in part, of the work of Jacques Derrida. In his essay "The Question of the Book," Derrida refers specifically to the connections between the condition of exile and territory when he states: "When a Jew or a poet proclaims the Site, he is not declaring war. For this site, this land, calling to us from beyond memory, is always elsewhere. The site is not the empirical and National Here of a territory. It is immemorial and thus also a future" (66). Derrida argues that the concept of land has no connection to either time or space—a point that is particularly problematic when we are dealing with exile. Such writing by Derrida has led some scholars of exile literature, like Michael Ugarte, to incorporate poststructuralism within their analysis. Specifically, Ugarte cites Derrida's work, where Derrida "refers to the nebulous place or site of the exile as the locus of linguistic activity which he describes as a journey to nowhere" (27). But I would argue that, if the theorist or the exile travels to nowhere and for no reason (because writing is "an eternally exilic search"), then such positions suppress "the very conditions of intelligibility within which the fundamental facts of our time can be theorized" (Ugarte 27; Ahmad 36).

One of the major issues that complicate an interpretation of the work of these exiles is that critics often describe their narrative as that of "counter-exile" or describe them as examples of poststructural culture—because the texts themselves point critics in such a direction. Since this literature attempts to narrate national identity in a new way, over and against the unifying, authoritarian visions of the nation that the exiled writers have been forced to leave, these texts often have complex, experimental aesthetics. Goytisolo's novel *Juan sin tierra* has provoked a plethora of articles which conclude that Goytisolo, also named Juan, has lost all ties to his nation through this narrative effort: he is splendidly landless. Ugarte writes: "The protagonist of *Juan sin tierra* is, as the title suggests, a landless being, in this case a writer whose wanderings from place to place and from text to text are emblematic of Goytisolo's own conception of writing" (*Shifting* 208). But I would suggest that we read between the lines and not take the novel's title at face value. Juan, the character, desires the loss of a nation that has caused him suffering. Such desire does not necessarily lead to a free-floating, landless identity. For example, in Goytisolo's previous novel *Reivindicación del conde don Julián* the narrator states: "La patria no es la tierra : el hombre no es el árbol : ayúdame a vivir sin suelo y sin raíces : móvil, móvil" (124–25) ["one's true homeland is not the country of one's birth: man is not a tree: help me to live without roots: ever on the move"; 104]. He desires unattached movement, but has not achieved it. So for Goytisolo "land" is not equivalent to the "nation" or the "fatherland." What Goytisolo seems to suggest is that obsessions about geographic space as the foundation for national identity miss the degree to which such affiliations are mainly ideological and not spatially motivated.

In addition, the participation of these writers in an international community of exiles that came to recognize common goals moves their narrative, as mentioned before, to a realm incorporating both national and transnational affiliations. The interrelation between exiles from Spain and Latin America has existed since the fifteenth century. In modern times, Randolph Pope refers to Paris as their mythic home, but exiles converged on a variety of metropolitan centers throughout the nineteenth and twentieth centuries (59). Among the most common were Berlin, Barcelona, Vienna, London, Montreal, New York, Mexico City, and Buenos Aires. Studies have documented the emigration of European exiles to Latin America as well as that of Latin Americans to Europe (in particular, see Moeller; Graham-Yooll). Intellectuals from the nineteenth century often voluntarily "exiled" themselves as part of their education. It was considered important to travel in Europe, and particularly in France, in order to expand one's basis of experience. Government-imposed "real" exile obviously changes the stakes in such mind-expanding travel, but the tradition of convening in different centers of intellectual activity remained. What this historical legacy meant to exiles like Goytisolo, Dorfman, and Peri Rossi was that they were able to participate in a community of intellectuals and that such interactions had ramifications in their literary work, due in large part to the shared fact of authoritarian rule in their countries. Both Dorfman and Goytisolo narrate experiences of the exile while in Paris and Peri Rossi has a complete book of poetry entitled *Europa después de la lluvia*.

When these writers realize that struggle can no longer be only national and one-dimensional, their narrative represents a fragmented struggle and occasionally surpasses merely national resonance. Such fragmentation has often been misconstrued as the annihilation of national ties. Paul Ilie documents the relationship between Goytisolo, other Spanish exiles, and a community of Latin American exiles: "All of these writers share a common Hispanic intertextuality, both in their language and in their varieties of political disaffection and exile from dictatorships" ("Exolalia" 226). While it is true that the simultaneous exiles of both Spaniards and Latin Americans caused these writers to recognize common bonds, such associations should not lead us to the conclusion drawn by Ilie: "Their discourse dislodges language from historical referentiality even though the linguistic matrix is tied to authoritarian ideologies" ("Exolalia" 226). The contradiction is clear: if the "linguistic matrix is tied to authoritarian ideologies" then it has historical referentiality. Ilie describes his theory of this literary language as "exolalia" i.e., non-referential language of writers who "converge from many nations upon the same alienated discourse" (226).

The observation that exiled writers produce narrative that maintains ties to a concept of nation and yet are supposedly part of postmodern cultural production has often been explained by marking them as the result of postcoloniality (see the introduction for Spain's relation to postcolonial theory). Fredric Jameson argues in "Third World Literature in the Era of Multinational Capitalism" that texts produced from the Third World cannot be compared on equal terms to those produced in areas of dominant culture such as New York and Paris precisely because they maintain national-cultural identities (69). Ashcroft, Griffiths, and Tiffin in *The Empire Writes Back: Theory and Practice in Post-Colonial Literatures* maintain "a major feature of postcolonial literatures is the concern for place and displacement. It is here that the special postcolonial crisis of identity comes into being; the concern with the development or recovery of an effective identifying relationship with self and place" (8–9). Therefore, it has been argued that in postcolonial texts the persistence of cultural nationalism relates to the fact that these writers are working from historical experiences that revealed their cultural marginality and created a desire to forge a connection between the self and its home. In the case of exiled writers, though, signs of cultural nationalism might be read as a literary defense against the annihilation of politics and its place for struggle posited by poststructuralist theories and challenged by the economic realities of transnational capitalism. Quite simply, the "national presence" is a reminder that the alienation experienced cannot be the source of celebration, nor can it be overcome. Even though these authors recognize that a search for national origins is mythical and potentially oppressive, this observation does not deny the reality that they are unable to occupy a space that was their nation and that such banishment is painful. Moreover, rejecting a myth of origins is not the same as rejecting history.

Neil Larsen, in the introduction to *Border Writing,* supports the notion that the connection in such texts to a national culture is not merely the product of postcoloniality. In his words, "the fact that [certain postcolonial] authors can continue to produce compelling narrative fictions rooted, at one level, at least, in an authentically national-cultural experience, is not simply to be explained as a consequence of a postcolonial pristine state still unsullied by an 'incredulity toward metanarratives.' Such a view of things is not only patronizing; it obscures the important sense in which the writer's ability to draw on the cultural experience of a national 'public sphere' represents a conscious resistance to postmodernism's *affirmative* alienations" (xii, my emphasis). The postmodern has indelibly marked the narratives of these authors but the result has not been a collapse into a poststructuralist narrative void where writing is no longer interested in history or its connection to cultural identity. The task of these exiled writers has been to face the challenge of a new era of narrative possibilities (or impossibilities) where national-cultural experience appears in these texts as a form of *alien nation.*

Describing the relationship between exile literature and cultural identity as *alien nation* implicates two opposing positions regarding the connections between literature and the nation: DissemiNation by Homi Bhabha and DetermiNation by Neil Larsen. Both scholars work in the field of postcolonial studies yet Bhabha incorporates poststructuralist critique and Larsen speaks from a Marxist position. Bhabha describes national identity as both pedagogical and performative. The pedagogical aspect of national identity is the "narrated" national essence: it is national tradition, continuous and constant (Bhabha 147). The performative aspect of national identity is the subjective, discontinuous narratable aspect of the nation. Bhabha argues that it is the disjunction between these two areas of national identity that produces an opening for the emancipatory agency of liminal space. (Bhabha 4; Larsen 40). The "liminal" is also referred to as the "hybrid" and it is the state which allows the colonized to challenge the colonizer through the construction of "counter-narratives." "Counter-narratives of the nation that continually evoke and erase its totalizing boundaries—both actual and conceptual—disturb those ideological maneuvers through which 'imagined communities' are given essentialist identities" (Bhabha 149).

The writing of exiles from authoritarian regimes also resists the attempt to unify and contain national identity by presenting it as homogenized and stable. Bhabha states that the liminal is the place from which "the minority, the exilic, the marginal, and the emergent" may speak (149). The main problem, though, with Bhabha's category of the liminal is that it is no place, and it therefore provides no ground from which to speak. The influence of Derrida on Bhabha's position, as well as on the title of his article, comes forth here: "pluralism of the national sign, where difference returns as the same, is contested by the signifier's 'loss of identity' that inscribes the narrative of the people in the ambivalent, 'double' writing of the performative and the pedagogical" (154). If the signifier ceases to signify, then it is hard to see how writing produced from this ambivalent space could possibly have the power to reverse the traditional, totalizing national identity created through colonization. Ahmad has argued that the combination of Third Worldism and poststructuralism in Bhabha's work, presented as the alternative to Third Worldism and cultural nationalism, leaves him stuck in a "theoretical *mélange*" where the possibility of politics has been radically diminished (68–69). Larsen, agreeing with Ahmad, locates Bhabha's possibility for change on the uneven ground of liminal space. The irony is that Bhabha seems to argue that by merely constructing "counter-narratives" one will be able to subvert the pedagogical aspect of national identity. Such a claim is idealist, according to Larsen, and suggests that merely exposing oppression will lead to its end (39).

The persistent use of poststructuralism within a critique of the postcolonial may be more aptly termed *halluciNation* rather than disseMiNation: the oppressive features of "the nation" will not vanish into thin air by re-writing them (Kaminsky suggests we consider the term "InsemiNation"; see *After* 28). The counter position represented by the Marxist critiques of Ahmad and Larsen rejects the category of totalized, authoritarian cultural nationalism as well. If cultural nationalism is seen as a political position that argues for the superiority and integrity of national identity over other national identities that are considered threatening, then the poststructuralist rejection is based on a rejection of totality and the Marxist rejection is based on the lack of collective class critique. Yet, separating further the Marxists from the poststructuralists, the rejection of cultural nationalism does not *ipso facto* abolish a concept of national identity and does not lead to the belief in a postnational border subject. Larsen argues that cultural nationalism cannot be "outflanked" by "postulating the capacity of purely abstract-discursive and . . . aesthetic mechanisms to produce a postnationalist 'border subject'" (Introduction, *Border Writing* xviii). The poststructuralist and the Marxist versions of postcoloniality share a critique of cultural nationalism. However, by avoiding a ground for critique (i.e., class) the poststructuralists conceive of the nation as discourse, which then leads them back to cultural nationalism since the linguistic games of "counter-narratives" merely reproduce the discursive nation, but in different words. What the Marxist position holds against the poststructuralist is that the latter "'never asks,' indeed, 'never poses' the 'awkward question' of the nation and nationalism as the historical *product* (neither origin nor *telos*) of capitalism" (*Determinations* 41–42). Larsen argues, then, that postcolonial critiques must *determine* the nation as the historical product of capitalism, as opposed to disseminating it into an ambivalent space of discourse. Only then can postcolonial theory "disavow the reactionary political logic of cultural nationalism" (47). Exposing the oppressive facets of cultural identity requires historical, and not merely linguistic, ground. But, as the writing of the authors in this study will show, class critique alone does not adequately account for the crisis of nationalism either. National identity in Spain, Chile, and Uruguay, while fundamentally marked by the expansion of capitalist modes of production, was also shaped by patriarchy, Catholicism, and compulsory heterosexuality. Class critique is central but not sufficient as the sole category of analysis.

The Marxists and poststructuralists, while both disdaining cultural nationalism, work within entirely different conceptual frameworks. The role of the exile, as has been explained, has been adopted by the poststructuralists as a celebratory figure. Such treatment occurs in the work of Bhabha, Derrida, Deleuze and Guattari, Hicks, Ilie, Ugarte, and Said. Said in "Reflections on Exile" ends by saying, "Exile is life outside of habitual order. It is nomadic, decentered, contrapuntal" (366). While Said is not a poststructuralist, per se, statements like this one associate him with such an epistemology. The image of the nomad as decentered also implicates the theory of the nomad from Deleuze and Guattari. Ironically, it is Said's own theory of Orientalism that demonstrates the pitfalls in celebrating the life of the nomad and equating this pre-modern figure with contemporary exiles. Such characterizations of the exile have led writers like Larsen and Ahmad to question the relevancy of the exile to theories of cultural identity. Larsen congratulates Ahmad on his "relentless exposure of the myth of the exile-as-subversive" (13). Larsen is referring to Ahmad's critique of Salman Rushdie and his chapter "Languages of Class, Ideologies of Immigration" from *In Theory,* where Ahmad makes a sharp distinction between exile and self-exile. The self-exile for Ahmad has the freedom to choose his audience and has lost a "community of actual praxis" (131–32, 158). Elsewhere Ahmad does recuperate the exile, the "true" exile. "Exile, in the true sense, is of many kinds besides the purely colonial, and in any case it rarely produces an enduring sense of great pleasure. Exile usually has, as Williams points out, a principle, and the principle prevents one from 'floating upwards' and denying the pain" (58). I would argue that the division is not so straightforward, and that even those exiles "with principles" often find themselves just "floating," albeit not necessarily "upwards." When one's principles have been shown to lead to more pain, the frantic search for new strategies of representation can cause a frustrating inability to make sense of the system responsible for one's condition. For example, consider the following section from Dorfman's "Habeas Corpus," included in the book of poetry *Pastel de choclo* (*Last Waltz in Santiago*):

a veces despierto en mi cuándo / en mi dijéramos despierto, en un quizá / que me aqueja, que me aleja / de mí, / a veces amanezco en mi ausencia, / y no lo puedo evitar, / no estoy en ninguna parte, / despierto en una cálida pradera de hielo / que vive, que flota, que respira, / pero nada más que eso, nada más que / eso. (67)

sometimes I wake up in my when, / in my what do you call it I awake, in a maybe / that grieves me, that moves me / away from me / sometimes I wake up in my absence / and I can't avoid it / I am nowhere, / awake in a burning field of ice / that lives, that floats, that breathes / but just that, just / that. (53)

A segment of a poem from Cristina Peri Rossi's *Descripción de un naufragio*:

Ya / por el mero hecho / pertenezco a un mar en fugitiva. (24)
Already / because of a mere fact / I belong to a fugitive sea.

Juan Goytisolo in *Reivindicación del conde don Julián:*

no es sordo el mar, la erudición engaña : y las coronizadas, a menudo también : despejado el camino, el día te pertenece : dueño proeteico de tu destino, sí, y, lo que es mejor, fuera del devenir histórico. (26)

the sea is not deaf, and the store of knowledge you've acquired may be deceptive: your premonitions are often wrong too: the road ahead is clear, the day belongs to you: you are the protean master of your fate, and better still, you've dropped out from the march of history. (16)

Each of these fragments reveals a sensation of being outside of history, where one's existence no longer matters. The emotional state is not sharp pain, but numbness. Although this feeling does not create free-floating identity, it leaves one disconnected from clear-cut revolutionary ideals and holds one in a frustrating state of flux. Such literary explorations demonstrate the way in which these texts challenge popular theories of cultural identity. In Dorfman's poetic excerpt, there is a connection between being unable to name one's condition and being unable to identify one's location. Peri Rossi suggests that her state of "deterritorialization" relates to random acts. Goytisolo specifically questions his protagonist's ability to understand history and interpret events. The only way for the protagonist to move forward in time is to drop out of history (i.e., time).

The sense that exile pushes one to live outside of the nation and outside of time/history is countered by the sense of nostalgia and loss. In the following examples these writers express this loss of the nation and suggest that exile has stripped them of their identity. The first is another poem from the same collection by Dorfman, "Ejército de ocupación" ("Occupation Army"):

En esta esquina de Santiago / —Calle Huérfanos con Ahumada— / se seca y acumula la distancia: / Cada vez que pasas por ella / —como un disco quebrado / que alguien trata de tocar / por una penúltima vez— / te salta a

> doler lo que allá / vivimos / y todo lo que día a día / has tenido que olvidar. / A mí también me vuelve este recuerdo. / Lentamente soy de pronto / El eco de un disco / Que se quiebra y que sólo ponen / Muy muy bajo / Cada vez que pasa un tren. / Tú cruzas en Santiago por aquella esquina / Por la cual yo no puedo cruzar. (74)
>
> On this street corner in Santiago / —Huérfanos and Ahumada— / distance dries out and piles up. / Each time you pass by / —like a broken record / that someone tries to play / just one more time— / what we lived there leaps out / to hurt you, / everything you've had to forget / day by day. / That memory comes back to me too. / Slowly suddenly / I am the echo of a record / That breaks and that is only played / Very very softly / Whenever a train goes by. / In Santiago you go past that corner. / I cannot. (58)

In these lines Dorfman draws a distinction between the experience of the nation of those living under dictatorship and those in exile. Those "inside" are like a "broken record" that someone else controls, which refers to the forced amnesia of those who live under authoritarianism. The exile, though, is only the "echo" of the record and does not have the ability to physically encounter the street corner that holds so many memories. The exile is forced instead to use poetry to "echo" the experience and to try to hold on to his ties to his homeland.

Goytisolo's nostalgia for his lost nation takes the form of violent revenge. As Bradley Epps has noted: "*Reivinidcación del conde don Julián* is a vicious, vindictive book" (22). The novel's protagonist imagines recreating the betrayal of Count Julian in 711, when the Moors invaded Spain:

> el árabe cruel blandea jubilosamente su lanza : guerreros de pelo crespo, beduinos de pura sangre cubrirán algún día toda la espaciosa y triste España acogidos por un denso concierto de ayes, de súplicas, de lamentaciones : dormid, dormid tranquilos : nadie desconfía de ti y tu plan armoniosamente madura : reviviendo el recuerdo de tus humillaciones y agravios, acumulando gota a gota tu odio. (16)
>
> the cruel Arab is joyously brandishing his lance: warriors with kinky hair, pureblooded Bedouins will one day occupy the entire length and breadth of Spain, that vast, sad land, and be welcomed by a great chorus of moans and lamentations and supplications: sleep, sleep in peace: no one suspects you in the least and your plan is taking shape nicely: to relive the memory of the affronts and humiliations you suffered, storing up your hatred, drop by drop. (7)

Unlike the previous example from the same novel, in this passage Goytisolo's protagonist does to want to live outside of history; rather he wants to relive the defeat of Spain to the Moors. His expulsion from Spain causes him humiliation and pain, sparking his hatred of its authoritarian, oppressive society. Here we see Goytisolo's counter-nationalism, where he imagines a different nation from that under Franco.

In *Descripción de un naufragio* Peri Rossi has a number of poems that deal with guilt about exile. Grinberg and Grinberg explain that guilt is a common response to exile: "exiles can be swamped by the guilt they feel toward companions who died" (158). Peri Rossi's anxiety over leaving her nation is visible in the following excerpt:

> Si fui amarga fue por la pena. / El capitán gritó «Sálvese quien pueda» / y yo sin pensarlo más, me lancé al agua, / como siempre hubiera estado esperando este momento, / el momento supremo de la soledad / en que nada pesa / nada queda ya / sino el deseo impostergable de vivir; / me lancé al agua, es cierto, sin mirar atrás. / De mirar atrás quizás no me lanzara / habría vacilado mirando tus grandes ojos tristes / . . . «Sálvese quien pueda» había gritado el capitán, / la vida era una hipótesis de salto, / quedarse una muerte segura. (87–88)

> If I was bitter it was because of the pain. / The captain shouted "Save yourselves, if you can" / and I without thinking of it more, threw myself into the water / as if I had always been waiting for this moment, / the supreme moment of solitude / in which nothing has weight / nothing remains / except for the undeniable desire to live; / I threw myself into the water, it's true, without looking back. / If I'd looked back I might not have thrown myself / I might have vacillated looking at your big, sad eyes / . . . "Save yourselves, if you can" had shouted the captain / life was a hypothesis of the jump / staying a certain death.

Although she emphasizes that staying would have meant certain death, her poem circles around her sense of loss and her survivor's guilt. Another repetitive trope in this collection of poems is the recurring general who comes looking for her: "Detrás dejé navegación, / puentes claros, / asechanzas, / el general y la prisión" (33). ["I left behind navigation, / clear bridges, / stealthy persecutions, / the general and prison"]. Peri Rossi emphasizes the forced nature of her exile and the losses it entails.

These examples have demonstrated contradictory depictions of nationalism. On the one hand, exile cuts one off from the ties of the nation. Yet, on the other, exile is a state of loss. This loss is so extreme that exiles respond by recounting their experience and imagining some sort of reaction. Dorfman focuses on memory and distance, Goytisolo seeks retaliation and Peri Rossi seeks forgiveness and understanding from those she left behind. In each case, they describe exile as a condition that extends beyond the personal and they suggest that exile can only be considered as a dialectic between the personal and the collective. The collective nature of exile incorporates the individual into a community that is both national and transnational.

Most theories of nationalism stop with industrialization and independence. The impact of nationalism under authoritarianism, where the individual has none of the rights typically associated with the modern state (due process, elections, and protected rights) must be taken into account here. Since nationalism in Spain, Chile, and Uruguay was assimilated under these authoritarian regimes to promote the success of capitalism, nationalism becomes an ideology at the service of economic goals. In order to understand the role of the nation in literature, it is necessary to recognize how historical developments have transformed the role of nationalism in narrative. For those writers exiled from authoritarian regimes, they cannot avoid a connection to this history and to the states that outcast them, just as exile pushes their sense of territorial affiliations in new directions. These words of Fredric Jameson from *The Political Unconscious* emphasize the connection between exile literature and its historical conditions: "History is what hurts, it is what refuses desire and sets inexorable limits to individual as well as collective praxis.... This is indeed the ultimate sense in which History as ground and untranscendable horizon needs no particular theoretical justification: we may be sure that its alienating necessities will not forget us, however we might prefer to ignore them" (102). These writers' history represents an integral link to their narrative, just as their *alien nation* binds them to a story that reaches beyond individual experience and ties them to a transnational collective.

CHAPTER FOUR
Exile's Time

Given that exile often forces travel to new lands that speak foreign languages, many scholars have focused on the problems of spatial displacement and linguistic estrangement in the cultural production of exiles. Amy Kaminsky, in *Reading the Body Politic,* draws the connection between spatial displacement and a crisis of language for the exiled writer: "Exile is dislocation, both physical and psychic. The exile is a stranger, not seen, misperceived. The departure into absence of exile contains and will foster a will to return to presence. The exile's writing aims to win back the land; its longed-for destination is that one place where it can never be" (32). While many scholars have researched the ramifications of the exile's spatial and linguistic alienation, the question of time, of the exile's time, has often been neglected. The following analysis proposes a theory of the exile's time and suggests that temporality for exiles from the latter part of the twentieth century often involves a dialectic between pre-modern myth and circularity, modern linear history, and postmodern ahistorical timelessness.

Previous studies of the exile's time have sparked contrasting and contradictory remarks. For instance, Paul Tabori cites József Wittlin, as stating: "In Spanish, there exists a word for describing an exile, the word *destierro,* a man deprived of his land. I take the liberty to forge one more definition, *destiempo,* a man who has been deprived of his time. That means deprived of the time which now passes in his country. The time of his exile is different. Or rather, the exile lives in two different times simultaneously, in the present and in the past" (32). Wittlin suggests that the exile lives in the present of his country of exile and in the past of his native land. The exile is *exiled* from the present time of his native land. Such a condition heightens the exile's remembrance of the past and creates a great nostalgia. But living in the past of your native land and in the present of your adoptive residence is not quite the same as living "*destiempo,*" which would literally mean outside of time.

Other scholars have posited that the exile's time is only the past, insofar as the exile dwells in nostalgic melancholy unable to engage with the present in any manner whatsoever. Additionally, other critics have described the existential crisis of the exile as a timeless state. Guillén argues that "even when the causes of banishment were political, its consequences were frighteningly cultural, for to be expelled from the center of the circle amounted to the danger of being hurled into the void or doomed to non-being" (275). This is Guillén's description of the timeless state of the ancient exile, yet, he maintains that even in the modern age of exiles, where the individual is expelled from a nation and not an empire, the "coordinates of [the exiles'] political fervor would become, one might say, increasingly *temporal*.... In our time the most terrible of banishments will often be the exile from the present—or even worse, from the future" (275). Guillén emphasizes that the exile has been removed from the historical time of his nation. Absent from national life, the exile is no longer physically *present* and therefore has been stripped of a temporal and historical connection to his or her land. Claudio Guillén also cites Wittlin as he argues that the exile's time is disconnected from the present: "la expulsión del presente; y por lo tanto del futuro— lingüístico, cultural, político—del país de origen" (*Múltiples moradas* 83) ["the expulsion from the present; and consequently from the—linguistic, cultural, political— future of the home country"]. Guillén suggests that exiles lose ties to future time in their homeland as well. There can be no reinsertion into the historical time of the lost nation.

Tabori has noted that the exile often has a greater impact on cultural developments in his adoptive land than in the country from which he has been exiled. In his words: "The contribution of his exile to his new country is always likely to be greater than his influence still sensible in his land of birth. His successes abroad are likely to be envied and derided" (38). Interestingly, Goytisolo, Dorfman, and Peri Rossi have all suffered the consequences of international success. In all three cases there are those who no longer consider them to be Spanish, Chilean, or Uruguayan. This rejection is exacerbated by the fact that they have not made a permanent residence in their "home land" now that the political constraints of their exile have been removed. That the exile has more of a cultural role on "foreign" soil also underscores the notion that the exile is cast out of the present and future of their homelands.

In addition to being outside of the present and the future of their former nations, exiles are also excluded from the past. In dictatorial versions of history, the exile is erased. For these reasons, exiles often find themselves obsessed with recording their version of history, one that accounts for those who opposed the dictatorship. Yet these memories of the past are always flawed, always tainted by the distortions of the exile's imagination and desire. The past is only understood in light of the present and vice versa. When one has experienced an extraordinary rupture in time, both views of the past and the present bear the marks of this disjunction. As Paul Ilie describes in *Inner Exile,* "temporal linearity intersects with emotional depth" (62). Ilie explains that as the time of exile lengthens, memory becomes atrophied and "time functions as a stifling force" (62).

Goytisolo, Dorfman, and Peri Rossi all narrate situations where time has become a problem for their characters. In each of the three novels of Goytisolo's trilogy, for instance, he begins describing time as boundless and without progression. In *Señas de identidad* he emphasizes an all-consuming sense of an endless and uncertain present: "suspendido como estabas en un presente incierto, exento de pasado como de porvenir, con la desolada e íntima certeza de saber que habías vuelto no porque las cosas hubieran cambiado y tu expatriación hubiese tenido sentido" (15) ["suspended as you were in an uncertain present, lacking a past as well as a future, with that desolate and intimate certainty of knowing that you had come back not because things had changed and your expatriation had had meaning"; 10]. This quotation describes a state of *destiempo*, a state of timelessness, which is not cyclical but rather, absent of time. Later in *Reivindicación del conde don Julián* time also does not appear to progress: "un día y otro día y otro aún : siempre igual" (11) ["one day, another, and yet another: ever the same"; 3]. The protagonist of this novel resides in Morocco, surrounded by exiles, outside of linear time: "La ciudad es crisol de todos los exilios y sus habitantes parecen acampar en un presente incierto" (20) ["the city is still a melting pot for all sorts of exiles, and its inhabitants seem to be living in an uncertain present"; 11]. In the third novel of the trilogy, *Juan sin tierra*, time is infinite and borderless: "según los gurús indostánicos, en la fase superior de la meditación, el cuerpo humano, purgado de apetitos y anhelos, se abandona con deleite a una existencia etérea, atenta sólo al manso discurrir de un tiempo sin fronteras" (11) ["according to Hindustani gurus, in the superior phase of meditation the human body, purged of its appetites and desires, abandons itself to an ethereal existence... attentive only to the gentle flow of time without end"; 2]. The anger and agony of timelessness experienced by the narrator of *Reivindicación del conde don Julián* is replaced by a liberating timelessness in *Juan sin tierra*, which allows the narrator to fantasize that exile has abolished his body's ties to time and space.

In Dorfman's novel *Viudas* the linear/historical relationship between family generations becomes blurred as time collapses, bringing together fathers and sons from different eras who have shared similar struggles. In his opening remarks, Dorfman explains that the novel was originally written under a pseudonym with the hope that such a ruse would gain the novel access to the Chilean public. The fictitious author, Eric Lohmann, supposedly wrote the text between 1941 and 1942, and was later arrested and murdered by the Gestapo. Years later his son found the manuscript and published it. This frame, Dorfman hoped, would help hide the true identity of the author, mixing fathers and sons locked in similar struggles from different eras. Dorfman explains in his introduction that the frame caused him to use a different language, one that might have come from a Dane in the 1940s but would reflect the situation in Chile in the 1970s as well: "De esa manera, quienes lean el libro podrán juzgar si también pudo haber sido escrito—y así fue, no se necesita nadie que lo certifique— por ese danés resistente, ese hermano mío cuarenta años mayor, ese padre que no alcanzó conocer a su hijo, y a cuya memoria dedico las páginas que él logró terminar unos días antes de morir" (8–9) ["This way, whoever reads the book can judge whether it could also have been written—and it was, nobody has to certify it so—by that Danish resistance fighter, that brother forty years my senior, that father who never got to meet his son, to whose memory I dedicate these pages he managed to finish a few days before his death"; iii]. Dorfman asks us to question who is the father/author of the text, thereby linking fathers, sons, and brothers in a non-linear fashion.

Upon completion of the manuscript, the publishing house that had agreed to the project found the material too risky for publication, and *Viudas* was published without the pseudonym in Mexico. Dorfman decided to keep the frame and in the fictitious son's introduction to the novel, Sirgud Lohmann gives the novel a timeless quality:

> El país que [mi padre] creó no es Grecia, sino que un lugar imaginario, equivalente de toda la Europa de su época. Escrita entre 1941 y 1942 la novela presagia lo que ha de ocurrir en su propio país, en Holanda, en Francia, en Italia, en Polonia, en los años que sobrevendrán. Pero más que eso, anuncia lo que ha de ocurrir justamente en Grecia después de la segunda guerra mundial durante la guerra civil. Y más aún, presiente, con una exactitud, lo que sigue sucediendo hoy, décadas más tarde, en tantas regiones del Tercer Mundo. (16)
>
> The country he created is not Greece but an imaginary place equivalent to all Europe of that epoch. Written between 1941 and 1942, the novel presages what was to occur in his own country, in Holland, in France, in Italy, in Poland, in the years to come. But more than that, it announces what was to happen in Greece itself after the Second World War, during the civil war. Beyond that, it prefigures what is still happening now, decades later, in so many areas of the Third World. (5)

Viudas tells a story about a small village in Greece around the time of World War II, but the above quotation suggests the notion that the dialectical relationship between a tyrannical military and its innocent victims has an ahistorical, cyclical pattern. The fact that time passes but nothing changes emphasizes the suffering of the powerless at the hands of the powerful. The novel highlights the cycle of oppressor and oppressed, resistance and its repression that has dominated human existence. This pre-modern description of time proposes that history is a myth. What is more, since the novel is written in exile in 1980, we note the way that time has collapsed, since what the novel suggests as prefiguration is both that as well as the recording of history.

Elsewhere Dorfman treats the concept of boundless time as the window to possible liberation. In *The Last Song of Manuel Sendero* children listen to a fairy tale which is meant to teach them to hope: "Once upon a time there was we ourselves in that country that never was. Once upon a time there was a land of meanwhile, a time between parentheses, a land of the back door, a land where they put women to sleep and take children prisoner" (407). The time of Pinochet's dictatorship is described as a "time between parentheses." This gesture takes the pain of exile and numbs it; the exile's time is outside of history. Concurrently, though, the novel's story of exile and of Chile's resistance to Pinochet is an important lesson and cannot be erased from history entirely if children are to learn from their fathers' mistakes. So, it is turned into a timeless fairy tale. Dorfman's *destiempo* then, is quite different from that seen in Goytisolo, because, while removed from historical time, the time of the novel still places hope in the future of the children who may learn from the past and break the cycle of tyranny and its victims.

In Peri Rossi's short story "La influencia de Edgar Allen Poe en la poesía de Raimundo Arias" (The Influence of Edgar Allen Poe in the Poetry of Raimundo

Arias), the notion of *destiempo* takes a somewhat comical turn when the daughter of an intellectual, fleeing into exile in Spain by boat, demands to know where her four hours went. As their ship crosses time zones the passengers are informed that they should set their watches ahead: "La primera vez, la niña resistió a la orden. Mantuvo su reloj pulsera en las doce, cuando todo el mundo en el barco corrió la aguja por el circuito de la esfera, con una manera tan frívola de tratar el tiempo, según opinión de Alicia" (51) ["The first time, the girl resisted the order. She kept her wristwatch at twelve, when everyone else on the boat ran the needle through the circuit of the sphere, with quite a frivolous way of treating time, in Alicia's opinion"]. She is incensed that the authorities have "stolen" her time and is dismayed when she finds out that she will never get her time back—that is, not until she is able to return to her country. Her father tries to explain: "'Hija, cuando regresemos te las devolverán, si es que algún día regresamos.' La respuesta no la consoló.... Pensó en barcos fantasmales llenos de hombres que custodiaban los recintos donde el tiempo robado estaba guardado, imaginó traficantes de horas que esperaban a los barcos en puertos sucios ... compraban horas, las vendían" (53) ["'Daughter, when we return they will be returned to you, if we ever return.' The answer did not console her.... She thought of ghost ships full of men who guarded pens where the stolen time was kept, she imagined time traffickers that waited for these ships in dirty ports ... they bought hours, they sold them"]. As she walks the streets of her European refuge, the clocks are all four hours ahead of her watch: "No es que yo esté atrasada, son ellos que están adelantados" (52) ["It is not that I am behind, they are the ones who are ahead"]. Nevertheless, her father points out, "ten en cuenta, hija mía, que cualquier rebeldía individual está destinada al fracaso" (51) ["bear in mind, my child, that any individual rebellion is destined to fail"]. Alicia's inability to accept the loss of time imposed by her forced travel reflects much more than a child's stubborn refusal to cooperate. Peri Rossi uses the figure of a child in exile in order to emphasize the way that the exiled adult has been conditioned to endure great hardships—what the adult passively accepts the child does not understand. Alicia's complaints, though, as they come in the form of childish queries and frustrations, illustrate the notion of exilic *destiempo* with a tone of humor and the images of "time traffickers" selling hours on the black market convert the notion of time into an object, a commodity, which this little girl is powerless to purchase.

In contrast, the poem "El tiempo" (Time) from Peri Rossi's collection *Europa después de la lluvia*, expresses the exile's time as a yearning for the past, an incessant, melancholic nostalgia. "Ahora que todo el mundo vive hacia el futuro / mi melancolía y yo hemos decidido / vivir en el pasado" (17) ["Now that everyone lives facing the future / my melancholy and I have decided / to live in the past"]. In another poem from the same collection, "Paisaje con isla" (Landscape with Island), Peri Rossi describes time in ways similar to that found in Goytisolo's text, where the exile has lost a connection to time entirely: "Fuera de la historia, / exonerada de cualquier anécdota, / de las cuentas de los hombres. / Es un gran espacio vacío y poblado como la memoria ... / Y el tiempo suspendido, antes del Diluvio" (23–24) ["Outside of history, / unburdened by any anecdotes, / and the accounts of men. / It is a great empty space populated by memory ... / And time suspended before the Flood"]. The exile is lost in time and space as described in "Naufragio" (Shipwreck): "Naufragó en una mancha de petróleo / que flotaba, como una isla / sin tiempo, / sin lugar" (37) ["She was cast away in an oil spill / that floated, like an island / without time, / without place"]. In her novel *La nave de los locos*, these themes continue. The exile has a distorted sense of time: "Equis no podía precisar cuántos [años]; a raíz de sus frecuentes viajes su sentido del tiempo se había perturbado y ora le parecía infinito —un tejido extensible que se extendía o se acortaba" (43) ["He did not know how many [years]; all this traveling had disrupted his sense of time until it now seemed like a piece of elastic, now stretching infinitely, now crisp, tight and full of knots"; 39–40]. The travels of the exile turn time into an object that can be contemplated and analyzed, from a distance. Outside of the normal progress of time, the exile becomes aware of its artifice and instability. Peri Rossi also describes the exile's time as stagnant: "En la historia no había ningún progreso, pero el hombre y Equis coincidieron en que la esencia de algunas historias es precisamente ésa: no modificarse, permanecer, como reductos estables, como faros, como ciudadelas, frente al irresistible deterioro del tiempo" (45) ["A story without progress, but then again the two men agreed that the essence of some stories lies precisely in this: they do not change, but remain like citadels or lighthouses facing the irresistible assault of time"; 41]. Here the translation does not reveal the play on words in Peri Rossi's original: "historia" means both story and history. Both narrative accounts of history (stories) and history itself are without progress. Peri Rossi's poetry and prose waver between expressing the experience of exile as one filled with nostalgia for the past and as a numbing state of *destiempo*.

Most noteworthy is the theme of temporal suspension in all three writers' work. Goytisolo describes his protagonist in *Señas de identidad* as "suspendido como estabas en el presente, exento de pasado como de porvenir" ["suspended as you were in an uncertain present, lacking a past as well as a future"], Dorfman narrates a time "between parentheses," and Peri Rossi describes "el tiempo suspendido" ["time suspended"]. Writing far from their nations, these authors' work suggests that the exiled individual exists, at least to some degree, in a state of suspended animation, disconnected from the present time of their non-exiled compatriots. The crisis of time, like that of space, then, is an important feature of exile literature. The protagonist of *Juan sin tierra* remarks "de la vasta latitud del espacio a la no menos vasta latitud del tiempo" (163) ["from the vast expanse of space to the no less vast expanse of time"; 150].

We might read these authors in relation to Jameson's notion of the "Nostalgia for the present" in *Postmodernism, or, The Cultural Logic of Late Capitalism*. In this chapter, Jameson describes how certain films of the postmodern exemplify a crisis in representing the present—a crisis he names "nostalgia for the present." Similar to the representational dilemmas facing these filmmakers, the writers under analysis here have difficulty narrating their relationship to history. They have a complex relationship to historicity: "Historicity is, in fact, neither a representation of the past nor a representation of the future . . . it can first and foremost be defined as a perception of the present as history" (284). As these writers explore the notion that they have been excluded from present history, or, rather, that their experience is not historical but a cyclical repetition, such ideas complicate their ability to connect their present experience to either synchronic or diachronic versions of their existence in any type of totalizing fashion. These words that Jameson uses to describe films from 1986 also resonate when thinking about the work of Goytisolo, Dorfman, and Peri Rossi: "they show a collective unconscious in the process of trying to identify its own present at the same time that they illuminate the failure of this attempt" (296). Such cultural products are read by Jameson as "symptoms" of postmodernism, where postmodernism marks a new "open space" for a distinct "mode of historicity." The temporal and spatial displacement of the exile heightens this cultural crisis.

Consequently, in each of these writers' work, exile is a condition which has created a complicated relationship to time, and, specifically, to the exile's ability to participate in linear history. I am interested in pushing the question of the exile's time further. What are some of the major concerns that the exiled writer faces as they attempt to produce texts that challenge the course of events in their native countries? The condition of exile creates a number of temporal conflicts—a focus on the past prior to exile (i.e., nostalgia), a sense that the exiled person has been removed from the present time of his or her country (but is able to live in the present elsewhere), a feeling of being a part of the cyclical repetition of banishment and exile, and the sense that the exile has been removed from history, and therefore, time altogether (*destiempo*), floating in an eternal void. How does the cultural production of exiles confront these different problems? And what types of issues complicate the question of time in exilic writing when such writing is also affected by the crisis of representation associated with postmodernism? Is the rejection of linear time that may be found in the cultural production of exiles from the latter part of the twentieth century a result of the exiles' desire to thwart the hegemony of linear history, or, is it rather a response to the exile's exclusion from the linear history of a particular nation?

As in Julia Kristeva's "Women's Time," where she argues that women have a complicated relationship to time, I would argue that the exile exists in multiple temporal categories. Toril Moi, in her introduction to Kristeva's collection of articles, explains its central point: "According to Kristeva, female subjectivity would seem to be linked both to cyclical time (repetition) and to *monumental* time (eternity), at least in so far as both are ways of conceptualizing time from the perspective of motherhood and reproduction. The time of history, however, can be characterized as linear time: time as project, teleology, departure, progression, and arrival" (187) Kristeva argues that feminists have tended to alternate between affirming women's right to participate in linear time, becoming active players in history, or rejecting the inclusion of women in linear time insofar as it is a male-dominated signifying system. (Amy Kaminsky draws a parallel between the role of women and of exiles in society; see her chapter "The Presence of Absence of Exile" in *Reading the Body Politic*.) Kristeva suggests that the most valuable description of women's time is one that sees it as fluctuating dialectically between these two poles of history and ahistory. I would argue that the exile, marginalized from linear/historical time as Kristeva claims women are, shares this complex temporal existence. The exile's time is cyclical, mythological, monumental, linear, and historical. The tension between these multiple time "frames" is a common thread throughout exile narrative.

This multifaceted dialectic can be partially explained by the fact that the condition of exile is both primordial (cyclical and eternal) and historically determined. In a cyclical fashion, each writer in exile becomes part of the tradition of exile literature. Equis, the protagonist of Cristina Peri Rossi's novel, *La nave de los locos,* believes that all exiles are related: "somos exiliados, y ése es un vínculo muy profundo, como un cordón umbilical" (107) ["we're exiles and this creates a closer tie than any umbilical cord"; 107]. Paul Tabori explains in his survey of exile that the first recorded exile was of Sinuhe in about 2000 BC. (Tabori's study points out that Sinuhe was the first "recorded" case of exile, but in his research he has determined that exile was most certainly a part of "primitive societies." According to Tabori, "political exile certainly pre-dates recorded history" and the words of Sinuhe "still echo in many an exile's memory"; 43.) Sinuhe begins a long legacy of exiles that all share the common bond of losing their place in the world. All exiles, despite the particularities of their historical circumstance, connect at some level with their fellow exiles across all ages. Greek mythology, Homeric poetry, and classical drama are crowded with images of exile and the themes present in these tales have affected exiles from all historical periods. We need only think of the figure of Ulysses to see how the theme of exile in Greek mythology reappears constantly in literature throughout the centuries. Upon being forced to leave one's land, these mythological figures of exile become part of the exile's cultural community and they pull the exile toward the historical void of primordial time.

In the work of Goytisolo, Dorfman, and Peri Rossi, many allusions to the common bonds of exile can be found. Juan Goytisolo's work takes up the myth of the pariah, or the outcast, who has wrongly been banished from his land. In *Señas de identidad,* for instance, Alvaro, the novel's protagonist, enters a community of pariahs from the Barrio chino in Barcelona: "Putas, carteristas, maricones.... Los demás no son personas son moluscos" (75) ["Whores, pickpockets, fairies.... The rest aren't people, they're mollusks"; 60]. Alvaro prefers the company of the marginalized: "aquella España errante, la España peregrina, sustituía en tu corazón a la España oficial" (342) ["That errant Spain, that vagabond Spain, substituted in your heart for the official Spain"; 284]. As the novel closes Alvaro dreams of the day "cuando también tú te has librado de ellos y navegas a solas / diciéndote / bendito sea mi desvío / todo cuanto me separa de vosotros y me acerca a los parias" (416) ["since you too have freed yourself from them and are sailing on alone / saying to yourself / blessed be my deviation / everything that separates me from all of you and brings me closer to the pariahs"; 347]. Yet his social exile still creates anguish for him precisely because the marginalized are defined and created in a dialectical relationship to the mainstream and the empowered. Even though he idealizes his role as outcast, he always returns to the painful signs of his social background which he is unable to completely erase: "tu casta (sí, la tuya) pese a tus esfuerzos por zafarte de ella" (67) ["your caste (yes, yours) in spite of your efforts to get away"; 54]

In the second and third novels of the trilogy, the theme of the pariah continues and Goytisolo's narrators prefer life as outcasts. In *Juan sin tierra*, the narrator reiterates the diatribe begun by Alvaro in *Señas de identidad:* "el odio irreductible a tus propias señas (raza profesión clase familia tierra) crecía, en la misma proporción que el impulso magnético hacia los parias" (94) ["your irremediable hatred toward your own marks of identity (race profession class family homeland) was growing, in direct proportion to your magnetic attraction toward pariahs"; 77]. The existence of the pariah as an outcast from the center of society is something that Goytisolo recognizes as timeless. Throughout history there have existed "grupúsculos de individuos que, fuera de los caminos trazados, han intentado mantener desde tiempos remotos un culto clandestino a los reptiles y otros animales lascivos, renegando a Dios, de su ley y sus santos para tomar por dueño y señor el diablo"(189) ["small groups of individuals who, straying far from the beaten path, have endeavored since the very beginning to perpetuate a secret worship of reptiles and of the lascivious creatures, denying God, His law and His saint and taking instead the devil as their lord and master"; 168]. Exile, as narrated by Goytisolo, is a condition that links all who experience it to an ageless community of heretics, traitors, and pariahs.

Dorfman's writing in exile conjures up the image of the Wandering Jew, the Jewish protagonist who has been banished by those intolerant of his beliefs. Tabori explains the history of the Wandering Jew: sometimes referred to as Ahasuerus or Cartaphilius, the Wandering Jew suffers exile because he refused to have faith in Jesus (58). The connection between this state of exile and that described in the literature of Dorfman lies in the recurring theme that the exile has been banished from his land by those intolerant of his beliefs. According to Tabori, the Jews were punished because they rejected the Messiah and "Jewish destiny was symbolized by . . . the Wandering Jew, one of the most tragic and enduring symbols of exile" (57). In Dorfman's work the beliefs of the exile are political, not religious, but the thematics are still quite similar. The exile for Dorfman is banished because he refuses to "worship" the authoritarian system, which has taken hold of his nation. The connection goes even further, since Pinochet, dictator of Chile, described himself as the nation's savior. After Pinochet named himself President of the Republic of Chile he delivered the following address: "El Presidente de la República debe ser el defensor de los más débiles, de los que muchas veces ni siquiera tienen organización suficiente para hacer oír su voz" (91) ["The President of the Republic should be the defender of the weak, of those that many times do not have sufficient organization to make their voices heard"]. Like a Messiah, Pinochet promised to deliver the poor souls of Chile to the gates of national reconstruction, i.e., Heaven. Pinochet's speeches are filled with similar rhetoric. As a consequence of resisting the image of Pinochet as the nation's messiah and of rejecting Pinochet's authority to govern Chile, Dorfman is banished from his home. Moreover, in Dorfman's own personal experience, as a child of Jewish descent whose family had been forced to move due to anti-Semitism, Chilean national identity did not arise from birth on Chilean land but out of a commitment to Allende's cause.

Consistent with the myth that the Wandering Jew suffers but grows though his experiences, Dorfman's work after the coup places faith in storytelling as an antidote to the anguish of exile. Wandering, forced wandering, comes as a result of the individual's refusal to renounce his beliefs. The fictitious author of *Viudas* is quoted by his son as saying in the months preceding his arrest and disappearance that "lo único que le faltaba para confirmar su fe en el futuro era escribir un libro, y en épocas como éstas había que hacerlo pronto, porque nunca se podía saber cuánto tiempo nos quedaba" (14) ["the only thing lacking was to write a book, and in times like these it had to be done fast, because no one knew how much time was left"; 3]. In an interview in 1991, Dorfman explained that exile brings great pain but can also have positive effects: "crossing the desert. It is a very Judaic image. You wander through the desert and you find out who you are. . . . I confronted these monsters head on and turned exile into a series of positive experiences. I turned the distance into language. I was able to look at some of the terrors and give them names" (qtd. in Incledon 96). Julio Cortázar also writes about the positive ways that exile can affect the writer's experience in "The Fellowship of Exile": "I believe that we writers in exile have the means to transcend the uprooting and separation imposed on us by dictatorships, to return in our own unique ways the blows we suffer collectively each time another writer is exiled" (14). This experience binds all writers to a transnational, transtemporal community of exiled and outcast writers.

The character of David in *The Last Song of Manuel Sendero* is Jewish, and is rejected, like the mythical Wandering Jew, because of his beliefs. His exile is double. He is first exiled from Chile when his comrades tell him that his presence poses a threat to their cause. Felipe, David's "friend," must tell him that he is to leave the country. He narrates their encounter: "I knew that if someone didn't muzzle David, didn't rein in his irresponsibility, they'd come for all of us that morning or the next" (327). But David does not want to be forced to leave the country and responds angrily: "I've already run away from too many places. Me, my old lady, my grandparents. Nobody's going to push me out of here" (327–28). He is later exiled, marginalized from that group of comrades (now in exile), when he decides to give an interview to a Chilean reporter, who is writing an article on how those who left Chile are enjoying an easy life. He hopes that the interview will help him to return to Chile and reinitiate contact with his son. Felipe believes that David should refuse the interview, since it makes a mockery of the hardships of exile. Felipe reminds him of the heroic acts of David's father when he lost his life saving people fleeing Austria in World War II: "You have no right to undermine the people who won't abandon ship" (393). David states that he will still send in the interview because all that matters to him is returning to Chile even if that means betraying the party. Felipe is disgusted with him: "I never should have invited you" (398). David's experience of not belonging and of exile immediately connects him to a long lineage of ancestors who suffered similarly.

Over and over again, Dorfman narrates in his novels protagonists who remain outside of the communities they desire. For instance, the protagonist of *Máscaras*, while not officially in exile, is totally isolated: no one is ever able to recognize him: "sus ojos pasarán sobre mi rostro como si estuvieran hechos de jabón, resbalando sobre mis rasgos como lluvia en una laguna oscura" (16) ["Your eyes will slip over my face as if they were made of soap, sliding through my features like rain on a darkened waterfall"; 8]. Even his own family leaves him outcast: "Gente que me conozco trastrabilla contra mi cuerpo, me empuja. Un día frente a nuestro hogar, me pegó un empellón mi propio padre. No sólo no me recordó. Además me insultó" (34) ["People I have known for years stumble against me, push me. If I'm lucky they'll apologize. One day, in front of our house my own father gave me a shove. Not only did he not recognize me, on top of that he insulted me"; 27]. In his third novel after Pinochet's takeover, *Máscaras,* Dorfman depicts the increased frustration of prolonged exile. Yet in each of the novels Dorfman has written in exile, the protagonist has felt a deep isolation from any sense of community (even in *Konfidenz,* a novel ostensibly written "post-exile," the protagonist is a solitary man whose main companion has been the fantasy of a woman). This motif highlights the experience of exile as a timeless and universal state, and in particular as a condition which has an even deeper history in the Jewish tradition. Unlike the case of Goytisolo, Dorfman's exiles never find inclusion in a "community" of outcasts to be liberating. While their characters share a disdain for those in power, and correspondingly, do not wish to be part of the central hegemonic system that rules their lands, Dorfman's characters find no joy in being described as traitors to their land. All of the exiled characters found in Dorfman's work place their faith in storytelling as the only remedy to the evils of tyranny. Such a strong belief in the education of children may also be a sign of the influence of the myth of the Wandering Jew in Dorfman's depiction of the exile's role.

The distinctions between Dorfman's version of the exiled outcast and that found in Goytisolo and Peri Rossi are also connected to issues of sexuality. As gay writers, both Goytisolo and Peri Rossi narrate character, whose marginality actually liberates their sexuality—a theme that is not part of Dorfman's literature. In particular, Goytisolo struggled with his bourgeois background and experimented with his sexuality while simultaneously rejecting the authoritarian state headed by Franco until he was forced to leave Spain (for a detailed account of these experiences see Goytisolo's first volume of memoirs, *En los reinos de Taifa* [*Realms of Strife*]). He states in an interview: "Mi exilio no era solo físico y motivado exclusivamente por razones políticas: era un exilio moral, social, ideológico, sexual" (Jesús Lázaro 22) ["My exile wasn't only physical and motivated exclusively by political reasons: it was a moral, social, ideological, sexual exile"]. Similarly, Peri Rossi did not leave a utopic community when she was forced to leave Uruguay. As a lesbian writer, she existed on the margins of society even when she actually resided in her homeland: "la política entra en mi propia literatura por el mero hecho de que soy víctima de la política desde el momento en que nací" (qtd. in Zietz 83) ["politics enters into my own writing because of the mere fact that I have been a victim of politics since the moment I was born"].

Peri Rossi's own experience as a lesbian feminist differentiates her characterization of the plight of the exile from that seen in Goytisolo and Dorfman. Goytisolo's exile narrative is angry and delusionally omnipotent, exploring freely non-traditional sexual desires, which include pedophilia, homosexuality, and sadistic practices on women. Contrasting the sexual liberation afforded by exile in Peri Rossi's work, the exile in Dorfman is emasculated in a way that is not depicted as liberating whatsoever. To cite an example, the character of David from *The Last Song of Manuel Sendero,* once in exile, loses the two women in his life: Patricia, his lover, and Cecilia, his wife. He loses Patricia when he is forced to leave Chile and he loses Cecilia when she leaves him alone in Paris and returns to Chile. During his relationship with Gringa (his companion in exile), David decides to get a vasectomy. Men in exile, for Dorfman, are men without manhood. Dorfman's exiles are frustrated at their exclusion from history and have a strong desire to educate future generations about the follies of authoritarianism and ostracism, in order to recuperate their masculinity.

In contrast, Goytisolo's exiled protagonists are free to pursue their sexual fantasies—forbidden in the homeland: "someterás la geografía a los imperativos y exigencias de tu pasión" (*Juan sin tierra* 82) ["you will submit geography to the imperatives and demands of your passion"; 68]. For Peri Rossi, exile is also associated with a departure from traditional heterosexuality and characters in *La nave de los locos* practice pedophilia, transvestitism, and lesbianism. They experience impotence and have sex with old, ugly prostitutes. But in contrast with the work of Goytisolo, the banished exiles of Cristina Peri Rossi's literature are neither joyous in their marginalized state nor angry. The pervading emotional response to the experience of exile in her work is that of numbness. Tapping into an ahistorical pattern of ostracism, Peri Rossi's exiles are all passengers on a "ship of fools."

The delusion of Goytisolo's characters relates to their sense of power and not only to their sexuality. Nevertheless, the tendency to move towards what is traditionally considered "perverse" is central to Goytisolo's work (see Paul Julian Smith). For instance, the protagonist of *Reivindicación del conde don Julián* enjoys seeing a female tourist who is bitten by a snake and then subjected to the humiliation of having her genitals urinated on by some Moroccan boys. In the same novel, the thrill of raping the land of Spain, which has been converted into a female body, is narrated in a misogynistic and sadistic fashion. A further example occurs at the end of the novel when the protagonist forces a child, named Alvaro, to engage in sex or else witness the rape of his mother. The narrator imagines himself the wolf in "Little Red Riding Hood" and fantasizes the following dialogue: "abuelita, qué bicha tan grande tienes! / es para penetrarte mejor, so imbécil" (209) ["oh granny, what a big snake you have! / the better to penetrate you with, you stupid little idiot"; 177]. In order to carry out his destruction of civilization, the narrator believes that society must be sexually abused: "(sólo el sexo y su violencia desnuda) eres Julián / conoces el camino / que ningún respeto, ni humana consideración te retengan" (214) ["(sex alone and its naked violence) / you are Julian / you know the way / let no respect, no humanitarian considerations stand in your way"; 181]. Following the path of the Marquis de Sade, who is quoted in an epigraph to the novel, the narrator seeks to destroy societal norms through sexual perversion. (For more on the misogyny of Goytisolo see Stephanie Sieburth; Smith.)

Peri Rossi's novel also narrates scenes with prostitutes and acts of pedophilia that contrast the cultural dominance of heterosexuality. Yet these scenes are never narrated with the anger and sadistic pleasure found in Goytisolo's work. When Morris falls in love with a boy, Percival, Equis and Graciela both write letters to Morris stating: "El infierno es no poder amar" (148) ["Hell is not being able to love"; 153]. The love between this man and child is not narrated as a violent and evil act, but one of love and affection. It is only in Peri Rossi's case that the condition of exile incorporates all types and all deviations from the norm, from pedophilia to transvestitism, from rapists to political radicals. For her, all of the marginalized are equal, which separates her work from that of her male counterparts in this study. Peri Rossi also fuses the alienation of the exile with the alienation of those victimized by patriarchy. According to Amy Kaminsky: "part of Peri Rossi's project is to shake loose the rigidity of existing gender categories" (*Reading* 120).

In this way, Peri Rossi fuses the oppression of authoritarianism with that of patriarchy. Moreover, as her definition of the "oppressed" enjoys a looser structure, so does her description of exile, which is often equated with involuntary travel, emphasizing travel to a foreign land as opposed to loss of the homeland. In her texts the trope of the trip is a recurrent theme and it is the bridge that links exiles across the ages. "La sola palabra *viaje* / convoca reminiscencias antiguas: / todos los viajeros que alguna vez emprendieron camino / y todos los poetas que cultivaron la metáfora / como ciudades de un viaje imaginario sin traslado" (*Lingüistica General* 47) ["The sole word *voyage* / summons ancient reminiscences: / all of the travelers that at some point entered upon the road / and all of the poets that cultivated the metaphor / like cities on an imaginary voyage without moving"]. Mabel Moraña explains that "El motivo del viaje funciona como eje narrativo en *La nave de los locos*. El desplazamiento constante de Equis, exiliado, tiene el carácter de una peregrinación que vincula su peripecia con el Éxodo bíblico y con viajes arquetípicos (*La Odisea, La Divina Comedia*)" (205) ["The motif of the voyage functions as a narrative axis in *The Ship of Fools*. The constant displacement of Ecks, exiled, has the character of a pilgrimage that ties his peripeteia to the biblical Exodus and to archetypal trips (*The Odyssey, The Divine Comedy*)"]. In Italo Calvino's *Invisible Cities,* Marco Polo describes his travels to Kublai Khan and explains the role of the traveler: "Elsewhere is a negative mirror. The traveler recognizes the little that is his, discovering the much he has not had and will never have" (29). Echoing this tone, the dreaming protagonist of *La nave de los locos* hears the command: "La ciudad a la que llegues descríbela" (9) ["You will come to the city—describe it"; 1]. Who is speaking? Who is asking Equis to describe the city? This invisible source of power is ambiguously related to Equis. What is clear is that Equis is subordinate to the voice and is being asked to obey a command. Peri Rossi's characters exist in a hostile world, cognizant of their marginality and of their fragile role as storytellers. In this sense her work greatly contrasts the literature of Goytisolo and Dorfman, who both produce narratives obsessed with the loss of territory due to exile, and with the need to use writing as a tool for vindicating the exile's loss. Peri Rossi, on the other hand, tends to focus more on the involuntary and painful experience of being forced to travel and on the difficult process of deciding how to narrate the story. Equis answers his dream's command to describe his new destination with the question: "¿Cómo distinguir lo significante de lo insignificante?" (9) ["How shall I know what is meaningful and what is not?"; 1]. The exiled traveler has lost his point of reference; without his point of departure, he does not know where to begin his story. Highlighting the connections between travel and exile, Peri Rossi begins her novel *La nave de los locos* with an epigraph from Fernando Pessoa: "La vida es un viaje experimental hecho involuntariamente" ["Life is a voyage of experiment made against our will"]. Here exile and life are equated, leading Peri Rossi's protagonist to assert that the human condition is one of exile: "Todos somos exiliados de algo o de alguien. En realidad ésa es la verdadera condición humana" (106) ["We have all been exiled from something or someone... I think this is the human condition"; 106].

In each of these writers' works there are recurrent tropes of exile literature: Goytisolo champions the pariah, Dorfman's alludes to the myth of the Wandering Jew, and Peri Rossi conveys the suffering of the outcast. Nevertheless, at each stage of history these universal themes of exile literature attain new meanings. For instance, banishment in the Middle Ages was quite different from exile in modernity. Tabori suggests that the notion of terrestrial banishment altered greatly during the modern period: "it was the eighteenth century that created the idea of nation as contrasted to homeland, of citizen as opposed to subject, and thereby totally changed the very conception of exile" (87). Each experience of exile is distinct, and corresponds to a particular set of historical circumstances, surprising the victim of exile and shattering their sense of time and space: "porque hay viajes involuntarios," Equis informs us, "que nos sorprenden en medio de nuestra candorosa hipótesis del tiempo y del espacio" (55) ["Leaving can become an involuntary act which catches us unexpectedly, just as we innocently postulate infinite time and space ahead"; 51]. Of great importance in the work of these writers is the tension between nationalism and transnationalism. The narrative of writers during the latter part of the twentieth century witnesses a dramatic change, one where the notion of nation and of citizen is called into question. If the exile has been denied citizenship, can such an experience be liberating? With the shift in emphasis in postmodernism away from the nation and the citizen and toward the multinational and the multicultural also comes a shift in emphasis away from the melancholy and nostalgia of the modern and toward the ludic, ahistorical, and depersonal of the postmodern. How does the exile at this historical crossroads describe existence in relation to the world? Is the exile no more than another in an endless flow of deterritorialized souls, or are exiles the victims of human rights violations? There are no easy answers. In fact, I have found that the work of Goytisolo, Dorfman, and Peri Rossi incorporates a linear, a cyclical, a historical, and a primordial notion of time revealing the influence of both pre-modern and modern cosmovisions. The work of these authors also represents postmodernism, on the one hand, as a key to liberation from the binds of the nation and patriarchy and, on the other hand, as a sign of individual annihilation, heralding the obsolescence of the struggles most central to the exile. The writers studied here do not emphasize one of these visions of time but waver between these positions, thereby making it difficult to assert that they favor one temporality over another.

Julia Kristeva in her aforementioned article "Women's Time" suggests that women have a complicated relationship to time and that such complications must be addressed if one hopes to subvert the heterosexist patriarchal system that, because of its emphasis on progressive/historical time, has made women temporally disadvantaged. Describing women and time she states: "In other words, we confront two temporal dimensions: the time of linear history or *cursive time* (as Nietzsche called it), and the time of another history, thus another time, *monumental time* (again according to Nietzsche), which englobes these supra-national, socio-cultural ensembles within even larger entities" (189). For Kristeva, and also for these writers, the most effective threats to the patriarchal system address the construction of identity in both monumental and linear time. First subversion requires the rejection of patriarchy "by demanding recognition of an irreducible identity, without equal in the opposite sex and, as such, exploded, plural, fluid, in a certain way non-identical, this feminism situates itself outside the linear time of identities which communicate through projection and vindication. Such feminism rejoins, on the one hand, the archaic (mythical) memory, and on the other, the cyclical or monumental temporality of marginal movements" (194–95).

Secondly there must be an "*insertion* into history and the radical *refusal* of the subjective limitations imposed by this history's time" (195). The literature of Goytisolo, Dorfman, and Peri Rossi grapples with the connection of the exile to both linear, historical time and mythical time (as both cyclical repetition and eternal timelessness). Simultaneously refusing to be forgotten by history and refusing to participate in the version of history being promoted within their nations' borders, these writers *insert* the protagonists of their texts into a temporal conundrum, one which requires that they act in a world that is both historical and mythical, while all the while rejecting any complicity with the ideological bases of authoritarianism. Their work takes up these issues with a specific political agenda in mind, one that means to directly challenge the authoritarian regimes that are the cause of their experience of exile. Therefore, the combination of myth and history in these writers' work is a result not only of the exilic condition's temporal paradox, but also of their particular response to the fascist-based ideologies favored by the military regimes in their homelands. (For more on the intersections of myth and history see Labanyi.)

In this way, the question of the exile's time, as I have modeled it on Kristeva's theory of women's time, becomes increasingly a question of how the exile chooses to define history and the individual's relation to the world. If the exile favors mythical, archetypal, and/or primordial visions of the exile's connection to world history, then what conclusions should be drawn? Michael Gillespie informs us that "Reality for the Greeks is a conjunction of the actual and the eternal.... Time in this sense is, as Plato's Timaeus asserts, the moving image of eternity" (2). Is the rejection of linear time, then, a movement back to the mythical visions of the Greeks or a movement forward to "The End of History" as the postmodern critic Jean Baudrillard describes it in "The Year 2000 Has Already Happened"? In this article Baudrillard describes his theory of how, in the postmodern age, history has come to an end. "It remains for us to accommodate ourselves to the time left to us, which is seemingly emptied of sense by this reversal. The end of this century is before us like an empty beach" (44). Best and Kellner, in their analysis of Baudrillard's work, illuminate his radical theories of the end of time. "Baudrillard suggests that we face a new, futureless future in which no decisive event can await us, because all is finished, perfected, and doomed to infinite repetition: the eternal recurrence of the same is the fate of the West.... There is no time to come.... We are frozen in a glacial present in which time is annihilated"

(134). What is most significant for the purposes of understanding the exile's time is to note the convergence between the description of time in theorists of the postmodern and that found in scholars of ancient mythology. For instance, Mircea Eliade points out that it is the Judeo-Christian eschatological visions that are responsible for the end of the cyclic theories of the eternal return. "Time is no longer the circular Time of the Eternal Return; it has become a linear and irreversible Time. Nor is this all: the eschatology represents the triumph of Sacred History" (65). Therefore, the pre-modern and the postmodern (at least in certain versions of their two world views) unite in their rejection of History, favoring cosmovisions which hold that life is "eternal recurrence" and that the notions of reason and progress are either unthinkable or in and of themselves mythical concepts. According to Gillespie, Christianity heralds the advent of modernity as it leads to the concepts of reason and progress (10). Progress is the seed concept of linear time. It is the basis of free will and of political goals. These concepts change throughout the modern period only to be radically challenged by theorists of the postmodern.

While I am pointing out remarkable similarities between the description of time in certain visions of the pre-modern and the postmodern, I do not want to argue that the pre-modern and the postmodern are actually one and the same. The most salient result of this connection, though, affects the way many postmodern critics describe their world views as heralding an "end" which actually seems to be a *return* to the pre-modern. This becomes even more noteworthy when we realize that many postmodern critics have been greatly influenced by pre-modern thinkers and utilize many of their models in their own work. For instance Lyotard's work points to pre-modern precursors of postmodernism in "The Stoics, Aristotle, and Greek Philosophy" (Best and Kellner 174). I am also, obviously, drawing a distinction between postmodern critics like Derrida, Lyotard, and Baudrillard whose work stems from an anti-historical position and critics, like Jameson, who have not abandoned "History" and see the postmodern as part of a continuous process of social development.

But what of the occasions where the exile favors a vision of progress, movement toward a goal, and a belief in human rights? Gillespie, in his survey of "The Question of History," further explains: "The doctrine of historical progress, however, not only establishes standards of justice and right by which to measure conduct and political institutions but also creates a goal or destination for humanity and a concomitant historical duty or moral imperative" (12–13). Caught between linear history and cyclical repetition, the exile's time exemplifies some of the most pressing questions facing critical inquiry today. Is the human condition continuous or discontinuous? Does time progress or is it eternal? If time does not progress, does that indicate a (paradoxically) progressive move forward to the postmodern or does it build a non-linear temporal bridge between the postmodern and the pre-modern? Most importantly how does the exile reconcile visions of the self in society that correspond to pre-modern, modern, and postmodern theories of time? Perhaps the answer may require a second look at the historical circumstances that prefaced the state of exile. How do Goytisolo, Dorfman, and Peri Rossi react to the visions of history being offered by the leaders in the homelands?

In the following sections of this chapter I explain the *exile's time* constructed in the literature of Goytisolo, Dorfman, and Peri Rossi. Inasmuch as these writers are specifically writing against their nation's regimes, it is necessary to understand the ways that right-wing dictatorships use a specific rhetoric of time. These regimes overwhelmingly coincide in their recourse to two specific time frames, the pre-modern and the modern, that will enable their national goals. The pre-modern suggests that the members of society are subjects of the state without civil rights. Leaders are preordained monarchs who should not be questioned and who demand blind obedience. This pre-modern use of time is then combined with the modern as authoritarian regimes promote the active insertion of their countries into the global capitalist market. Consequently Goytisolo, Dorfman, and Peri Rossi create narratives that disrupt these visions. Their texts present alternative myths that challenge the use of myth in their respective countries. In order to compete with the official versions of the nation and its history, these writers' alternative myths challenge the pre-modern and modern sources of political legitimacy constructed by each of their country's authoritarian regimes. Their critique also suggests a postmodern use of time where the individual has lost agency and must recognize irreducible difference. For these writers, this promiscuous vision of temporality represents the strongest attack of the system. As the following analysis demonstrates, the work of these writers is a complex response to a complex problem. The depiction of the exile's time is a carefully constructed counterattack to the social hegemony of authoritarianism.

In the next section of this chapter I explain the ways that fascism served as an ideological role model in Spain, Chile, and Uruguay. The role of fascism has a significant impact on the exile's sense of time, because fascism relies on pre-modern myths of regeneration and a return to origins as well as on modern notions of citizen participation in nation-building. I then analyze how Goytisolo, Dorfman, and Peri Rossi each counter these versions of national identity. Goytisolo challenges Franco's privileging of the time of the Catholic Kings, Dorfman critiques Pinochet as the father of the nation, focusing on the myth of David versus Goliath, and Cristina Peri Rossi counters the myths of creation with myths of expulsion. In each case, these writers confront the ways that authoritarian regimes control national time, mandating a single version of national history and national origins. Working against this oppressive manipulation of national identity, these writers respond by creating multifaceted, multitemporal versions of their nations. The last section of the chapter "Crossing Time Zones" argues that pre-modern, modern, and postmodern notions of time co-exist in these writers' work in dialectic tension. Analysis of their narrative technique reveals how their writing is affected by exile, postmodernism, fascist authoritarianism, and globalization.

MYTHS OF EXILE VERSUS MYTHS OF FASCISM

Writing of fascism without referring specifically to the cases of Hitler or Mussolini, is fraught with problems, precisely because the term "fascism" has been taken so often to refer to the specific system of government found in Germany and Italy prior to World War II. Nevertheless, as an ideology, fascism has had much broader usage.

Scores of scholars have dedicated much research to isolating a concise and clear definition of fascism only to leave us with a myriad of different answers. Roger Griffith dedicates his book *The Nature of Fascism* to weeding out these definitions and combining them into a working model: "Fascism is a genus or political ideology whose mythic core in its various permutations is a palingenetic form of populist ultra-nationalism" (26). The key word here is "palingenetic," which Griffith tells us "derives from *palin* (again, new) and *genesis* (creation, birth)." So the term "refers to the sense of a new start or of regeneration after a phase of crisis or decline which can be associated just as much with mystical (for example the Second Coming) as secular realities (for example the new Germany)" (33). What fascism, as an ideology, combines, then, is both a linear and a primordial vision of time. As a truly modern phenomenon, fascism incorporates notions of progress and also of a return to origins, suggesting that modern forms of society do not imply a total absence of pre-modern ideologies. Even in non-fascist modern forms of government there are many pre-modern myths like that of the "hero" (i.e., "the new communist man") or that of "regeneration" (i.e., "the New Deal") (Griffith 33–35).

The authoritarian regimes from which Goytisolo, Dorfman, and Peri Rossi were exiled were not strictly fascist, but all had strong connections to fascist ideology—a significant factor for the writer interested in countering the dominant ideology of a nation. The most important of these factors, apart from the obvious stress on a militaristic society, are the notions that the military government will return the nation to its origins (or will place it back on its natural historical course), will accomplish this by creating order from chaos, and will remove all subversive elements, thereby creating cultural homogeneity and ultra-nationalism.

The actual terminology that best describes the state of government in Spain, Chile, and Uruguay during the dictatorships has provoked a great deal of debate. In the case of Spain, most scholars agree that Franco's regime had fascist tendencies, but was not strictly fascist (Caudet and Bertrand 194). Spain's particular history of fascism is complex and begins with the Falange party founded by Ramiro Ledesma Ramos and Ernesto Giménez who published a magazine called "La conquista del Estado" (The Conquest of the State), which began publication in 1931. As Caudet and Bertrand note, the publication was influenced by Hitler, "but his racism had been replaced by the mystical notion of Spain's glorious imperial past" (194). Jo Labanyi in *Myth and History in the Contemporary Spanish Novel* states that, in the case of Franco's regime, pre-modern myth played a crucial role: "The Falangist intellectual Pedro Laín Entralgo . . . would claim that fascism saved man from the inauthenticity of history by restoring him to lost eternal values: 'we are thrust into time—into history—but our substance is eternity'" (36).

One of the key elements of this ideology was the creation of order out of the chaos caused by the Second Republic, which led Spain from 1931 until the end of the Civil War in 1939. "The new culture claimed to provide stability after the discontinuity of the immediate past, to go back to the imperial age of the 16th century and the old tradition" (de Muñoz 215). In Goytisolo's novel *Señas de identidad*, the protagonist, Alvaro hates the fascist influences he notices in Spanish life: "origen y fuente del actual progreso y bienestar es obra de un hombre y un Régimen" (370) ["the origin and source of current progress and well-being is the work of one man and a Regime"; 307]. Under Francoist fascism the nation would be returned to the normal course of history that had its origins with the Catholic Kings and all citizens of Spain would be forced to unite under a banner of Spanish nationalism. As Franco declared in speeches:

> La obra de los Reyes Católicos no tiene par en la Historia. Constituyó la más honda y gloriosa transformación que en su vida puede sufrir un pueblo. ... Dando cima a la Reconquista, alcanzaron la unidad de los hombres y de las tierras de España, instaurando el poder real; liberaron al pueblo de los abusos y de la anarquía de los nobles ... incorporaron todas las fuerzas sociales y políticas de la nación en un todo orgánico.... Y todo esto en el siglo XV, cuando todavía la mayoría de los pueblos no había logrado forjar su nacionalidad. (153–54, 5/20/45)
>
> The work of the Catholic Kings has no equal in History. It constituted the most glorious and profound transformation that a people can endure in this life.... At the height of the Reconquest, they achieved the unity of the men and lands of Spain, installing royal power; they liberated the people of the abuses and anarchy of the nobles ... they incorporated all of the social and political forces of the nation into an organic whole.... And all this in the fifteenth century, when the majority of communities had not even been able to forge their national identity.

In this one quotation, Franco unites his three main doctrines of order, unity, and an emphasis on the founding moment of the Catholic Kings. By combining a mythical return to the origins of the Catholic Kings and the modern goals of improving the national economy through tourism, Franco's government rested on primordial and modern ideologies.

Goytisolo's three novels written in exile—*Señas de identidad* (1966), *Reivindicación del conde don Julián* (1970), and *Juan sin tierra* (1975)—coupled with his extensive critical writings reveal a complex, almost obsessive, critique of Spanish nationalism. While some scholars have suggested that *Juan sin tierra* signaled Goytisolo's complete break from his Spanish heritage, his writing suggests otherwise (see Ugarte, *Shifting*). In *España y los españoles* (Spain and the Spaniards), published in 1979, Goytisolo retraces Spanish history, attempting to destroy the false myths of Spanish essences. His principle thesis is that official versions of Spanish culture erase the truth of Spain. "No existe una sola España, sino varias Españas de diferentes niveles económicos, sociales y culturales: toda tentativa de reducirlas a un denominador común nos lleva a sacrificar la realidad a la arbitrariedad de un método" (8) ["A single Spain does not exist, but rather a variety of Spains each of a different economic, social and cultural level: every effort to reduce them to a common denominator leads us to sacrifice reality to the arbitrariness of a method"]. Consequently Goytisolo attacks official Spain—the Spain of the Catholic Kings and of Franco—only to replace this false version of the nation with a more accurate picture of Spain as multicultural and diverse.

Goytisolo is well aware of the ways that Spain has been shaped by totalizing and oppressive myths and he writes *España y los españoles* in order to counter appearances with reality, and myths with anti-myths (21). He specifically targets the myths of the Falange, claiming that they and other fascist groups worship the ideal of imperial, military Castilla exemplified by the figure of the "caballero cristiano" (Christian gentleman). "Para José Antonio Primo de Rivera, el español es un ser dotado de 'esencias perennes' y, como tal, destinado a influir y dominar a los demás" (156) ["For José Antonio Primo de Rivera, the Spaniard is a being endowed with 'perennial essences' and, as such, is destined to influence and dominate others"]. Writing against this legacy, Goytisolo tries to provide an image of Spain that can unmask this false vision. He also seeks to expose the ways that myths of nationalism have negatively influenced society: "El lenguaje y estilo de la Falange son totalmente anacrónicos" (156) ["The language and style of the Falange are totally anachronic"]. This anachronism is a method of social control, which appeals to the powerful role of the church and of the military in Spanish life.

Goytisolo's reaction to the cultural violence during Franco's regime can be noted throughout his trilogy of novels. In particular, in the last scene of *Señas de identidad* Alvaro visits Montjuich in Barcelona. The castle there dates back to the Middle Ages and the fortress was used as a prison during the Spanish Civil War. Important historical figures, like Luis Companys, an advocate of Catalan nationalism, were imprisoned and murdered at the site. Brochures are being handed out in four languages so that the many tourists can read about the historical site they are visiting. As Alvaro reads the brochure that the tourists receive, he notices that in the description of the importance of the place in Barcelona's past there is no mention of the Republic or the Civil War. In order to create a myth of cultural homogeneity and national unification, Franco forbade mention of the Civil War, preferring to refer to his rise to power as a Crusade. Countering Franco's plan, Alvaro, rebelliously, remembers with the help of a whispering guide that it was at this location that Luis Companys was shot. Companys was an advocate of Catalan nationalism and had been an enemy of Franco's Nationalists in the Civil War. He is a symbol of Catalan regionalism and his death was testimony to the intolerance of difference under Franco. Raymond Carr describes his execution along with that of other Spaniards who represented political dissension:

> Between 1939 and 1950 at least 22,000 Spaniards were executed—schoolmasters, trade union leaders, mayors, Republican commanders, and politicians like Companys, handed over by Vichy to his executioners.... What was called a "pact of blood" bound the victors together and made reconciliation inconceivable. Those who did not accept the new Spain of Catholic unity were neither Spaniards nor Christians; the firing squad and prison replaced the dungeons and fires of the Inquisition. (719)

The erasure of Companys's execution from the historical site visited by these tourists only reinforces Alvaro's fear that tourism will effectively establish the Spain of Franco. Believing that capitalism will commodify his country through tourism, Alvaro becomes desperate. Alvaro visits Montjuich in 1963, ten years after the Pacts of Madrid established U.S. military bases in Spain and improved Spain's foreign relations policy, paving the way for heightened tourism. While Alvaro looks for clues to his past and an understanding of his relationship to Spain, tourists from Europe and the United States accompany him. The fragmented narrative presents the reader with Alvaro's thoughts mingled with the trivial chitchat common to tourists. The tourist group looks at a monument to the Civil War dead and Alvaro overhears a French tourist saying "prend moi une photo" (417) followed by "de quelle guerre s'agit-il" (418). Alvaro asks himself: "La ciudad que contemplaban, ¿era la tuya?" (406) ["The city they contemplated, was it yours?"]. What happens to nationalism when it becomes a commodity for sale to tourists? Goytisolo's last words in the novel are *Introduce the coin* in the four most common languages of tourists visiting Spain.

Moments before, Alvaro hears "Voices" telling him to leave, that he does not belong. "olvídate de nosotros y te olvidaremos / tu pasión fue un error repáralo / salida / sortie / exit / Ausgang" (421) ["forget about us and we will forget about you / your passion was a mistake / remedy it / salida / sortie / exit / Ausgang"]. Now the invitation to leave is in the four common languages of the tourists. But another set of voices that contrasts the voice of "official" Spain tell Alvaro's *not* to forget. "No olvides cuanto ocurrió en él no te calles" (422) ["do not forget what happened there do not be silent"; 351]. He is still troubled by what has happened to Spain and he will tell his story. Throughout his novels Goytisolo's narrators attempt to counter the fascist-based myths that form the foundation of Franco's ideology through remembering real deaths in real history.

Franco's form of government was very influential in the creation of Pinochet's political rhetoric. On 20 November 1975 Augusto Pinochet, dictator of Chile, attended the funeral of Francisco Franco. During his visit, Pinochet declared:

> España...ha sufrido, como nosotros sufrimos hoy, el intento perverso del marxismo que siembra el odio y pretende cambiar los valores espirituales a un mundo materialista y ateo....Al expresar estos sentimientos lo hago consciente de la pérdida que lamenta el mundo hispano....Después de vencer a las fuerzas que pugnaban por destrozar a su pueblo y alejarlo de su tradición histórica, España reconquistó su grandeza. (103)
>
> Spain...has suffered, as we suffer today, the perverse intentions of Marxism that sows hate and pretends to alter spiritual values towards a materialist and atheist world....As I express these feelings, I do this conscious of the loss that the Hispanic world laments....After conquering the forces that sought to destroy her people and separate them from their historic tradition, Spain reconquered her grandeur.

Pinochet, like Franco, desired the return of his nation to its "glorious past." As is common in authoritarian takeovers of leftist governments, Pinochet explained his suspension of Chile's constitution and civil rights as a necessary solution to the chaos of socialism. Pinochet's government was based on a myth of national reconstruction and a return to the "normal course of history" that the socialists had attempted to obstruct with their brief period in office. While Pinochet did not have the legacy of the Catholic Kings on which to base his image, as did Francisco Franco when he assumed power in Spain, he did refer to mythical figures from Chile's past to legitimate his dictatorship. In particular, he associated himself with Bernardo O'Higgins, known as the Liberator of Chile. By connecting himself with O'Higgins, Pinochet described himself as the "Father of the Nation." He, like O'Higgins, would bring control of Chile into the hands of Chileans. O'Higgins fought to free Chile from the Spanish colonizers and Pinochet would free Chile from the colonization of socialism.

In Spanish the word "patria" a word etymologically linked to "padre," or father, is commonly used to refer to "nation" and as Benedict Anderson has noted such language introduces a "vocabulary of kinship." This language suggests that the ties between people and their leaders are natural, i.e., not chosen, and governing is equated with parentage (Anderson 143). Pinochet, in his speeches, uses the term "patria" more frequently than "país," a word that does not convey the sense of nation as family, thereby furthering his image as father of the nation. Pinochet, like Franco, associated his project closely with the Catholic Church. Pinochet considered himself both the head of state and the pre-ordained protector of Catholic values in Chile. In this way, Pinochet's ideological base for his role as dictator combines pre-modern and modern notions of, on the one hand, a monarch/spiritual leader who was destined to rule the land, and, on the other, a president who heads a nation of citizens. This combination of modern dictator and pre-modern monarch was made brazenly clear by a caricature published in *Apsi* magazine in 1987 that depicted Pinochet as Louis XIV. All issues of the magazine were confiscated and its editors were imprisoned (Valenzuela 176). The Pinochet regime's connection (similar to Franco) with Catholic values made his version of fascism distinct from Hitler's regime—a distinction that exposes the persistence of pre-modern forms of non-secular thinking within modern Spain and Latin America. In "Repression and State Security" Patricia Weiss Fagen explains: "This contemporary military rule in Latin America was reminiscent of the fascist regimes of Europe in that they all linked concepts of national well-being with justifications for the extensive, illegal repression of certain groups of citizens.... The military ruler in Latin America, in terms reminiscent of those used by Nazis in Germany, openly proclaimed their intention to eliminate subversives from the body politic" (39). The similarities between Pinochet and Franco's rhetoric have been noted by Hernán Vidal, who states: "You will note that the Declaration of Principles [of Pinochet's Military Junta] corresponds to a mythical discourse ... that reproduces, at times, the canonical language of the Peninsular Reconquest. This language was adopted and reproduced in Chile by groups sympathetic to Francoist Fascism" (109). As Vidal points out, both Franco and Pinochet combine mythical and mystical discourse: they would return their nations to their origins and into the hands of God. Vidal further notes: "Next [Pinochet] makes a call... for the participation of every Chilean in national reconstruction... this message is sustained by references to ... the genuine expression of the 'nation's essence': its Spanish origin and... Christian tradition. At the same time... he proposes a 'national project' which... will result in the development of capitalism and in the modernization of Chile" (112). So, at every turn these premodern linguistic registers referring to a religious legacy and a return to origins have modern and modernizing goals as Pinochet tries to force Chile into the international capitalist marketplace. Manuel Antonio Garretón states in "Fear in Military Regimes" that "the military regimes [in the Southern Cone] were committed to restructuring their respective capitalist systems and then reinserting them into the global capitalist system" (15).

Dorfman, in an article on the tragic murder of Rodrigo Rojas Denegri, who was burned alive in 1986 by Pinochet's police, describes life under Pinochet as life during the Holocaust. The youth, the fiercest opponents of Pinochet, suffer because the regime will not tolerate any threats to its ideal of cultural homogeneity: "El régimen ha respondido redoblando su barbarie. A los jóvenes se los fuerza a extinguir barricadas con sus pies descalzos... miles son arrestados y golpeados... lo que sea para contagiar el miedo en todo el país" (*Araucaria* 16–17) ["The regime has responded by redoubling its barbarism. They force the youth to extinguish barricades with their bare feet... thousands are arrested and beaten... anything in order to make fear in the country contagious"]. Dorfman associates the situation in Chile with ghetto life under Hitler, where any threat to the forced sense of unity the regime required was exterminated. Pinochet's government, like that of Franco, utilized the fascist-based myths of a return to origins, the creation of order from chaos, and a goal of national unity. In his writing, Dorfman attempts to counter these myths and offer a different vision of national identity.

In an interview, Cristina Peri Rossi responded to the problems of cultural production in Uruguay prior to and during the military regime:

> La lucha entre el fascismo y el socialismo—o entre la revolución y la contra revolución, como se prefiera—salpicó la vida y la obra de casi todos los escritores... de modo que nadie continuó escribiendo como antes... ¿cómo no cambiar, cuando todo fue dado la vuelta? En cuanto al porvenir de la literatura uruguaya: Ya existe una literatura cuyo tema es el exilio. Yo, por ejemplo, la hago. Y creo que no se necesitarán muchos años para que aparezca. El porvenir estará en relación directa con la suerte del país, y que yo sepa, cuando el fascismo oye la palabra 'cultura' saca el revólver. Sucederá lo mismo que en España: una gran cantidad de artistas uruguayos en el exilio, y los de adentro callados, silenciados; ah también habrá—es seguro—una literatura oficial: pomposa, con botas, sable y uniforme yankis. (qtd. in Zeitz 87)
>
> The struggle between fascism and socialism—or between revolution and counter-revolution, whichever one prefers—touched the life and work of almost every writer... to the extent that no one continued writing as before.

...How could we not change, when everything was turned upside down? As far as the future of Uruguayan literature is concerned: There already exists a literature whose theme is exile. I, for example, work in it. And I think that it won't take many years for it to appear. The future will be in direct relation to the fortune of the country, and as far as I know, when Fascism hears the word "culture" it takes out its revolver. The same thing will happen as happened in Spain: a huge quantity of Uruguayan artists in exile, and those inside quiet, silenced: oh, there will also be—it is certain—an official literature; pompous, with boots, saber and Yankee uniforms.

Peri Rossi connects the events in Uruguay with those in Spain. Fascist-like intolerance of cultural creativity was a problem in all three of these writers' countries.

Peri Rossi's last text prior to exile, *Indicios pánicos* (*Panic Signs*) (1970), presages the Fascist influences that affected her country. Interestingly, both Peri Rossi and Dorfman produced texts just prior to exile that foreshadowed the authoritarian governments that were on the verge of controlling their homes. Dorfman's *Moros en la costa* (*Hard Rain*) is a novel that senses the impending crisis that Allende's regime was to face. In an epigraph to her novel Peri Rossi cites Benito Mussolini: "Es tiempo de decir que el hombre, antes de recibir los beneficios de la cultura, debe recibir los beneficios de la orden. En cierto sentido, se puede decir que el policía ha precedido, en la historia, al profesor" (7) ["It is time to say that man, before receiving the benefits of culture, should receive the benefits of order. In a certain sense, one could say that, in history, the police have preceded the professor"]. In a footnote to her epigraph, Peri Rossi writes: "Después de Mussolini, muchos pensadores en América Latina han sostenido la misma tesis, aunque llevándola a la práctica quizás con más esmero aún" (7) ["After Mussolini, many Latin American thinkers have maintained the same thesis, although they have perhaps practiced it with even greater conscientiousness"]. All three writers, then, describe life under authoritarianism in their countries with references to fascism. Peri Rossi's case is distinct, though, specifically because a visible dictator, as in the cases of Spain and Chile, did not rule Uruguay. "Uruguay under military rule was not a history of a *líder máximo*" (Weinstein 50). Because the military Junta chose to remain somewhat anonymous, much of the official propaganda that can be found in the speeches and decrees of Franco and Pinochet is not present in the case of Uruguay. President Juan María Bordaberry, who was central to the rise of the military in the Uruguayan government and held power from 1972–76, did meet with Pinochet, though, and they publicly declared the compatibility of their regimes' ideologies since both leaders wanted to "salvar la esencia misma de la patria" ["save the essence of the country"]. Bordaberry affirmed: "Y fueron sus Fuerzas Armadas, al igual que en Chile, quienes [empezaron] este verdadero proceso de reconstrucción nacional que debió iniciarse para [guardar] lo nuestro, salvar lo que heredamos de nuestros mayores y asentar más que nunca el emblema de libertad, paz y trabajo" (Pinochet 119) ["And it was their Armed Forces, the same as in Chile, who began the true process of national reconstruction and who had to begin in order to protect us, to save what we have inherited from our forefathers and to establish now more than ever the emblem of liberty, peace and work"].

Despite the less leader-oriented sources of authoritarianism in Uruguay, the fascist-based desires for a new order and for cultural homogeneity persisted (Sosnowski 4–5). In 1975, Bordaberry, under the direction of the Armed Forces, published in the press two memorandums justifying the suspension of the constitution. In one of these he explains the importance of creating a new order and of uniting the youth of the nation: "En fin, en lo concerniente a la educación y la promoción social, el nuevo orden debería respetar la libertad de los docentes y educados, promoviendo los valores de familia y encuadrando bajo una dirección 'unitaria' el tiempo ocioso de la juventud" (Lerin and Torres 63) ["Finally, as far as education and social promotion is concerned, the new order should respect the freedom of teachers and students, promoting family values and framing under a 'unitary' direction the free time of the youth"]. Just as in the cases of Spain and Chile, the Uruguayan military relied heavily on myths for legitimacy. "The ordering of time was accomplished chiefly by means of an official history, which was created gradually beginning in the late nineteenth century.... The idea of Uruguay as a 'model country' persisted as a systematic construct... and [implied] the creation of a 'perfect city'" (Rial 69). In the work of Peri Rossi, the evils of the city can be read as a response to the highlighted importance of an advanced city life organized around the model of Montevideo under military rule. Peri Rossi's characters have trouble navigating life in the city. Morris, a character from *La nave de los locos*, visits a metaphorical city, El Gran Ombligo (The Great Navel), and is completely alienated: "En el Gran Ombligo, a Morris le lloran los ojos, se le obstruye la nariz, los músculos se contraen y la cabeza le pesa, como si llevara un casco" (125) ["In the Great Navel Morris suffers from watering eyes, blocked nose, muscle cramps, and a heavy head as though he were wearing a helmet"; 126].

The authoritarian governments in Spain, Chile, and Uruguay can be called, according to Gino Germani "functional substitutes for fascism" (73). What is most important about the presence of fascist overtones in these regimes is their use of myth and history. As he explains: "What is essential in modern authoritarianism... is that the aim of this planned socialization and resocialization is the transformation of the population into ideologically 'militant', active participants" (9). In the cases being studied here, this action is directly connected to the modernization of the national economy and the insertion of the country into the international marketplace. But these modern goals are combined with a pre-modern concept of the "subject" as it existed during monarchies:

> The legitimacy of the rulers need not be formally approved by the subjects. Insofar as the nation becomes the prescriptive nucleus on which social integration rests, and the active presence of all members of the national community is functionally necessary,... some form of active political participation will also be required, even if to some extent it remains purely formal and symbolic. Here we find one of the most paradoxical aspects of the totalitarian system. (10)

Inasmuch as the governments in Spain, Chile, and Uruguay required that their citizens live in the temporal paradox of the pre-modern and the modern, Goytisolo, Dorfman, and Peri Rossi endeavor to combat these versions of time in their nations by offering alternative myths, alternative histories and alternative temporalities. In the following analysis I will examine the way each of these three writers launched their individual attacks on three temporal fronts: the pre-modern, the modern, and the postmodern.

Goytisolo: El conde don Julián Battles the Cid

Like the classical Ulysses, Goytisolo's narrators desire to overthrow those who have usurped their homeland. Unlike Ulysses, Goytisolo's protagonists will never satisfy their desire for vindication because they operate within a system that constantly exposes their marginality and dubious power. As Michael Ugarte explains in *Shifting Ground,* Goytisolo, similar to James Joyce, who also transforms the classical figure of Ulysses, is obsessed with the homeland, despite the influence of postmodernism on his work (205). Ugarte categorizes Goytisolo's writing in *Reivindicación del conde don Julián* as postmodern. I will be arguing, differing from Ugarte, that this text is a promiscuous dialectical combination of pre-modern, modern, and postmodern worldviews. Both Joyce and Goytisolo challenge classical forms of narrating the experience of exile. Yet, in keeping with traditional exile literature, for them, home and nation cannot be mentally separated. The following analysis demonstrates that Goytisolo's novels, while having ties to other tales of exiles, provide their own distinct versions of the quest for home. The "quest myth," which suggests that it is possible to be successfully returned to one's origins by searching for one's home, undergoes a significant revision in Goytisolo's writing to reflect his particular experience of exile (see Labanyi for more detail on different versions of the "quest myth" in her chapter "The Historical uses of Myth").

It is Goytisolo's position as an exile of Spain in the 1960s and 1970s that leads him to confront the exile's loss of a homeland in a seemingly contradictory fashion. On the one hand, Goytisolo's texts create an alternative concept of the nation which opposes that being promoted under Franco. On the other hand, he wholeheartedly dismisses the notion of nation as repressive and restricting to identity because it forces one to assimilate into a group, conform to traceable territorial affiliation, and participate in a society that requires the establishment of rules of conduct. In this sense we can note the influence of Roland Barthes's critique of myth in Goytisolo's work. Labanyi, in her analysis of the influence of myth on post-Civil War writers in Spain, explains the central point of Barthes's work as it relates to these writers: "For Barthes myth is always authoritarian in that it denies ambiguity and the possibility of alternatives, and creates a world of solid, fixed 'eternal' values" (23). Agreeing with Barthes's view of myth, Goytisolo, at times, rejects the use of myth, preferring to emphasize ubiquitous relativism. His work oscillates between a position that requires that myth be used to counter myth, and one that suggests that such projects are intrinsically authoritarian and are always doomed to fail when they challenge, from a marginalized position, dominant power structures. The use of myth in Goytisolo's work is paradoxical: he adopts an Eliadean view of myth as the basis of primordial social constructs (i.e., myths are useful ideological tools for constructing the relationship between the self and the world), a Freudian view of myth as the mind's unconscious efforts at seeking release from oppressive civilization (i.e., myths are an important act of mental liberation), and a Barthesian view of myth as authoritarian (i.e., myths are something to be rejected). In this way his novels hold the concept of myth in a dialectical tension between the primordial, the modern, and the postmodern.

Jo Labanyi explains that myth always accompanies nation-building (8). The myth of national essences allows the association of the State with timeless cultural practices, which gives the nation necessary roots and legitimizes the role of its leaders. Francoist rhetoric justified dictatorship by asserting that Franco's government was necessary to return Spain to its original cultural state. Labanyi also argues that such constructions of the nation generally are used as antidotes to decadence (9). In the case of Spain, the "decadence" of the Second Republic (1931–39) is overcome by a return to Spain's roots, the roots of the Catholic Kings. Franco is able to use the chaos of the Second Republic as proof that democracy is alien to Spain, thereby clearing the path for a return to Catholic values and to a non-participatory form of government, like the monarchy of the Catholic Kings. Labanyi sees Franco's emphasis on unity as a common practice under totalitarian regimes, and, in particular, fascist ones. Luis Torres, the Vice-Secretary of Franco's National Delegation of Popular Education, an institution that housed the Department for the Censorship of Books, outlined the following goals of his office: "to spread The Culture to the entire nation through all possible means, so that in this way, we may orient the people towards the form of good habits and customs and the healthy concept of the ideas that inspired *el Movimiento Nacional* and propagandize the healthy and traditional Spanish Culture as well as Catholic Doctrine" (Veciana 25). The goals of Franco's regime are by no means subtle in this regard. There will be one culture for the entire nation.

By contrast, Goytisolo champions fragmentation over unity. He also argues that the return to essences that Franco emphasizes with a return to the Spain of the Catholic Kings is misguided: for him, there are different roots of Spanish culture that should be privileged. These roots pre-date the Catholic Kings, an important part of Goytisolo's argument, and they refer to the Spain of the Christians, Jews, and Moors. Influenced by the work of Américo Castro, Goytisolo argues that Spain's heritage is multicultural and that national culture is not single or unified. (For Castro's description of Spain's cultural roots see *La realidad histórica de España*.) In Goytisolo's introduction to *España y los españoles* he describes the power of Spain's unifying myth of origins based on the Catholic Kings: "Mito real, por tanto, que da un aspecto inevitablemente engañoso al término 'España' y actúa permanentemente sobre la realidad nacional. Pero esta realidad—compleja, cambiante, contradictoria—encaja difícilmente en el molde uniforme y estático de la palabra 'España'" (8) ["Royal myth, therefore, that gives an inevitably deceptive aspect to the term "Spain" and that affects national reality permanently. But this reality—complex, changing, contradictory—fits uncomfortably in the uniform and static mold of the word 'Spain'"). Since multiculturalism has been labeled a postmodern phenomenon, it is interesting to note that Goytisolo highlights that in Spain's case multiculturalism preceded the forced cultural homogeneity imposed by the Catholic Kings and the Inquisition. In particular, Goytisolo's second novel of the trilogy is primarily concerned with revising the founding date of cultural nationalism. Where for Franco 1492 marks the pinnacle of Spanish history and also the cultural roots that he favors, Goytisolo's date will be 711. This date marks the invasion of Spain by the Arabs. Spain had been part of the Roman Empire until the Visigoths were able to take advantage of Rome's weakening hold and establish a new kingdom. In 711 the Arabs invaded and overthrew the reign of Visigoth King Rodrigo, beginning the era of Arab control of Spain. During the years 711–1492 Spain was the home of Arabs, Jews, and Christians. Goytisolo attempts to divert emphasis from 1492—which symbolizes the unification of Spain, the expulsion of the Jews and the Moors, and the success of Columbus in the Americas—to 711, which symbolizes Arab triumph and multiculturalism.

In *Reivindicación del conde don Julián,* history is mixed with myth and the choice of the nation's cultural founders is a political battle. The contrasting desires to break with the past and also transform our understanding of it plague the narrator. The ambivalence of the narrator of *Reivindicación del conde don Julián* is caused by the uncertainty of his position: he finds his alienation no longer something he is "certain" he wants to overcome. Five years have elapsed since the publication of *Señas de identidad,* and the state of affairs has not improved. The rabid narrator of *Reivindicación del conde don Julián,* who has been denied a place in history, spends his days fantasizing about a different Spain, one where pariahs like him are not banished, and one where difference is not cause for execution or exile. I should add that many critics have addressed the connections between the novels of the trilogy. Some see a clear break between *Señas de identidad* and those that followed based on the absence in the last two of a named narrator as well as any formal rules of punctuation. Many, though, consider the novels to represent the development of one single protagonist and often refer to the unnamed protagonists of the latter two novels as Alvaro as well. I will respect Goytisolo's decision to not name them. Even though there is a link that connects all three novels, it does not justify an assumption that the same narrator operates in all. The narrator of *Reivindicación del conde don Julián* has ties to Alvaro, but they are not the same character.

The narrator of *Reivindicación del conde don Julián* leads a seemingly simple life. He gets up, checks that the coast of Spain is still there and that his battle must wage on and then prepares to leave the small room he rents. He then wanders the streets of Tangiers, reveling in the carnavalesque chaos of the marketplace, which gives him a chance to observe a few tourists, whom he despises and imagines being destroyed. He then proceeds to the library where he takes out texts of Spain's canon and smashes bugs between the pages. This small victory over Spanish culture achieved, he leaves. On the day we follow him, he also stands in line to give blood to the Red Cross, which he fantasizes will return to Spain and infect the recipients of it with rabies. Later he meets an Arab and goes to smoke hash where Spanish TV allows his drugged mind to fantasize about invading the country. Next he returns home, alone, to begin similar activities the next day.

The testimonial efforts of Alvaro in *Señas de identidad* are abandoned in *Reivindicación del conde don Julián* in favor of fantastic assaults on Spanish culture. In this second exile novel, the protagonist is delusional and such a state aids his fantasies of destruction and revenge. Freud associated the fantasies of the unconscious with myth. It is in these fantasies that the human mind seeks release from the repression of civilization. Freud suggested that myth functioned in a way similar to dreams (Labanyi 12; see, in particular, Freud's *Interpretation of Dreams*). *Reivindicación del conde don Julián*'s delusional protagonist supports my theory that the novel is obsessed with the connections between myth and history: the protagonist's mental state wavers between connecting him with the outside world and present time and sending him into a dream-like timeless state.

The act of entering the library in Tangiers, retrieving books from Spain's canon, and inserting insects into the pages is possibly one of the most powerful images of the book. *Reivindicación del conde don Julián* links the politics of Spain directly to the chosen discourse of official culture: the inheritance of the ideology of the Catholic Kings and their cultural legacy. Goytisolo attacks Franco's version of the nation by focusing on the image of Sacred Spain. His novel also continues to present an alternative nation: "la violencia, la violencia siempre ... anulando de golpe el orden fingido, revelando la verdad bajo la máscara, catalizando tus fuerzas dispersas y los donjuanescos proyectos de invasión : traición grandiosa, ruina de siglos : ejército cruel de Tariq, destrucción de la España Sagrada" (52) ["violence, inescapable violence ... instantly destroying the illusion of order, revealing the truth hidden behind the mask, catalyzing your scattered forces and your [donjuanesque] plans for invasion: a grandiose act of treason, the collapse of entire centuries: the cruel army of Tariq, the destruction of Sacred Spain"; 39]. He will annul the "pretend order" and expose the truth beneath the mask. By destroying the mask of Sacred Spain, the narrator can let the "real" Spain show its face. At the same time that the novel undertakes such grandiose plans of destruction, the narrator recognizes the flaws of his plan and his deluded desires referring to his "donjuanescos proyectos" ["donjuanesque plans"]. (See Epps for more on the violence in this novel.)

The battle to destroy Sacred Spain enacted by Goytisolo's second novel in exile can be characterized as a battle between Count Julian versus the Cid. The Cid, Rodrigo Díaz de Vivar, is the legendary hero of Spain, who was immortalized in the medieval epic poem *Cantar de mio Cid* that dates back to approximately 1140 and narrates historical events from the end of the second century during the Christian Reconquest. The tale of the Cid begins with his exile from Vivar when he was falsely accused of taking tributes that he had collected on behalf of King Alfonso VI from the "pariahs" and Moors of Andalusia. After bidding farewell to his wife and two daughters, he begins a series of conquests. He successfully captures areas of Muslim Spain and installs himself in Valencia (1094), all the while sending tributes to Alfonso VI. In the second section of the poem, his daughters marry, attracting suitors because of the new-found wealth of their father. In the third section, the Cid humiliates his sons-in-law, who retaliate by physically abusing their wives. The Cid asks permission of the King and gets his revenge.

The connection between the Cid and Franco's ideological agenda is clear. Franco, in a speech, refers to the Cid, claiming:

> El Cid es el espíritu de España. Suele ser en la estrechez y no en la opulencia cuando surgen estas grandes figuras.... Lanzada una nación por la pendiente del egoísmo y la comodidad forzosamente tenía que caer en el envilecimiento.... ¡El gran miedo a que el Cid saliera de su tumba y encarnarse en las nuevas generaciones!... Este ha sido el gran servicio de nuestra Cruzada, la virtud de nuestro movimiento: el haber despertado en las nuevas generaciones la conciencia de lo que fuimos, de lo que somos y de lo que podemos ser. (1955, 154)

> The Cid is the spirit of Spain. It is usually in moments of hardship and not in opulence when these great figures come forth.... Launched from a nation steeped in egoism and forced comfort that had to fall into vileness.... The great fear that the Cid would leave his tomb and incarnate himself in new generations!... This has been the great service of our Crusade, the virtue of our movement: having awoken in new generations the consciousness of who we were, of who we are and of who we can become.

Inaugurating a statue of the Cid, Franco names him as the forefather to his version of Spanish society.

The Cid, like the classical Ulysses, is symbolic of the man who has been cast out of his home and who, through great acts of masculine strength and wisdom, manages to return. He is the paradigm of the exile for Spanish literature and he represents the Spanish values of Christianity over Islam. Official history exalts the Visigoths, deprecating the Arabs and the Jews, making the Cid the perfect precursor to the Spain of the Catholic Kings. Goytisolo makes specific reference to the power of the Cid's legacy in *España y los españoles,* explaining how the Cid has often come to reflect the characteristics of the "ideal Spaniard" (39). *Reivindicación del conde don Julián* constantly associates the figure of the Cid with the current state of Spain: "nuestras figuras gloriosas y efemérides patria suscitan el bostezo pulcro y cortés, la amable, comedida sonrisa : ... don Pelayo, Guzmán el Bueno, Ruy Díaz de Vivar! el deslumbrante progreso industrial la mirífica sociedad de consumo" (136) ["our glorious figures and national ephemerida provoke politely stifled yawns, affable, discreet smiles: ... Pelayo, Guzmán el Bueno, Ruy Díaz de Vivar! The prodigious rate of industrial growth, the glorious consumer society have undermined traditional values"; 113–14]. The glorious figures of Spanish culture are responsible for the acrid conformism of Spanish society. They do not foster rebellion, but instead lead society toward greater forms of subservience. The Cid is part of the mask that, once placed on Spain, helped align society with consumer culture: "y he aquí que la máscara crece y se transforma en un desmesurado mascarón que articula talismánicos nombres sin perder un ápice de su rigidez ... y crece y crece, adquiere proporciones monstruosos, se extiende y acartona, rivaliza en inmovilidad con las estatuas : genio y figura, figura y genio : Manolete, Séneca, el Cid" (175–76) ["and now the mask grows even larger and turns into an enormous, grotesque *mascarón* which utters talismanic names without losing one iota of its rigidity . . . it becomes bigger and bigger and bigger, takes on monstrous proportions, stretches and stretches, and then dries up, its immobility rivaling that of statues: genius and the appearance of genius, and vice versa: Manolete, Seneca, the Cid"; 148]. Through the statuesque image of the Cid, official culture has managed to form a rock-like base, which serves as a foundation for the artifice of Sacred Spain.

Count Julian was also exiled, but he has little in common with the Cid. In his case, his exile has no honor, for he truly did betray his country. As the Christian Lord of Ceuta he allowed the Muslim armies of Tarik to enter and begin to conquer the peninsula in 711. Unlike the glorification that the Cid receives, the story of Count Julian is not part of the canon and was not made into a Hollywood movie starring Charleston Heston. Two of the opening epigraphs to the novel represent radically different descriptions of Count Julian, thereby establishing early on that his place in history is ambiguous at best. Goytisolo embraces this ambiguity and uses it to frustrate the sterile, perfect image of the Cid. In fact, the first citation which refers to Count Julian emphasizes that few facts exist regarding him: even his name is not clear, "probablemente se llamara Julián o quizás Urbano, Ulbán o Bulian . . . en realidad no sabemos si era berberisco, godo o bizantino . . . si gobernaba Septum . . . si era un exarca o gobernador" ["his real name was probably Julian, or perhaps Urban or Ulbán or Bulian. . . . We are not certain whether he was a Berber, a Visigoth or a Byzantine . . . he may have been the ruler of Septum . . . he may have been an exarch or a governor"]. The second epigraph, clearly from a perspective favoring the image of Sacred Spain begins: "Maldita sea la saña del traidor Julián ca mucho fué perseverada; maldita sea la su ira, ca mucho fué dura et mala" ["Accursed be the fury of the traitor Julian, of which we were long the victims; accursed be his wrath, for it was cruel and evil"]. This is taken from the chronicles of Alfonso X el Sabio, King of Leon and Castilla, in the thirteenth century. The last quote from the Marquis de Sade dreams of a crime with the perpetual effect of agitation: "Je voudrais trouver un crime dont l'effet perpétual agît, même quand je n'agirais plus" ["I should like to discover the crime the effect of which would be actively felt forever"]. Goytisolo exhumes the story of Count Julian as a model for the perfect crime: his act of betrayal caused seven centuries of unrest in Spain.

But the nostalgia for a past moment when such acts of betrayal were possible is constantly exposed as a fantasy. The narrator wishes he were Count Julian, but he is not. He must perform his betrayal mentally and through his narrative, hoping that these fantasies have the strength to challenge the myths behind Francoism. He destroys the Spanish classics with bugs, but other copies are available. He destroys tourism by imagining the grotesque death of the U.S. tourist, Mrs. Putifar, who is bitten by a snake charmer's snake and lies on the market floor dying while Moroccan boys lift her skirt to urinate on her genitals, but other tourists arrive after her. This sense of futility connects to theories of the postmodern which question the validity of representation. The protagonist of the novel has one vision, one that is constantly exposed as flawed. Like Michel Foucault and Deleuze and Guattari, Goytisolo challenges the modern notions of representation and reason with an emphasis on difference and fragmentation (see Foucault's *The Order of Things* and Deleuze and Guattari's *Anti-Oedipus*).

The desire for destruction continues throughout the novel and turns on the people, language, and religious values of Spain. The narrator fantasizes that his rabid blood will reach Spain and infect her inhabitants, but his "rabia" or anger will be filtered out as it has been by Spain's "limpieza de sangre" (purity of blood) for centuries. This is a reference to the emphasis on Christian blood under the Inquisition. Even those Muslims and Jews, who converted to Catholicism, were never considered to have "pure blood." There was a caste system regarding one's religious bloodlines, where only those who had pure Christian family heritage could hold the most privileged places in society. It is worth thinking about the way that spreading infected blood also reflects on issues of HIV and homophobia, an issue that was less central in 1970, when *Reivindicación del conde don Julián* was published. Nevertheless, the connections between homosexuality and infected blood date back farther than the onset of HIV fears. The protagonist will destroy the official culture of Sacred Spain—the Cid, Seneca, and the Generation of '98—by substituting an alternative, but he knows that an alternative culture will not ultimately solve the problem. Seneca, because of the value of his stoicism for Francoist ideology, was considered to be a Spaniard by official culture. Américo Castro exposes this as a complete myth by first making a distinction between the region, which is now known as Spain but was then a part of the Roman Empire: "Sólo una alucinación, explicable por una especie de psicosis colectiva, pudo hacer de Séneca y de su filosofía un fenómeno español. Aun admitiendo que el pensar estoico hubiese tenido hondas y originales repercusiones en el pensamiento español (no las tuvo), de ahí no cabría deducir ningún españolismo en Séneca" (147) ["Only a hallucination, explained as some sort of collective psychosis, would turn Seneca and his philosophy into a Spanish phenomenon. Even if we admitted that stoic thought had had profound and original repercussions in Spanish thought (which it didn't), from there one could not deduce any Spanishness in Seneca"].

The narrator will also try to destroy order by narrating a dense text and remembering that "la duda es tu única certeza" (89) ["doubt is your only certainty"; 73]. He will try to destroy the Spanish language through new modes of writing: "prosa anárquica y bárbara, lejos de vuestro estilo peinado, de vuestra anémica, relamida escritura! ... en abrupta ruptura con la sintaxis oficial y su secuela de dogmas y entredicho" (152) ["anarchical and barbarous prose, the very opposite of your carefully kempt style, your anemic, prim and proper, overrefined writing ... breaking away altogether from the official syntax and its attendant procession of dogmas and interdicts"; 128]. Yet, despite his anarchistic prose, he will not have a completely chaotic text: he still yearns to communicate. He is caught in a paradox since only a syntax that is readable can counter the official syntax. So his writing is different from the sterile prose of the Generation of '98 and critics like Menéndez Pelayo, but it is not completely opaque.

Reivindicación del conde don Julián does battle on pre-modern terms, exhuming the figure of Count Julian and suggesting a different manichean schema from that offered by Franco's use of the values of the Catholic Kings. The novel also uses modernist strategies, suggesting a totalizing version of the nation that is a rejection of Franco: after invading Spain, the armies led by the narrator will forge a new nation. Furthermore, it is the haphazard and chaotic battle that is totally fragmented and revealed as delusional which suggests Goytisolo's postmodern influences. The sources of power have become dispersed which leads Goytisolo to use an irrational approach, attacking everything Spanish. Franco, or a dictatorial figure, is no longer the clear source of evil. Goytisolo questions whether the problem is intrinsic to Spain or is even capable of repair.

Perhaps one of the best demonstrations of this dilemma takes place when he attacks the Catholic Church by turning the sacred image of Isabel la Católica into a dancing, sex-crazed woman when she listens to the music of the Rolling Stones (162–65). Later, the region of Spain is transformed into the body of Isabel la Católica whose vagina has been mutated into a tourist attraction: "el Antro que van ustedes a visitar es sin duda alguna una de las curiosidades históricas más típicas y pasmosas de nuestro privilegiado paisaje peninsular / sus implicaciones metafísicas / su configuración moral / su espiritualidad rica y densa" (166) ["The Cavern that you are about to visit is undoubtedly one of the most typical and most fascinating historical curiosities of our unique Peninsula / its metaphysical implications / its moral configuration / its rich, intense spirituality"; 140]. Here the blows are two fisted: the Catholic Church's embrace of tourism's material benefits is critiqued at the same time that Goytisolo debases the exaltation of the Virgin and her "pure" sex. Goytisolo shows that the chastity of the Virgin has been sullied through the follies of her protectors. Consumerism has made the glorified symbols of the past items to be sold. This is both liberating and destructive for him. Through the commodification of Isabel la Católica, the deep meaning of the icon will be stripped and she will have no more value than a pack of Benson and Hedges. The problem for Goytisolo's project is that such flatness of meaning will make the myth of Count Julian equally insignificant. Exposing the way that commodification of Catholic values ultimately renders them meaningless will not help to combat the spread of capitalism in Spain. At this level, Goytisolo's critique lacks a way out of the dominance of materialism on Spanish land. One can only assume that, as his goal is to destroy Sacred Spain, it is less important to him whether it is vanquished due to a counter narrative of non-Sacred Spain or due to hypercapitalism. Yet it remains clear throughout all three novels of the trilogy that Goytisolo does not support capitalism and that materialism is also one of the evils he endeavors to destroy. Beginning with *Señas de identidad,* the tourist is presented as the ultimate consumer of national identity. "Los millones de extranjeros que visitan la Península la contemplan ya a través del telón alienador de la moderna sociedad de consumo" (*España* 205) ["The millions of foreigners that visit the Peninsula already contemplate it through the alienating veil of modern consumer society"]. The tourist wants to purchase a memory of a nation that often does not exist, but will be fabricated for their pleasure. As was noted in the scene at Montjuich from *Señas de identidad*, the tourist strips the nation of meaning, gliding over the surface of national monuments and histories, translating historic events and memories into cheap souvenirs to be purchased, taken home, and forgotten. The critical dilemma for this novel seems to be that no matter which tack Goytisolo chooses—counter-narrative or nihilism—his project for liberation is fraught with obstacles and his methods, if successful, may only lead to more problems.

So, if tourism does not undo the sacred value of official Spain, then to rid the country of the Catholics and capitalism, we must go back to the Middle Ages. The narrator, fancying himself a contemporary Count Julian, leads the invasion of Spain by a new Muslim army headed by Tarik. In his fantasy, time has turned back and he is able to live in the past. The novel repeatedly returns in a cyclical fashion to the possibilities of the vindication of Count Julian and it repeatedly recognizes that such possibilities are hallucinations. It is the connection between these two gestures—a belief in the power of myth and a disbelief in the ability to counter omnipotent official ideology—that demonstrate the novel's bridge between the postmodern and the premodern.

By converting the physical geography of Spain into a tool for mental acts of betrayal, the narrator transforms the land into a primordial myth. The nation, for instance, is a scar, a wound that cannot be forgotten. The sea is soothing and separates him from the "acuciante, venenosa cicatriz" (68) ["painful, poisonous scar"; 55]. Elsewhere, he states that language is the only tie that binds him to Spain, "la patria no es la tierra, el hombre no es el árbol : ayúdame a vivir sin suelo sin raíces : móvil, móvil : sin otro alimento y sustancia que tu rica palabra : palabra sin historia, orden verbal autónomo, engañoso delirio" (124–25) ["one's true homeland is not the country of one's birth: man is not a tree: help me to live without roots: ever on the move: my only sustenance your nourishing language: a tongue without history, a hermetic verbal universe, a shimmering mirage"; 104]. He desires words without history—through a postmodern rejection of myth—but the ever-present cultural umbilical cord cannot be severed. Moreover, in contrast with the modern impulse to substitute Sacred Spain with the reinstallation of Muslim Spain and her multicultural values, the narrator also dreams of a transnational, free-floating existence without nationality. From this perspective, the nation, by definition, controls our identity: all nations must be betrayed. Betrayal extends beyond the particular treason committed by Count Julian to all organized society and liberates the self from any of the constraints of civilization. The narrator dreams of chaotic anarchy where individuals are stripped of the baggage of national culture.

Reivindicación del conde don Julián's structure reveals the combination of premodern, modern, and postmodern modes of rebellion. First, the text challenges the myths that the Franco regime relied on by offering a counter-myth centered on the figure of Count Julian. The exiled Count Julian's story becomes the mythical origin that should form the basis of Spanish society. Then the text appears to seek, nostalgically, to recreate the Spanish nation and to reform Spanish culture. The narrator, through brave acts of will and determination, can beat Franco's regime and replace it with a society where individuals are not forced to conform to cultural homogeneity. At the same time, though, the text, through its nontraditional grammar and language, its fragmented narrative, and its questioning of the narrator's ability to progress through time, reveals a postmodern view of the exile's place in society. The narrator lives in *destiempo,* unable to engage in society whatsoever, destined to remain on the margins and to suffer the consequences of multinational capitalism. He has no ethical ground from which to fight, and no sense of history from which to move forward. Revenge, while still desired, is futile. In fact, the pleasure of fantasizing about successful revenge is the only option left to the exile.

We are left to wonder how to read the last sentence of the text: "Mañana será otro día, la invasión recomenzará" (240) ["Tomorrow will be another day, the invasion will begin all over again"; 204]. Time is cyclical for the exiled protagonist who told us in the first few pages, "un día y otro día y otro aún : siempre igual" (11) ["one day, another, and yet another: ever the same"; 3]. To what state does the text return to each morning? To the pre-modern, the modern, or the postmodern? The narrator awakens each day to three world visions. For it is only by combining them that he has a chance of challenging Francoist ideology. Moreover, despite such combinations, there is no certainty in the narrator's ability to succeed. Such a sense of futility only makes sense when it is read as a postmodern condition. Only after a crisis in the modern truths of free will and self-determination can the loss of agency experienced by the exile be seen as part of a postmodern condition. Such an eclectic version of society has the sufficient, necessary force to turn the founding principles of the modern authoritarian state upside down and ask the reader to question the basis of modernism's (i.e., the Francoist government's) need for legitimacy, social homogeneity, and order.

Dorfman: David versus Goliath

Augusto Pinochet came to power almost forty years after Francisco Franco. Pinochet could not create a national economy based on autarchy, as did Franco in the first phase of his regime. Instead, he came to power as the champion of capitalism over socialism. Capitalism is a modern form of economy and required the formation of the nation-state as the entity within which capitalism was regulated and from which it was disseminated. In modern times, therefore, history witnesses the birth of the nation. Individuals are conceived of as citizens and they choose their leaders as opposed to inheriting them. Technically the nation-state, then, is modern and secular. Modernity also refers to the transition from feudalism to capitalism. And the nation was the center for the development of capitalist modes of production. What makes these notions slippery when dealing with Augusto Pinochet, though, is that he was an advocate of capitalism, but, as a dictator, he also expected unconditional obedience from the populace. Economically, Chile practiced modern capitalism, but socially, Chileans were expected to remain pre-modern with none of the rights associated with modern society. Hence, we find the paradox of modern authoritarianism (see Gino Germani).

Pinochet was the central figure for the pre-modern and modern ideologies that formed the basis of his regime. The image of Pinochet was crucial to the foundation of his authoritarian government. In fact, in 1993, during the twentieth anniversary of the coup, many of these images persisted. Flyers called "all Thankful Chileans with Good memories" to congregate at the house of Pinochet—"Liberator of Chile"—in order to celebrate the "20th Anniversary of our Second National Independence." Elsewhere on the flyer Pinochet is referred to as the "Second Father of the Nation"

(O'Higgins was the first). It is important to bear in mind that in 1993, Pinochet was no longer dictator of Chile and the elected president was Patricio Aylwin, a member of the moderate Christian Democrat party who assumed office in 1990. But Pinochet was not gone and he certainly was not forgotten.

As he viewed from a distance the construction of Pinochet's image, Dorfman felt a need to combat it. In fact, in an article written after the 1989 plebiscite which called for a presidential election to be held in 1990, Dorfman explained the persistent centrality and complexity of the image of Pinochet sixteen years after his initial takeover: "In all cases, the general weighs at the center of one's life, a dark anchor narrowing the range of every choice.... He is burned into our memory, in our customs, into the way we speak, into our dreams. How are we to exorcise him?" ("Adiós General" 76). Here Dorfman describes Pinochet as a devil inhabiting the body of the Chilean nation. Yet, at the same time that Dorfman writes hoping to challenge Pinochet's image as a savior by describing him as a devil, he also combats his modern image, as a statesman, an advocate of capitalism, and a father of the nation: "Even for exiles, Pinochet, by taking possession of our landscape and the people we loved, became the owner of our future" (75). The above quotation emphasizes Dorfman's vision of Pinochet as the ultimate capitalist consumer, one who not only purchases land, but also people and their dreams.

In *The Last Song of Manuel Sendero* Dorfman's critique of Pinochet occurs on every symbolic level which Pinochet himself tries to occupy. For instance, he counters Pinochet's image as a pre-modern savior and he also critiques Pinochet's capitalist goals for modernizing Chile. In so doing, Dorfman rejects the concept of nation that Pinochet represents. The nation should not be a space of oppression. The leader should not be an authoritarian father and its people should not be treated as naive children. When Dorfman works on these issues he does not reject the concept of nation, but instead argues for a different nation that contrasts the nation of the military regime. In *The Last Song of Manuel Sendero,* Dorfman narrates two alternative nations. The first refers to Chile under Allende and is nostalgic for the past: "You take charge of the government, the poor take over, and one of those unique and miraculous periods opens up for the first time ever, and there's a real possibility of putting an end to the misery of all of those kids" (32). But as we know this utopic nation came to an end and was replaced by tyranny: "they throw you out. And these sons of bitches take your place." So the vision of Chile under Allende does not provide a solution to Pinochet's nation. Elsewhere in the same novel Dorfman narrates a mythical, manichean nation where the good are able to defeat the forces of evil:

> Once upon a time, ... on the frontier of a fairy tale, there was a singer whose name was Manuel.... Once upon a time there was a land of meanwhile, a time between parentheses, ... Once upon a time Manuel Sendero had dreamed that his voice could rescue his beloved from Hell and resurrect his son and move the beasts to pity. Once upon a time ... Manuel Sendero believed that he was immortal. (407)

In this quotation Dorfman equates nation with myth, as did Pinochet. Similar to the way that he contrasts Pinochet with Allende, Dorfman tries to suggest a version of the nation that is benevolent and holds the possibility of peace. Interestingly, Dorfman chooses to narrate two separate alternatives to Pinochet's Chile. The first refers specifically to Allende's Chile, but the second version of the nation has no temporal or spatial markers. Dorfman's narrative answers Pinochet's version of Chile on both a national and a transnational level.

In comparison with Goytisolo, whose mythical, borderless nation is made up of pariahs, outcasts, and social misfits, Dorfman's pre-modern vision of community has heroes, martyrs, and happy families. These differences evoke the disparity between their experiences of exile: Goytisolo's "self" exile after decades of life under Franco contrasts that of Dorfman who left Chile shortly after the experience of being a part of a successful socialist government. Consequently, Goytisolo's ideal community is defined by its separation from normalizing, hegemonic social structures and Dorfman's is characterized by manicheism and the triumph of good over evil. While their images of these communities differ, their desire to imagine and narrate them is similar. Not only do both authors conjure alternative nations free of the repressive characteristics of their former nations, but both also spend considerable time combating the false images of the nation perpetuated by the Franco and Pinochet regimes. Goytisolo's descriptions of republicans from the Civil War and Dorfman's memories of Allende rescue important historical events from the collective amnesia imposed by authoritarian censorship. Goytisolo and Dorfman create counter-versions of national identity in response to the pre-modern and modern national images constructed by Franco and Pinochet.

Yet, as Dorfman endeavors to provide an alternative view of his nation's history, his ultimate critique of Pinochet's patrimony of Chile is postmodern. In this case, a postmodern perspective argues that the nation is no longer the source of identity as it was under modernism. Because of the effects of technology and multinational corporations, information, culture, and people flow across national borders, thereby reducing the importance of the nation. So, on a postmodern level, Dorfman rejects the image of Pinochet by defining him as a puppet of multinational corporations. For instance in *The Last Song of Manuel Sendero* the figure of the Caballero, an evil tyrant, is about to shoot the son of Manuel Sendero when the narrative breaks. Who gave the order to shoot? "The Caballero, or someone identical to him—there were so many of them, so many of his twins in this universe" (403). In postmodernity the source of evil is dispersed and fragmented; the only solution is to radically question the basis of modern civilization. David, an exile from Chile in *The Last Song of Manuel Sendero,* sums up a fellow exile's thoughts on Pinochet's persistent presence:

> He said . . . that revolutions have failed because we haven't taken into account that the ones who made them were old men. That exploitation starts in everyday life, in the family, in sexual relationships, in emotional unhappiness, in the authority of the father over the child and the husband over the wife. That

while that wasn't changed, revolutions would go on reproducing the same old structures of domination. (264)

So domination is a function of modern civilization, and it is doomed to pre-modern cyclical repetition, because modernity relies on the pre-modern social organization of the center and the margin. (See Foucault's *Madness and Civilization* and *The Birth of a Clinic* for a description of the connections between center/margin social organization in pre-modern and modern times. His main point is that modernity continues the pre-modern practice of expelling or confining those that do not conform to the dominant order.) Such critiques of modernity are the most forceful features of Dorfman's attack on Pinochet's regime because he does not simply argue for substituting Pinochet with a symbolic Allende. Dorfman suggests that domination is a function of modern civilization and that any form of nationalism inherently includes social repression. In this version of the nation, Dorfman favors the destruction of all versions of nationalism.

For writers, the postmodern has also meant a deep distrust in language's ability to represent as well as communicate. Because Dorfman recognizes that language is also a source of authority, his writing leaves gaps where readers are meant to draw their own conclusions. *The Last Song of Manuel Sendero* is not a linear narrative with closure. It has many levels of narrative including the myth of Manuel Sendero, the dialogue between the Chilean exiles David and Felipe, the story of the comic strip David is writing, a series of critical footnotes from scholars analyzing the dialogue between David and Felipe thirty thousand years later, and the legend of David and the Dragon Pinchot. One of the footnotes states that the text under analysis is "of uncertain authorship and obscure national origin" (79). While the author and national origin of the novel are not totally occluded in the text, Dorfman has tried to problematize the connections between authority and writing by fragmenting his narrative and questioning the notion of fathering a text.

Dorfman's ultimate fear is also of the postmodern, specifically of the ubiquitous presence of transnational capitalism, and its potential ability to destroy cultural differences and take away all hope that another economic basis to society is possible. If Pinochet replaced Allende as the Father of the Nation due to the demands of transnational capitalism, and not because he was simply born to be a despot, then transnational capitalism is unstoppable and the Allende years were just a terrible farce. What if the Allende years were only an illusion of political possibility? David and Felipe debate this issue while stuck in a traffic jam in Mexico. David says: "I hope you told them that our experiment failed." Felipe: "Failed? I wouldn't say that. You learned a lot. People were educated." David responds: "Failed, Felipe. [Nothing we did] has any permanent value.... Not valid. And I don't see where we did much consciousness raising, do you?" (83). David characterizes capitalism as an uncontrollable force that the individual is powerless to stop—ideas which are Dorfman's worst nightmare, but which are a nightmare that he refuses to dismiss. Later, he describes Pinochet's Chile as a postmodern space of hyperconsumerism: "Ex-Chile: it was, but is no more. A trademark, a copyright, a department store more than a country. Like a supermarket of underdevelopment.... Third World Shopping Center, continuous show.... Who will buy the first Chil-child?" (92–93). This is the version of the postmodern, with its homogenizing potential and its conversion of people into goods, which Dorfman tries to undermine through parody. Once again we can note similarities between Goytisolo and Dorfman's strategies. Where Goytisolo mourned the loss of the nation to the hyper-consumerism of tourism, Dorfman reads transnational capitalism as the harbinger of the devastating social effects of multinational corporations. Goytisolo imagines a Spain where everyone performs Spanishness for an endless parade of photo-snapping tourists and Dorfman envisions a Chile turned into an enormous sweatshop.

And yet, ironically, it is his postmodern critique of Pinochet that may be the most persuasive. For instance, Dorfman describes his vision of Chile under Pinochet in a scene where a cartoonist, Carl Barks, has been asked to help in the project of national reconstruction. In the following quote Barks watches TV, which speaks directly to him. "God, announced Reverend Rex, is like a giant computer, a screen filling infinity, ... The faithful have to facilitate God's labor, so that his work will be advanced. That's why His ideal man is being fashioned in this exceptional country ... what better imagination for that man than your own? ... To live forever, my dear friend, is to colonize the Great Beyond" (369). Barks will create the perfect citizen and help God as well as Chile's leaders to successfully rule the world. Here Dorfman critiques the role of God while also attacking colonialism, cultural imperialism, and postmodern levels of technology. Therefore, to confront Pinochet, Dorfman's narrative uses a mixed bag of pre-modern, modern, and postmodern cultural referents. For instance, in *The Last Song of Manuel Sendero*, to counter the pre-modern image of Pinochet as national savior and predestined monarch, he tells the myth of Manuel Sendero suggesting him as a hero for Chileans. The son of Sendero calls out to his father and reaffirms that he believes in his father and not in the evil Caballero: "Tell [the Caballero] he doesn't exist ... that he has all of the power and none of the love ... he'd have to be left all alone on the planet in order to be successful ... tell him that my father your father our father who art on the earth that is not yet ours will find us ... Do anything but surrender" (412–13).

Manuel Sendero's song is able to deeply affect all who hear it and he has been asked by the Caballero to sing on behalf of the regime. If he refuses, he, his wife, and his unborn son will all die. There are many versions of this tale told throughout the text, but in each one it is clear that Manuel represents good and the Caballero represents evil. Even later, as the son of Sendero returns to finish the battle that his father lost, the son of Sendero represents good. When the son of Sendero returns, he still lives in the time of his father's mythical legend, but the rest of the country has forgotten about him: "He tried to calm himself down, thinking that the same thing happens to every traveler who returns with anticipated nostalgia after years of distance and finds that someone has poisoned the wells in his holy places" (177). Now it is Eduardo, part of the first rebellion of the unborn, who has the chance to overcome the Caballero. The Son of Sendero thinks: "it was the country Eduardo had inherited and the one that would be his grandchildren's if he were lucky, and if things went badly, it would be the Caballero's grandchildren, depending on who was stronger and more cunning" (177). Strength and cunning are the tools of mythical heroes. This story, as it is told to children of the future, is meant to teach children about the evils of tyranny. Dorfman uses this pre-modern form of myth, where good fights evil in a timeless, nameless place to counter the image of Pinochet as the benevolent leader of the Chilean land.

In the same novel he offers two competing visions of a modern leader, each wishing to be the symbolic father of the nation: Pinochet and Felipe. Felipe represents the new generation of the Unidad Popular, one that, after the tragic death of Allende, recognizes the need for compromise and caution. David, on the other hand, represents the idealist who is unable to adapt to the new realities of the Pinochet government: "his imagination knew no bounds" (322). Felipe describes David after the coup: "I confess I was fed up with him. That failure to observe the norms of security was typical of David, who went on living as if we still had the government in our hands, as if the coup hadn't happened, not to mention the terror that followed it" (321). The novel suggests that it is the conflict between David and Felipe—representative of leftists unable to reach a unified position—that allows people like Pinochet to remain in power. The crisis for Chile is that only those willing to advocate repression and order seem to remain in power; because Felipe and David bicker over the correct role for their party—because they are fragmented—they are unable to pose a true threat to Pinochet (386–98). David is no longer a member of the party: "If you only knew what a relief it is to not be connected to anybody.... I'm going back and I can't do anybody any harm.... What happens depends on me and nobody else." Felipe counters: "If everybody felt like that we'd have Pinochet for a thousand years" (387). The political idealism of the Allende years has been shattered. Political activism, in crisis, gives way to Machiavellian leaders like Pinochet. Pinochet is the modern statesman, making deals with foreign corporations and increasing tourism. He knows that to succeed, he must present himself as the perfect leader capable of bringing peace and prosperity to all "good Chileans."

In *The Last Song of Manuel Sendero* the transnational reach of both pop culture and technology has made the notions of individual and cultural identity extremely fragile. For instance, in a comic strip written by David, technological achievements have made it possible to create perfectly capitalist societies. Medical advances have been able to locate the source of individual will, the X-factor, which causes people to rebel, and governments have learned how to sap it from the populace. Carl Barks explains to his wife: "The total solution.... A scientific model for conduct, finally, for the improvement of the human race" (308). Hitler's Final Solution becomes the "total solution." In this version of postmodernity, it is no longer a question of choosing between Allende and Pinochet, but of recognizing that now the Allies and the Axis powers are all in favor of capitalism.

One of the best examples of the complex ways in which Dorfman's work emphasizes the tenuous place of writing and yet still struggles for political change by challenging Pinochet's image on pre-modern, modern, and postmodern terms, can be noted through a comparative analysis of one section of Pinochet's memoirs and one small narrative segment from *The Last Song of Manuel Sendero*. During the second year of the military regime an ad-hoc commission on human rights petitioned to enter Chile. Pinochet denied them access to the country and in a speech delivered in June of 1975, during a trip to the North of Chile, Pinochet declared:

> I should tell my country that I have made a resolution: I have refused entrance to Chile for the Commission on Human Rights. This will bring violent reactions not only from the Marxist World, but also from their sympathizers. It's unfortunate that the world is unable to defend us, they are invaded by indifference... they hide their heads to leave this small David alone fighting against the Giant Goliath, but don't forget that David defeated Goliath. (87)

Pinochet describes Chile as a nation of victims who will only survive if they work together to defend themselves from the evil threat of Marxism. Artfully he manages to slide over the fact that many human rights were being violated daily by twisting the argument to refer once again to the evils which he, and he alone, as a symbolic David, can rectify. Later in the same piece he explains that shortly after the above speech he was able to implement programs that would help Chile leave the financial "hecatomb" created by the failures of the Allende government.

What we have, then, is an example of his rhetorical recourse to the pre-modern and highly persuasive tale of David and Goliath, a timeless tale of the powers of resistance. The story is then altered to include the modern realities of international politics, in this case the Commission on Human Rights, and of national economics, specifically the entrance of Chile into the capitalist marketplace. Interestingly, Dorfman also re-writes the tale of David and Goliath in his novel *The Last Song of Manuel Sendero*. Whether or not Dorfman was specifically aware of Pinochet's use of the same tale, it is interesting to note the way in which the same language is used by discourses with opposing politics, each of which argue that their version of history is the right version. In *The Last Song of Manuel Sendero*, the legend of David and Goliath becomes the legend of David and the Dragon Pinchot. Through this tale Dorfman constructs an alternative hero to that being offered by Pinochet: he combats the pre-modern image of Pinochet as David, offered by Pinochet himself, by turning Pinochet into the Dragon Pinchot. In the second epilogue of the novel, the legend is described in detail and is mixed with two other narratives lines. The three pieces of narrative intertwine and each version has a character named David.

In one of these narrative lines David is an exile from Pinochet's Chile who is visiting a fellow exile, Felipe, in Mexico. This narrative line represents a modern David, who is struggling to return to his country and to his family. David is especially concerned about his son, Alejandro, living in Chile without him. Because David is exiled from fatherhood, he is terrified that Alejandro's grandfather, a military man, is replacing him: "And with that grandfather, they're really impressionable, easily taken in. The fatherland, the little soldier, the military band, the big he-man" (214). The battle over cultural identity is reduced to a battle over who will be Alejandro's father figure. Later, when David finally must return to Chile because of reports that Alejandro has committed suicide, David experiences the exile's worst nightmare—complete loss of agency, pure historical voyeurism with all of the pain and none of the pleasure. This David is a modern hero who feels great pain and alienation and who believes that his presence at his son's side might have kept him from taking his life.

Thirty thousand years later a mother tells her children the legend of David and the Dragon Pinchot. The story is essentially the same as the above tale and yet its historical displacement turns what we might consider today to be a modern tale of exile, into a pre-modern myth of expulsion with legendary possibilities for the success of good over evil. The legend tells us that "[David] believed that if he went back with a little air from the future, he'd be able to rescue [his son]" (430). As the children being told this tale are tucked into bed, their mother says: "while you're sleeping kids, breathe a lot in the direction of the past. Blow really hard and let's see if a little bit of your air doesn't reach David" (431). By turning the tale of the exiled David into the pre-modern legend of David, Dorfman suggests both a cyclical and a linear sense of history. He also shows that, over time, many of the same struggles persist. It is in this pre-modern vein that Dorfman tries to provide an alternative hero for the future that can combat Pinochet's pre-modern self-definition as savior. In so doing, Dorfman also indicates the primordial origins of exile: the pre-modern David has been banished from his land.

The last narrative strand leaves us in postmodernity. Here David is nothing more than a character in a Mexican soap opera. What in the other narrative strands had been a compelling story of pain and anguish is now merely a flat product of commercialized culture. We have moved from pre-modern legend, to modern novel, to postmodern transnational pop culture. "The last scene of the first episode of the soap opera takes place in the same place as the first one: the Mexico City airport.... On camera David and Felipe" (432). In this narrative line there is no Dragon Pinchot or Dictator Pinochet. The actors are saying good-bye and yet the source of their pain is visibly absent as the director searches for the appropriate facial expression for his cast. It is not hope, nor rage, nor defiance. He tells us that there is sadness: "But something else too. Something I can't get a handle on. I don't know what to call it" (432). What is most interesting about the character of David is that, in each narrative line, he is fighting against something that has caused him to suffer exile. Yet, in this last version, both the concepts of nation and of politics have been left out. The modern values of culture and nation have been stripped of meaning. Exile has become fragmentation and does not refer to a specific political struggle.

Why did Dorfman narrate these three versions? Perhaps, because in each version of the story of David, Dorfman is able to represent the historical shifts in the notion of individual will and the corresponding shifts in theories about the communicability of language. In the legend, David had to "run away to a foreign land" (427). Good fights evil and there is a sense that faith and good intentions are the keys to success. There is also an atmosphere of confidence that, if children are told these stories, they will learn right from wrong. In the case of the exiled David, who hopes to return to Chile to be with his son, there is a modern sense of the nation and the dictator. The exiled David exemplifies the tensions between a modern notion of historical agency and alienation from society. While language is questioned, it is still able to represent. In the last version, there are no words to describe the expression that the director is looking for. There is no concept of historical agency: everyone is part of the set of a Mexican soap opera. The source of evil has become nebulous: there is no evil dragon or terrible dictator, no king or statesman. Evil is nameless and ubiquitous. Even though Dorfman provides us with these three versions of history, which challenge the official cultural history being offered by Pinochet, it is important to bear in mind that there is no sense of progression. By presenting these different levels of narrative, each of which provide a distinct aesthetics of resistance, Dorfman hopes to reach the reader. And yet these multiple fragments with their competing versions of the self and its representation through language may ultimately deflate the political force of his argument. Dorfman is caught in a double bind: he wants to reject Pinochet but he does not want to resort to using authoritative rhetoric.

Analyzing Ariel Dorfman's exile narrative is difficult because of the hybrid temporalities his work occupies and because of the contradictory strategies he uses to challenge the power of Pinochet. Most critics prefer to focus on only one aspect of his project, disregarding the rest. For instance, Salvador Oropesa has described *The Last Song of Manuel Sendero* as a postmodern novel with none of the manichean impulses of Dorfman's previous work (16). Yet, as I have shown, *The Last Song of Manuel Sendero* is a novel which has elements of pre-modern manicheism and postmodern relativity. It is necessary to consider all of the elements of his narrative, even when some of them seem to contradict each other. *The Last Song of Manuel Sendero* narrates myths that compete with those proffered by Pinochet, it tries to give a different view of history and the nation, and it questions the value and meaning of such quests: Dorfman's novel simultaneously faces, defaces, and effaces the image of Pinochet as father of the nation.

Peri Rossi: Myths of Expulsion versus the Myth of Creation

The process of militarization of the Uruguayan government had none of the media attention or international recognition that Franco or Pinochet received as they assumed power in their countries. As Juan Rial explains, "The process that culminated in the 1973 coup was a long one. In reality, Uruguay had only a quasi-constitutional government from 1968 on" (73). Unlike the cases of Dorfman and Goytisolo, Peri Rossi's use of myth and history in her work in exile does not allude specifically to the Uruguayan regime's official discourse, as in the case of Franco's use of the figure of the Cid or Pinochet's use of the tale of David and Goliath. In Goytisolo's revision of history, where he champions Count Julian over the Cid, his work has a direct connection to Spanish history. Dorfman's use of David and Goliath critiques Pinochet's official discourse and is further applied to all authoritarian systems. Peri Rossi's work widens the field of critique even farther: her narrative highlights the battle between myths that support official order and myths that pose a challenge to all forms of patriarchy (as both a system of government and a social practice).

Rubén Yáñez explains that there were differences in the fascist-based ideology found in Uruguay after the coup and that "Fascism in Uruguay operated very differently from fascism in Chile. Instead of mounting a homogenous offensive against the people and attacking the entire spectrum of instruments involved in a struggle for a national program, the Uruguayan fascists attacked progressively and selectively" (140). One of the most significant results of this attack was the "systematic repression of culture, its creators, and its organizations" (140). As a result of this repression, the Uruguayan government created a new version of Uruguayan culture and identity, one which forced the exile of Peri Rossi due to the requirements of what she has described as a "fascismo difícil de detener" (qtd. in Zeitz 86) ["fascism difficult to stop"]. The result of this cultural repression in Uruguay, according to Peri Rossi, is that "su literatura está aplastada bajo el peso de las botas y del silencio obligatorio" (qtd. in Zeitz 86) ["its literature is plastered under the weight of boots and obligatory silence"]. For instance, in *La nave de los locos*, cultural production under authoritarian regimes is critiqued as mere propaganda: "Vercingétorix observó que los oficiales y los soldados tenían no sólo predisposición a la violencia sino a la poesía y al relato. Los poemas versaban sobre el amor a la patria, la belleza de la bandera, el honor de las Fuerzas Armadas, la encarnizada lucha contra los Oscuros Enemigos, el sol, el apostolado militar, las buenas costumbres y el espíritu cristiano" (61–62) ["Vercingétorix noticed that the soldiers and officers were not only predisposed to violence but to poetry. [The poems were about] love of country, the beauty of the flag, the honour of the armed forces, their bloody battle against the Enemy, the sun, the military calling, strong family values, and the Church"; 58]. These words echo the speeches of Pinochet and Franco.

To contrast this cultural suffocation, Peri Rossi's work in exile confronts new issues: "Lo que ocurre es que en los últimos años, y a causa del exilio, se vuelven más claras las raíces culturales.... No se nos ocurre pensar en nuestras raíces hasta que salimos del país" (qtd. in Golano 48) ["What has happened is that in the last years, as a result of exile, my cultural roots have become clearer.... It doesn't occur to us to think about our roots until we leave our country"]. Exile forces Peri Rossi to make the political situation in Uruguay a central issue in her work, while simultaneously reconnecting her to the immigrant past of her Italian ancestors who were also forced to flee their nation by boat. Peri Rossi explains the connection between her situation and that of her ancestors:

> Una generación más atrás que la de mis padres, encontramos a los infaltables emigrantes italianos, por ambas ramas. Llegados a América en barcos hacinados, pobres y laboriosos. (No deja de ser irónico que buena parte de sus descendientes, en los tristes años de fascismo latinoamericano, hayamos reemprendido el viaje, en barcos igualmente hacinados, pobres y dejando atrás las raíces). (Moraña 205 note)

> A generation before my parents we find indefatigable Italian immigrants on both sides. They arrive in America on boats overcrowded, poor and hard working. (It does not cease to be ironic that a good part of their descendents in the sad years of Latin American fascism, have had to reinitiate the trip, on boats equally overcrowded, poor, leaving behind our roots).

This history, combined with the cyclical repetition of being banished from one's land, becomes one of the central concerns of Peri Rossi's first novel in exile, *La nave de los locos*. Time for the exile is a problem, precisely because the exile has become a victim of authoritarianism's version of history. In an article describing life in exile, Peri Rossi explains how exile caused her to reconsider the ways in which authoritarianism alters time:

> I became aware of one of the most terrible effects of dictatorships: the isolation in space that they cause has a function of *destroying the dialectic element of time*. Dictators aspire to make themselves eternal, they create an arbitrary but illusory notion of time: before them, nothing; afterwards nothing. The extermination, the persecution of a whole generation emptied of the time of the essential relation of history, the interchange and the replacement of the old by the young. Time, immobilized, crystallized, in an apparently perpetual duration, history turns to a fixed picture hung on the wall: an eternal present that is fundamentally a very remote past. ("Exercise in Return" 224, my emphasis)

Peri Rossi contends that the notion of linear history became radically altered for the Uruguayan populace as a result of the military regime. Dictators steal the possibility of historical agency from their nations, thereby warping present time by turning national attention toward a mythical and glorious past. To combat the way in which dictators usurp time and remove people from history, Peri Rossi's novel *La nave de los locos* demonstrates that those excluded from official history are still *present*, albeit on the margins of the nation, either in prison or exile. Her work emphasizes the dialectic between center and margin, where the center's official history necessarily implies the margin's alternative history, and she hopes, through her focus on the margins, to alter the balance of power between the center and the margins.

Specifically, in *La nave de los locos,* official history relies on the pre-modern tale of Judeo-Christian creation. Peri Rossi counterbalances the Judeo-Christian myth of creation with the pain and suffering caused by the myths of expulsion. She argues that the myth of creation has required that society accept the corresponding myths of expulsion. In her novel, children are asked to describe Eve and the majority of students find her "guilty" of excessive curiosity and a lack of loyalty which caused humanity to suffer expulsion from Paradise: "39 alumnos la juzgaron excesivamente curiosa, 33 charlatana y, 25 consideraron que tenía mal carácter" (160–61) ["39 pupils described her as excessively curious; 33, a gossip; and 25 thought that she had a bad temper"; 164]. Only one student demonstrates a critical mind which does not blindly accept the story of Eve: "Dios como era muy machista lo primero que hiso dise mi mamá fue inventar al hombre y después ensima dise que Eva le nasió de un costado que dise mi mamá que ojalá todos los partos del mundo fueran ashí" (158) ["God since he was very macho the first thing that he did says my mom was invent man and later on top of it all says that Eve was born from a rib that says my mom wouldn't it be great if all births in the world were like that"]. *La nave de los locos* asks the reader to question the ideological basis of such tales, where expulsion is justified, and male domination requires female subordination. By exposing the fact that the isolated self suffers, her novel points at the tyranny of the myth of creation and its corresponding emphasis on harmony and cultural homogeneity.

Peri Rossi uses the myth of the Ship of Fools as a timeless tale of banishment and suffering to counter the peace and perfection of the myth of creation. As Foucault explains: "[The concept of the Ship of Fools] symbolized a great disquiet, suddenly dawning on the horizon of European culture at the end of the Middle Ages. Madness and the madman became major figures, in their ambiguity: menace and mockery, the dizzying unreason of the world, and the feeble mockery of men" (*Madness* 13). *La nave de los locos* presents the mythical ships of fools who departed in the fifteenth century as the pre-modern precursors to many other cases where society has turned away those who threaten a system based on order, reason, and progress: the novel connects the political prisoners and exiles of the 1970s from the Southern Cone to the case of the Jewish people in World War II (especially to the labs where pregnant Jewish women were sent, experimented on and left to die) (169). We can note the influence of Foucault's *The Birth of the Clinic* on the work of Peri Rossi here. Peri Rossi, like Foucault, focuses on the ways in which medicine has been used at the expense of human life and in favor of progress. Dorfman also focuses on medicine as an abusive aspect of civilization in *The Last Song of Manuel Sendero*; where similar to the case of the Jewish people in World War II, people are used for experiments that will create a better race. Peri Rossi also links these cases to the myth of Eve, to the plight of women seeking abortion in Europe, to African women who must undergo infibulation—in essence to all types of marginalized people who suffer social exile to some degree. As Maria Rosa Olivera-Williams observes: "Este viaje simbólico y circular, 'ya leído', tiene por objeto introducirse críticamente en las catástrofes que acosan al ser humano de hoy.... En un tiempo circular, los espacios repiten, a pesar de su variación, una cadena de tragedias" (82) ["This symbolic and circular trip, 'already read,' has as its object the critique of catastrophes that pursue humanity today.... In a circular time, spaces repeat, in spite of their variations, a chain of tragedies"].

Another feature of Peri Rossi's attack on authoritarianism's appropriation of the individual's connection to historical time is to reestablish that connection. Even though she repeatedly refers to the cyclical, repetitive facets of marginalization, she returns to history as an antidote. In her article "An Exercise in Return" she states that the Uruguayan public has "the feeling of having been stolen from history" (224). Her work, then, tries to give them back their history. Moraña points out that "Múltiples indicios marcan, a lo largo del texto, la referencia al clima de violencia y represión del Uruguay posterior al golpe de estado de 1973" (206) ["Multiple indices mark, throughout the text, the reference to the climate of violence and repression of Uruguay after the coup d'état of 1973"]. For instance, the character of Vercingétorix, who was held prisoner in an unnamed country that fits the description of Uruguay, represents the multitude of disappeared Uruguayans who *officially* did not exist. Vercingétorix "desapareció, metido a golpes en la parte posterior de un auto sin matrícula, pero de una marca a cuyo paso la ciudad se vaciaba, presa del pánico" (57) ["he disappeared, brutally pushed into the back of a car without license plates, whose type was well known and feared throughout the town"; 53]. He is thrown into a concentration camp: "Los dos años siguientes (si es que todavía tenía sentido computar el tiempo con los relojes normales; a él le parecieron diez, y uno que agonizó cerca suyo creía que eran veinte) los pasó en un campo de desaparecidos, lejos de la ciudad, en un lugar apartado" (58) ["The next two years (if there was any point in measuring time by the clock, when it seemed like ten years to him and twenty to his friend suffering agonies about him) Vercingétorix spent in a camp for the disappeared"; 54]. By telling the story of the exiles and prisoners of the military regime, Peri Rossi reinserts these events into Uruguayan history: narrating life in a concentration camp brings both the space of the margin and the painful confinement of its prisoners back into the historical picture. Like passengers on a ship of fools, all threats to the military regime must be kept on the margins so that they do not disrupt the plans for the city and civilization. The political prisoners and exiles are removed from historical time and become atemporally connected to all those who have suffered social exclusion. Vercingétorix can not avoid thinking that "en otro lugar, no muy lejos de su cama estrecha... hubiera otro campo, otro infierno, separado del mundo, con su pueblo de fantasmas que morían violentamente y no dejaban rastros, porque eran lanzados al mar o enterrados en fosas comunes, sin nombre, sin memoria. Y esta sospecha no le dejaba vivir" (61) ["somewhere, not far from his narrow bed... there would be another camp, another hell, with its inmates dying without a trace, either thrown into the sea or buried in common graves, no name, no memory. And he couldn't live with this thought", 57].

So, once again, Peri Rossi mixes history with eternal repetition. The novel recreates the dialectic tension between these two poles that has been collapsed by authoritarian conceptions of time. As Elia Kantaris explains: Peri Rossi "attempt[s] to work through to the root mechanisms underlying the phenomenon of dictatorship, seen as a particularly crude expression of a more insidious, generalized oppression. Specifically, [she] examine[s] the mechanisms which appear to link the monopoly of power to the process of alienation—the way the construction of one's group's 'self-identity' appears to depend upon the denial and destruction of another's" (248).

Peri Rossi underscores the way in which dictatorships usurp time in order to force their nations into modernity, leaving their inhabitants temporally bewildered: "a temporal suspension the dictatorship provoked, upon subverting itself, the development of a modern society and turning it back into an earlier sphere of time" ("An Exercise in Return" 224). The sphere of an earlier time is the pre-modern story of Judeo-Christian creation. This myth is relayed to the reader through the memory of Equis who recalls seeing a tapestry in Gerona depicting the Biblical story of creation. Referring to the tapestry, Equis comments: "Todo en él está dispuesto para que el hombre se sienta en perfecta armonía, consustanciado, integrado al universo" (20) ["Everything is so arranged that man can feel in harmony with the design, become part of its embroidered universe"; 13]. Moreover, "se podría vivir" (one could live) in the tapestry, as if under a dictatorship, "si se tuviera la suficiente perseverancia" ["if one had sufficient perseverance"]. "Hay cuadros así donde todo está dispuesto para que el hombre viva exonerado del resto del mundo" (13) ["Art like this beckons man to live within its world, freed from the sins of the other one"; 14]. By challenging the representation of creation in the tapestry, Peri Rossi is able to critique the myth of origins, of order, and of homogeneity, inasmuch as they comprise the founding principles of modern authoritarianism, which allows dictators to exonerate themselves from the injustices they commit.

The tapestry functions as a metaphor for the authoritarian state, which feigns harmony and depicts order over chaos. In the voice of an unidentified "we" the text informs the reader about the comforting aspects in the tapestry's representation of the Creation myth:

> Lo que amamos en toda estructura es una composición del mundo, un significado que ordene el caos devorador, una hipótesis comprensible y por ende reparadora. Repara nuestro sentimiento de la fuga y de la dispersión, nuestra desolada experiencia del desorden.... En telas así sería posible vivir toda la vida, en medio de un discurso perfectamente inteligible, de cuyo sentido no se podría dudar porque es una metáfora donde todo el universo está encerrado.... Lo que nos asombra y nos asombrará siempre, es que una sola mente haya podido concebir una estructura convincente, placentera y dichosa como ésta; una estructura que es una metáfora, sin dejar de ser por ello también, una realidad. (21)

> What one admires in the work, besides the fine execution, handsome texture and harmony of colours, is this structure—a structure so symmetrical, so dependable that even when it is incomplete, it is possible to recreate the whole, if not on the cathedral wall, then within the framework of the imagination.... Immersed in such art one could live one's life, engaged in a perfectly rational discourse whose meaning cannot be questioned because it resides in an image containing the whole universe.... [W]hat surprises us and will always surprise us is the notion that a single mind could conceive of such a convincing and pleasing structure, moreover a happy one, a structure which as well as being a metaphor is also a reality. (14–15)

Like dictatorships, the tapestry presents a world order which is complete and perfect, making its inhabitants content and at peace, pleased by the depiction of unity and structure. Furthermore, a populace that believes in monotheism (where the world, like the tapestry, has been created by a single mind) may more readily accept the political leadership of a single man. The above description mirrors the official rhetoric of regimes like those found in Spain, Chile, and Uruguay, which, as the text demonstrates, have precursors in the official voices of the Catholic Church who describe God as the single mind which created all and whose voice is unquestionably capable of perfect, true communication. These military leaders, then, portray themselves as God-like figures, thereby bolstering their legitimacy through a manipulation of their nation's spiritual beliefs. Describing life under dictatorship, the novel makes a connection between the tapestry's version of the world and that found in military regimes: "La vida en su apariencia, continuaba su ritmo y se comía en los restaurantes o se iba al cine, se celebraba un cumpleaños o se bautizaba a un niño, las escuelas estaban abiertas y los generales, solemnes, anacrónicos como muñecos a cuerda, realizaban pomposos discursos, bajo la luz de los reflectores y las banderas de la patria" (61) ["in the meantime people would carry on as normal, on the surface at least, eating in restaurants, going to the cinema or to school, celebrating birthdays, christening the newborns, and the generals, solemn and anachronistic as wind-up dolls, delivering their speeches by the lights of arc lamps and national flags"; 58]. Meanwhile, elsewhere on the margins of this society, victims of the system, like the incarcerated Vercingétorix and the exiled Equis, exist.

Such versions of history, like that found in the tapestry, are perversions, the novel suggests, precisely because they neglect to represent the existence of those expelled from the system. The tapestry "corresponde a esa religiosidad medieval capaz de construir un mundo perfectamente concéntrico y ordenado. Pero cualquier armonía supone la destrucción de los elementos reales que se le oponen, por eso es casi siempre simbólico. Equis contempló el tapiz como una leyenda cuyo ritmo nos fascina, pero que no provoca nostalgia" (20) ["the product of a [medieval] religious system, a world, that is perfectly concentric and ordered. But such harmony assumes the destruction of those aspects of reality which oppose it; thus it is almost always symbolic. Ecks studied the tapestry as one might read an old legend whose rhythm fascinates, but which evokes no nostalgia"; 13]. The mission of the novel is to debunk the overvalorization of order and harmony. In fact, Equis shows us that even the tapestry itself can be deconstructed to reveal its own contradictions "esta inclusión de los vientos, en los cuatro costados, sugiere que en el universo, todo es movimiento, nada está quieto" (162) ["the inclusion of the winds, so close to the circle of Creation, suggests that all is moving; nothing in the universe remains still"; 165]. So the perfect harmony that the tapestry seeks to represent is shown to be false. Instead, in a description of life as flux and dialectic that evokes the words of Heraclitus, Peri Rossi asserts that any effort to describe life as static and unified is oppressive.

It is important to note that the tapestry, like this novel, is also a representation. The tapestry suggests to its viewers its representation of the world's origins and hopes that the viewer will believe this version. The novel, by contrast, tries to subvert the tapestry's persuasive power by appealing to its reader's sense that the world is not perfectly ordered. For instance, the novel includes a brief section called "Las confesiones de Eva" ("The Confessions of Eve"), which contradicts the version of creation presented in the tapestry and also challenges the beliefs of the school children who condemn her actions. According to Eve, the gods' vision of the world is flawed but requires her to cooperate with its myths and falsehoods. She must "colaborar en la extensión de los mitos que sostienen la organización y el espíritu de la tribu, sus ideas dominantes y ocultar para siempre los conflictos que esta sujeción plantea" (153) ["collaborate in perpetuating the myths which sustain the structure, ideology and spirit of the tribe. Any conflict arising from our forced condition must be hidden"; 158]. Once again the perfect mirror of society, the tapestry or the creation myth, is shown to have cracks that reveal its contradictions and their effect on modern society. In contrast to the desired harmony and order of the tapestry, this novel appears to us in fragments and disorder. Unlike Eve, the novel is not bound by the laws of the system because its author has been expelled from society already. Or, at least, that is the premise upon which the narrative's battle against authority rests.

One of the ways that the novel challenges the representational power of the tapestry is by emphasizing its flaws and inaccuracies. For instance, the tapestry's order is shown to be false since certain pieces of it are missing. In a final page of the text the reader is told "Faltan enero, noviembre, diciembre y, por lo menos dos ríos del Paraíso" ["The tapestry is missing January, November and December and at least two of the rivers of Paradise"]. The totalizing impulse of the tapestry is revealed as a farce. There has been some debate about the actual role of the tapestry in the text. Some scholars consider the tapestry to represent a harmony that Equis yearns for and they connect the text with the tapestry claiming that the text is also seeking harmony (see Invernizzi 53; Olivera-Williams 84). In Gabriel Mora's opinion: "Enfrentando pues al tapiz de la inmutable armonía, se encuentran en el libro de Peri Rossi todos esos episodios que ilustran de una u otra manera el agresivo ejercicio del poder junto con la resistencia que, en forma de transgresores arreglos sociales, genera en sus víctimas. ¿Y no es la resistencia a la agresión una manera de restaurar el equilibrio (armonía) perdido?" (350) ["Facing the tapestry of immutable harmony, we find in Peri Rossi's book all of these episodes that illustrate one way or another the aggressive exercise of power together with the resistance that, in the form of transgressing social arrangements, it generates in its victims. And isn't resistance to aggression a way to restore lost equilibrium (harmony)?"]. In agreement with Hugo J. Verani, I consider the tapestry to represent the origin of suffering and not a sought after origin of harmony. It also seems clear that the tapestry depicts the creation myth as the painful precursor to the alienations of modern society. "La religiosidad medieval construyó un mundo de ideología única y de placenteras afinidades.... [El tapiz] reproduce un orden armónico contrapuesto al caos de la realidad actual, el mundo de 'la nave de los locos'" (81) ["Medieval religion constructed a unique ideological world of pleasing affinities.... [The tapestry] reproduces a harmonic order contrapuntal to the chaos of present reality, the world of the 'ship of fools'"].

In the tapestry, the creation myth, which is one of the principle ideological sources of fascist-based governments (see Griffith's definition above), is founded on a patriarchal system that provides order, harmony, and a clear source of humanity's origins. This type of myth is the pre-modern foundation for the modernizing goals of fascist-like military regimes that seek to control their country's economy. As we have seen, Peri Rossi combats this myth by challenging its emphasis on harmony and revealing such a notion to be a falsehood—one that requires the expulsion of all "undesirables." Her attack also takes place on the historical ground of modernity, where her text challenges the modern values of economic success and technology as the necessary paths to individual happiness and social bliss.

Kantaris explains that the novel exposes the "sexually driven power complexes and stereotypes of modern Western society" (261). Not only do we read of the clitoral castration of African girls and the Holocaust experiments on Jewish pregnant women, but we also read of women who travel in desperation to London to get abortions. In a key scene that explores the ties between sex and violence, Equis goes to see the film *Demon Seed,* where Julie Christie is raped by an invisible and omnipotent machine, that behaves "como las dictaduras" (23) ["The dictator is unseen yet ever present"; 17]. To contrast these evils of modern society, the novel offers us the character of Graciela, a "liberated" woman, who dedicates her life to researching the mistreatment of women and travels to Africa to try to protect young girls from clitoral castration. Vercingétorix, similarly, is concerned with human rights and is unable to surrender to official order. Rescuing Equis from a scuffle in a public park where Equis refuses to pay for a seat on a bench, we are told that Vercingétorix was about to deliver a speech: "acerca de las libertades, el individualismo, los derechos humanos y la noción de autoridad" (66) ["on freedom, human rights and the meaning of authority"; 63]. These types of ethical struggles happen on the ground of modern society and in the realm of linear history.

Nevertheless, as in the work of Goytisolo, Peri Rossi's texts spend little time in modernity, preferring to see the modern period as nothing but the source of capitalism and bourgeois society. Morris, a fellow outcast of Equis, reflects on the critiques of modernity made by the modern thinkers Marx and Freud: "Un secreto mecanismo hace que los más oprimidos sean, a su vez, los más represores. Sutil mecánica. ¿Quién había descubierto eso, Freud o Marx?" (127) ["There is a secret subtle mechanism which ensures that the more one is oppressed the more repressive one becomes. Who had thought of this? Freud or Marx?"; 129]. These musings demonstrate the relevance of modernism's critique of bourgeois capitalist society, while also suggesting that those critiques were unsuccessful in altering the course of official history. Dorfman's work, in particular *Viudas,* on the other hand, remains deeply concerned with a crisis in the modern notions of justice and democracy—notions which his novels continue to champion, fighting for the power to be placed in the hands of a collective and not in the hands of the military. Goytisolo and Peri Rossi, however, narrate texts that take place primarily in pre-modern and postmodern worlds. For instance, in a section that indicates the link between the pre-modern and the postmodern in *La nave de los locos,* a boy by the name of Percival, goes to a park. He goes to the park for two reasons; one is to connect him with pre-modern idealism, when man was in harmony with nature. He looks at ducks in a pond, and "Mirándolos sentía como si una dulce hipnosis fuera dominándole los sentidos, desplazando el presente hacia un pasado que él no conocía con la memoria ni con la razón pero que indudablemente había existido. En ese pasado muy antiguo él no sabía quién había sido, pero estaba seguro, en cambio, de su afinidad con el agua del lago y con los patos era mucho mayor" (134) ["Looking at them he was overcome by a kind of hypnosis which transported him to a past, unknown and unremembered, yet definitely real. He did not know when he had been in that remote past, but he felt a strong affinity with the lake and the ducks"; 136]. The second reason is that the park connects him to the postmodern. He goes to an old bandstand that has been destroyed by time and is now a useless place: "Los marcos eran grises y Percival los encontraba hermosos, con esa rara belleza de las cosas que subsisten fragmentadas, vacías de la finalidad, desprovistas de función" (135) ["These decaying structures seemed beautiful to Percival, with that rare beauty of things which survive only in part, empty, unable to function"; 137]. He learns from his mother that the bandstand is "decadent" and he decides that he likes the idea since he is certain that it relates to questions of time. And yet, unlike the work of Goytisolo, where Spain under the Moors is a wonderful place, Peri Rossi's novel does not find the pre-modern to be a source of utopic ideals: the pre-modern is merely the source of the dialectics between center and margin, harmony and suffering. Instead, she favors relativism, fragmentation, and chaos over the manichean impulses that some of Goytisolo's characters represent. For this reason, Peri Rossi's attack on the system omits any battle scenes similar to those described in *Reivindicación del conde don Julián* or in *The Last Song of Manuel Sendero*. Unlike Goytisolo and Dorfman, Peri Rossi does not narrate an alternative to authoritarianism that is systematic in any way. Her only solution resides in ambiguity and an emphasis on difference.

At the end of the novel a King, representing the ultimate pre-modern patriarch, is destroyed because Equis answers the enigma, "¿Cuál es el tributo mayor, el homenaje que un hombre puede hacer a la mujer que ama?" (183) ["What is the greatest tribute and homage a man can give to the woman he loves?"; 188) with the answer: "su virilidad" (196) ["his virility"; 203]. Such an answer destroys the system because it refuses to place more power in either of the sexes, which, according to Peri Rossi, is the fundamental "original sin" of society. Equis functions as an anti-hero on a quest for a mode of destruction capable of demolishing patriarchy. His exile and impotence make him the perfect representative of those outside of the phalologocentric order. Influenced by the work of Lacan, Peri Rossi's protagonist tries to destroy the center and replace it with a multiplied margin where identity is not fixed along any traditional lines, and where the symbolic phallus is not the prime producer of meaning. In a later novel, *Solitario de amor* (*Solitaire of Love*), Peri Rossi begins with an epigraph from Lacan. "Amar es dar lo que no se tiene a quien no es" ["To love is to give what one doesn't have to the one one isn't"]. Despite Peri Rossi's references to Lacan, I would argue that in the same way that she is influenced by the work of Foucault, Lacan's notion of the phalologocentrism is important to her work, but that she moves beyond his theories to posit a world where the phallus simply does not exist. Her work suggests that the only possible method for destroying oppressive power is through the ambiguity of gender because the concept of virility is the basis of power structures. This ambiguity is the only true threat to the modern system, which is comprised of capitalism, dictatorship, fascism, and sexual repression. In this way, Peri Rossi, like Dorfman and Goytisolo, finds a persuasive critique of the modern to be found in theories of the postmodern.

In the chapter "El hombre es el pasado de la mujer" ("Man Is Woman's Past"), Equis describes his experience viewing the film *Demon Seed*: "una máquina bestial y omnipresente, a la cual era imposible identificar porque se trataba, en realidad, de un símbolo, un símbolo que estaba en todas partes y contra la que Julie Christie, el porvenir del hombre, nada podía hacer, pues esa máquina pesada y torpe, tosca y ensoberbecida, no conocía el límite ni la resistencia, gran símbolo fálico, estructura del poder invencible" (24) ["a brutish omnipresent mechanism, impossible to identify because it is in fact a symbol, against which Julie Christie, man's future, can do nothing, for it is massive, coarse, enraged and its enraged obscenity knows no limits; a phallic structure of unlimited power"; 18]. This description of man's power as it is converted into technology depicts the postmodern as the most extreme form of social oppression. This view of the postmodern is contrasted by the ambiguity of gender, which Equis suggests as the postmodern solution to the pain of modernity. In this sense, as in the case of Goytisolo and Dorfman, the postmodern is simultaneously capable of freeing the marginalized from suffering and also of imprisoning all those who challenge the system with no possibility of escape.

The postmodern, through its emphasis on ambiguity, suggests a total lack of political agency, insofar as the connections between beliefs and acts are completely ambiguous and uncertain. Morris states that politics has been reduced to two positions, which nevertheless are basically identical and politically impotent: "podríamos decir, en la actualidad, que hay sólo dos: *una* política y la *otra,* cuyas diferencias, por lo demás, son mínimas. El tránsito, por otra parte, entre *una* política y la *otra* es harto frecuente, de modo que se puede vivir la mitad de la existencia proclamando *una* y ejecutando la *otra*, y los años que restan, al revés. Llamado también la fluidez de ideologías" (130) ["Nowadays there are but two politics and the differences between the two are minimal. It is easy to pass from one to the other; you can spend the first half of your life proclaiming the principles of one and acting according to the other. This is what is called ideological fluidity"; 132]. The fluidity of ideology is a counterpoint to the fluidity of gender roles. The novel suggests that fluid gender roles are necessary in order to destroy patriarchy. Nevertheless, such a fluid identity cannot be relegated to gender roles and spills over into the realm of politics. Therefore the potentially liberating fluidity of sex also implies, through its stress on ambiguity and relativity, the politically debilitating fluidity of political action and the ambiguity of ideology. Impotence in Equis is liberating: "Hace mucho tiempo que no tengo una erección.... Y no me importa" (188) ["I haven't had an erection for a long time.... And I don't mind"; 194]. On the other hand, political impotence is devastating.

These two parallel postmodern possibilities convey completely distinct visions of the world: one that is liberating and one that is eternally incarcerating. There are two parallel primordial times: that of creation and that of expulsion, that of harmony and that of suffering. There are two modern times: that of progress and that of the exile of Equis, the imprisonment of Vercingétorix, and the abortion of Lucía. Vercingétorix thinks that two worlds exist: one which he occupies and another which is oblivious to his suffering: "sentía en su conciencia, todavía despierta, la existencia de dos mundos perfectamente paralelos, distantes y desconocidos entre sí" (59) ["this awareness would bring him a clear image of two distinct worlds, parallel yet unknown to each other, remote and independent"; 56].

The existence of parallel worlds relating to distinct time frames is an important feature of the text's description of time, because each temporal vision produces more than one description of society. One salient example of Peri Rossi's dialectics of time in relation to multiple worlds is the description of a painting representing the departure of a ship of fools during the fifteenth century. The painting functions as a partial mirror to the tapestry, even though the tapestry is described to the reader in segments throughout the novel and the painting is described in one chapter. "El viaje, VIII: La nave de los locos" ("The Journey, VIII: The Ship of Fools") tells of the forced departure by boat of "undesirables" while upper-class society, dressed up on the shores, watches the spectacle. The binary existence of humanity depicted in this painting undermines the "harmony" of the tapestry. Both of these examples of the visual arts emphasize the segment of society favored by the patriarchal system. Countering the painting, which focuses on representing the spectators who have dressed up to watch the departure of the fools, the novel recounts the testimonial of Artemius Gudröm, a "sane" crewmember on a ship of fools, from the sixteenth century. He narrates the tragic story of Glaucus, who trusted Gudröm and died trying to swim for shore following Gudröm and the rest of the crew. The other passengers on the ship died at sea, too afraid to jump into the water and even try to swim. So while the painting focuses on the way in which the privileged took pleasure in watching these ships set sail, the novel exposes the perversity of their pleasure and includes a testimonial which reveals the history of these ships to be deeply disturbing (53). In the painting and in Gudröm's testimonial, society is divided in two: the center and the margins.

The text furthers this binary vision of society by presenting a variety of references to the theme of the ship of fools, and by adding to this list other marginalized groups which have been cast out of society as well. Lucía Invernizzi has done a thorough analysis of the references to other "ships of fools" in Peri Rossi's text: "La de Sebastian Brant, el conocido cuadro de Hieronymous Bosch, otro no tan conocido y para mi no identificado sino por la descripción que de él se hace en el Capítulo—'El viaje, VIII: La nave de los locos,' atribuyéndolo a 'anónimo pintor'; la novela de Katherine Anne Porter; la obra de Pedro Gómez Valderrama en la que *La nave de los locos* es título del conjunto de relatos que componen el libro y de una de las narraciones en él incluida" (32) ["The one by Sebastian Brant, the well known painting by Hieronymous Bosch, another painting less known and for me unidentifiable except for the description of it in the Chapter 'The Journey, VIII: The Ship of Fools,' attributed to an 'anonymous painter;' the novel by Katherine Anne Porter; the work of Pedro Gómez Valderrama on *The Ship of Fools* in his short story collection by that name, where one of the stories carries the same name"]. In her analysis of these references Invernizzi points to the historical distinctions present in each "repeated" tale of the ship of fools (33–34). The ship of fools is a metaphor for all those who have been rejected by society: "Hospitales especiales para heridos de guerra. Hospitales militares, para prisioneros políticos. Selvas apropiadas para arrojar opositores incómodos. Naves de locos. La nave, sustituida por el manicomio. Cárceles hediondas donde encerrar a los transgresores. Clínicas privadas" (176) ["Field hospitals for the wounded. Military hospitals housing political prisoners. Woods where troublesome opponents disappeared. Ships of fools, the ship as substitute for the madhouse. Evil smelling prisons to lock up transgressors. Private clinics"; 181]. Peri Rossi follows Foucault's assessment of the outcasts in society: the insane asylum replaces the ship of fools (*Madness* 38). The exiles and political prisoners from Uruguay are only one more example of those who threaten the order of the system. Moraña explains the constant mix of history and timelessness in the novel: the theme of the ship of fools, "se vincula por un lado a constantes... por otro lado... [tiene] sus raíces en la situación política del Uruguay de la dictadura.... La historia fluye" (211) ["is connected on the one hand to constants... on the other hand,... it has its roots in the political situation of Uruguay under dictatorship.... History flows"]. History exists, but it is in dialectical flux, turning the text back to myth and forward to ubiquitous relativity.

Nevertheless, many critics have not appreciated the complexities of this novel's theory of time. For instance, Gabriela Mora argues at one and the same time that Peri Rossi searches for harmony, but conducts her search following the footsteps of Foucault, Lacan, and Deleuze and Guattari. She claims that the novel represents decentering, heterogeneity, and multiplicity (343). By contrast, as I have argued, Peri Rossi's text, while certainly emphasizing a postmodern critique of modernity, still relies heavily on using alternative primordial myths to challenge official history as it was constructed by the military regime in Uruguay. To battle official history Peri Rossi does not use a non-hierarchical, multiple, heterogeneous vision of the world, as suggested by Mora, because such a state of political relativity is incapable of posing a true threat to authoritarianism. For this reason, like Dorfman and Goytisolo, Peri Rossi rejects those visions of the postmodern which abandon history in favor of a ludic, free-floating existence: such positions make the types of political battles central to these writers' work futile. Kantaris states that Peri Rossi's works "address the problem of re-integration: the possibility of re-engaging with the other in the face of violence and death; the need to define a place for oneself in which to *act*, socially and politically" (256). Peri Rossi's concerns with women's issues, human rights, sexual freedom, etc. problematize characterizing her as a practicant of the rhizome. The emphasis in Peri Rossi on the structures of power, which are the cause of exile, exclude her work from following the format of rhizome analysis, since rhizomatics rejects any type of structural analysis whatsoever. Despite the fact that Deleuze and Guattari's work is in large part a critique of fascism, because they remain relativists, they do not support any replacement for the fascist system of government. In agreement with Best and Kellner in their analysis of Deleuze and Guattari, I would argue that the concept of rhizome analysis is suggestive, but ultimately is doomed to fail as a true strategy of resistance. "If we can speak of frenzied, permanent self-revolution as the Deleuzo-Guattarian 'ethic,' it is not clear that this position radically breaks from capitalist and consumerist behavior.... There are no ideological battles to be fought and won, no critical consciousness to achieve, no basis for political agency; politics primarily involves the liberation of desiring bodies from which everything else apparently follows" (107–108; see Deleuze and Guattari's *A Thousand Plateaus*). Similar to the way in which Peri Rossi has been influenced by Foucault, the influence of Deleuze and Guattari is just that. She does not mirror their strategy of rhizomatics. Much in the same way that Kristeva argues for women to be reinserted back into historical time, but on their own terms, while all the while retaining the values of *monumental* time, Peri Rossi's text dialectically flows across the pre-modern, the modern, and the postmodern as it searches for a way to narrate the crisis of exile.

CROSSING TIME ZONES

The work of Goytisolo, Dorfman, and Peri Rossi tries to suggest alternative myths that compete with the mythical visions of the nation provided by the fascist-based ideologies associated with the authoritarian regimes in their homelands. In order to compete with the official versions of the nation and its history, these writers' alternative myths challenge the pre-modern and modern sources of legitimacy that the regimes constructed. The myths these writers offer incorporate pre-modern, modern, and postmodern conceptions of cultural identity and social formation. Each worldview relates to different conceptions of time and offers distinct philosophies of identity and existence: the pre-modern is characterized by manicheism, feudalism, monotheism, and monarchy; modernism focuses on rationality, free will, liberalism, democracy, and capitalism; and postmodernism suggests the loss of historical agency (without the ethical ground of manicheism or of liberalism), transnational capitalism, the instability of meaning, gender ambiguity, and the exaltation of difference. For these writers, this promiscuous vision of temporality is the only viable challenge to the system, and the only meaningful way to describe their relationship to the world. Given their experience of exile at a moment in history where fascist-oriented dictators endeavored to move their countries into the transnational capitalist marketplace, these writers were confronted with a time warp that required that they combine these temporalities in their narrative strategies of resistance to the system. Nestor García Canclini argues: "Sobre todo en el período más reciente, cuando la transnacionalización de la economía y la cultura nos vuelve 'contemporáneos de todos los hombres' (Paz), y sin embargo no elimina las tradiciones nacionales, optar en forma excluyente entre dependencia o nacionalismo, entre modernización o tradicionalidad local, es una simplificación insostenible" (*Culturas* 80) ["Above all in the most recent period, when the transnationalization of the economy and culture makes us 'the contemporaries of all men' (Paz), and nevertheless does not eliminate national traditions, to opt in an exclusive way between dependence and nationalism, between modernization and local traditions, is an unsupportable simplification"]. Simplification, clearly, is not part of the narrative project of Goytisolo, Dorfman, or Peri Rossi. Only through a complex interweaving of many different narrative threads, each corresponding to distinct world visions, can these writers aspire to write texts that represent their experience of exile.

All three of these world visions appeared in the texts analyzed. Goytisolo narrates a manichean world where the good Moors conquered the evil Christian Spaniards, Dorfman narrates a world where the small David tries, because of his great virtue and courage, to overcome the Dragon Pinchot, and Peri Rossi narrates a world where the myth of creation, which was purported to be good, requires that large segments of the population be deemed insane. In this way the myths of the authoritarian regimes, which argued that they were returning their countries to the natural course of history, are challenged and revealed as falsehoods. Kantaris, describing the work of Peri Rossi and Marta Traba states: "Firstly, as a way of countering any authoritarian claim to a monopoly of 'natural' order, it is imperative on both writers to expose the mechanism of exile and alienation underlying the 'naturalisation' of all such discursive constructs as 'self,' 'masculinity,' 'femininity,' 'patriotism,' 'morality,' etc." (249). Goytisolo, Dorfman, and Peri Rossi utilize just these tactics as they attempt to undermine the foundational myths that the military regimes require for the fabrication of their legitimacy.

It is noteworthy that all of the alternative myths narrated in their texts try to challenge the Judeo-Christian hold on identity. The Cid has been heralded as the most important figure leading to the Christian Reconquest of Spain and Goytisolo contrasts this figure with the alternative hero of Count Julian. Dorfman's myth comes from the Old Testament, where he uses the tale of David as a way to inspire the marginalized to fight. In a different section of the same novel he critiques the notion of an omnipotent God as he is incarnated in the form of the Reverend Rex. Reverend Rex speaks to the cartoonist, Carl Barks (a cartoon character in David's comic strip) and calls on him to "colonize the Great Beyond." The association between Christian ideology and cultural imperialism is exposed as Dorfman argues that authoritarianism has a great need for spiritual myths that support tyranny. Peri Rossi also specifically attacks Judeo-Christianity in her novel, focusing on the myth of creation and on its many ramifications in the construction of both national and personal identity, especially in terms of gender and sexuality. Through their questioning of the founding principles of Judeo-Christianity these writers recognize the need to confront the ideologies reigning in their nations on distinct temporal levels. As Julia Kristeva writes: "At best one is guilty of naivety if one considers our modern societies as simply patrilinear, or class-structured, or capitalist-monopolist, and omits the fact that they are at the same time (and never one without the other) governed by a monotheism whose essence is best expressed in the Bible: the 'paternal Word' sustained by a fight to the death between the two races (men/women)" (144).

In addition to the direct references in their work to the founding myths of Christianity, these novels have multiple Biblical references, which attempt to challenge the authority of the Sacred Word. As *La nave de los locos* opens, Exodus is quoted: "Y no angustiarás al extranjero: pues vosotros sabéis cómo se halla el alma del extranjero, ya que extranjeros fuisteis en la tierra de Egipto" (10) ["Also thou shall not oppress a stranger: for ye know the heart of a stranger, seeing ye were strangers in the land of Egypt"; 2]. The Bible teaches that exile should not produce anguish, but Peri Rossi's novel proves that the Bible is the source of alienation and oppression, that the "Sacred Word" is a lie. Exile is suffering: "extranjero. Ex. Extrañamiento" (10) ["stranger. Ecks. Estranged, Expelled from the womb of earth"; 2]. Both Equis and Vercingétorix are thirty-three years old, yet they do not die, as did Jesus Christ, saving humanity: they live in pain and uncertainty (78, 60). *The Last Song of Manuel Sendero* is replete with references to threes, challenging the Holy Trinity: the footnotes that accompany the dialogue of David and Felipe are "Commenting on a text which is more than thirty thousand years old" (79). The second rebellion takes place thirty years after the first, and the son of Sendero asks the government for three conditions (362). "Thirty-three years later" (408). "Thirty thousand years later" (425). The number three repeats and undermines the Bible's version of the importance of three as the door to salvation, because the use of three in Dorfman's novel reveals the suffering to continue endlessly. Goytisolo's narrator, in the first chapter of *Juan sin tierra*, wants to replace Catholic values with Cuban *santería* and Caribbean sensuality. He replaces the Christian emphasis on purity with an emphasis on the anus. Catholicism will be destroyed by Cuban culture: "la eterna manzana brillante y lustrosa que se ofrece al mordisco con rubores mentidos : la banana aún mejor : la piña tropical : la sugestiva pera" (25) ["the eternal, bright shiny apple inviting one to sink one's teeth into its deceitful rosy blush: or better still the banana: the tropical pineapple: the suggestive pear"; 15].

These texts demonstrate the minute and grand ways in which Catholicism continues to be a central guiding factor in Hispanic identity: it has not been thoroughly replaced by a modern notion of the secular self. The pre-modern continues to be a source of contemporary cultural ideology in Spain and Latin America. As Nestor García Canclini explains: "Esta *heterogeneidad multitemporal* de la cultura moderna es consecuencia de una historia en la que la modernización operó pocas veces mediante la sustitución de lo tradicional y lo antiguo" (*Culturas* 72) ["This *multitemporal heterogeneity* of modern culture is the consequence of a history in which modernization rarely operated through the substitution of the traditional and the ancient"]. For this reason, these writers cannot avoid addressing the importance of the myths central to Catholicism in identity/nation formation.

In modern times, Dorfman and Peri Rossi's texts are concerned with politics and human rights. Central to Dorfman's work is the question of free will and the possibilities of historical agency, notions affected by the brief success of Salvador Allende's regime. Peri Rossi mixes politics in the Southern Cone with a concern for women's rights and finds that systems based on patriarchy and capitalist gain leave little hope for changing the center/margin dialectic. Also concerned with free will and political agency, Peri Rossi, unlike Dorfman, posits a world where such questions still remain but are shown to be increasingly rhetorical with little hope for effecting action. Goytisolo's modernity is exemplified by the fight over which version of history will prevail. How will the Spanish Civil War be remembered? His entire novel *Señas de identidad* circles around that question, where the protagonist, Alvaro, desperately tries to challenge Franco's version of history, and believes that were he successful, political change might follow. Kantaris's thoughts from the aforementioned article can be applied to Dorfman and Goytisolo as well: "[these] writers perceive that a centralising patriarchal system, such as dictatorship, exerts its prohibitory power not only by institutionalising abduction, torture, rape and murder as means of social control, but also by tightly controlling systems of *signification*" (249).

Through their concern for the control of discourse common in authoritarian regimes, these writers look for insight from poststructural theories of language. These poststructural theories and their connections to postmodernism cause the greatest dilemmas for these writers. For the postmodern, like the pre-modern and the modern, has both a conservative and a liberating version. As John Beverley has pointed out: "one must recognize that, because by virtue of postmodernism's very critique of essentialism there is no necessary connection between it and the left, a postmodernism of the right ... is also flourishing in Latin America" (121). These texts reveal the tensions between the apolitical and groundless version of the postmodern, most often described as the ludic postmodern, or as textualism, and a politically inspired resistance postmodernism, which does not abandon a concept of the self and of history—notions central to the identity of the exile—even though it recognizes that the modern ways of defining these notions need to be radically reassessed. As Fernando Calderón explains: "Beginning in the 70s, with the military dictatorships and the consequent reappraisal of private life and then of democracy, it becomes possible to think that various processes and systems of thought coexist in Latin America, some complementing modernity, others developing a confused postmodernity, and others maintaining pre-modernity, but all in a mixed and subordinate manner" (59). The leftist struggles of modernity and the battle field for those struggles have been significantly altered, meaning that the most effective resistance to an oppressive system will require guerrilla tactics which combat every aspect of identity as it has been predetermined by a still intact hegemonic system.

Arguably, it is just this type of temporal promiscuity, or dialectic flux of the pre-modern, modern, and postmodern, that characterizes postmodern cultural production by Hispanics. In fact, as many have argued, "uneven modernity" like that found in Spain and Latin America, seems to be answered by a postmodern condition of hybrid temporalities. (See Stephanie Sieburth for "uneven modernity" in Spain and Julio Ramos and Fernando Calderón for an analysis of Latin American modernity/postmodernity as an example of "mixed temporalities.") Modernity in Spain and Latin America is uniquely modern—precisely because many pre-modern ways of thinking and of organizing society persist—as in the importance of Catholicism, the legacy of authoritarianism, etc. As Nestor García Canclini explains, many of the cornerstones to modern ideology have not been fully developed in Latin America, complicating the notion of the postmodern in the region: "No hemos tenido una industrialización sólida . . . ni un ordenamiento socio-político basado en la racionalidad formal y material" (*Culturas* 20) ["We have not had a solid industrialization . . . nor a social political ordering based in formal and material rationality"]. As he points out, Latin America has a mixture of both the pre-modern and the postmodern. In postmodern cultural production there is no necessary break with modernity or with pre-modernity. To pre-modern and modern culture another layer of cultural consciousness is added, that of the postmodern: "coexisten múltiples lógicas de desarrollo" (25) ["Multiple logics of development exist"]. So Goytisolo's, Dorfman's, and Peri Rossi's work does not fit easily into common temporal categories used to describe literature. Their work draws on myth and epic, realism and existentialism, poststructuralism and political postmodernism. In their case, though, writing across the pre-modern, the modern, and the postmodern is a consequence not only of Spanish and Latin American history, but also of their experience of exile. The sense that history is not neatly linear is connected to the exile's pre-modern legacy. The complex notions of time in their texts are strategically employed in order to describe and challenge the experience of exile. The myths narrated by these novels respond to both their historical and universal condition. So "exile's time" in these texts is connected to the experience of exile, of fascist ideology, and of Hispanic cultural identity. Exile's time, then, is a dialectic flow between the pre-modern, modern, and postmodern.

Nevertheless, it is important to highlight that myth as used by these writers does not ever truly provide a complete replacement for the totalizing myths behind authoritarian regimes: myth does not always refer to a totalized pre-modern world vision. As Labanyi points out, myth is used by writers of Goytisolo's generation in Spain with an ironic tone and the same could be said for Peri Rossi and Dorfman (52). Myth appears in their texts as a challenge to the notion of linear history. Yet, myth also appears in these texts as a response to its use by writers of the Latin American boom in the 60s, where myth and history combine, thereby forming an alternative version of the region's cultural past (Goytisolo has explained to Julio Ortega the impact of these boom writers on his work; 13). The myths of the boom novelists were meant to replace the hegemony of the Western myths implicit in colonization. Western history was described as a "deviation from roots" (Labanyi 27). Labanyi further explains: "The concept of myth put forward by Latin American writers is almost exclusively based on Eliade's insistence on myth as a return to origins, fused with the Jungian notion... of the quest myth as a return to the 'womb' of the unconscious in search of rebirth" (30). Even so, Labanyi recognizes that even the authors associated with the boom acknowledged that their totalizing efforts at narrating an alternative cultural identity were fraught with difficulties (31). In the work of Goytisolo, Dorfman, and Peri Rossi, all readers of the boom, the use of myth becomes even more problematic and must be understood through the historical filter of modern authoritarianism and exile as well as postmodern theories of the loss of historical agency and the ubiquitous relativism of meaning. Post-boom writers like Dorfman and Peri Rossi reject the totalizing impulses of the boom writers and the boom's connection to the commercialization of Latin American literature and the exportation, for Western consumption, of Latin American exoticism (see Zeitz 83). Dorfman has spoken of the importance of the boom in the establishment of an autochthonous literary heritage for his generation, but he also states: "You have to kill the fathers. I mean, you have to kill the literary antecedents every time you start to write. That's very important" (qtd. in Incledon 99). In fact, like the modern use of myth by the boom writers, what occurs in the texts of Goytisolo, Dorfman, and Peri Rossi may be more aptly termed a postmodern use of myth, where their works simultaneously challenge myths of hegemony with non-hegemonic myths while debunking the universalizing and eternal truths implicit in myth by resorting to postmodern tactics of deconstruction and relativity.

The literature of these three writers, as it develops such complex notions of time, demands that those theories which seek to fit literature into precise categories be reevaluated. Goytisolo, Dorfman, and Peri Rossi were forced to cross time zones—they were forced to leave the time of their homelands—and their literary response to such temporal displacement signifies an even greater cultural crisis that affected many artists with roots in Spain and Latin America. Postmodernism as it appears in the work of these writers has been altered from its "First World" context, even though, or, because, Goytisolo, Dorfman, and Peri Rossi all spend time in these centers of postmodern theory while seeking political asylum. As George Yúdice argues, referring to postmodernism in Latin America: "My argument as regards Latin America is not that informal economies or narcotraffic *are* postmodern phenomena but, rather, that they are simultaneously responses and propositions that pose alternatives to the *grand récit* of postmodernity as it has been constructed by Lyotard, Jameson, and their predecessors" (4). What is most crucial to gather from Yúdice's point is that the exile from Latin America or Spain, because of their cultural context, was unlikely to emulate entirely the "First World"-oriented theories of the postmodern. Instead, these ideas influence their exile writing, but are only one of many contributing factors to these narrative projects. The complex combination of the circumstances of exile, of alienation from fascist-based versions of official history, of Hispanic cultural roots, and of influence by theories of the postmodern emanating from France, Germany, and the United States led these writers to produce texts which lie at a crossroads where many ways of interpreting the world intersect dialectically.

CHAPTER FIVE

To Be Is Not to Be: Exile and the Crisis of Linguistic Representation

Ser es dejar de estar.—Octavio Armand

Spanish expresses "to be" with two distinct verbs: "ser" and "estar." The dichotomy that the exile faces of, for instance, being Chilean—ser chileno (to be Chilean)—and not being in Chile—no estar en Chile (to not be in Chile)—seems to be exacerbated by these two verbal forms: soy de donde no estoy (I am from where I am not). Or as the Cuban exile Octavio Armand has put it, "ser es dejar de estar" ("to be [someone] is not to be [somewhere]"). In the case of the Spanish-speaking exile, to be is not to be, and that is the problem.

The result of this fragmented identity has led certain exiles to produce texts that directly confront this linguistic crisis. Goytisolo, Dorfman, and Peri Rossi are among those writers who consider the crisis of language to be integrally connected to the political and cultural dilemmas facing the exiled writer. As Cristina Peri Rossi explains in "An Exercise in Return": "There is no *here* without a protagonist and without interlocutors: my here moves with me, it is transitory and circumstantial only in the measure by which I move. The richness of Castilian allows us the subtle distinction between the verb *ser* and the verb *estar: soy de aquí* (I am from here) and *estoy aquí* (I am here) can include all discourse on the human condition" (223). To be, then, is *both* a transitory and a fixed concept. To be Uruguayan is not to be in Uruguay for Peri Rossi. This split in identity connects the exile's problems of defining who the self "is" with the exile's lack of faith in linguistic representation.

Such a connection between language and the self was made clear in the work of the linguist Emile Benveniste, who stated: "Language is marked so deeply by the expression of subjectivity that one might ask if it could still function and be called a language if it were constructed otherwise" (225). Indeed, what this chapter will make clear is that the connection between subjectivity and language becomes extremely complicated in the narrative of exiled writers. For Goytisolo, Dorfman, and Peri Rossi, the crisis of language, while revealing a crisis in the subject, does not lead to the end of representations of the subject. Rather it suggests that the connection between language and the subject must be radically reconsidered. The problems of style and representation in these writers' works lead to a mixture of many aesthetic codes, but the result is not an apolitical pastiche of gibberish. The crisis of representation that these authors face is not reduced to merely a "rhetorical issue." Insofar as these writers are committed to representing their own personal and collective histories, they are excluded from the playground of the ludic postmodern's linguistic games. In Peri Rossi's *La nave de los locos*, Equis refers to his exile and states: "Este viaje ya lo leí más de cinco veces" (11) ["I've already read about this journey five times over"; 3]. But can reading ever prepare the exile for the experience? Is reading about exile the same as exile? As we read about the exile of Equis, Peri Rossi underlines the difference between reading, writing, and experience. And it is a difference that matters. There is an exile that exists beyond the textual.

Claudio Guillén has remarked on the significance of the rupture in meaning between the verbs "ser" and "estar" in the work of exiled writers. He states: "It is possible for the poems of counter-exile... to move like other elegies between the poles of *ser* and *estar*" (279). Guillén is implying that certain texts can choose to highlight either the fixed or the transitory states of being. Yet the problem for exiles like Goytisolo, Dorfman, and Peri Rossi is that, due to the poststructuralist turn, which affected their concept of writing, they are also questioning the rupture of "ser" versus "ser." What is? Or, rather, can language represent what is?

As discussed in the previous chapter, the works of Goytisolo, Dorfman, and Peri Rossi resist conventional critical categorization because they incorporate elements of pre-modern, modern, and postmodern aesthetics. Language alternately is fixed and unmediated, questioned and representational, and free-floating and self-reflexive. In *Lingüística General* Cristina Peri Rossi writes: "El poeta no escribe sobre las cosas / sino sobre el nombre de las cosas" (9) ["The poet doesn't write about things / but rather about the names of things"], a statement which seems to reflect a poststructuralist position on language. Yet elsewhere in the same book, she writes: "Eludir el nombre de las cosas / es convocarlas de manera más elocuente" (39) ["To avoid/ evade the name of things / is to summon them in a more eloquent way"]. In these lines she suggests that even if literary language is incapable of perfectly reflecting reality, it is still representational. Or another reading of these lines might be that literary language is more powerful and evocative than the direct address of authoritarian language. Yet, in another poem from the same collection she writes: "En la nostálgica distancia que va / del sueño a lo real / se instala a la alquimia del poema / y del amor" (31) ["In the nostalgic distance that goes / from the dream to the real / is installed the alchemy of the poem / and of love"]. Language is the chemical connection between dream and reality: it is the key to connecting the physical and the mental. In just these three short examples we have seen that Peri Rossi's poetry reflects diverse and contradictory positions on language. These dialectical contradictions are the crux of the linguistic crisis for exiles. Exile is the condition which has exacerbated these linguistic dilemmas. In an example from the same collection of poetry, the condition of exile is shown to affect writing deeply: "Escribimos porque los objetos de los que queremos hablar / no están" (14) ["We write because the objects of which we want to speak / are not there"]. So writing is an act of reclaiming "being." By writing, the exile tries to conjure up the place where she cannot "be." "El poeta se parece al profeta, / es verdad, / no sólo en el hecho de ser oído por escaso / número de gentes, / sino porque como aquél, / aspira salvarse de la muerte / a través del verbo. / Aunque sea un verbo profano" (16) ["The poet is like the prophet, / it is true, / not only in the fact that he is heard by a scant / number of people, / but also because like the prophet, / he aspires to save himself from death / through the word. / Even if it is a profane word"]. In this poem, Peri Rossi speaks of truth and of writing as the exile's means of survival.

Hence, writing in exile is an act of self-recuperation and a simultaneous effort to construct an identity that struggles against extinction. Guillermo Cabrera Infante, exiled from Cuba, refers to the exile as an invisible being (34). Without his writing he would no longer exist. Yet, ironically, Cabrera Infante is in exile precisely because he is a writer. Writing, then, is directly connected to these authors' notion of self and their notion of nationality. As exile complicates this situation, the texts produced reflect the struggle to prevent personal and collective histories from disappearing. Julia Kristeva has suggested: "The symbolic order—the order of verbal communication, the paternal order of genealogy—is a temporal order. For the speaking animal it is the clock of objective time: it provides the reference point, and, consequently, all possibilities of measurement by distinguishing between a before, a now, and an after. If *I* don't exist except in the speech I address to another, *I* am only present in the moment of that communication" (153). Insofar as exiles, like women, are subject to "the paternal order of genealogy" they too must use speech and writing as a means of resistance, or else face invisibility and disappearance, i.e., non-being. Such acts of resistance require a belief in the ability of language to communicate and to affect the world in which we live.

It is important to recognize that, in addition to the influence of poststructuralism on these writers, their work resists transparent language because of the authoritarian realities to which they respond. Authoritarian regimes control language in order to maintain power. In these situations the use of propaganda and censorship highlight the difference between what is experienced and what language describes. As a result, certain exile texts struggle to narrate; yet their authors have lost faith in language's ability to account for their history. The exiled subject must confront the loss of identity at a moment in history when, due to authoritarianism in their nations, the notion of the self and its relationship to language has become extremely fragile.

In a world where dominant forms of cultural production leave little space for the margins, the exiled writer has often experimented with a narrative style that seeks to resist tradition. These texts, when charged with a political message, attempt to restore the repressed dimensions of identity that have become overshadowed by the objectifying practices of those in power. In the case of the Hispanic writer, the writing must resist the conventional narratives that dominate mainstream culture and find a new voice. Of course this practice becomes even more imperative when the writer is forced to leave his or her country.

Is there a common discourse of exile? Many scholars of exile literature have chosen to focus on whether the condition implies either a loss or a gain of language. For Andrew Gurr, "Distance gives perspective, and for exiles it is also the prerequisite for freedom in their art. Freedom to write is a major stimulus to exile, and exile creates the kind of isolation which is the nearest thing to freedom which the twentieth century artist is likely to attain" (17). Paul Ilie describes the language of exile as "graphocentrism," which is the "indeterminate language of exile." "Everything passes uncritically into the vortex of language for its own sake.... [Graphocentrism] denationalizes Spanish and encourages language to float unanchored to any particular nation" ("Exolalia" 246). Edward Said joins the chorus of those who see the experience of exile as aesthetically liberating: "Seeing 'the entire world as a foreign land' makes possible originality of vision.... [T]his plurality of vision gives rise to an awareness of simultaneous dimensions" ("Reflections" 366). Indisputably, the condition of exile exposes the writer to a new linguistic environment, one that may provide greater creative possibilities, but to see such acquisitions as a step toward "freedom" or merely as a positive experience is highly problematic. In fact, it contradicts the deconstructive motivations behind the statements made by critics like Ilie and Said. Can experience be connected to a "positive" linguistic outcome? Moreover, doesn't such a position contradict the notion of a language divorced from reality? Ilie refers to the discourse of exile as language that "floats unanchored." Said, on the other hand, mixes deconstruction with historicism and states: "both the new and the old environments are vivid, actual, occurring together contrapuntally. There is a unique pleasure in this sort of apprehension" (366). According to Said, one environment has been stripped of its historical time, while the other, that of the exile's present residence, is historical and actual. What is most significant about these positions on the discourse of exile is the fact that these critics all seem intent on determining whether the experience is either a loss or a gain of language. Discourse studies of exile writing attempt to delimit the use of language to either a positive, transcultural, original, and free use of language; or a negative, nostalgic, and limited use of language, as in the case of Guillén's two categories of exile and counter-exile literature. Perhaps, once again, the desire to fit the work of these writers into neat categories fails, and highlights the shortcomings of binary theories about the discourse of exile literature. We find, rather, that these contrary notions of language can be found to coexist dialectically in much exile writing. Speaking of language and cultural displacement Angelika Bammer claims that "For, at once carrier of national and familial traditions and emblem of cultural and personal identity, language functions equally as an identity-grounding home under conditions of displacement and a means of intervention into identity-fixing cultural agendas" (xvi). Bammer describes the language of displacement as a dialectic between cultural fixity and cultural relativism.

The early exile texts of Goytisolo, Dorfman, and Peri Rossi do not represent the condition of exile as a literary advantage. In fact, the early exile texts of Goytisolo and Dorfman more closely approximate linguistically testimonial narrative, as these writers were first intent on re-telling history. For instance, the matriarch of the Greek family in *Viudas* is named Sofía, not Sophia, a clear flag that the text is not strictly referring to Greece, but to places where "ph" is not used in the name Sofía. This observation is made relevant by the fact that all of the other characters' names have been translated from the Greek alphabet, without a corresponding translation in spelling into

Spanish. For instance, the captain's name is Gheorghakis and the orderly's is Emmanuel, spellings that are not typically Spanish, unlike "Sofía" with an "f" and an accent mark. Yet in the case of Dorfman's second novel in exile, *The Last Song of Manuel Sendero,* Dorfman himself helped translate the text into English and in the process made some changes. He prefers the English version to the Spanish, which demonstrates that, over time, his experience of exile affected his need to privilege Spanish as it is spoken in Chile. Or, in Goytisolo's case, *Señas de identidad* is stylistically a combination of neo-realism and poststructuralist interior dialogue. When other languages appear in the text, such as French, English, or German, they make sense contextually. For instance, as Alvaro is looking for work for fellow exiles in Paris, the text communicates what Alvaro hears during the conversation in French: "Alvaro evocaba las mañanas pasadas junto al teléfono, proponiendo el servicio de alguna Vicenta a exquisitas damas de Auteuil y Neuilly que insistían en averiguar si 'cette fille a un bon rendement' o si 'elle est propre'" (241) ["Alvaro thought about the mornings spent beside his telephone, proposing the services of some Vicenta to elegant ladies of Auteuil and Neuilly who insisted on finding out whether '*cette fille a un bon rendement*' or whether '*elle est propre*'"; 200]. Such a use of French cannot be considered a linguistic move away from Spanish. Throughout *Señas de identidad* Goytisolo's narrator remains very committed to "Spanish" Spanish:

> oh patria / mi nacimiento entre los tuyos y el hondo amor que / sin pedirlo tú / durante años obstinadamente te he ofrendado / separémonos como buenos amigos puesto que aún es tiempo / nada nos une ya sino tu bella lengua mancillada hoy por / sofismas mentiras hipótesis angélicas aparentes verdades / frases vacías cáscaras huecas / alambicados silogismos / buenas palabras ... mejor vivir entre extranjeros que se expresan en idioma extraño para ti que en medio de paisanos que diariamente prostituyen el tuyo propio. (420)
>
> oh my country / my birth among yours and the deep love that / without your asking / for years I have obstinately offered you / let us part like good friends while there still is time / nothing joins us except your beautiful language stained today by sophistry lies / angelic hypotheses apparent truths / phrases empty as hollow shells / distilled syllogisms / good words... better to live among foreigners who express themselves in a strange tongue than / in the midst of countrymen who prostitute you every day. (350)

In his later works, where Goytisolo more thoroughly abandons his use of punctuation and begins to use Cuban and Mexican expressions, the effects of exile on his language are more pronounced. Nevertheless, Goytisolo never loses ties to Castillian Spanish.

In Peri Rossi's case, one of her first texts written in exile, the short story "La influencia de Edgar Allen Poe en la poesía de Raimundo Arias" (The Influence of Edgar Allen Poe in the Poetry of Raimundo Arias) devotes an entire section to the different words used in Spain versus the Southern Cone for food. "En el país de donde venían, a los melocotones los llamaban duraznos.... Las fresas eran frutillas; las frutillas eran fresas, en el país donde habían decidido ir por hablar el mismo idioma" (51) ["In the country they came from, they called *melocotones* [peaches] *duraznos* [peaches]. ... *Fresas* [strawberries] were *frutillas* [strawberries]; *Frutillas* [strawberries] were *fresas* [strawberries] in the country they had decided to go to because they spoke the same language"]. In these lines she emphasizes the fact that exile in Spain, despite the "common" language, does not mean that the Uruguayan characters avoid a linguistic crisis. Yet, as her exile progresses, Peri Rossi's writing becomes less regionally identifiable: "Escribo contra la realidad. Empecé a hacerlo porque la realidad que veía a mi alrededor—en mi casa, primero; luego en mi país—no me gustaba. En este sentido, poco importa cuál sea la realidad geográfica" (qtd. in Schmidt 218) ["I write against reality. I began to do it because I didn't like the reality I saw around me—first in my home; later in my country. In this sense geographical reality has little importance"]. Therefore the later works produced in exile of Goytisolo, Dorfman, and Peri Rossi reflect a broader linguistic context and depict the discourse of exile as *both* a loss and a gain.

The language of exile texts crosses borders or becomes more nationalistic, at times within the same text. It has been argued that Juan Goytisolo, exiled from Spain in the 1950s, now writes using "Latin American" Spanish—an argument that speaks to the universalization of Spanish as a result of the intellectual diaspora (see Paul Ilie). In contrast, Cristina Peri Rossi, an Uruguayan exiled in Spain, has a story in the collection *El museo de los esfuerzos inútiles* entitled "Las avenidas de la lengua" ("The Avenues of Language") which compares the use of different past tenses to express the past, focusing on the preterit versus the present perfect. The narrator has a friend who states: "He subido arriba y no te encontré" (93) ["I was ascending up and didn't find you"; 78]. This use of the present perfect is common in Spain but would sound out of place in Uruguay. The narrator then wonders: "¿Por qué no dijo simplemente: 'subí arriba y no te encontré'?" ["Why hadn't he simply said, 'I ascended up and didn't find you'?"; 79]. This discrepancy in the use of the past tense causes the narrator great anguish: "No hay sintaxis inocente" (92) ["There is nothing innocent about syntax"; 78]. She continues to be disturbed by her friend's words: "Me pareció que no iba a poder dejar de pensar en esto, que la situación se iba a prolongar indefinidamente, si él no modificaba la frase que había pronunciado" (93–94) ["It seemed like it would be impossible to stop thinking about this, that the situation would go on and on indefinitely unless he recast his sentence"; 79]. For the Uruguayan the use of the present perfect instead of the preterit seems to prolong the action without giving it a definite end: "todavía peor hubiera sido que él dijera, por ejemplo: 'He subido arriba y no te he encontrado.' Con esa frase, me habría hecho desaparecer de aquel lugar; toda mi persona no hubiera alcanzado para llenar esa ausencia" (94) ["It would have been even worse had he said something like: 'I have ascended up and I haven't found you.' With that sentence, he would have made me disappear from the place. All of me taken together would not have been enough to make up for my absence"; 80]. Because her friend has not specified an end to the act of looking for her and not finding her, the narrator fears disappearance. In this way, the story "Las avenidas de la lengua" underlines the distance between the language Peri Rossi learned in Uruguay and that which she encounters in Spain, because in Spain the use of the present perfect is equivalent to the use of the preterit in the sentence "I went up and didn't find you." Moreover, the sentence she focuses on also links language to the self. The shift of past tense verbs in this sentence threatens her sense of identity. How does the narrator exist within this foreign use of language?

Angel Rama, in "Founding the Latin American Literary Community," argues that writers can become transcultural or more regional in their use of language while in exile. For instance, according to him, the writing of the Argentine Julio Cortázar becomes regional: "The long self-imposed exile of Julio Cortázar in Paris led him to such total concentration on the language of Buenos Aires (even more than that of Argentina) that all his characters, regardless of origin, are linguistically homogenous in their use of *porteño* speech" (12). In contrast to Rama's perception of regionalism of Cortázar's writing, Jorge Edwards argues that Pablo Neruda's language changes due to living outside of Chile. *Residencia en la tierra* (*Residence on Earth*), written in Rangoon, uses, according to Edwards, "odd" Spanish. "He heard chiefly English, as spoken in the English colonies, and his use of verbs is not altogether Chilean or Spanish. It was something new, and he made of it something very creative in the Spanish language" (70). In this sense, exile texts can be examples of transculturation, where they reflect the resulting cultural change induced by the introduction of elements of foreign culture. On the other hand, exile texts are also an example of regionalism in as much as their language maintains ties that can be traced back to their authors' country of origin.

It is important to note that Rama attributes to the artist the capacity to choose which foreign elements and which regional elements will be part of the process of transculturation. He clearly believes in the artist's free will (*Transculturación* 38). Adding to the notion of transculturation as postulated by the Cuban Fernando Ortiz Rama explains that the author is able to employ criteria of selectivity and invention (38). The notion that the artist has the free will to choose which elements of foreign or regional culture to include reveals Rama's connection to the aesthetics of the boom. Speaking of the boom writer Juan Rulfo, Rama argues:

> buscamos ejemplificar dos cosas: la presencia activa en una literatura, no sólo de asuntos de una determinada región cultural americana y al mismo tiempo la tarea redescubridora, inventiva y original del escritor situado en el conflicto modernizador. Edifica una neoculturación que no es la mera adición de elementos contrapuestos, sino una construcción nueva que asume los desgarramientos y problemas de la colisión cultural. Quizás no deberíamos olvidar nunca que el escritor es, ante todo, un productor. (116)

> we look to exemplify two things: the active presence in literature not only of issues associated with a determinant American cultural region but also at the same time the work of inventive and original rediscovery by the author situated within the conflict of modernity. It constructs a neoculturation that is not the mere addition of counterpoising elements, but rather a new con-

struction that covers the forceful separations and problems of cultural collision. Perhaps we should not forget that the writer is, above all, a producer.

In addressing the elements of transculturation and regionalism in the work of these writers, it is important to consider that for post-boom writers, like Dorfman and Peri Rossi, and for Post–Civil War writers, like Goytisolo, there can no longer be such faith in unmediated creative production, and specifically in the artist's free will to create. As Ariel Dorfman explains in the introduction to his collection of essays *Some Write to the Future,* which contains essays written in the 1960s and early 1970s and translated into English in the 1990s, these essays reflect his desire to see literature as having an important role in the liberation of the people of Latin America. Yet, after Pinochet, these thoughts have become altered and such idealism is no longer possible. After Pinochet, Dorfman sees creative production as integrally connected to the issue of power: it either subverts the prevalent power or submits to it, and the author is not always "free" to choose the path of his text and more importantly, of his readers, even though he can try to guide them (xii).

The issue of language for these writers is complex, then, for a variety of reasons. First, these writers are faced with producing texts in Spanish outside of the regions where either Spanish is not the national language or in places where their particular version of Spanish is not spoken. Second, because of the official discourse propagated by the authoritarian regimes in their nations and the resulting censorship and control of free expression, these writers are sensitive to the notion of "free, unmediated communication." Goytisolo remarks on the impact of Franco on Spanish in *España y los españoles,* where he states that, even after Franco's death, language continues to be restricted: "Años y años de posesión ilegítima y exclusiva destinada a vaciar los vocablos de su genuino contenido . . . a fin de esterilizar la potencia subversiva del lenguaje o convertirlo en instrumento dócil de un discurso voluntariamente amañado, engañoso y adormecedor" (213) ["Years and years of illegitimate and exclusive possession destined to empty words of their genuine content . . . in order to sterilize the subversive potential of language or convert it into the docile instrument of a discourse voluntarily manipulated, deceptive and soporific"]. The adjectives Goytisolo uses to refer to language—manipulated, deceptive, and soporific—could evoke a poststructuralist position on language. But for Goytisolo, this linguistic state is the direct result of Francoist policies. Goytisolo suggests that the reconstruction of Spain requires that language be re-infused with meaning and historical specificity. Writing shortly after Franco's death he states: "Frente a tal situación de envenenamiento y asfixia, el sistema actual significa el reajuste del lenguaje a los hechos" (*España* 213) ["Faced with such a poisoning and stifling situation, the current system signals the readjustment of language to facts"]. Third, these writers are influenced by theories of poststructuralism, which leads them to question the representational ability of language, most specifically, the ability of language to represent reality, and causes doubt that there can be *any* communication that is able to change the course of history. And finally, insofar as these writers are political exiles, they are faced with the dilemma that writing is their only weapon in these battles. Exiled from the battlegrounds of their nations, they must fight with words. They must write in order to challenge the "order of things." They also must write to exist. As exiles, they have been excised from their nations: they are now invisible, non-existent. Therefore, as exiled writers, they also embrace, at times, the notion: I write, therefore, I exist. Through writing, they challenge their national absence and create a textual presence. Dorfman explains his interest in writing *Viudas* under a pseudonym so that the novel could be released in Chile: "Me obsesionaba la necesidad... de ser leído en mi propio país, supliendo con mi presencia literaria, aunque fuera bajo un seudónimo, la forzada ausencia física que tanto nos duele" (7) ["I was obsessed with the necessity... of being read in my own country, replacing with my literary presence, even if it were under a pseudonym, the forced physical absence that causes us so much pain"]. If he could not *be* in Chile, perhaps his writing could *be* there instead.

But to be is not to be, both because of the rupture between "ser" and "estar" and because of the fear of an unbridgeable rupture between the signifiers "ser" and "estar" and their signifieds, and that is the problem. So once again, each effort at positive action (belief in writing, communication, and political change) and self-determination is counterbalanced by doubt and frustration. All three of these writers have great insecurity about their ability to represent history through writing. Cristina Peri Rossi's character, Equis, from *La nave de los locos* exemplifies this doubt. After dreaming that he has been told to describe what he sees, "La ciudad a la que llegues descríbela" (9) ["You will come to a city—describe it"; 1], he is lost in confusion and can no longer tell the significant from the insignificant: "quedé confuso. La paja me parecía más bella y los granos, torvos. La duda me ganó" (9) ["I was confused. The straw seemed more beautiful and the grain, unyielding. Doubt overwhelmed me"; 1]. Nevertheless, despite great doubt, these writers do not give up, they write, and such a simple fact is testimony to their hope that they can communicate.

"I'm interested in something else David. All of a sudden I wonder who in the devil are you writing that for, David?' ... 'Who for?... I wish I knew. Who for? I don't have the slightest fucking idea" (*The Last Song of Manuel Sendero* 109). Another significant linguistic dilemma for the writer in exile is the problem of audience. Angel Rama explains that the exiled writer addresses three publics: "that of the country or culture in which he has temporarily settled; that of his native country, with which he tries to maintain communication in spite of dictatorial restraints; and the public of his compatriots, who make up the people of his diaspora" ("Founding" 12). The history of Dorfman's *Viudas,* with its attempted pseudonym, is an excellent example of an exiled writer who hopes to still reach the audience of his native country. Dorfman, in the prologue to the novel, states that he had tried the pseudonym ploy, "para que el hijo creciera allá donde debía hacerlo: en su tierra verdadera, entre los suyos" (7) ["so that the son grew up over there where he should: in his true land, among his own"]. Later in the prologue to *The Empire's Old Clothes,* Dorfman explains how exile changed his opinion about the appropriate audience for his writing: "these years of exile and defeat have taught me some new things. It is essential, above all, to go beyond the sphere of those who are already convinced" (11). But as Morris learns in *La nave de los locos,* "cada día hay más autores y menos lectores" (126) ["every day the number of authors increases and the number of readers diminishes"; 127]. These writers, then, also have complicated connections to a readership. Cristina Peri Rossi has been anthologized as both a Latin American and as a Spanish woman writer, Dorfman's play *La muerte y la doncella* (*Death and the Maiden*) was more successful in Europe than in Chile, and, lastly, Goytisolo fits uneasily into the category of contemporary Spanish writers due to the influence of Latin American and Arabic culture in his work.

Given the complex and contradictory theories of language in these writers' work, it has become exceedingly difficult for scholars to analyze their literature. The common practice has been to emphasize either the instability of meaning, i.e., the elements of poststructuralism and also transculturation in their work, or to focus on the regional, i.e., nationalist and political features of their writing. Speaking of Goytisolo, Carlos Fuentes writes: "[Goytisolo] is the prisoner of all of the verbal chains of the Spanish language only to make them evident" (73–74). Fuentes sees language in Goytisolo's literature as regionally tied in its political project of challenging Franco's appropriation of the Spanish language. In contrast Paul Ilie argues: "[A] disentailment from national prerogatives is announced in the title of a novel by Juan Goytisolo *John the Landless* (*Juan sin tierra*), where cultural loss reaches the final extremity of surrendering the native language in exchange for a foreign tongue" (*Inner Exile* 8). Ilie asserts that Goytisolo has been able to "free" himself from the regional ties of his linguistic origins because the last paragraph of the novel is written in Arabic. Referring to *Reivindicación del conde don Julián* many scholars have noted the influence of Argentine, Mexican, and Cuban Spanish, which they attribute to Goytisolo's affiliations with Julio Cortázar, Carlos Fuentes, and Severo Sarduy and which they see as reflecting a "new" side of Spanish (see Doblado 144; Gould Levine 175). Such "new" Spanish suggests Goytisolo is a transcultural writer, no longer restricted to the language of his native land. This position contrasts that articulated by Fuentes, who sees Goytisolo as a prisoner of his native tongue. I would argue that neither position completely accounts for the use of language in his work. In fact, Goytisolo himself has described his linguistic approach as a paradox: "El mundo en que vivimos reclama un lenguaje nuevo, virulento y anárquico ... [S]ólo podemos crear destruyendo: una destrucción que sea a la vez creación; una creación a la par destructiva" (*Furgón de cola* 56) ["The world in which we live calls for a new, virulent, anarchic language ... [W]e can only create destroying: a destruction that is also a creation; a creation equally destructive"]. Goytisolo's writing depicts a constant dialectic between affirming and denying the ability of language to represent.

Ariel Dorfman's work also projects a theory of language full of contradictions, and consequently difficult to assess. Dorfman has described his linguistic aesthetic as "social irrealism": writing full of hope where there often seems to be no reason to have it (see Boyers and Lertora 11). Unlike Goytisolo, Dorfman does not choose destruction as his creative method. Instead, his work provides many visions of the same story, fragmenting the narrative line. In his opinion, "language is what allows us to reveal reality and to hide reality. In other words, language is full of lies and full of revelation" (qtd. in Wisenberg 199). Dorfman is far more of an idealist than either Goytisolo or Peri Rossi, but such idealism does not result in a belief in unmediated and untainted representation. The entire novel *The Last Song of Manuel Sendero* questions the validity of the tale of Manuel Sendero. Did he sing or didn't he? As the son of Sendero returns to his country and confronts his father's friend, Skinny, the latter denies both his story and his existence: "The first thing is that things didn't happen the way you said.... The fact is, young man, that Manuel Sendero never had a son. The only one he had, the one he and Doralisa were going to have, they killed" (21–22). The narrator in this part of the novel, the son of Sendero, an exile, is denied both his ability to represent history and his existence. But, as the novel begins, these problems of being and representation are counterbalanced by the children, who are listening to the tale of their great-grandfather, Manuel Sendero, from their grandfather, the son of Sendero, and are sure that they know the true story. They blurt out: "How do we know all this? Very simple. I found it out, we all did, from the mouth of my grandfather ... and he was *unquestionably* present in the middle of the story from beginning to end" (7, my emphasis). So truth and fabrication are at constant odds in Dorfman's work, even though he retains an aesthetics of hope, a hope in communication, that is far stronger than that found in Goytisolo and Peri Rossi.

Scholars of Cristina Peri Rossi's work have also chosen to categorize her work as either linguistically regional and structural or transcultural and poststructural. Mabel Moraña states in reference to *La nave de los locos:* "los personajes hablan idiomas diferentes, y la comunicación se limita a un intercambio de gestos o a un lenguaje que flota sin posibilidad de recepción" (208) ["the characters speak different languages, and communication is limited to an exchange of gestures or a language that floats without the possibility of reception"]. Jorgelina Corbatta, in contrast, refers to Peri Rossi's writing and argues that "la patria del escritor es la lengua materna" (169) ["the fatherland of the writer is the mother tongue"]. In her poem "Diálogo de exiliados" (Exile's Dialogue) from *Europa después de la lluvia* Peri Rossi's dialogue is between a Spanish-speaking exile remembering a conversation with someone and random expressions overheard in France. "Aquí la vida vuelve a comenzar / *(Je partis de Deauville un peu avant minuit).* / No serás torturado / No serás lanzado al mar / Otra ciudad" (42–43) ["Here life begins again / *(I left Deauville a little before midnight).* / You will not be tortured / You will not be thrown into the sea / Another city"]. Here language is not "floating without reception." It is meant to convey the anguish of life in a foreign land, where words and faces are unfamiliar, and where the notion of "dialogue" has been altered. Yet as the poem ends she writes: "Lentamente / te acostumbrarás a amar este otro mar / y entonces, quieras o no, comprenderás / Que nous venions cependant de naître" (44) ["Slowly / you will become accustomed to loving this other sea / and then, whether you like it or not, you will understand / That we have just however been born"]. So the exile's language has been changed and French no longer functions as background noise. In the last poem of the collection, "A los amigos que me recomiendan viajes" (To My Friends Who Recommend Travel to Me), Peri Rossi writes: "Hay tres cosas que quisiera decirte, / pero la segunda contradice la primera / y la tercera es un malentendido. / Preferible es el silencio" (97) ["There are three things that I wanted to say to you, / but the second contradicts the first / and the third is a misunderstanding. / Silence is preferable"]. Contradicting this statement, Peri Rossi opens her novel *La nave de los locos* with an epigraph from George Steiner: "Nada nos destruye más certeramente que el silencio de otro ser humano" ["Nothing destroys us more surely than the silence of another human being"]. So once again, the notion of language in Peri Rossi's work is slippery. At every instance she vacillates between a belief and a denial of representation and communication. Her work also displays the effects of regionalism and transculturation, as both are used to construct the complex linguistic identity of the exile.

As discussed above, the crisis of language is a constant element in exile texts and it plays a particularly significant role in the texts analyzed in this study. These texts trace territories as they attempt to narrate an experience in relation to geographical space. They cannot reproduce "the reality" of this history, but they can trace it, using language as their tool. At the same time that they outline the spatial and historical lines of their experience, they also strike out into new and unmapped territory, making marks in the margins. Now the borders of identity are blurred, not reinforced. Culture becomes a notion that avoids description and escapes location. Therefore, at the same time that these texts construct visible signs of a former identity characteristic of their national, political, and gendered origins, they also mark the spaces beyond those lines that now represent the instability and incommunicability of their experience and their identity.

The history of the multiple dictatorships that have plagued the Spanish-speaking world in this century demands that these authors approach their narration with a new sensitivity. The ability of these texts to communicate a certain degree of this experience is testimony to the connection between language, the self, and history. While that connection may radically alter from one moment to the next, the narrative strategy which ebbs and flows between affirming the writeable territory of experience and emphasizing the disjointed signs of the margins is the most critically pertinent example of exile writing after the postmodern turn.

The following sections of this chapter explore the dialectics of language in exile writing by focusing on three main tensions in the writing of Goytisolo, Dorfman, and Peri Rossi. The first deals with the problem of linguistic authority and the ties between authoritarianism and linguistic fixity. The second analyzes the multifarious functions of naming in these texts: names are alternatively absent, symbolic, and deconstructed. The third section addresses the tension between politics and play in the use of language. Understanding their competing and contradictory discursive efforts requires that we read the language of exile literature dialectically.

WHO IS THE AUTHOR(ITY)?

Does language represent reality? Must it be fragmented in order to avoid authoritarianism? Each of the writers included in this study has problems with the notion of authority and authorship. In part, this can be attributed to the exile's experience that language is treacherous and that "lo que era ya no es" (what was no longer is). According to Abigail Lee-Six, Goytisolo in *Juan sin tierra* tries to prove that the system of conventions in modern society is purely arbitrary (99). In her opinion, Goytisolo does this specifically by arguing that the "culo" (ass) replace the "cara" (face) as the central signifier for individual identity: "the *cara-culo contra-pied* highlights the arbitrary nature of social conventions; just as logical a case can be made for *culo* to stand as a dignified symbol of humankind as for *cara* to do so" (101). Nevertheless, while the cara/culo debate betrays the arbitrary nature of signs (reminding the reader of the work of Sausurre), by substituting one signifier for another, Goytisolo does not effectively displace meaning: he merely shifts it. This tactic is similar to the way in which Dorfman's novel constantly questions whether Manuel Sendero sang. In so doing, Dorfman does not question whether Sendero's story is important; he merely questions whether we need to be certain of all of the details in order to communicate history. In this way, the effects of dictatorship are exposed as the exile's writing tries to fragment the totalizing hold on language observed under authoritarianism. Peri Rossi writes in a short story: "De la guerra había surgido un sentimiento de seguridad para unos y un sentimiento de inseguridad para otros, y muchas cosas habían cambiado de signo" (*La tarde del dinosaurio* 84) ["From the war there had surged a sense of security for some and a sense of insecurity for others, and many other things had changed signs"]. For each of these writers the authoritative connection between signifier and signified must be challenged.

Additionally, these exiles are also influenced by the postmodern turn in discourse analysis. Poststructuralism, following the linguistic analysis of structuralism, focused attention on the way in which identity is constructed through language. In exile, these writers are only capable of countering the identities being forged in their nations through language, which accounts for the importance of theories of discourse in their work. The poststructuralists pay particular attention to the institutionalization of discourse as a signifying system that predefined identity. Moving away from the rigidity of semiotics, many poststructural theorists practiced "discourse theory." As Best and Kellner explain: "much postmodern theory follows discourse theory in assuming that it is language, signs, images, codes, and signifying systems which organize the psyche, society, and everyday life" (27). Foucault explained the shift in his work from archaeology to genealogy as a move made necessary after 1968: "What was missing from my work was the problem of a 'discursive regime,' the effects of power proper on the enunciative play. I confused it too much with systematicity, the theoretical form, or something like a paradigm" (qtd. in Dreyfus and Rabinow 104). He later focuses on the construction of power and knowledge in modern society (see *Discipline and Punish* and *The History of Sexuality*). Therefore, at the same time that studies of discourse and its connections to power and authority were becoming central to new critical inquiry, these writers were exiled from nations practicing censorship and propaganda. They are exiled from their ability to communicate "freely" in their language precisely at a time when such notions themselves are being questioned.

As described earlier in the introduction, many poststructural theorists have exalted the condition of exile as the prime opportunity to explore the connections between discourse and an absence of communication. Because exile is centered on a condition of absence and emasculation (loss of power), it immediately connects to issues of desire and lack, conjuring up the work of Lacan. Furthermore, Derrida in his article "Edmond Jabès and the Question of the Book" equates exile with writing: "We must be separated from life and communities, and must entrust ourselves to traces.... Absence attempts to produce itself in the book and is lost in being pronounced; it knows itself as disappearing and lost, and to this extent it is impenetrable" (68–69). Kristeva states, in reference to the work of Freud and Lacan: "castration is, in sum, the imaginary construction of a radical operation which constitutes the symbolic field and all beings inscribed therein" ("Women's" 198). For Kristeva, men and women's relationship to language is always a question of desire and lack (198). Inasmuch as these conditions are exacerbated by the experience of exile, where the exile's relationship to language is severed from native land and native tongue, these theories appear to transfer easily to the study of the literary language of exiles. Nevertheless, despite the exile's desires and lacks, Dorfman, Goytisolo, and Peri Rossi never abandon the hope that their writing may communicate their experience to others.

Dorfman and the Unsung Hero

Viudas, Dorfman's first novel in exile, begins with the problem of authorship and authority. The frame of the novel and the attempted use of the pseudonym already mark the text as an investigation into how to tell a story without being authoritative, while also wanting to reach a public living under authoritarianism. The author and the authoritarian are linked in their efforts to communicate, and Dorfman is aware of this dilemma from the onset of his work in exile. *Viudas* asks: Who has the authority to tell the story? Who is the author of the story? Who has the authority to alter history? And most importantly, which version will prevail? These questions continue to weigh heavily in his second exile novel, *The Last Song of Manuel Sendero*. As Dorfman explains: "I've always felt that the struggle against the dictatorship of the author upon the reader is one of the central questions in my work" (qtd. in Incledon 99).

Beyond the frame of the novel and the issue of the pseudonym, *Viudas* is a novel that, throughout the narrative, constantly questions the authority of communication. The novel's setting is a small village in Greece where all of the men have disappeared. One day, a dead body appears in a river and the central conflict revolves around who has the right, and the authority, to explain the existence and identity of this body. The body functions as a signified and the text embarks on a tale of war, where two sides fight for control of the signifier.

Sofía Angelos appears in the office of the Captain after hearing about the appearance of a body, before she has actually seen it. She comes to his office requesting the right to bury her father, Karoulos Mylonas, who has already been buried by the soldiers. They declare that the dead man is not her father—not even her relative (27). She hears them but does not pay attention: "El capitán se concentró en ella, para ver si reaccionaba ante estas palabras, pero era como si no contaran, como si ya las hubiera escuchado antes y ahora no tenía sentido perder el tiempo volviendo a atenderlas o siquiera darles una respuesta" (27) ["The captain scrutinized her to see how she would react, but it was as if she'd heard the words before and now it made no sense to waste time listening or responding to them"; 14]. Whose version is right? These are different discourses that do not intersect: what means father to her is a dead revolutionary to them. Her response finally is to reaffirm her authority to claim the body as her father: "¿Usted cree, capitán, que no voy a reconocer a mi propio padre?" (28) ["Do you think, Captain, that I can't recognize my own father?"; 15]. Dorfman then complicates the issue even further when the reader learns that the body found was totally unrecognizable.

Two weeks later, Sofía appears in the same office requesting the right to bury her husband, Michael Angelos, even though, once again, she has not even seen the cadaver: "No puede ser eso, primero porque el marido no está muerto, segundo porque nadie podría atreverse jamás a identificar a ciencia cierta ese cadáver, tercero, porque, en este caso como en el otro, no corresponden las edades" (49) ["Which is impossible, first of all because Michael Angelos isn't dead, second because nobody could ever positively identify a body in that state, and third because, in this case, as in the other, the ages don't match up"; 32]. The novel continues to stress the crisis of signification for those living under dictatorship. Sofía substitutes a body for her husband and feels peace: at least he can have a proper Christian burial. But the government wants scientific proof, even though the Captain admits that such proof is impossible. By focusing on the notion of disappeared bodies, Dorfman stresses the linguistic crisis that is a result of such atrocities.

Who has the right to decide if Sofía can claim this man as her husband? As Sofía and the government battle over the right to choose which signifier fits the body of the dead man, Dorfman's novel reveals the way in which history challenges the claims of poststructuralism: the sign is not freely arbitrary. Sofía is challenging the authorities, i.e., those who have the power to decide what this body signifies. In this case the instability of the sign is only disempowering for those who endeavor to challenge authority. Because it is not clear who or what the body signifies, it is even more difficult for the women to claim that they "know" the name of the dead man. The politics of signification are made clear by the appearance of the unnamed body. No matter who claims the right to name the body, the problem remains that a man has been brutally murdered. The issue of language is important but cannot overshadow the horrible fact that this town has lost every man capable of threatening the authoritarian government.

In the beginning of part five of the novel, another woman from the village, Katherina, goes to claim that the second body is actually her husband, thereby further complicating the question of who can name this body. As she speaks to the Captain, she undermines his authority by using his own rhetoric: "Capitán—dijo ella—yo soy una mujer. Debo suponer que un oficial del Ejército de la Nación no utilizará métodos violentos o un lenguaje bajo contra una mujer. Yo sólo ejerzo mis derechos. Y cuando yo me casé, juré ser leal a mi marido hasta que la muerte nos separara" (89) ["Captain, I am a woman. I would expect that an officer of the nation's army wouldn't use violent methods and foul language against a woman. I'm merely exercising my rights. When I married, I swore to be faithful to my husband until death us do part"; 61]. As in the case of The Mothers of the Plaza de Mayo in Argentina, who began to organize some years after the publication of this book, the women, because of the profound absence of men, are forced to take charge and rebel against authority. But the foundation for their arguments rests on their self-identification as mothers and wives. Even though the women attempt to challenge the patriarchal government, they do not employ radical feminist tactics nor do they challenge the patriarchal biases of language. Their actions stem from their roles as wives and mothers, which actually coincides with the rhetoric of the Captain, himself: "Las mujeres, en casa, o en la cama. Ahí señora es donde las mujeres deberían estar" (181) ["A woman's place is in the home. Or in bed. That's where women belong, madam"; 129]. The Captain believes that women should do nothing to endanger their families. Yet the women, following Sofía's lead, are acting on similar principles because they believe that claiming these dead bodies is the only way to protect the souls, through Christian burial, of their families.

Being and language are inextricably linked, as Benveniste has described. Nevertheless, through the disappearance of these men, their names have become detached from their beings. *Viudas* emphasizes that this crisis of language is also a crisis in identity. Who will identify these bodies? These men have been robbed of their existence—like the exile who cannot return or be read by the public in his or her homeland. The power to choose the signifier for the signified is not merely a rhetorical game; it is a matter of life or death. The women of the village challenge the authorities, but the Captain has more power. He will erase the conversations he has had with these women. He can even erase their existence as well, as he arrests Sofía and her grandson, Alexis: "Y esta conversación jamás existió. La borro así. No va a quedar ni su recuerdo porque ustedes, ustedes no cuentan para nada. Para nada, ¿entiende? Mire a lo que han llevado sus esfuerzos. Mire. A esto. Mire" (190) ["And this conversation, this conversation never took place. I'm erasing it like that. Nobody's going to remember it. Because you people, you people don't count. You don't count understand? Look at what your efforts have accomplished. Look at this. Look"; 136]. As the novel concludes, the women have gathered around yet another body. But this time there will be no talking. The Captain arrives at the beach with a large group of soldiers and proclaims: "Es hora de poner orden teniente. Proceda de una vez" (202) ["It's time to put things in order, Lieutenant. Proceed at once"; 145]. The reader never learns the outcome of the Captain's orders, but one can only assume that these women were massacred. Nonetheless, the open ending of the novel leaves the reader to ponder yet another question: Will the children of these women come to the captain and claim the authority to bury their disappeared loved ones? How will the battle over the signified end?

Salvador Oropesa has described *Viudas* as a modern novel, and he also describes it as manicheistic because it appeals, according to him, to the reader's emotions instead of to reason: "son los sentimientos, la parte no racional (debido al maniqueísmo), la que se moviliza para la causa de los derechos humanos y la justicia social" (65) ["it is feelings, the non-rational part (due to manicheism), that is mobilized to the cause of human rights and social justice"]. In Oropesa's opinion, the central conflict in *Viudas* is good versus evil, but as we have seen, the battle over the authority to name the dead bodies is far more intricate. Many women claim the same body as their kin. Moreover, Sofía, as the matriarch of her family, is equally as authoritative in her decisions as the captain. Many members of her family resent her making decisions on their behalf. In particular, Alexis, her grandson, feels that his father is still alive and does not want Sofía to sign his death certificate: "papá estaba vivo, abuela, y si ella lo proclamaba muerto, capaz de que lo mataran de verdad" (183) ["but papa was alive, grandma, and if she declared him dead, they might really kill him"; 131].

The Last Song of Manuel Sendero, according to Oropesa, is not allegorical like *Viudas*. "No es una alegoría como *Viudas*, ya que estas se caracterizan por no problematizar el referente" (63) ["It is not an allegory like *Widows*, given that they are characterized by not problematizing the referent"]. Instead, he states that in *The Last Song of Manuel Sendero* "el giro es radical. Como nos pronostica Derrida, no vamos a encontrar tranquilidad en su lectura" (65) ["the turn is radical. As Derrida forecasts, we are not going to find tranquility in reading"]. Contrary to Oropesa's assessment of Dorfman's literary project, I would not consider *Viudas* to be an allegorical, manicheistic novel with no concern for the status of the referent. In fact, in my opinion, the connection between the notions of "good" and "bad," "victim" and "authoritarian" are most definitely problematized in the novel. Moreover, while I agree with Oropesa that *The Last Song of Manuel Sendero* takes these issues and complicates them even further, I would dispute the use of Derrida's notion of *différance* as the backdrop for Dorfman's theory of writing in his second exile novel. In *The Last Song of Manuel Sendero* Dorfman does not abandon a literary message and a political project. In 1991, Dorfman explained the problem of language and politics as a persistent dilemma in his work: "I think that Pinochet is going to be a central issue weighing on our country for a long time.... [In *The Last Song of Manuel Sendero*], [h]e seeps into the language, contaminating it to the point that he becomes part of the dictionary" (qtd. in Incledon 96). Language, for Dorfman, is not divorced from the reality of Pinochet's dictatorship. Therefore Oropesa's quoting of Derrida where the poststructuralist calls for "a strategy without finality, What might be called blind tactics" (65) is misplaced when applied to the narrative of *The Last Song of Manuel Sendero*.

Similar to the frame that begins *Viudas*, *The Last Song of Manuel Sendero* begins with a disclaimer: "I am always suspicious of authors who, at the opening of their books, without flinching, separate fact from fiction in what is to follow. How can they be so sure?... Like myself, and so many characters in my novel, [David, the protagonist] is submerged in historical circumstances and hounded by political figures who, alas, are not the product of my imagination" (n.p.). Dorfman associates himself with his characters, connecting being and writing. Yet the connection does not, as Oropesa might have us believe, "tener su parelelo en la influencia que el estructuralismo transformacional—Barthes—tuvo en la neovangurdia" (68) ["have its parallel in the influence that transformational structuralism—Barthes—had on the neovanguard"]. Oropesa further states: "Una vez que la posibilidad telos político-religioso queda descartada,... nos movemos en el terreno de la contingencia" (68) ["As soon as the possibility of the political-religious telos is discarded... we move in the terrain of contingency"]. (It is noteworthy that Oropesa considers Goytisolo as a literary antecedent to the work of Dorfman, insofar as Goytisolo explores the problems of language, nation, and exile in his trilogy; 68–70.) And yet, even though Dorfman, in his disclaimer, begins his novel with a profound insecurity about authorship and the authority to tell history, he still writes a novel that attempts to give an alternative view of the connections between Chilean history and humanity's history of tyranny and resistance. What Oropesa misses in his analysis, then, is the fact that postmodern theories such as those of Barthes and Derrida influence the work of Dorfman but appear in his work with a twist, an adaptation. Poststructuralism complicates language and formally affects the structure of narrative in Dorfman's work, but Dorfman does not become an unquestioning disciple of these theories. His own experience makes such an apolitical approach to language impossible.

Adding to the disclaimer, Dorfman includes a variety of textual twists that undermine what appears to be the principal narrative line. First, the novel is divided into two parts: "Inside" and "Outside." The "Inside" is the story of Manuel Sendero, while the "Outside" refers to the exile of David from Chile. Nevertheless the "Inside" and the "Outside," while *supposedly* representing opposites, do not literally. The two tales are actually quite similar and parallel in many respects. Both tell of a terrible despot and resistance to him: one is Pinochet (Outside) and the other is the Caballero (Inside). Both tell of exile: David (Outside) and the son of Sendero (Inside). These two sections simultaneously question how it is possible to form a collective and find peace from tyranny, both ask how far you must compromise with power in order to defeat oppression, and both pose the dilemma of how much you can trust your comrades. One of the clearest connections between the "Inside" and the "Outside" occurs when David remembers speaking to his friends the night that Allende won the presidency of Chile: "Build the city inside yourselves, *compañeros*, if I can do it, you can do it, since you've had more practice and more patience, always remember it like it was tonight, tell it freely, syllable by syllable, *along the senderos, the pathways; explain it right away and in a voice that will travel as far as your great-children*, because tomorrow we are going to have to pay dearly for standing upright and for this walk we are taking" (148–49, my emphasis).

In addition to the linguistic trick where "Inside" is not opposite to "Outside," Dorfman complicates the narrative even further by including footnotes to the dialogue between David and Felipe which supposedly accompany a text used in a course 30,000 years later for Prehistoric Amerspanish III, "commenting on a text which is . . . of uncertain authorship and obscure national origin" (79). In another part of the novel, the tale of David and the Dragon Pinchot is also told 30,000 years after the dialogue between David and Felipe. Therefore the events of 1973 in Chile yield two distinct textual accounts which remain 30,000 years later as part of cultural history: one is the dialogue itself as it appears in a textbook and the other is the mythical tale of a hero who fights an evil Dragon Pinchot.

As the title reminds us, the central question of authority and authorship revolves around Manuel's last song. Did he sing or did he not? Did he refuse to sing and thereby condemn himself, his wife (Doralisa), and his unborn son to death? Manuel has a powerful voice. He is able to move those who hear him, like an author who is able to eloquently inspire his reader. Yet Manuel has gone mute. "He had tried to change the world with his song... and when the world, far from changing, had gotten worse, Manuel Sendero had fallen back on that extreme recourse of muteness, in order not to have to collaborate" (406). Eduardo believes that Manuel lost his voice because of his failure with a fellow comrade, Gringo. Manuel inspires Gringo to join him and then Gringo is killed. So according to Eduardo, Manuel loses his voice: "Because he wasn't prepared to continue the struggle, at least not with the politicians who had guided so many innocents—... to the slaughterhouse.... But he had not taken responsibility for his voice. Gringo wasn't the only one he had involved in this mess" (73). At least this is one version of the story.

Skinny provides another version: "He spoke of Manuel Sendero's last song, confirmed that he had heard it. It makes no difference that there aren't any proofs or traces left, he said" (10). In these lines Skinny rejects the importance of both scientific proof and Derridean traces. He also rejects the existence of the son of Sendero, who he claims matter-of-factly, was never born (22). Yet, the reader is supposedly reading the account of the son of Sendero's experiences as he himself has told them to his children and grandchildren. Moreover, the last song was supposed to be sung by Sendero to save his family's life.

There are more than two versions to this story, as Skinny explains: "People make up a lot, especially about Manuel Sendero" (20). In a scene where the son of Sendero narrates his encounter with the Caballero thirty years after "the question of the song," the son tells the children: "He could have sung. But he didn't, kids. I remember now that he didn't" (405). This revelation would then imply that the son never was born, and yet, the son is the one telling his story. The novel, by questioning the connections between existence and storytelling forces the reader to ask how history is preserved: What are the connections between language and life? How important is it for such stories to be factual? Moreover, given the multiple versions of Manuel's story, the novel asks how a story can be told in a way that is not authoritative and yet still manages to provide hope for the future. The story of Sendero is "ever-changing" yet it also manages to instill hope. Pamela, the girlfriend of the son of Sendero, uses the tale to inspire her and, significantly, she is the storyteller at the end of the novel who has passed the legend on to her children: "Pamela had repeated that legend like any other child, to give her strength when things were going badly and nobody understood her" (435).

Nevertheless, although Skinny, Pamela, and Papa Ramón believe that Manuel sang, "the world had not changed by Manuel's last song" (444). In this sense the novel grapples with the difficult and tenuous hope that an act of rebellion could succeed in transforming the world. Such a notion requires a sense of free will and a belief that the future is not pre-determined, but the novel refuses to promote such a notion with any sense of certainty. As Skinny puts it, "Exile is like being in an insane asylum. Everybody believes he's been in the Battle of Waterloo" (20). There can be no certainty about one's ability to remember the past and consequently there can be no certainty that one can tell stories that will affect the future. *The Last Song of Manuel Sendero* is a novel full of hope, full of dreams that Manuel Sendero's story will build a better future, "when pretty little men and pretty women are born who can't understand that there was once a time when such monsters were the only masters of the next to the last word" (412). The novel fights to have the last word, but undermines its success by making the "Last Epilogue" the "First Prologue," sending the novel on a circular path to find the "sendero" (path) which will end the cycles of tyranny.

Goytisolo and the Battle to Be Master of the Spanish Language

Questioning the interactions between language and authority is a central element of the narrative in Goytisolo's trilogy of exile. *Señas de identidad* begins the process, demonstrating the difference between Alvaro's memory of Spain and the official discourse of Spain's past. (We may recall, for instance, the last scene at the tourist site in Barcelona.) *Reivindicación del conde don Julián* continues to challenge the ties between language and power when the narrator attempts to re-narrate Spain's "origins" and fantasizes that such a re-narration is capable of overturning Franco and, most importantly, Francoist ideology, derived from the myth of the Catholic Kings. *Juan sin tierra* attempts to create a new cultural community for the narrator, specifically through the act of writing. Writing allows the narrator, who essentially remains isolated working in a small room, to construct a new past, present, and future for himself. As the novel ends, the last words appear in Arabic claiming that the narrator is now free, "on the other side" with his fellow pariahs, sharpening a knife. The knife, like the pen, is the weapon that the novel fantasizes will destroy the power over language and identity that has caused the narrator to suffer.

But there is another side to this story. As Edward Said has claimed: "Much of the exile's life is taken up with compensating for disorienting loss by creating a new world to rule.... The novel [according to Lukács]... exists because other worlds *may* exist, alternatives for bourgeois spectators, wanderers, exiles" ("Reflections" 363). Goytisolo's novels, progressively from *Señas de identidad* to *Juan sin tierra*, fantasize new worlds and new world orders. Goytisolo's obsession with the Spanish language and his efforts to attack what he considers to be the sterile prose of the Generation of '98 and of Franco's regime complement his narrative effort to exercise linguistic power as a response to his loss of power due to exile. His inability to change Spain from within makes his efforts at changing Spain from outside her national borders even more intense.

Nonetheless, the novels that comprise Goytisolo's trilogy of exile are not communicated transparently as confident literary attacks on Spain nor are they linear and complete narratives. For each moment of linguistic security and certainty there is a moment of fragmentation and instability that undermines the ease with which the linguistic battle is fought. We remember, for instance, that in the last scene of *Señas de identidad*, after the narrator has seemingly been successful in counteracting Franco's version of the past, the text immediately reverts to the "voices" of Spain which tell Alvaro to leave, that his birth was an error and that he never has belonged and never will belong in Spain. Similarly, in *Reivindicación del conde don Julián,* as the novel closes, the narrator's fantasy of a victorious attack on Spain is exposed as meaningless, because tomorrow the invasion will have to begin again. Each day brings no progress and the narrator's words lack sufficient authority to make a difference. Even

Juan sin tierra does not conclude with certain victory. While the narrator writes in Arabic and claims he is finally among his own—his writing has transformed his identity and he now has a new language—he is still sharpening a knife. He has not ended his battle. He is still struggling with Spain. He is not done writing.

In each of these texts there is a dialectic between success and failure to use language as an effective weapon to overthrow authority. Carlos Fuentes has referred to *Juan sin tierra* as a novel "in debt to everything it denies.... Goytisolo takes on his peculiar inheritance in order to wage war against it, and this is one of the secrets of his tortured and torturing prose, pure and impure at the same time" (72). Therefore, for every victory, there is a failure. For every instance of "unfettered" language there is a corresponding example of Goytisolo's obsession with Peninsular Spanish. However, critics have chosen to see only one side of these linguistic maneuverings. Abigail Lee-Six has written that as early as *Señas de identidad* the language of Goytisolo's narrator "breaks barriers" and demonstrates linguistic "non-fixity" (36). Severo Sarduy has argued that Goytisolo's language in *Juan sin tierra* is "deterritorialized" and that his narrators "systematically plunder" and "deconstruct" Spanish, leaving the reader to experience "deterritorialized signification" (106).

Once again, it is necessary to emphasize that Goytisolo is reacting, through his writing, to the usurpation of language practiced by Franco's regime. As he explains, under dictatorship, one cannot speak clearly and signifiers begin to refer to new signifieds, or else they cease to appear connected to any "reality whatsoever." To give one example, residential incarceration (house arrest), a common practice under Franco, which is exemplified in the character of Antonio in *Señas de identidad*, made "home" equal "prison": "libertad y prisión se confunden" (Goytisolo, "Review" 221–22) ["freedom and prison are confused"]. Antonio is even made to shave off his beard, changing his signs of identity (*Señas* 232).

In response to what Goytisolo perceives as Franco's control of language, each novel of the trilogy becomes increasingly concerned with the connections between power and language. Moreover, like Dorfman, Goytisolo's novels question the notion of the "author" as the "authority" to tell the story. In *Señas de identidad*, *Reivindicación del conde don Julián*, and *Juan sin tierra* the narrator speaks to himself and to the reader directly in the second person, immediately implicating the reader as author. This undermines the role of either an omniscient or a third person narrator. Benveniste describes the use of the second person singular as an emphasis on the connection between language and the self. Each instance of "tú," the second person familiar, holds the possibility of creating a new identity. Nevertheless, when Goytisolo uses "tú," such self-construction is constantly thwarted by the "voices" of *Señas de identidad* that have the last word and the greater authority, or by the isolated and solitary hallucinations of the narrator of *Reivindicación del conde don Julián*, whose dementia leaves him too weak to threaten the authorities in Spain.

Perhaps one of the best examples of Goytisolo's novelistic representation of the connections between language and authority is the scene from *Juan sin tierra* where a representative of "Peninsular Order," Colonel Vosk, confronts the narrator. Vosk attacks the narrator with a list of his novelistic errors, which he states must be changed:

"todos los críticos sinceros lo dicen : tu universo actual es monótono : los personajes son excéntricos, escasamente representativos : las situaciones que describes, inverosímiles y desorbitadas : créeme majo : tienes que cambiar" (271) ["all sincere critics say the same thing: your present universe is monotonous: the characters are eccentric, scarcely representative at all: the situations that you describe are wildly improbable: believe me, my boy: you must change"; 240]. For Vosk, the narrator's style is unacceptable, specifically because it challenges "pure" Peninsular Spanish through its "falta de rigor lingüístico [y] ... incesante erosión del idioma" (272) ["lack of linguistic rigor [and] ... continual erosion of his native tongue"; 240–41]. As this scene is narrated to us, we encounter both Vosk's "pure" and the narrator's "impure" Peninsular Spanish, which makes it difficult to assert that the novel's discourse is destroying Goytisolo's native language. In fact, it would be more apt to consider this scene as a demonstration of a linguistic battle, where neither side is a clear winner.

Some pages later the narrator is placed in a psychiatric ward where Vosk appears, once again, this time as the Doctor of the "Instituto de Normalización" (277) (Normalization Institute). Vosk tells the narrator that he will learn to change his terrible narrative ways: the Institute has successfully gotten most writers to destroy their manuscripts and repent (280). Vosk then tells the narrator that he must write according to the "norms" and that he must also engage in reproductive sex, thereby linking writing and identity. But the narrator writes and defeats Vosk at least in the "placer solitario de la escritura" (282) ["the solitary pleasure of writing"; 249]. Vosk is destroyed by the narrator's writing and converted into a slave to his literary master: "ahora no soy nada más que una voz : me ha reducido usted al murmullo de un vago e inidentificable discurso : ni voz mía siquiera, sino de usted, de mi amo" (290) ["I am nothing but a voice now: you have reduced me to the murmur of a vague and unidentifiable discourse: not even my voice, but yours, the voice of my master"; 256]. The narrator victimizes Vosk, and turns him into a linguistic entity, with no other existence outside of language. Most importantly, it is a language that the narrator controls.

The narrator, victorious, then reveals to the reader his theory of writing: "transformarla en discurso sin peripecia alguna : dinamitar la inveterada noción de personaje de hueso y carne ... indiferente de las amenazas expresas o tácitas del comisario-gendarme-aduanero disfrazado de crítico" (295) ["to transform it into a discourse without a trace of a plot: to explode the inveterate notion of the character of flesh and blood ... indifferent to the threats of the police commissioner-gendarme-customs officer disguised as critic"; 260]. The narrator then continues to fantasize that through writing he is able to change the world and increase his authority. The author is now the authority, and he will invoke a system which is anarchic and, consequently, liberating. The reader is told that only through the chaos of the signifier can there be freedom for the signified, or the self: "el fascinante caos emborrone la blancura del papel de una enigmática, liberadora proliferación de signos" (296) ["fascinating chaos scribbles an enigmatic, liberating proliferation of signs all over the whiteness of the page"; 260]. Such a liberating proliferation of signs is meant to lead to the "autonomía del objeto literario : estructura verbal con sus propias relaciones internas, lenguaje percibido en sí mismo y no como intercesor transparente de un mundo ajeno, exterior"

(296) ["the autonomy of the literary object: a verbal structure with its own unique relations of signs, a language perceived in and of itself and not as the transparent intercessor of an alien, outer world"; 261]. Nevertheless, even though the narrator finds such a vision of literature as utopic and liberating, the novel actually demonstrates that it is neither Vosk's nor the narrator's vision of literary discourse that motivates the narrative: it is the conflict between the two positions. In many ways, the text reveals that both positions are authoritative as they argue, albeit in different manners, that their vision of language's interaction with the external world is the *right* one.

When the novel ends it returns to a letter written by a slave owned by the narrator's ancestors in Cuba. The text reproduces the letter, again, while the narrator fantasizes that by including this text within the novel, he is able to repay the slave for the harm inflicted by his family. Such writing is the driving force behind his life: "da sentido a una vida (la tuya?) organizada (en función de ella) como un ininterrumpido proceso de ruptura y desprendimiento... saldada la deuda puedes vivir en paz" (297) ["give meaning to a life (yours?) organized (as a function of this letter) as an uninterrupted process of breaking off and breaking free... having paid a debt you owe, you may henceforth live in peace"; 262]. What is most interesting here is the shift in the narrator's theory of language from the preceding page. Not only does the narrator propose poststructuralism as the antidote for the structural realism of Vosk, he also makes a complete shift and argues that through testimonial, the testimonial of a slave, he is able to rectify his guilt over his family's past. This leads Goytisolo to wondering if such a thing is possible, then what is the connection between writing and the external world? Once again, Goytisolo complicates the issue of language and of authority. Can merely reproducing a letter and repenting absolve the descendent of the Master? Is the author enough of an authority to effect such change? The issue of authority, authors, and language remains elaborate throughout the trilogy.

Nevertheless, these complex literary tactics have led critics like Ilie to state: "Goytisolo reports that the word's failure to represent reality imposes an unexpected instability of perception. There ensues an experience of deepened estrangement that dislodges language from the world of shared external reality, an unmooring that also rescues language from history" ("Exolalia" 243). In a common example of poststructuralist practice, Ilie at one and the same time argues that Goytisolo's work language divorces language from external reality, while also rescuing "language from history." Goytisolo's literary discourse is full of dialectical contradictions. In general, though, these dialectics are overlooked and most critics describe these tensions as mutually exclusive binaries. Ilie hints at a discursive dialectic when he states that words "fail" to represent reality for Goytisolo at the same time that he "rescues language from history." Rather than stress the opposition between these two poles, it would seem more appropriate to stress the tensions and interpenetrations. Goytisolo's work alternatively strives to represent and to deconstruct. Moreover, he does neither totally, but constantly wavers between both poles.

Peri Rossi and the Desire for Authority

Peri Rossi's work, even before exile, focused a great deal of attention on the representational ability of language and on the connections between authorship and authority. In *Indicios pánicos* she includes an "advertencia" (warning) which precedes the text stating: "Todas las historias que componen este volumen son rigurosamente reales. Cualquier parecido o semejanza con personajes, episodios y obras literarias es meramente casual e involuntario" ["All of the stories that comprise this volume are rigorously real. Any similarity or likeness to characters, episodes or literary works is merely casual and involuntary"]. Yet, as one may guess, the text that follows is an elaborate combination of history and fiction. The warning serves to poke fun at the notion that literature's connection to history and history's connection to literature can be easily determined.

After exile, Cristina Peri Rossi's first published work was a collection of short stories entitled *La tarde del dinosaurio* (1980) (The Afternoon of the Dinosaur). In this collection, various stories have child protagonists who challenge the adults' authority to fix the meaning of language. Remember, for example, the case of Alicia from "La influencia de Edgar Allen Poe en la poesía de Raimundo Arias" who mistrusts the words used in Spain for fruits. In the story homonymous with the collection, a young boy has two fathers who each represent distinct relationships to authority and language: "su padre número dos era muy autoritario.... No como su padre número uno, que era mucho más amable y más suave" (83–84) ["his number two father was very authoritarian.... Not like his number one father, who was much nicer and more gentle"]. The boy faces the conflict of having two distinct types of fathers, but his most pressing dilemma is the sense that he is not in control of his own history, or his own story. "[N]o había podido elegir el año, ni la época, ni el país... antes de descolgarlo violentamente en éste" (88) ["He had not been able to select the year, the epoch or even the country... before being dropped into this one"]. Peri Rossi creates a character who, through his youth, is able to question things that adults accept. His two fathers have distinct roles to play in the dictatorial state; one is the winner and the other the loser, and each of them plays their role to perfection, unquestioningly. It is the son who asks the questions. The authoritarian father, "daba pocas explicaciones. No como su padre número uno... que vivía dando explicaciones de todo" (83–84) ["gave few explanations. Not like his number one father... who lived by explaining everything"].

Later, when the boy is asked to write an essay on "mis padres" ("my parents" or "my fathers"), he decides to write about the two men. When his teacher asks why he did not mention his mother he responds: "Entendí que sólo se refería a los hombres.... Es el problema de los plurales que engloban a ambos sexos.... El lenguaje es imperialista" (92) ["I understood that it only referred to men.... This is the problem of plurals that encompass both sexes.... Language is imperialist"]. The teacher angrily responds that he is too young to have such an opinion. But he replies that he has had no choice: "Antes de que tuviera uso del razón el lenguaje se había metido con él, imponiéndole sus leyes, obligándolo a llamar a las cosas de determinadas maneras, haciéndole creer que eran las únicas posibles" (94) ["Before he even had the use of reason, language had gotten into it with him, imposing its laws, obliging him to speak of things in determinate ways, making him believe that these were the only possibilities"]. Through the crisis of this boy, who is living in the Southern Cone under a dictatorship, Peri Rossi exposes the tension between authority and linguistic fixity. This child, like most of Peri Rossi's literary children, is extraordinarily precocious. Or, perhaps he is less repressed and less afraid than the adults that surround him, allowing him to voice questions the adults cannot face. "Hoy de mañana mamá llamó al médico y le dijo que nos encontraba muy preocupados por el lenguaje" (107) ["Today, in the morning, Mom called the doctor and told him that she found us very worried about language"]. His mother is afraid that he and his sister are obsessed with language because they spend hours playing with the dictionary and creating new words. By focusing on the way in which children react to the authority of language, Peri Rossi is able to threaten the hegemony of the signifier's tie to an authoritarian signified. When dictatorships determine what can exist and what words can be used to describe what is permitted to remain, the ties between language and authority become blatant.

By using the perspective of children, Peri Rossi also suggests the connections between language and repression and ties her discourse analysis to psychoanalysis. Her work has been clearly influenced by the work of Lacan. He appears in countless references throughout her work and she even uses one of his statements as an epigraph to her novel *Solitario de amor*. Nevertheless, the influence of Lacan does not push Peri Rossi to wholeheartedly adopt a poststructural linguistic position. Much in the same way that Slavoj Žižek reads Lacan, I would argue so does Peri Rossi. Despite Lacan's three categories of representation (the symbolic, the imaginary, and the real) many critics pass over the last and read Lacan as suggesting that there is nothing beyond language. Similar to the way that Masu'd Zavarzadeh draws a line between those postmodern thinkers who stem from the work of Nietzsche and fall into the ludic postmodern and those who are influenced by the teachings of Marx and advocate resistance postmodernism, Žižek argues that it is a mistake to read Lacan as a disciple of Nietzsche: "Lacan always insists on psycho-analysis as a truth experience: his thesis that truth is structured like a fiction has nothing to do with a post-structuralist reduction of the truth-dimension to a textual 'truth-effect'" (154). What is most significant for a study of Peri Rossi's exile literature is her use of Lacan's concept of "the lack" in representation. According to Žižek: "it is a signifier which introduces a void, an absence in the Real" (170). Language, then, desires to represent the Real, but knows that it lacks the possibility of complete success.

Language also is incapable of adequately representing identity. In the story "En la playa" (On the Beach), a young girl speaks to a couple of tourists on vacation. The adult woman tells the girl: "Parece que te importa mucho el lenguaje" (35) ["It seems that language is very important to you"]. As the couple attempts to find "a sign of her identity" she claims that her name is "Euuuuyllarre." "Eso no es un nombre. No significa nada" (37) ["That isn't a name. That doesn't mean anything"]. But unwilling to be controlled by the adults, the girl defiantly claims: "Significa lo que quiero que signifique" (37) ["It means what I want it to mean"] At the end of the story, the girl has convinced the adults to use her name and they have invited her stay with them. Yet we know that, once again, Peri Rossi is playing with the fantasy that the less repressed child may be able to challenge the ties between signifier and signified and consequently disrupt the authority of language. If she is able to define herself, then she is able to free herself of the linguistic power of the adults. If she is able to decide what a word refers to and convince others, then she can threaten the entire signifying system. The fantasy ending of "En la playa" contrasts greatly with the end of "La tarde del dinosaurio," where the little boy tells of his recurring nightmare of a dinosaur that emerges from the sea. He dreams that he wishes to stop it from hurting his loved ones, that he will "Apaciguarlo. Domesticarlo" (110) ["Pacify it. Domesticate it"]. But in the end of the dream, when the dinosaur emerges, he becomes terrified and screams for his father. Which father? The authoritarian or the intellectual? For the boy "papá" has a double meaning and within this linguistic confusion Peri Rossi emphasizes the desire and lack, which are inextricable elements of writing and linguistic expression.

Elia Kantaris has written about "The Politics of Desire" in *La nave de los locos,* Peri Rossi's first exile novel, which continues to investigate some of the same issues present in *La tarde del dinosaurio.* As he explains: "Words never allow themselves to be pinned down to a univocal or conventional meaning. . . . In the context of exile and alienation, all meanings become inherently terroristic" (260). Nevertheless, despite the terrorism of the signifier, Peri Rossi continues to narrate and attempts to provide an alternative discourse to that which reigns in her homeland. It is this motivation that constantly returns any discourse analysis of her work back to the category of the "real." Even if language cannot reach the "real," it can try.

The exile, removed from the linguistic battleground of her censured nation, has only the weapon of words. Equis, the exiled protagonist of *La nave de los locos,* loves to look at maps and remember countries that have long since been destroyed, or conquered. Memory and writing are weapons against absence and disappearance: "Igual que después de una larga dictadura, muerto el tirano o derrocado el régimen, de las ciudades desaparecen sus huellas más visibles (los nombres de las calles, los bustos, los monumentos)" (36) ["As after a long tyranny, the tyrant once dead and his rule broken, all visible traces disappear from the cities (street names, busts, monuments)"; 31]. The same lands remain, but their signifiers have been changed. For the exile, existence is even more precarious, given that he does not remain. The exile is absent and must fight to be remembered. Equis, unlike the child protagonists of *La tarde del dinosaurio,* is not confident about his ability to challenge the authority of the signifier. As an adult, he appears far more resigned to his inferior position in the power relations that govern linguistic meaning. He still rebels, though, reading "naughty" books on the bus. "A veces, Equis lee solamente para provocar" (69) ["There are times when Ecks reads on the bus simply to provoke"; 66]. He attempts to challenge authority by being authoritarian himself. He brings a large book and rests it on his neighboring passenger's arm, and his neighbor inevitably glances at the text.

> A este sistema de lectura a la fuerza, Equis lo llama su plan particular de alfabetización. . . . En épocas especialmente difíciles (cuando por ejemplo hay una serie de televisión muy exitosa que además se vende en fascículos o

> cuando el gobierno establece una censura muy rigorosa sobre los libros interesantes), ... [d]e inmediato aprovecha para recomendar muy seriamente, otros libros pornográficos, entre los cuales se encuentran las novelas de Salinger, los cuentos de Cortázar y las obras de Foucault. (69)
>
> Ecks describes this system of enforced reading as his literacy campaign.... During periods of greatest public deprivation (for example when some novelized soap opera is all the rage, or when the government of the day imposes its censorship on the more challenging books), ... taking advantage of the interest aroused, Ecks goes on to recommend other equally pornographic works by J.D. Salinger, Foucault, Cortázar. (67)

Equis is enacting a micro-struggle: abandoning the belief in the possibility of collective rebellion, he attempts to upset the system in minute ways. If one can change the reading material of the public, perhaps one can change the system that controls it. The only problem is that substituting one book over another does not help teach the public how to challenge the system themselves. In this case the authority comes from the exiled Equis, who, because of his marginal position, is unlikely to change the power relations of signification.

At times Equis reads Nabokov or *Tristram Shandy* on the bus and, on one particular occasion, his neighbor leans over and says that when she was young she was an anarchist, too. Equis replies: "El placer es el deseo" (70) ["Pleasure is desire"; 67]. Such an ambiguous response leads the reader to question the meaning behind his words. Of course, much of Peri Rossi's linguistic literary strategy is to include such phrases, leaving them open to multiple interpretations and thereby deflating her role as the master of the novel's meaning.

It is interesting to note that Goytisolo writes about "el placer solitario de la escritura" ["the solitary pleasure of writing"] and Peri Rossi states: "el placer es el deseo" ["pleasure is desire"]. Roland Barthes and his theories about the "pleasure of the text" have influenced both writers (see *The Pleasure of the Text*). Such pleasures become even more necessary for the self in exile, who feels even less involved in the external world. Nevertheless, in Barthes's terms these writers' work falls between the strategies of *plaisir* and *jouissance,* because they refuse to seek pleasure for pleasure's sake and are unable to break with their cultural context. The ending of the novel certainly suggests such an interpretation of Equis's desire. As an impotent man, a man without control of the signifier, Equis has a recurring dream. In this dream he is able to destroy the "King," the source of signification, the man who has been able to destroy countless suitors who have sought out his daughter because he has provided them with an enigma that they have not been able to answer correctly. But Equis does not answer the enigma with the response the King seeks. Rather he finds an answer that is so powerful that it actually destroys the King and turns him into a pathetic toy that dies as Equis watches with pleasure. This dream reveals the desire of Equis to have the authority to destroy the authoritative source of signification that controls all linguistic expression, particularly that found in countries ruled by patriarchal, authoritarian systems. What is most significant is that his answer to the enigma "¿Cuál es el tributo mayor, el homenaje que el hombre puede hacer a la mujer que ama?" (183) ["What is the greatest tribute and homage a man can give to the woman he loves?"; 188] is "su virilidad" (197) ["his virility"; 204]; he responds with an ambiguous answer, which is unambiguous in its threat to patriarchy. The ambiguity lies in whether he should forfeit his virility or whether both he and his lover should be virile. (Kantaris has also noted this reading of Equis's response; 262). Does the answer suggest the end of the phallic signifier or does it seek the equal distribution of the power to signify among all who use language?

It is precisely this linguistic ambiguity mixed with a clearly defined desire to overthrow authority that exemplifies Peri Rossi's position on language and authority. She refuses to fix the meaning of Equis's response, but she also refuses to write a novel that is disinterested in the ties between language and power relations in the "external world." She is the author of texts that struggle with the role of the author and of the author's role in subverting the authoritarian's desire to control the bond between signifier and signified.

Heroes, Masters, and Desire

In each of these writers' work in exile, the structure and style of their writing reveals their suspicions about authoritative discourse. Yet, such suspicions do not impede their interest in communicating their versions of history and their alternative visions of the expressive potential of language. What follows, then, is often a disguised strategy—paradoxical in nature and full of contradictions. Interestingly, all three writers have a noticeable lack of dialogue in their works and their novels are full of many voices and fragments. Where dialogue appears, it is altered. Goytisolo's narrator speaks to himself, or to the reader. In *The Last Song of Manuel Sendero,* the dialogue between David and Felipe is fragmented and interrupted. Peri Rossi's works have very little dialogue—most of the characters keep their thoughts to themselves. Perhaps the lack of traditional literary dialogue combined with the multiple voices is a key to the quandary these authors face as they write novels that argue against the authority of the signifying system.

It is interesting to note that Peri Rossi (*Indicios pánicos*), Dorfman (*The Last Song of Manuel Sendero*), and Goytisolo (*Reivindicación del conde don Julián*) include opening statements or quotations that reinforce the notion that there is a connection between their stories and history. Moreover, in the cases of Peri Rossi and Dorfman, it is also noteworthy that both pieces include a tone of humor and irony: Peri Rossi uses the phrase "*rigurosamente* reales" (*rigorously* real) and Dorfman states that, aside from the character of Carl Barks, every other character is "*absolutely* fictitious" (my emphasis). Goytisolo includes three opening epigraphs, two of which present the figure of Count Julian from different perspectives, and one, from the Marquis de Sade, which dreams of the perfect crime. The first two accounts are "historical" and the last is "literary," yet all three seem to only partially represent the story of Count Julian. In this way, all three writers play with the connections between fact and fiction. The following section comparatively analyzes the ways each author challenges linguistic authority through specific attention to the structure of their texts.

Dorfman's strategy includes recuperating a sense of hope through the use of heroic role models who can overshadow the monstrous figures of authority, be they Dragons or dictators. But in conjunction with his interest in challenging the authoritarian's official history, he problematizes his role as author. Beginning with *Viudas*, Dorfman set out to complicate the notion of narrative authority: he tried to use a pseudonym, but also called the novel his "son." The novel is stylistically complex as well. One part of the novel is missing, part ten, making it clear that the reader does not have a "total" text. Moreover the narrative voice shifts, undermining the idea that the narrator is the authority, i.e., the linguistic leader, of the text. In the first chapter, the narrative voice shifts from Fidelia to an omniscient narrator. In the second, Fidelia narrates in first person singular, but also narrates in first person plural, and later refers to herself in the third person (which she also does in chapter five, part viii). In chapter seven, part ii, as Alexis and Sofía are taken prisoner, the narrative is in the second person, placing the reader in the role of Alexis. Even the flow of sentences disrupts the traditional, consistent position of the narrator: "Él, Alexis, iba a sobrevivir. Me iba a la capital a encontrar a mi papá" (192) ["He, Alexis, was going to survive. I was going to the capital to find my father"; 137]. The text shifts from third to first person, suggesting the interaction between personal and collective history, and fragmenting the authority of the narrator. By using this complex strategy, Dorfman suggests that only through a multiplicity of perspectives can one appreciate history. Moreover, even if the story is not complete and seamless, it must be told. Despite the novel's ambiguous ending, the message of the story is still clear: we must struggle to remember those that die at the hands of authoritarians.

Dorfman continues to use the tactic of shifting the narrator's voice in *The Last Song of Manuel Sendero*. During a segment of omniscient narration, David's voice erupts in first person: "'Good idea,' I say" (112). As in *Viudas,* the end to the story is not clear and the "Last Epilogue" is the "First Prologue." In addition to these twists, Dorfman's second novel in exile is a significantly more complex narrative. There are the two narratives corresponding to "Inside" and "Outside." The "Outside" is further fragmented by the footnotes and the inclusion of the story line from the comic strip, which David is working on for Felipe. The comic strip, ostensibly a subtext to the dialogue between the two exiles, at times overshadows the dialogue and overtakes the narrative drive of the novel.

This type of stylistic challenge to the authority of the author is continued in *Máscaras,* where the novel is in three parts, each narrated by a different character. In the first part the narrator is speaking to a doctor who cannot hear him. "Pero ya que no me podrá escuchar, me voy a dar el gusto" (19) ["But since you can't hear a word I'm saying, I'll take my time"; 11]. In part, the narrator appears to be confessing, or giving a testimonial, yet it is clear that he does not expect to be heard by anyone. The second part begins with the narrative of Oriana, an amnesiac, who has taken refuge from two men trying to capture her and who is hiding with the narrator of the first part. Yet while the first narrator addresses himself to the Doctor and the Doctor addresses himself to the faceless man (in the third part), Oriana's audience appears vague, almost as though she is merely speaking to herself. In the end of the novel—which, not surprisingly, Dorfman names "Una especie de epílogo" ("A Sort of Epilogue")—the outcome of the story also remains unclear.

Despite these narrative maneuvers meant to undermine a totalizeable text, Dorfman's novels in exile repeatedly attack the power of authoritarianism. In *Viudas* the fight for the disappeared reveals the evils of dictatorship. In *The Last Song of Manuel Sendero* the different narrative lines all converge upon tales of evil men who are challenged, but not necessarily conquered, by benevolent heroes. And in *Máscaras* two men desire to increase their authority, one over a nation and the other over a woman. Each of Dorfman's exile novels progressively treats the problem of evil men and finally suggests through the representation of ambiguous heroes that evil is intrinsically connected to power. Like Dorfman, Goytisolo employs narrative devices that challenge his authority as author, but which still seek to leave a message for the reader. Goytisolo's texts challenge the authority of official Spanish by attempting to replace the discourse of the masters with a different one. As has been made clear, these narrative efforts are consistently exposed as unlikely threats to the hegemony of discourse. Yet, it remains noteworthy that Goytisolo's challenge to authoritarianism is itself full of sadistic fantasies of being the Master to the weak and humiliated Servant (remember, for instance, the scene with Vosk from *Juan sin tierra* or Mrs. Putifar from *Reivindicación del conde don Julián*).

One of the most striking features of Goytisolo's style is his use of a narrative in the second person in *Señas de identidad, Reivindicación del conde don Julián,* and *Juan sin tierra*. The texts are like autobiographical narrative, and yet they are also full of commands directed at the narrator himself, and/or the reader (in his two autobiographies Goytisolo intersperses his account of his life with italicized sections, which also use the "tú" form). Benveniste has commented on the use of the second person: "It is necessary and sufficient, that one envisage a *person* other than 'I' for the sign of 'you' to be assigned to that person.... What differentiates 'I' from 'you' is first of all the fact of being, in the case of 'I,' *internal* to the statement and external to 'you'" (201). Because, in Goytisolo's novels, the reader and the author become linked at the same time that their difference is highlighted, Benveniste's analysis of the use of the second person does not describe the manner in which it is employed in Goytisolo's novels. When Goytisolo writes for instance: "entre los tuyos al fin" (*Juan sin tierra* 87) ["among your own, at last"], the reader does not tend to identify with the phrase. In fact, the isolation and fantasy of the narrator seem to be emphasized in these cases. He speaks to the reader as though the reader were a reflection of the narrator, wishing that he were not alone, but emphasizing his solitude in the process. By shifting the meaning of "I" and "You," as Benveniste has analyzed them, Goytisolo questions the notion of an internal identity and an external one. Such a challenge is a significant threat to a system that requires that identity remain fixed and determinate.

In addition to Goytisolo's use of the second person, his second and third novels of the trilogy also include many random phrases with uncertain enunciators. He shifts the narrative voice of these phrases as well and intersperses them with phrases that seem like signs or graffiti: the reader supposes that these other discourses are those overheard or seen by the narrator. Nevertheless, their interruption serves to fragment the text, suggesting that, given that these words are all involuntarily filtered through the mind of the narrator, individual identity is itself a linguistic conundrum. It is also significant that in the second and third novels of the trilogy, Goytisolo abandons the sentence and its punctuation. Most ideas are separated by a colon that has a space on either side of it, instead of only having a space following it. Goytisolo had begun to experiment with punctuation in *Señas de identidad* but still had a narrative style primarily controlled by traditional punctuation. This abandonment of the traditional structure of the sentence is a further attack on the hegemony of a structured and fixed symbolic system of meaning. Nevertheless, despite Goytisolo's alternative style, his narrators still desire to be linguistic masters. Only now the rules will be different; the standardized practices of hegemonic discourse will be replaced.

Peri Rossi's writing in exile does not demonstrate the same desire for mastery and heroism that can be observed in the work of Goytisolo and Dorfman. Her poetry, short stories, and novel represent many distinct literary approaches to the issue of linguistic determination. Focusing on her novel, *La nave de los locos,* many of those approaches converge. The words "El viaje" ("The Journey") are contained in the titles of twenty-one of the chapters in the novel. This repetition of "el viaje" within different contexts and referring to different characters manages to unsettle the word from any fixed meaning. In each case "el viaje" refers to alienation and marginality, but each chapter approaches this topic from a different perspective. So the word "viaje" does not float free of signification, nor is it fixed. Intercalated between these chapters are eleven segments that describe the tapestry seen by Equis in Gerona on one of his travels. There are also fragments of the diary of Eve, which respond to the story described in the tapestry. In addition, footnotes, lists, and other textual fragments complicate reading the novel as a totalizeable and complete narrative. Even the tapestry itself, which is meant to be the mirror of unity and stylistic perfection, is not complete because at the end of the novel we are told that three months, "enero, noviembre, diciembre" (January, November, December) and two rivers are missing. The months represent the winter months, and are also relayed to us out of order, indicating that the tapestry itself imposes a false order that requires the suppression of certain elements of history.

Lucía Invernizzi, commenting on the fragmented style of the narrative maintains that "Sin embargo, la lectura percibe que toda esa multiplicidad y fragmentarismo se integran en una unidad" (31) ["Nevertheless, the reading suggests that all of this multiplicity and fragmentarism is integrated into a whole"]. She argues that the fragments and the tapestry do not challenge the novel's unity but actually contribute to the "whole." I would suggest, instead, that the novel critiques the idea of a perfect and complete structure through irony—"lo que admiramos en la obra...es una estructura; una estructura tan perfecta y geométrica, tan verificable" (21) ["what one admires in the work...is this structure—a structure so symmetrical, so dependable"; 14]. Such language in its hyperbole cannot be interpreted as a sign of the textual poetics of the novel.

Like Dorfman and Goytisolo, it appears that Peri Rossi also narrates a fragmented text as a response to her desire to thwart the authority of official discourse and its effects on cultural production. When Morris is asked to fill out a form at a publishing house in order to submit his manuscript for consideration, he is asked to summarize in ten lines the content of the book; he writes: "Manual práctico para extraviarse de la ciudad. Manual de circulación.... Mi obra trata de todo.... O sea: del todo minimizado" (128) ["Practical instruction on how to get lost in the city. Traffic regulations.... The work deals with everything.... That is, the whole in its infinitesimal particles"; 129]. This description of Morris's book could aptly describe the narrative of all three of the writers analyzed in this chapter. Each of these writers write fragmented, yet meticulously structured, texts that indicate the uneasy way in which these authors combine a fragmented critique of authority and a politicized, total narrative project aimed at changing the basis of authoritarianism.

WHAT'S IN A NAME?

> *No escribo sobre las cosas sino sobre el nombre de las cosas.*
>
> *I don't write about things, but rather about the names of things.*—Peri Rossi

It is remarkable that Dorfman, Goytisolo, and Peri Rossi all narrate texts with many unnamed characters. The issues that they confront regarding language and authority are highlighted by their refusal to name, to signify, and fix with a word the identity of their characters. The connections between language and identity are further questioned as proper names cease to be the central signifier for the self. Why this lack of names? How can these texts refuse to name and still communicate? Not naming characters seems to run counter to theories of language that advocate that only through a linguistic challenge can official discourse be disrupted. Can one challenge through an absence of signs? Kristeva in her article "About Chinese Women" discusses the important relationship between the names in a family's lineage and history. She argues that "The symbolic order functions in our monotheistic society by means of a *system of kinship* that involves transmission of the name of the father... and a *system of speech* that involves an increasingly logical, simple, positive and 'scientific' form of communication" (151). Such a linguistic system, she asserts, prohibits women from being producers of signification. To challenge this order, women must recognize that "an ostensible masculine, paternal identification... is necessary in order to have a voice in politics and history" (156). bell hooks has argued that "Moving from silence into speech is for the oppressed, the colonized, the exploited, and those who stand and struggle side by side, a gesture of defiance that heals, that makes new life, and new growth possible. It is that act of speech, of 'talking back' that is no mere gesture of empty words" (340). Nevertheless, these writers, while trying to challenge official discourse, opt, at times, to avoid signification altogether. How can they expect to provide alternatives through silence? What could account for such a convergence in their literary projects?

Perhaps a clue to this practice on the part of these writers lies in their literary predecessors. The exiled writers of the Spanish Civil War wrote many autobiographical narratives in a realist style, testifying to their experience fighting against Franco. Goytisolo's generation began to seek new ways of narrating the experience of dictatorship. As Michael Ugarte has commented: "What sets Goytisolo's exilic search apart from that of most Spanish writers who left during or immediately after the war (with the possible exception of Cernuda) is not only the self-conscious nature of his search but its attention to language" (*Shifting* 194). Goytisolo's experience of living under Franco and suffering censorship also contributes to his disbelief in the representational possibilities of language. In Goytisolo's trilogy of exile many characters remain unnamed. In *Señas de identidad,* the protagonist is Alvaro, yet the "voices" which haunt him are not connected to any particular people. In *Reivindicación del conde don Julián* the narrator is never named, as is also the case in *Juan sin tierra*. Such a project may appear to mirror the convictions of Deleuze and Guattari, who, in their article "What Is a Minor Literature," call for "an asignifying, *intensive use* of language. Here again, there no longer is any subject of utterance nor subject of statement" (22). Yet in *Reivindicación del conde don Julián* the narrator states: "idioma mirífico del Poeta, vehículo necesario de la traición, hermosa lengua tuya" (70) ["the marvelous language of the Poet, the linguistic vehicle most appropriate for treason, your beautiful native tongue"; 56]. Language cannot be destroyed because it is necessary for revenge. Moreover, for revenge to be possible, the narrator must have a signified object of his revenge.

Kessel Schwartz has argued that in *Reivindicación del conde don Julián* Goytisolo is unable to destroy the bonds of language (157), but that he successfully betrays Spain and destroys her language in *Juan sin tierra* (171). Nevertheless, both texts contain a dialectic between using language as a weapon and attempting to free language from any bond to the external world. This paradoxical linguistic approach is revealed in the following lines from *Reivindicación del conde don Julián:*

> palabra liberada de secular servidumbre : ilusión realista del pájaro que entra en el cuadro y picotea a las uvas : palabra-transparente, palabra-reflejo, testimonio ruinoso yerto e inexpresivo : cementerio de coches, oxidada hecatombe en las orillas de la gran ciudad : guadalajara verbal que ensucia y no abona, deyección maloliente e inútil : discursos, programas, plataformas, sonoras mentiras : palabras simples para sentimientos simples : las tuyas Julián en qué lenguaje forjarlas? : palabra extrema de pasión extrema. (125)

> the Word freed after centuries of bondage: the illusion of the bird who flies into the canvas to peck at the painted grapes: language-as-transparency, language-as-reflection, witness that is worthless, sound and fury, signifying nothing: a wrecking yard, rusting junk on the outskirts of a great city: a verbal Guadalajara, a river of excrement that befouls without fertilization, stinking, a useless garbage, speeches, programs, platforms, lies couched in lofty language: simple words for simple feelings: your, Julian: in what language can they be cast?: the extreme language of extreme passion. (104–05)

It is Goytisolo's extreme passion for language that exposes his desire to be Master and author, capable of extreme acts of destruction. His narrator is uncertain of which language to use to forge his revenge, but such uncertainty does not lead him to abandon his project. Such linguistic uncertainty cannot be read as an apolitical practice of linguistic poststructuralism.

The case of writers exiled from Latin America is distinct from that of the Spaniards in large part due to the problems of language and identity that are part of the post-colonial condition. Naming has an extremely important history in Latin American writing. Even as early as the colonial period writers grappled with the problem of naming. The Spanish language seemed inadequate to describe the Latin American region. What names would be used for flora and fauna that did not exist in Spain? Centuries later, the writers of the boom used naming as a means to reclaim conquered territory. Semiotics and the theories of the structuralists were integral to the literary project of creating an autochthonous language. The figures of Ariel and Calibán from Shakespeare's *Tempest* have grown to exemplify the debate over language in Latin America. In 1971 Roberto Fernández Retamar wrote *Calibán* as a reaction to José Enrique Rodó's *Ariel* (1900). (For a detailed analysis of the Ariel/Calibán debate see José David Saldivar's *The Dialectics of Our America*.) "The School of Caliban" included third world, postcolonial writers, like George Lamming and Aimé Césaire, who advocated the notion that to sever the ties with colonial imperialism, it was necessary to focus on the ramifications of using the language of the colonizer. Fernández Retamar suggests that Calibán should become the symbol of Latin America, a symbol exemplified by Calibán's exclamation that, having been forced to speak the language of his conquerors, his only recourse is to use that language to curse them.

The legacy of Calibán is part of the reason why language is a complex issue for writers like Dorfman and Peri Rossi, who cannot advocate First-World versions of poststructuralism because of their experience that language is always tied to relations of power that have real consequences in the external world. These writers employ a different approach to language from those associated with the boom. In agreement with Angel Rama's theories of transculturation, the boom authors considered writers to be an important part of the process of renaming Latin American history through an autochthonous literary language (*Transculturación* 43). This type of literary confidence is no longer possible for Dorfman and Peri Rossi. The influence of such postmodern theories of language on Dorfman's writing is made clear in the following interview, where he states that exile has had positive effects on his writing: "I turned the distance into language. I was able to look at some of the terrors and give them names" (qtd. in Incledon 96). Yet, as his texts show, naming has become a problem for him—a problem that demonstrates a crisis of representation and a crisis in linguistic confidence.

Beginning with *Viudas* and the unnamed bodies of the dead men that appear in the town's river, Dorfman's work investigates the crisis of naming under authoritarianism. The bodies are unnamed and yet Sofía, whose name is not revealed to the reader until page 83, wants to bury her father with his *name:* "Lo voy a enterrar con su nombre, con todas las letras del nombre que él me dio" (33) ["I'm going to bury him with a priest and with his name. With all the letters of the name he gave me"; 18]. Yet, it is not clear that this body-signified can be represented by the name-signifier of her father. Dorfman continues to complicate these issues in *The Last Song of Manuel Sendero* when the son of Sendero is never named. "Grandfather had no name. He'd had no baptism, religious or pagan. Nobody had received him with a couple of syllables so he'd know when to answer, when to obey commands, or when to declare himself guilty" (342). The lack of name for this character allows Dorfman to pursue the notion that those without names are not ruled by the symbolic order. Yet, as the novel makes explicit, the nameless son is incapable of threatening the system, if the system is unable to recognize him.

In Dorfman's third novel in exile, *Máscaras,* the protagonist remains nameless throughout the text. He is also faceless. In contrast with the emphasis on sound, song, and voice in *The Last Song of Manuel Sendero,* in *Máscaras* Dorfman focuses on the eyes and the image. The protagonist explains: "No es tan despreciable vivir solamente para darle de comer a los ojos, doctor.... [S]oy absolutamente incapaz de olvidar un rostro.... Nadie puede disfrazarse.... No vivimos en el siglo de los sonidos.... El sonido es un triste acompañante de segunda categoría" (25–26) ["There's nothing wrong in living for the nourishment of our eyes, Doctor.... I am absolutely incapable of forgetting a face.... Nobody can slip on a disguise that I won't see through. ...This is not the century of sounds.... Sounds are like maids: they travel second class"; 17–18]. Names have less value in this bleak world: "Todo nombre —...no es más que un triste conjunto de sonidos" (67) ["Any name —... which is no more than a sad jumble of sounds"; 60]. To a certain degree *Máscaras* can be read as a black vision counterbalancing the hopeful possibilities of *The Last Song of Manuel Sendero.* Oriana, the amnesiac woman, is unable to remember her past but travels from house to house collecting the memories of those who are about to die. "Mientras en algún rincón de esa ciudad a la que yo no puedo llegar, mi mamá y todas las madres del mundo se mueren sin nadie que les escuche su canción" (125) ["While in some corner of this city where I cannot walk, my mother and all the mothers of the universe are dying without anybody to listen to their song"; 121]. Those who sing in this novel are not heard at all. Throughout the text no one uses their real name, and those who attempt resistance are hunted. Oriana has been given a false name because she cannot remember hers. Even the setting of the novel remains nameless.

Cristina Peri Rossi also refuses to name the settings of her novel, *La nave de los locos.* For example: "En sus conversaciones y apuntes de viaje, Equis omite deliberadamente el nombre de ésta y de otras ciudades, con el evidente propósito de no herir susceptibilidades: caro precio pagaron Dante y Virgilio, por no ser complacientes, sin tener en cuenta ejemplos más modernos" (37) ["In his conversation and travel notes Ecks deliberately avoids naming the city of A and other cities, apparently to escape offending anybody's susceptibilities. Virgil and Dante, to give only two examples, paid dear for their lack of discretion on this point"; 32]. In this way, Peri Rossi's refusal to name these sites is a clear reaction to her experience as an exiled writer who mistrusts the ties between signifier and signified and also has experienced the fear that naming can lead to persecution. It is the authoritarians who name: "Cuidado... me parece que con el cambio de gobierno, los nombres de las calles se han modificado" (119) ["Remember... that the names of streets have changed since the last government"; 120]. Hugo J. Verani has commented on this feature of Peri Rossi's novel, stating: "Se omite deliberadamente toda cronología y espacio reconocible: la novela se desarrolla en la isla de M, en las ciudades de A o B, en Trampa, Pueblo de Dios, o Gran Ombligo. El lector se ve obligado a relacionar los sucesos a situaciones concretas de su propia experiencia" (82) ["Every chronology or recognizable space is omitted: the novel takes place in the island of M, in the cities of A or B, in Trick, Town of God, or the Great Navel. The reader is obligated to relate the events to concrete situations from their own experience"]. Consequently, by not naming, Peri Rossi widens the realm of representational possibilities for her text while simultaneously reflecting her particular experience as an exiled writer.

The protagonist of the novel is practically nameless: "Me llamo Equis.... Por circunstancias especiales, que tienen más que ver con la marcha del mundo que con mis propios deseos, desde hace años viajo de un lugar a otro, sin rumbo fijo" (78) ["My name is Ecks.... Due to special circumstances that have more to do with the way the world turns than with my personal wishes, I have traveled from one place to another without any firm direction"; 76]. Yet as Verani has noted, Equis's name, in its absence, signifies a great deal: "El protagonista se llama Equis—la Equis de ex, exilio, extranjero, extraño, excentricidad" (81) ["The protagonist is named Ecks, the Ecks of ex, exile, *extranjero* [stranger], *extraño* [strange], eccentric"]. Equis, though, reinforces the notion that his name is not of great relevance: "En cuanto a los nombres, Equis piensa que en general son irrelevantes, igual que el sexo, aunque en ambos casos, hay gente que se esfuerza para merecerlos" (25–26) ["Ecks thought that names were irrelevant, as was gender, although in both cases people did their best to live up to them"; 19]. Agreeing with him, his friend, Graciela, states upon meeting him: "Si quieres, puedes llamarme Graciela, dado que hay que dirigirse a las cosas y a la gente por un nombre" (87) ["If you like, you can call me Graciela, given our necessity to refer to people and objects by name"; 86].

Both Dorfman and Goytisolo also play with the fixity of names: Julián's name is not clear, as exemplified in one of the opening quotes: "Los historiadores musulmanes llaman casi siempre Ulyan y que probablemente se llamara Julián o quizás, Urbano, Ulbán, o Bulian" ["Moslem historians almost always refer to as Ulyan, though his real name was probably Julian, or perhaps Urban or Ulbán or Bulian"]. The name used for the protagonist of *Señas de identidad* reappears in *Reivindicación del conde don Julián* but refers this time to a typical Spaniard who is a lawyer in Morocco: Don Alvaro Peranzules. Later the narrator echoes the uncertainty of Julián's name, "Ulyan, Urbano, o Julián" (Ulyan, Urbano, or Julian) emphasizing that some signifieds have multiple signifiers and other signifiers can represent multiple signifieds. At the end of the novel, the name "Alvaro" reappears, but this time it refers to a small boy who has fallen victim to the narrator's fantasy of being Julián. In the narrator's fantasy, Julián rapes Alvaro, telling him that it is either him or his mother. The name "Alvaro" comes to refer to quite distinct personalities (the narrator of *Señas de identidad*, a traditional

Castilian lawyer, and a young boy who is a victim of the pedophilic desires of Count Julian in *Reivindicación del conde don Julián*), thereby aiding Goytisolo in his attack on the rigidity of peninsular rhetoric.

In *The Last Song of Manuel Sendero* David is asked by Felipe to change the name of one of the cartoon characters in the strip they are working on from Carl Barks, who really did illustrate for Walt Disney, to Carl Starks. Yet the change of name is insignificant, because the name still represents the same thing. Similarly, in *Máscaras* the narrator constantly changes the doctor's name: "Marivelli, o como quiera que llame" (11) ["Mavirelli, or whatever your name is"; 3]. It is noteworthy that Dorfman changed the name in the translation; the change emphasizes my point that the signifier may shift but its signified remains constant. He is alternately named Marvirelli, Maravelli, Mentirelli, Moronevi, Mearelli, etc. (Salvador Oropesa has analyzed each distinct variation of the doctor's name; 86). The narrator changes the doctor's name according to his wishes, attempting to challenge the connection between political power and linguistic power. In this small way, by renaming him again and again, the narrator attempts to threaten his identity. Yet, as the novel ends, it is not clear whether the protagonist was able to effectively challenge the doctor's power. Oropesa reads these name shifts as the deconstruction of the connection between name and referent and as a sign of Dorfman's practice of Lyotard's theory of the "differend." Oropesa states: "De aquí se puede deducir que la violencia verbal y la física se ponen en esta novela en el mismo plano" (90) ["From this one can deduce that verbal and physical violence are put on the same plane in this novel"]. Yet, I would argue that we must read these shifts in name as attempts to reveal that linguistic non-fixity does not lead to an equation between language and the physical world. In fact, the name shifts reveal that an unnamed or a multiply-named character can still retain a coherent identity, one which may be read as a challenge to the historical relations of power and its need for linguistic control.

In addition to refusing to name characters and to pointing to the irrelevance of names by shifting them or by simply naming a protagonist "X," all three writers also include figures of evil who receive names which are general or non-specific. Dorfman's Lieutenant (*Viudas*) is like the Caballero (*The Last Song*) who is like the Doctor (*Máscaras*). Goytisolo's figures, while not evil, per se, represent those elements of Spanish society which must be destroyed: the "voces" of *Señas de identidad,* the lawyer, Alvaro Peranzules, who represents "el hombre carpetovetónico" (the Spain-obsessed man), "un caballero cristiano" (Christian gentleman), i.e., the perfect Spanish gentleman, and Coronel Vosk, who reappears throughout *Juan sin tierra* in various authoritarian roles. In *La nave de los locos,* Peri Rossi's male figures of evil are represented primarily by the King, who controls language through the enigma.

Beyond the generic/general names that are used to represent evil male figures, these writers also use names with great symbolic meaning. In Dorfman's *Viudas* the matriarch is named Sofía, for wisdom, and her last name is Angelous (angelic/messenger), the priest is named Father Gabriel (Messenger), the orderly is Emmanuel (God with us), and Fidelia (Faithful), the granddaughter of Sofía, is the trustworthy narrator of much of the novel. Goytisolo in both of the last two novels of his trilogy uses historically symbolic names like that of Count Julian, Tarik (the Muslim Soldier), Lawrence of Arabia, Ibn Turmeda, and Reverend Père de Foucauld (these last three form the triumvirate of pariahs with which the narrator associates). The best example of symbolic naming in Cristina Peri Rossi's exile writing is the character of Percival, the young, precocious boy with whom Morris falls in love. When they first meet, Percival waits before disclosing his name: "El niño parecía estudiar muy atentamente el aspecto de Morris, antes de realizar un acto de confianza como es entregar el nombre" (139) ["Carefully the boy examined the stranger once more before entrusting him with something so important as his name"; 142]. He then states: "Me llamo Percival.... La gente cree que los nombres no tienen ninguna importancia, por eso lo preguntan enseguida. Pero nombrar las cosas es apoderarse un poco de ellas... Percival fue un caballero muy famoso" (139) ["I am called Percival. People always ask one's name because they think that names are of little importance. But to name something is to some extent to own it.... Percival was a famous knight"; 142]. Percival believes that names are very important as well as powerful, which contrasts with Equis's and Graciela's position that names are irrelevant. Elsewhere, Peri Rossi stresses the political importance of names in her poem "Relación de tripulantes que participaron en el naufragio" (Relation of Crew Members Who Participated in the Shipwreck) from the collection *Descripción de un naufragio*, where she writes "me vienen a la memoria ardida / como olas a bordo / los nombres de los compañeros muertos—desaparecidos / en travesía de mares y de países / lanzados a la noche" (96) ["they come to my burning memory / like waves over the side / the names of *compañeros* dead—disappeared / crossing seas and countries / launched into the night"]. Here she makes the issue of naming an important political crisis, one that the exiled writer must face.

The problem of naming takes many distinct forms in the work of Goytisolo, Dorfman, and Peri Rossi. Their main characters lack names, names are repeated, the same character changes names, and names are important symbols. Nevertheless, such similarities should not overshadow the differences in their projects. Goytisolo's approach to naming is tied to his desire for mastery and his will to destroy Peninsular Spanish. Dorfman continues to have a clear political project aimed at overthrowing the evil sources of power responsible for human suffering. Peri Rossi's project is less specific in designating the object of attack. She, like Goytisolo and Dorfman, also wants to challenge official discourse by changing the order of symbolic signification. But the object of her attack is more broadly defined and, unlike the work of Goytisolo and Dorfman, she does not suggest a clearly defined alternative to the system she is challenging. She wants to defy the established linguistic categories that define gender by undermining the authority of a "phallic" signifying system. What is most significant is that, as exiles, these writers find it necessary to approach the issue of naming from a variety of perspectives.

POSTMODERNISM AND THE CRISIS OF LANGUAGE: POLITICS OR PLAY?

> *Language is a river and the word an oar for a voyage without destination and without rescue.*
>
> —Augusto Roa Bastos

Although Dorfman, Goytisolo, and Peri Rossi narrate unnamed characters, their works communicate. This communication is possible because these writers have reacted specifically to the historical conditions that forced them to work in exile. The fragmentation and linguistic games in their texts do not lead to a plurality of meaning where each version has equal value. The use of language in these texts never loses sight of its object of desire and, despite narrative fragmentation, each writer privileges a particular version of the story. Moreover, each version has a political project: in each case these writers are attempting to use language as a weapon of defense against the extinction of their existence and of their history. Recall, for instance, Peri Rossi's use of Steiner as an epigraph to *La nave de los locos* calling for expression over silence, or Dorfman's emphasis on storytelling in *The Last Song of Manuel Sendero*, or Goytisolo's passionate need to rewrite history and deconstruct Western values in *Reivindicación del conde don Julián* and *Juan sin tierra* respectively. Another constant in these texts has been a continuous questioning of a systematic approach to such political projects, a questioning that has served to shatter any firm political grounding for their arguments.

Julia Kristeva suggests in "About Chinese Women" that the solution to such linguistic dilemmas is a form of speech which "is a constant alternation between time and its 'truth', identity and its loss, history and that which produces it: that which remains outside the sign beyond time. An impossible dialectic of two terms, a permanent alteration: never the one without the other" (156). In these lines Kristeva suggests that it is only through such a dialectical process of writing that texts can be political without resorting to authoritarianism and patriarchy. Kristeva, often considered a poststructuralist and occasionally writing pieces that clearly support a playful poststructural position, in the above lines articulates a position more appropriately described as resistance postmodern because of its political goals. She advocates resistance, and resistance to a clearly defined opponent. This approach differs from that articulated by Derrida in "Structure, Sign, and Play," where he states:

> Turned toward the lost or impossible presence of the absent origin, this structuralist thematic of broken immediacy is therefore the saddened, *negative*, nostalgic, guilty, Rousseauistic side of the thinking of play whose other side would be the Nietzschean *affirmation,* that is the joyous affirmation of the play of the word and of the innocence of becoming, the affirmation of a world of signs without fault, without truth, and without origin which is offered to an active interpretation.... There are thus two interpretations of interpretation, of structure, of sign, of play. The one seeks to decipher, dreams of decip-

hering a truth or an origin which escapes play and the order of the sign, and which lives the necessity of interpretation as an exile. The other, which is no longer turned toward the origin, affirms play and tries to pass beyond man and humanism, the name of man being the name of that being who, throughout the history of metaphysics or of ontotheology—in other words, throughout his entire history—has dreamed of full presence, the reassuring foundation, the origin and the end of play. (292)

Derrida, disclaiming the symbolic exile's search for interpretation, concludes that such an act is empty of linguistic play and seeks the unmediated discovery of an origin. Yet Goytisolo, Dorfman, and Peri Rossi attempt to interpret history through an exchange between linguistic play and linguistic interpretation.

In their play with language, Goytisolo, Dorfman, and Peri Rossi all parody the act of writing. Such parodies are self-indictments that refer to their relative safety in exile and their guilt about avoiding the "real" political battles being waged in their homelands. Nevertheless, it is important to recognize the limits of such parodies; they do not suggest that these writers have embraced ludic postmodern positions. Language is a source of power, and ridiculing its power demonstrates its limitations. Goytisolo's protagonist from *Reivindicación del conde don Julián* believes that he can challenge the Spanish literary canon by squashing bugs between the pages of these books in the Moroccan library. In *Juan sin tierra* the character of Vosk is a parody of the sterile approach to literature, which Goytisolo considers to reign in his homeland. When his narrator fantasizes that he has conquered Vosk, Vosk asserts: "LA NOVELA ES EL REFLEJO OBJETIVO DE LA REALIDAD SOCIO-HISTORICA. / ABAJO LOS MITOS OCULTATIVOS! / LAS OBSESIONES DEL ESCRITOR MISTIFICAN. / NO A LAS EXPERIENCIAS FORMALES Y ONIRICAS! / EL REALISMO ES LA CUMBRE DEL ARTE" (255) ["THE NOVEL IS THE OBJECTIVE REFLECTION OF SOCIOHISTORICAL REALITY. / DOWN WITH MYTHS THAT HIDE THE TRUTH! / THE WRITER'S SUBJECTIVE OBSESSIONS ARE A MYSTIFICATION. / NO TO FORMALIST AND ONEIRIC EXPERIMENTS! / REALISM IS THE ACME OF THE CROWNING GLORY OF ART"; 225]. In contrast to Vosk's ideals, the narrator is in favor of texts which are "mera expresión enajenada, a menudo esquizofrénica, de obsesiones y complejos personales que, en lugar de ser reflejo objetivo del mundo, postulan tan sólo el intento de liberación, desesperado y parcial, de una mentalidad enferma" (250) ["merely the deranged, frequently schizophrenic, expression of personal obsessions and complexes, which, rather than being an objective reflection of the world, represent nothing more than a desperate and incomplete attempt at liberation on the part of a sick mentality"; 220]. Through these two opposing positions on the role of literature, Goytisolo parodies both approaches and consequently parodies his work itself.

The best example of Dorfman's parody of literary endeavors appears in the footnotes to the dialogue between David and Felipe in *The Last Song of Manuel Sendero*. Here he critiques the act of interpreting texts and thereby questions the notion that literature can provoke readings that are both relevant and meaningful. Commenting on the difficulty of using the fragments of the dialogue as the basis for a study of ancient history, the authors of the footnotes remark: "to have to reconstruct an entire epoch of human effort by means of these fragments can be compared to the task which would face an extraterrestrial visitor from a superior civilization attempting to recreate our entire present culture by examining a kitchen recipe" (79). Dorfman pokes fun at the notion that literature can ever adequately represent history and he also parodies literary scholars, historians, etc., who attempt to interpret such texts as insights into the human condition. In the footnotes we learn that there are two main schools of thought dominating the theoretical scene 30,000 years after Pinochet's coup. The first is the Historical School, which seeks to read this text as realistic testimonial, and the second is the Abolitionist School, which sees the text as pure fantasy and argues that the dialogue should cease to be read in universities (81). This breakdown seems quite similar to the debate between advocates of identity politics, who support the testimonial genre, versus poststructuralists, who approach the entire world as text without any connection to an external "reality." What is most significant is that Dorfman's work is caught between advocating both schools of thought and also recognizing their limitations. We know that the text these critics are commenting on is both a combination of testimonial and fantasy. Dorfman plays with the idea that these critics are still at odds so many years later. Is there any point to entering into the debate at all?

Referring to *La nave de los locos,* Verani explains that the heterogeneous narrative produces a polyphonic discourse that reveals a ludic attitude (88). Perhaps the scene that best parodies the act of writing occurs during Morris's visit to the publishing house. He has to fill out a form describing his book and is constantly boggled by the specific and limiting questions he is expected to answer. In particular he is uncertain about the genre of his text: "No sé muy bien si mi libro es una novela corta, un cuento largo o un ensayo narrativo. Para decirlo en otros términos: me parece que se trata de una obra. Con algunos fragmentos poéticos, para ser más precisos, dentro del carácter épico del conjunto" (127) ["I don't know whether my work is a short novel, a long story or a narrative essay. It is a piece of prose, with some poetic fragments, to be exact, perhaps an epic"; 128]. Peri Rossi appears to be describing her own novel here, parodying the act of writing such a complex text and believing that it will be accepted by a large publishing house. Textual ambiguity is unacceptable in the business/editorial world, the secretary explains, and Morris must choose the genre of his work. He responds: "Me parece una triste, lamentable simplificación de la realidad.... Desde antiguo la épica y la lírica se han combinado, igual que la mimesis y la fantasía" (127) ["This seems to me a lamentable simplification.... Epic and poetry have merged from time immemorial as have realism and fantasy"; 128]. Peri Rossi recognizes that literature requires readers, and literature that is difficult to categorize and that also desires to challenge the central sources of signification in society is in a tenuous, perhaps ridiculous, position.

Recognizing the potentially ludicrous nature of their literary projects does not imply that these authors necessarily support the linguistic theories of ludic poststructuralism. Their language games are signs of the interaction between play and politics because they narrate a historical moment that has grown out of the crisis of modernity and out of theories of poststructuralism. Nevertheless, it is their consistent return to history and politics that marks their games as games which are not just for play but also for power over the ability to signify an alternative version of cultural life.

Each of these writers continues to link writing with existence: to be is (not) to be. Dorfman emphasizes that a fragmented story and an impartial representation are not the problem. The problem occurs when the writer has no hope of linguistic agency. As an author he is committed to the belief that he must write and that writing is his only weapon against the dominant ideologies attempting to control cultural identity. The son of Sendero's main concern is not "that his story was a partial reconstruction, depending on the accounts of the other fetuses.... No, it was the fear that someone... would say: it wasn't his voice Manuel Sendero lost, it was his hope; that they would say that, and he would have no answer for them" (49). In this way, Dorfman's writing confronts the exiled writer's problems with agency. Language and identity are linked. Through his writing Dorfman demonstrates the need to believe that linguistic battles can be won and that the oppressed can willfully challenge those that attempt to define the confines of human existence.

Unlike Dorfman, Goytisolo links language and identity primarily at the personal level. Language and the self intersect through the metaphor of writing as masturbation and sexual pleasure. Stephanie Sieburth states that in *Reivindicación del conde don Julián* "Language is inseparable from sex in the narrator's discourse" (165). In *Juan sin tierra* the equation between sex and writing becomes blatant. The narrator explains his literary desires: "el inveterado, improductivo acto de empuñar la pluma y escurrir su filiforme secreción genitiva según las pulsiones de tu voluntad" (209) ["the inveterate, unproductive act of clutching the pen and letting its filiform generative secretion flow in accordance with the impulses of your will"; 185]. But these sexual acts are not for mere pleasure; they also have grander goals. Writing is the only possible means of redemption from the sins of "our fathers." The novel constantly repeats the phrase "basta un simple trazo de pluma" (50, 85, 96, 215) ["a mere trace of the pen is sufficient"]. Writing is the means by which the narrator becomes liberated from the pre-defined identity that Spanish society has imposed upon him. Realist literature that attempts to have an unmediated connection to the world is equated with reproductive sex, which gives the narrator no pleasure, and condemns him to suffer. There is no pleasure in such writing (263). Only his pen/penis is capable of achieving his "desvío moral y artístico, social, religioso, sexual" (298) ["moral, artistic, social, religious, sexual deviation"; 263]. His writing, then, is not without political ramifications. If the narrator can liberate himself through writing, then he is capable of using language as a weapon against all of the evils of Western civilization. In the end, writing, for the exiled author, is the ultimate battleground. Goytisolo wonders whether a subversive story can be told. Can the literary text be a source of liberation? Uncertain of the answer, he writes, and, in his own way, he hopes.

The bond between language and being also emblematizes the crisis of representation in Cristina Peri Rossi's work. Equis, a constant dreamer, dreams about the theater: "No es raro que los hombres que han inventado el teatro como un simulacro de la vida, a su vez tengan pesadillas con el teatro, multiplicando así el juego de espejos:

sueño que represento y en la representación a veces estoy dormido" (173) ["I imagine that, if the theatre is a representation of life, theatrical nightmares are images of images, twice removed from reality: I sometimes dream that I am acting and in my role I am often asleep"; 177]. Is literature a mirage of power, where many mirrors play with the text's ability to represent? Are the producers of literature merely characters in their own works, characters "asleep" and incapable of any agency? These dilemmas plague the texts produced by Peri Rossi in exile. Nevertheless, she never abandons a sense of optimism. Every text, "por el mero hecho de existir" (by the mere fact of existing), has the potential to create a change in power relations. The self needs communication. La nave de los locos narrates the tale of a girl from the Midwest who commits suicide in New York after spending eight hours with a sign reading: "Me siento muy sola, por favor, hable usted conmigo" (70) ["I'm very lonely. Please, someone talk to me"; 67]. Why is this story in the novel? The suicide, silencing, and extermination of this life must not be forgotten, just as the disappeared and exiled must be remembered. Only through a belief in language's ability to represent the self and vice versa, can the exiled writer narrate in a way that challenges official discourse.

Language is the triumph and the limit for these writers. It represents their potential to create change and reveals the ways in which such endeavors fall short of their goals. Most importantly, though, language is never left on the plane of ubiquitous relativism. Such a state is not possible for writers who have borne witness to the results of authoritarian discourse. Returning to this chapter's play on the famous words of Hamlet, I would like to cite the words of Julio Cortázar:

> Polonius says of Hamlet: "There is a method in his madness." And he's right, because by applying his method of madness, Hamlet triumphs in the end. He triumphs as a madman. A sane person would never have been able to bring down the despotic system which was choking Denmark. His own life and the lives of Ofelia and Laertes are the terrible price of that madness, but Hamlet does away with his father's assassins, with power based on terror and lies, with the junta of his time. There is method in that madness, and an example we can learn from. Let us invent rather than accept the labels we wear. Let us define ourselves by opposing the predictable, the conventional. (18)

Following this line of reasoning, the practice in these writers' work of focusing on the crisis "to be is not to be" is not a futile exercise in rhetorical games. It is, perhaps, the only viable alternative to the official discourses that these writers are challenging. So *there is method in this madness*: there is a coherent linguistic strategy employed by these writers, despite paradoxes, oppositions, and complexities. For these writers the representation of human existence through language is a problem, but it is a problem they must address. As Slavoj Žižek explains:

> symbolic representation always distorts the subject, . . . it is always a displacement, a failure. . . . The subject tries to articulate itself in a signifying representation; the representation fails; instead of a richness we have a lack, and this void opened by the failure *is* the subject of the signifier. To put it

paradoxically: the subject of the signifier is a retroactive effect of the failure of its own representation; that is why the failure of representation is the only way to represent it adequately. (175)

Therefore, while the ability to "perfectly" represent the subject might be a failure, the result of the narrative project might not. Or rather, through the representation of the gaps between the communicability of language and the experience of exile and alienation the narrative effectively presents the crisis as a problem which escapes facile resolution: this can be noted by the untotalizable narratives of these writers, which at the same time display totalizing impulses. They endeavor to present the complete realm of linguistic interactions that occur within society and they engage in such practices through fragmentation, silence, and exaggeration. Consequently, the representation of "representation" as a crisis is the only way to depict the dilemmas facing these writers as they struggle with the fragile connections between language and life.

CHAPTER SIX
Lost in Space: The Geography of Exile

> *It is easy to say: My homeland is where I was born. But you have returned to the place of your birth and found nothing. What does this mean? It is easy to say: My homeland is the land where I shall die. But you can die anywhere. Possibly you will die on the border between two countries.*
> —Mahmoud Darwish (qtd. in Ammiel Alcalay's *After Jews and Arabs*)

A frequent theme in science fiction is that of the lost community unable to return to its original home. The spaceship-wrecked, although they are dreaming of return, must learn to create an alternative "home." For instance, the television series *Lost in Space* revolved around the travails of a family on a space mission that, due to faulty technology, was unable to return home. The extraterrestrial home that the Robinson family created seemed to function fairly well; and this appeased concerns over the integrity of the traditional family that plagued U.S. society during the 1960s. Nevertheless, this recurrent theme in science fiction of a group cut off from its territory and forced to encounter a new land and survive within it has taken many variations over the years as different social fears have mirrored changes in the social and economic construction of society. Like science fiction, much exile literature has also been obsessed with similar issues and these obsessions reflect changing trends in social organization. Perhaps the main difference between these two forms of cultural production is that in science fiction the element of technology is always a central issue: it is either a threat or the means by which the group will survive, will have hope of return, etc. Science fiction is also, always, spatially fantastic: the spaces in which the stories occur are extraordinary and bizarre. What makes this reference to science fiction relevant in the case of the texts studied here is that exiled writers in the latter part of the twentieth century were also affected deeply by changes in technology and spatial relations, particularly with regard to the increasing internationalization of capitalist modes of production. Therefore, technology and its connection to space are issues that affect the construction of an alternative cultural community in the work of Goytisolo, Dorfman, and Peri Rossi—all of whom see technology largely as a threat to the survival of marginalized populations whose spaces of cultural existence are greatly diminishing.

In the latter part of the twentieth century, technological innovations occur at an ever-increasing rate, resulting in a corresponding shift in economic relations as well as social-spatial relations. Doreen Massey explains in her article "A Place Called Home" that "[t]he internationalization of capital is a process with old roots, but in recent decades it has increased in intensity and scope and changed in its nature.... The most recent, quite newly emerging, form of spatial structure is that of the 'global corporation'" (3–4). Massey traces the connections between social-spatial relations and economic modes of production and argues that "each geographical place in the world is being realigned in relation to new global realities" (6). The question, then, is, how does such a shift influence the creation of a cultural community in the writings of exiles? How does transnational capitalism affect the exile's notion of home? Where is home for the exile who has left a nation governed by an authoritarian system influenced by the internationalization of capital? How does the exile reconcile nationalism and transnationalism? Further, how does the exiled writer represent the conflict between these two spatial visions of culture? What is most significant about the work of Goytisolo, Dorfman, and Peri Rossi, is that, faced with the choice between two cultural theories which appear to represent polar opposites, they choose to represent the dialectics and intersections between these positions rather than favoring only one view.

As in the case of these writers' representations of nation, language, and time, the spaces of their work are extremely complex. For Goytisolo, the best example of a complex textual space is *Juan sin tierra,* where the reader travels to many lands and many eras through the imagination of a narrator confined in a room. Dorfman's *The Last Song of Manuel Sendero* is spatially complicated by the distinction between "Inside" and "Outside"—spatial referents that do not refer strictly to space but rather to the distinction between timeless myth and historical fiction. In the case of Peri Rossi's *La nave de los locos* there is a tension between the metaphor that the marginalized are confined to the closed quarters of a ship and the metaphor that all outcasts and marginalized people are a part of every aspect of modern society, dialectically connected to the global condition of capitalist production as it is linked to phalogocentrism. In each writer's work the space of exile is both a condition of confinement and of limitless movement. I would argue that, as these writers negotiate the complexities of their condition, they construct versions of cultural identity which are "lost in space," neither wholly national nor transnational, not completely territorialized nor deterritorialized.

In cultural theory, the notion that both the national and the transnational may be used to describe the spatial relationship one has to the world has been highly contested. Edward Said states: "Because exile, unlike nationalism, is fundamentally a discontinuous state of being, exiles are cut off from their roots, their land, their past.... Exiles feel, therefore, an urgent need to reconstitute their broken lives, usually by choosing to see themselves as part of a triumphant ideology or a restored people" ("Reflections" 360). He argues further that the condition of exile free of this "triumphant ideology," i.e., nationalist sentiment, is "virtually" impossible. Is that really so? Is it not possible that exiles may see such ideology as inherently deceptive and false—

desiring it and yet compelled to deny those desires? Aijaz Ahmad sees no room for compromise on this issue either. He states that certain literary theories from the 1960s onward have posed the questions of empire, colony, nation, migrancy, post-coloniality "first under the insignia of certain varieties of Third-Worldist nationalism and then, more recently and in more obviously poststructuralist ways, *against* the categories of nation and nationalism" (3). Not only does Ahmad see the intersection of these two notions as impossible, he believes that any argument that integrates a notion of nationalism and a simultaneous rejection of it is not only suspect, but outright foolish. "The two moments—politically, for and against nationalism; theoretically, Third-Worldism and poststructuralism—remain discrete and epiphenomenal, even though the more outlandish of the poststructuralists have tried to combine them" (36). We may read this statement as a potential critique of the work of the writers analyzed in this study, or more to the point, of my reading of these authors. Yet it seems that the fundamental difference between the work of Goytisolo, Dorfman, and Peri Rossi and that of Homi Bhabha, Edward Said, and other subjects of Ahmad's attack, is that the writers studied here are acutely aware of the contradiction and implausibility of fusing these two political impulses, yet they consistently feel impelled to repeat the same narrative gestures.

These writers are caught between two contradictory visions of cultural identity and, consequently, two seemingly incompatible political positions. For instance, Xavier Albó in "Our Identity Starting from Pluralism at the Base" argues in favor of the connection between nationalism and a precisely defined political project: "What remains clear in all of this, however, is that nationalism involves seeking a primordial identity that the group feels to be above other loyalties and from which it is prepared to fight. For the same reason, nation, in and of itself, implies some kind of political project" (23). He argues that nationalism implies political goals. The exile, expelled from a nation and interested in the future of that nation, cannot avoid nationalist sentiment. However, insofar as poststructuralist and postmodern theories influence these writers, they are also loath to advocate any type of totalizing systemic change, a method associated with nationalist ideology. Like the proponents of Deleuze and Guattari's schizoanalysis and rhizomatics, these writers are also interested in the liberating possibilities of an existence which is able to destroy all rigid aspects of identity, including those of nationality (see Best and Kellner 88–89). The paradoxical situation, though, is that they are at one and the same time attempting to establish the roots, or the grounding, of a political struggle while also suggesting that any type of struggle truly capable of liberation must avoid any fixed, i.e., authoritarian, ideological base.

Goytisolo, Dorfman, and Peri Rossi each create metaphorical constructions of a nation that expose the tension between nationalism and transnationalism in their visions of a cultural community. Moreover, "nation" as a concept, in each case, also shifts from a notion that specifically refers to spatial boundaries. The nation-state is not the only type of nation these writers describe: their definition of the term enjoys a much looser structure. In fact, "nation" for them, is a closer approximation to the word's etymology, which derives from the Latin *natio-*, birth, and does not refer specifically to a territorial base. Their metaphors for the nation might also be thought of in terms of the Greek *ethnos*, which is the contemporary term used for nation in the Greek language and is also the etymological root of the term "ethnic," thereby reflecting primarily the cultural connections between a group of people. Many marginalized groups wishing to construct alternative cultural communities regardless of spatial boundaries have utilized such a less restricted usage of the term "nation." We need think only of the Jewish people, of the Nation of Islam, and even of such pop cultural referents as TV Nation, to recognize that the term "nation" as it has been rigidly used in much cultural theory actually has a much broader application. One that, most importantly, does not imply that the concept refers to strict geographical borders.

Nevertheless, as exiles, these writers' notion of nation is also spatially determined. We recall the significance for Alvaro in *Señas de identidad* of returning to Spain to die, or the angry exiled narrator of *Reivindicación del conde don Julián,* who is obsessed with observing the border of Spain from his vantage point in Tangiers as he dreams of invading his homeland. In *The Last Song of Manuel Sendero* the footnotes to the dialogue of David and Felipe represent distinct interpretations of the dialogue, which is being studied 30,000 years later. The text tells us that "the only matter upon which there is virtual unanimity among the critics is that the most obsessive, recurrent, one might say, annoying theme is the quest for permits to leave and enter countries" (79). Visas and passports are very real aspects of the exile's life and they underline the fact that geographical territories are not merely imaginary symbols, but powerful signs of the containment of one's free will to move. Cristina Peri Rossi has a story entitled "Aeropuertos" ("Airports") in her collection *El museo de los esfuerzos inútiles.* The story describes the space of the airport as a unique construct which holds many possibilities for the exile: "Otros aman los aeropuertos porque les gusta sentirse suspendidos entre una ciudad y otra, entre un horario y otro diferente, la sensación de no haber partido aún, ni haber llegado tampoco. Algunos, quedándose, sueñan que pueden escapar" (104) ["Other people love airports because they enjoy feeling suspended between one city and another, between one time zone and another, that ongoing sensation of having neither left nor arrived. Some of those who stay behind dream of escaping"; 87]. The airport, then, comes to symbolize the way station between entrance to and expulsion from a nation-state, where the exile waits floating between departure and arrival, and, in the meanwhile, creates an alternative national space which is the airport itself.

In this way, the nation becomes less a spatial referent and more of a cultural referent in the work of these writers. For each writer the "nation" is the space of commonality for struggle, which is, at times, geographically specific and at others is not. Even so, each alternative nation is also the source of oppression; it represses difference and emphasizes commonality. The alternative nations narrated by these authors, taken alone, do not adequately represent their theory of cultural identity. In addition to their metaphorical alternative nations, these writers also represent the effects of transnationalism on the condition of exile, and they attempt to represent the intricate ways in which nationalism and transnationalism are necessary facets of the experience of exile in the latter part of the twentieth century. The following analysis will demonstrate the paradoxical manner in which these writers incorporate these contradictory strategies of representing the individual's relationship to a concept of the nation. The exile's dialectic of space turns on the location of cultural communities and the ways that these communities alternate between dependence and independence on the nation-state. Each writer focuses on a spatial metaphor that facilitates an investigation into the ways that communities are constructed and in each case such communities are shown to be both comforting and confining.

JUAN GOYTISOLO: THE HOME

Doreen Massey in her article "A Place Called Home" points out: "The link between place and culture, it is argued, is being ruptured" (5). This link is purportedly vanishing due to the effects of globalization on the world's economy. She goes on to state that these changes have lead to "much talk of postmodern geographies of fragmentation, depthlessness and instantaneity" (7). By looking at the work of exiled writers who produced novels during the dawn of transnational capitalism, the connections between place and culture can be investigated. For instance, Juan Goytisolo's protagonists cross borders incessantly as they search for a proper solution to their pain. Yet such geographic flights resolve nothing: the presence of Spain in the narrators' identities persists throughout the course of each novel.

The work of Goytisolo in exile demonstrates a great interest in the connections between the concept of home and of nation. Goytisolo's trilogy progressively deals with this theme as each novel constructs alternative nations that are increasingly metaphorical. In *Señas de identidad* the protagonist returns home to die and desires, through the will of his memory, to construct an alternative vision of Spain, which can challenge the one being promoted by Francoist ideology. In *Reivindicación del conde don Julián* the protagonist fantasizes about re-claiming his home after successfully invading his homeland with the help of a Muslim army. Following his novels of returning to home, and re-claiming home, *Juan sin tierra* is a novel about reinventing home by constructing an extra-national community of pariahs. His last novel of the trilogy emphasizes the symbolic "home" of the homeless and social misfits, cast away by the requirements of a rigid and conservative world. As the novel ends, the protagonist joyously pronounces that he has joined the "other" side and is free of the ties that bind him to his Spanish past. Yet the same character is waiting and sharpening a knife, indicating that he is not free of his connections to his Spanish homeland. It is this conflict that best symbolizes Goytisolo's approach to the problem of the nation for the exiled writer. Yet, scholars of his work often downplay the contradictions in his theories of cultural identity. Michael Ugarte writes in *Shifting Ground* about "the protagonist of *Juan sin tierra,* a landless being, in this case a writer [who] wander[s] from place to place and from text to text" (208). The protagonist of *Juan sin tierra* fantasizes about a landless state, hence the title of the novel. Nonetheless, as we recall that the text is actually written in the confines of a small room and is fed only by the narrator's peripatetic imagination, the immobility and territorialization of the narrator are then placed in direct contrast with the textual deterritorialization of his narrative accounts.

Therefore, the notion of the homeland as a symbolic referent for the nation enjoys contrasting descriptions throughout Goytisolo's trilogy, where *Juan sin tierra* exemplifies the most extreme form of the dialectic that the nation is at once fixed and geographical and also free-floating and incessantly transformable. The theme of the nation as homeland is first made clear through the connections between the nation and a mother/stepmother figure. This connection is made manifest in the second novel of his trilogy of exile, *Reivindicación del conde don Julián*. The narrator begins saying good-bye to his stepmother: "adiós, Madrastra inmunda, país de siervos y señores ... y tú pueblo que los soportas" (15) ["farewell, foul Stepmother, land of masters and slaves and ... you people that support them"; 7]. He is in exile, viewing his country from the shores of Tangiers and planning for his return. Later the stepson reveals his *modus operandi*. He will dedicate himself to destroying the hold of his symbolic stepmother as he struggles to reconstruct his home. Each morning he begins the day by "comprobando una vez más ... que la invectiva no te desahoga : que la Madrastra sigue allí, agazapada, inmóvil : que la devastadora invasión no se ha producido : llamas, dolores, guerras, muertes, asolamientos, fieros males : paciencia la hora llegará" (16) ["realizing once again ... that invective doesn't ease your pain: that the Stepmother is still there, lying in wait, motionless, ready to spring: that the invasion which will lay waste to everything has not yet taken place: flames, suffering, wars, death, desolation, evil deeds: patience the hour will come"; 7].

The complex connection between the concept of both fatherland and motherland is important in the narrative of Goytisolo. Most critics focus on his equation of the nation with the mother or stepmother. They point out the misogynistic behavior of the protagonists demonstrated by their desire to violate the female body, which is repeatedly associated with the nation (see Sieburth 163). Yet, in so doing, they overlook the role of the father. In the first novel of the trilogy, *Señas de identidad,* the protagonist, Alvaro Mendiola, tries to understand his past as it relates to his nation's history. One of the most significant questions he has regards the murder of his father at a massacre in Yeste, which no one who survived seems willing to discuss (134). It is the suppressed memory of the Civil War that haunts Alvaro and hinders his ability to trace his past. The mysterious and brutal death of his father leaves him isolated from the Spain that emerged after the Civil War, because in post–Civil War Spain his father's story disappears and Alvaro is orphaned from history.

The absent father is recurrent throughout the three novels of the trilogy. In *Señas de identidad* he is dead and in *Reivindicación del conde don Julián* and *Juan sin tierra*, he is never mentioned (while the father is not mentioned in *Reivindicación del conde don Julián*, we know that Alvarito, the protagonist's alter-ego, is fatherless and lives alone with his mother). The figure of the mother is also absent, except in the case of Alvarito's mother in *Reivindicación del conde don Julián,* who is threatened with rape by the narrator. She does not "appear" in the text but is only alluded to when the narrator speaks to Alvarito (229). Primarily the mother figure functions at a symbolic level when she is equated with the nation or when Goytisolo's narrators fantasize about returning to the womb and being reborn. While these maternal images are crucial to the crisis of cultural identity central to these novels, they are entirely symbolic. The absence of a "real" mother connected to a home leaves the protagonists with an enormous sense of loss. The connection between the figure of the father and the mother as symbolic of the nation is seen in the following quotation from *Reivindicación del conde don Julián:* "la patria es la madre de todos los vicios" (134) ["the fatherland is the mother of all vices"]. The figures of father and mother are inextricably linked to the nation and are responsible for all of the nation's vices. Inasmuch as the nation has officially orphaned the protagonists of these novels, their attempt to recover home is commensurate with their desire to destroy the nation under Franco. Family structure is associated with the structure of the state and its corresponding ideological institutions.

Goytisolo's position as a Spanish exile in the 1960s and 1970s leads him to confront the crisis of the nation in a seemingly contradictory fashion. On the one hand, Goytisolo's texts create a concept of the nation that opposes the one being promoted under Franco. On the other hand, he wholeheartedly dismisses his alternative notion of nation as repressive and restricting to identity because it forces one to assimilate into a group, conform to traceable territorial affiliation, and participate in a society that requires the establishment of rules of conduct. Jesús Lázaro points out that Goytisolo responds to the regime of Franco as well as to the events of the Cuban Revolution (1959), the Vietnam War (1964–76), and the Algerian War (1954–62) (126). Claudia Schaefer Rodríguez states that Goytisolo comes to associate revolution with repression after the events in Cuba (in particular the Padilla affair), Angola, and Nicaragua: "Todos los ejemplos de auténtica revolución... están destinados a fracasar a causa de que la característica fundamental e intrínseca a toda revolución es que genera represión" (88) ["All of the examples of authentic revolution... are destined to fail because the fundamental and intrinsic nature of revolution is that it generates repression"]. On account of these observations Goytisolo becomes progressively more uncomfortable with suggesting an alternative society. What begins as a critique of Sacred Spain, capitalism, and authoritarianism turns into a disdain of Western civilization.

In *Reivindicación del conde don Julián* home has two meanings. On the one hand it is a place that invariably stifles independence and on the other it is necessary for survival. The narrator of *Reivindicación del conde don Julián* is obsessed with invading Spain and reinstating Islam because he needs to believe that there is a way to counteract Franco's version of the nation. Jo Labanyi states that Goytisolo's text is more dependent on Francoist Spain than any other postwar novel (211). His dependence, though, is centered on his need to use the images promoted under Franco as targets for his attacks. Even though he yearns to forget and free himself of his past, the line "el país de cuyo nombre no quieres acordarte" ["the country whose name you don't want to remember"] echoes throughout the text as a constant reminder of the power of memory (60, 72, 214). He is unable to forget willfully. His imagination will not produce a new Spain, and it will not cut the cord. For him, home is no place.

The notion of home as fantasy and fetish is carried on in *Juan sin tierra*. In this novel, home becomes even more dispersed and elusive. It is no longer found in the marginal sectors of society inhabited by non-conformists like that found in *Señas de identidad*, or in the reconstruction of Spain into an Islamic nation. Now it is more clearly a no-space that is formed solely by a fraternity between the narrator and other pariahs. It is multicultural and extra-territorial: territory and culture matter but are not as constitutive of identity as in the prior novels. This novel remains committed to the destruction of the Spain of the Catholic Kings, but it is equally dedicated to the construction of a utopia, where writing is the only way to liberate oneself. In *Señas de identidad* Spain was the basis for memory and was to be challenged through testimonial; the concept of home requires that others listen to the story and change. *Reivindicación del conde don Julián* creates a fantasy Spain where the narrator can betray the nation and return it to the age of Muslim domination. An overthrow of the cultural authoritarianism of the Catholic Kings is the prerequisite to success in *Reivindicación del conde don Julián*. But in both of these novels, there has been a counter-current to the desire to create a concept of the nation; the narrators have sought to be liberated of any signs of cultural identity. Alvaro Mendiola wants to be "Alvaro Mendiola, a secas, sin señas de identidad" ["Alvaro Mendiola, plain and simple, without marks of identity"] and the narrator of *Reivindicación del conde don Julián* insists: "rehusar la identidad, comenzar a cero" ["refuse identity, begin at zero"]. This gesture of stripping oneself of links to the nation reaches its apogee in *Juan sin tierra,* where the narrator yearns to be landless: Juan the landless.

In keeping with its companions in the trilogy, *Juan sin tierra* sends a mixed message about the role of the nation in cultural identity. The narrator desires complete liberation from the confines of a national identity, but these goals are thwarted. The novel begins mentioning "un tiempo sin fronteras" ["time without end"] where the narrator is "absortas en la leve contemplación del mar" (11) ["absorbed in the remote contemplation of the sea"; 2]. He seems much less limited than the two prior narrators, who begin their narratives by invoking, in anger, official Spain. Shortly following the mention of time without borders and contemplating the sea, the narrator mentions that he is "hijo de la tierra y a la tierra unido" (11) ["an offspring of the earth, to earth forever united"; 3]. One page later we learn that the narrator is "sólidamente arraigado en el mundo inferior por unos pies" (12) ["solidly rooted in the inferior world thanks to a pair of feet"; 3]. So the paradox is present again. The narrator frees himself from worldly ties through contemplation, but is always thrust back into the reality of his own gravity.

What sets the critique of official Spain in *Juan sin tierra* apart from the prior two novels is that the regime of Franco is considered more the symptom than the cause of his nation's political malaise. The novel delves even deeper into the historical obsessions of mainstream Spanish culture. It focuses on the myth of purity associated with Catholic values. The narrator sitting alone in his room in 1973 writes about Cuba, Istanbul, Tangiers, Cairo, Spain, New York, etc. His project does not have the structure of either of the first two novels. The attack is multifocal, at one moment addressing Spanish culture, at others, civilization in general. During the course of his writing, the narrator of *Juan sin tierra* reviews the Spanish obsession with cleanliness and highlights the hypocrisy of a nation that can commit atrocious crimes in the name of religious values. Beginning in the moment that the narrator writes, 1973, the novel takes a journey back to the Middle Ages, questioning the repressive basis of civilization. Gloria Doblado comments that this return to the pre-modern highlights a series of crimes, corruption, cruel acts, and humiliations that were perpetrated in the name of religion and moral values (158). History cannot be remembered without guilt: Spanish history holds the dark tales of the Inquisition, Imperialism, and the Civil War. Moreover, the ideological basis for all of these acts has been the sterile morality of the Catholic Church and the basic repressions of civilized society.

Juan sin tierra is particularly critical of the connection between reproductive sex and productive society. Characters similar to the Figurones of *Reivindicación del conde don Julián* are also present in this novel. There is the "Parejita Reproductora" (Reproductive Couple) and the character of Colonel Vosk, who, like Alvaro Peranzules of *Reivindicación del conde don Julián,* represents the perfect Christian gentleman. Speaking with the narrator, Vosk complains about the increase in pornography and sexual display appearing in Spain. Privately the narrator rejoices, because he believes that the replacement of the spiritual with the material will inevitably lead to the demise of Christian values. Transnational capitalism has brought culture from all corners of the world to Spain, upsetting the forced homogeneity maintained for so long under Franco. These changes are "tratando de contaminar el país con las drogas, la confusión de sexos, la proliferación de salas de mala nota, amenaza mortal a nuestro luminoso futuro, a nuestro patrimonio más noble y más santo" (167) ["endeavoring to contaminate the country by way of drugs, the confusion of sexes, the proliferation of unsavory public dance halls, a mortal threat to out bright future, to our most noble and sacred patrimony"; 153]. The narrator continues to attack Sacred Spain and its assumptions of moral superiority.

The utopian possibilities of writing allow the narrator spatial and temporal latitude. While he is physically stuck in his room writing, he gains access to all nations and cultures. Nonetheless, he still centers much of his interest on the nation he repeatedly maintains is no longer "his." He tries to counter the official version of culture: "La hoy unificada Península era un espacio poblado de seres varios, multicolores, corruptos, pasado vergonzoso que había que ocultar ... época funesta de creencias funestas" (163) ["The now-unified Peninsula was an area populated by various multicolored, corrupt beings, a shameful past that it was necessary to hide ... a dismal era of different beliefs"; 150]. Before the forced cultural homogenization of the Catholic Kings, Spain was multiracial and multicultural, and the novel argues that this must be remembered. Yet there are other things that also bear on memory, like the international contributors to Spain's current condition or the slavery in Cuba that links the narrator's family, as prior slave owners, to economic imperialism. Profound shame over the past and disgust at current events demonstrate intertextuality with *Señas de identidad* and *Reivindicación del conde don Julián*: "en el país de cuyo nombre no quieres acordarte" (14) ["in the country whose name you do not care to remember"; 5]. The narrator, like Alvaro Mendiola and the narrator of *Reivindicación del conde don Julián,* has deep hatred for his signs of cultural identity. The difference is that now they are not only Spanish, but are more broadly the products of "civilized" society. "El odio irreductible a tus propias señas (raza profesión clase familia tierra) crecía en la misma proporción que el impulso magnético hacia los parias y toda la violencia impuesta en nombre de la grey civilizadora (a la que exteriormente pertenecías)" (94) ["Your irremediable hatred towards your own marks of identity (race profession class family homeland) was growing, in direct proportion to your magnetic attraction toward pariahs, and all the violence in the name of the civilizing flock of the faithful (to which you at least outwardly still belonged)"; 77]. He is in search of anarchy as an antidote to society; yet, paradoxically, he desires a community, albeit one of pariahs.

Goytisolo's narrators' problems with Spain are, then, the result of Western civilization. The critique of tourism and capitalism in *Juan sin tierra* is magnified to address the international phenomenon of transnational capitalism. In *Juan sin tierra* tourism represents the evils of capitalism and its corresponding ideologies of national pride. It strives to "galvanizar la emoción nacional, satisfacer los gustos ancestrales del pueblo, mantener el prestigio exterior del país, preservar la afluencia de turistas extranjeros" (186) ["galvanize our traditional predilections, maintain the country's prestige abroad, ensure the continued influx of foreign tourists"; 166]. Successful tourism is founded on placing value on national cultural uniqueness. Each country must be able to claim that it has something special to offer the tourist, who will be able to purchase cultural experience in an exotic setting. "Yes, our country is different / esta expresión, popular hoy en el orbe entero gracias a la próvida y eficiente labor de nuestros consulados y agencias turísticas, no es un simple lema acertado de propaganda sino que corresponde a una realidad indisputable que sólo los insensatos o ciegos osarían poner en duda" (173) ["Yes, our country is different / this expression, popular throughout the globe today thanks to the careful and efficient labor of our consulates and travel agencies, is not simply a highly successful advertisement: rather, it is a reflection, alas, of an indisputable reality that only the mad or the blind would dare question"; 158]. Of course the voice behind these words is referring to the valuable difference of Spain. But what is most disturbing to the narrator is that this difference is artificial because the singularly most important shared characteristic between Spain and the rest of the World is civilization. *Juan sin tierra*'s narrator wants to destroy the nation as it has existed under Franco, but he is uncomfortable with positing an alternative nation, such as the Muslim nation that tried to replace Sacred Spain in *Reivindicación del conde don Julián*. Goytisolo, in *Juan sin tierra*, appears to move increasingly toward an anti-national stance, where nation always means a way to control identity and there is no liberation in a national context. In spite of these efforts, his narrators never seem to conquer the gravitational effects of national identity and their feet always lead them back to the dilemma of Spain.

Searching for a home, the narrator of *Juan sin tierra* broadens his quest for a community. Instead of trying to replace his lost home with a new Islamic culture or a group of marginalized Spanish outcasts, the narrator of *Juan sin tierra* creates his own unique community. Like his counterparts, the desired community is of non-conformist social pariahs, but this time he includes a hodgepodge of characters, the three most important of which are T. E. Lawrence, Père de Foucauld, and Anselm Turmeda: "El desierto te invita de nuevo, vasto y tenaz como tu deseo... alcanzarás el oasis más próximo... Anselm Turmeda, Père de Foucauld, Lawrence de Arabia? : entre los tuyos al fin, inmerso en su denso caldo humano" (87) ["The desert beckons to you once again, as vast and stubborn as your desire... you will reach the next oasis... Anselm Turmeda, Père de Foucauld, Lawrence de Arabia?: amid those of your kind at last, immersed in their teeming human broth"; 72]. The desert functions as a welcoming mother whose arms protect him from the hostile, fertile world that causes him pain.

He reaches an oasis and finds comrades. But the question mark after "Arabia" signals his doubt that such union is possible.

Who are these three historical figures that the narrator has chosen to form his cultural community? T. E. Lawrence (1888–1935) was a British officer who was sent to organize the Arab war against Turkey during World War I. His experiences led him to shun his Anglo background through attempted cultural conversion into the Arab world. His political and cultural failures do not bother the narrator, who exalts Lawrence's textual successes in the writing of his memoirs, *The Seven Pillars of Wisdom*. Anselm Turmeda (1352–1432) also sought assimilation into Arab culture and actually converted to Islam. Coming from Spain as an ordained Franciscan, Turmeda was later called Ibn Turmeda. He was not the political figure Lawrence was, but he was a prolific writer. His theory of the falsity of human dominance over nature is crucial to the tenets of *Juan sin tierra*. Turmeda's theory was that the human was not superior to the animal because, while he did eat animals, other animals, small microbes, eat him. This theory proves for the narrator that civilization is artificial and that the justification of violence over other creatures cannot be logically proven. The last of the three, Charles de Foucauld (1858–1916), was a monk who traveled to Africa to convert the Arab "infidels" to Christianity. The narrator's fascination with this figure rests on his quest for martyrdom and his obsession with the desert. Michael Ugarte, in an excellent analysis of the relationship between these historical figures and the narrative of Goytisolo, explains that the inclusion of Foucauld, who contrasts the Islamophile practices of the other two figures, serves to create an even tighter bond between the narrator and his chosen community precisely because all were pariahs, all were travelers, and all were fascinated by the geography of the Arab world (*Trilogy of Treason* 120–29). Furthermore, Ugarte states: "The differences in the spiritual concerns among Turmeda, Foucauld, and Lawrence, not to mention their disparities in time and place are superficial in Goytisolo's eyes" (120). The narrator visits the graves of these comrades, he traverses the same deserts, and he dreams of the same frustrated victories. The sea of *Reivindicación del conde don Julián* is replaced by the arid desert, and the cemeteries of *Señas de identidad* return. *Juan sin tierra* goes beyond any preconceived notion of what constitutes a cultural community and the narrator founds his own atemporal, global village.

The narrator dreams of liberated wandering: "te sentirás totalmente perdido y caminarás cabizbajo y sin rumbo por entre la fauna cerril de Manhattan : pero el destino no te desampara y, al elevar los ojos al cielo mientras aguardas las luces del tráfico, serás bienaventurado testigo de una brusca y fulgurante Aparición" (73) ["you will feel totally lost and will wander about aimlessly, with bowed head, amid the untamed fauna of Manhattan: but fate is still watching over you, and on lifting your eyes heavenward as you wait for the traffic light to change, you will be the fortunate witness of a sudden and resplendent Apparition"; 59–60]. Each wayward step makes him witness to yet another feature of modernity. He dreams of deserts and winds up in cities. He goes underground in Manhattan and finds the reptiles in the sewers as interesting as the inhabitants above (78). He is an itinerant narrator embarking on imaginary voyages and envisioning the transnational transculturation of the Empire: "tu imperialismo amoroso no conoce fronteras" (128) ["your amorous imperialism recognizes no frontiers"; 114]. His writing is able to transcend geographic limitations: "someterás la geografía a los imperativos y exigencias de tu pasión" (82) ["you will subject geography to the imperatives and demands of your passion"; 68], and he can annul history with "un simple trazo de pluma" (85) ["a simple stroke of your pen"; 71]. But he knows that this feeling of liberation is fleeting: "el espartano ciclo recomenzará" (82) ["the Spartan cycle will begin all over again"; 68]. Echoing the cyclical sense of time in *Reivindicación del conde don Julián*, these transgressions must be endlessly repeated.

Many critics read the narrative of *Juan sin tierra* as testimony of Goytisolo's ability to unleash his territorial confinement and construct narrative that is deterritorial and unbounded, no longer burdened by the anguish and anger of *Señas de identidad* or *Reivindicación del conde don Julián*. Lázaro, in his book *La novelística de Juan Goytisolo,* suggests that after the anguish and displacement of the two prior novels, *Juan sin tierra* unleashes irony, humor, and hyperbole in a jubilant celebration of freedom (237). There is no doubt that there are discernible mood swings in each of the narrators of the trilogy: Alvaro Mendiola is mainly anguished and isolated, the narrator of *Reivindicación del conde don Julián* is enraged and psychotic, the narrator of *Juan sin tierra* is less encumbered with a desire to change the world and tries to satisfy his needs through narration. In each case, though, the chasm between the community sought and the reality of alienation is never bridged. The narrator in *Juan sin tierra* cannot be described as ecstatic over his solitude and he is not free. As mentioned, Ugarte in *Shifting Ground* states that the narrator of *Juan sin tierra* is just what the title suggests, "a landless being" (208). Yet, in each text the title has been the wish of the narrator, not the achievement. Alvaro was unable to completely trace and alter his signs of identity, Count Julian is not avenged in *Reivindicación del conde don Julián*, and *Juan sin tierra* does not create a landless self.

It is clear, however, that the narrator of *Juan sin tierra* experiences the contrasting conditions of travel and exploration versus exile and banishment. As in Ovid's *Metamorphoses,* travel changes the self and the imaginary travels of the narrator make possible the explorations of new communities. But the condition of exile is not eradicated and the travels provide a false sense of cultural assimilation into a new community, or nation, a fact of which the narrator is only too aware. Michael Seidel explains that modern writers were often more at home in the conjured space of exile than in the homeland. He explains that these writers made an artistic virtue of exilic necessity (5). Goytisolo's protagonists would prefer to feel "more at home" in *any* conjured space, which is the motivation behind their relentless pursuit of such a place. But these narrators are not members of modern society and they do not feel at home anywhere.

Therefore, despite the transnational, multicultural community of pariahs that the narrator fabricates for himself, he cannot erase the legacy of Spain. In a section returning to the crisis of culture and history in Spain, the narrator describes precisely his limitations: "tu cuerpo no abonará el suelo : excepto sí, investido de poderosa sustancia intoxica : pero si la realidad no se pliega a tus agresiones oníricas deberás decidir desde ahora la suerte que le reservas" (301) ["your body will not fertilize its soil: or will do so only if possessed of a powerful toxic substance: but should reality not yield to your oneiric assaults you must decide as of now what fate you consign to this body"; 265]. He knows that he will never be able to free himself of his past. His body will not forget its ties to Spanish soil. His one consolation is the thought that he is part of a legacy of Spanish heretics "tierra fecunda de herejes... a la vez que de santos y sabios... grupúsculos de individuos que, fuera de los caminos trazados, han intentado desde tiempos remotos un culto clandestino" (189) ["a land fertile in heretics... as well as saints and wise men... small groups of individuals, who, straying from the beaten path, have endeavored since the very earliest times to perpetuate a secret worship"; 168]. The nation is split in two: heretics and saints. Goytisolo does not abandon his nation or his quest for home. Instead, he redefines it as a space which houses many nations within the same borders, while also positing a concept of the nation which has no spatial borders, which links him across time and space to other pariahs.

ARIEL DORFMAN: THE FAMILY

Parallel with Goytisolo's focus on the legacy of the Catholic Kings as the cultural ideology central to Spanish nationalism, Dorfman's exile writing critiques the image of Augusto Pinochet, dictator of Chile, self-proclaimed father of the nation and supreme protector of Catholic values. In Dorfman's work the father figure is rewritten and reinscribed into a context that reaches beyond the traditional family and its connection to political ideology's construction of the national leader as a "father of the nation." Associations between God and Father, nation and family are challenged as Dorfman draws parallels between Pinochet and evil authoritarian leaders who disguise their tyranny by projecting themselves as benevolent fathers. Yet, what makes analysis of the father figure in Dorfman's work so interesting and so complicated is the multiple levels on which he works. First, he critiques the concept of the father by demonstrating that power always leads to oppression. Second, he suggests an alternative benevolent father to the evil authoritarian. And third, he describes the father as an abstract and nebulous symbol of both evil and love. These complex and contradictory images of the father are a recurring motif in Dorfman's exile literature.

Hernán Vidal in *Cultura nacional chilena, crítica literaria, y derechos humanos* explains that in Chilean ideology the national leader is the father of the nation and the members of that nation function as the leader's family. Critiquing Hernán Godoy's *El carácter chileno*, Vidal describes the way in which Godoy exalts the period of Diego Portales's regime (1831–61), which was a period of great presidential power that emphasized a strong central government (205). For Godoy this period represents a "classical age" for Chilean history characterized by equilibrium and an elite which led the nation, "unidos por un espíritu de familia, arraigados a la tierra y representativos de una poderosa individualidad nacional" (218) ["united by a spirit of family, linked to the land and representative of a powerful national individuality"]. The family spirit which drove the Portalian regime is reinscribed into the ideology of Pinochet, and Vidal comments that in Godoy's conservative account of the coup of 1973, "queda implícito que atribuye el golpe de estado al surgimiento de héroes con voluntad de reafirmar el carácter chileno y la identidad nacional" (207) ["it remains implicit that he attributes the coup to a surge of heroes with the will to reaffirm Chilean character and national identity"]. These heroes heralded by Godoy are meant to be the role models for the Chilean populace, who, due to the chaos and decadence of Allende's presidency, require leaders who can return "family values" to the national scene.

As Dorfman challenges the image of Pinochet as the symbolic father of Chile, he also investigates the notion of "family" as a monad for the modern nation. If the concept of a collective requires a social organization similar to national structure, then how do different versions of the family represent different national possibilities? Or, must the "family" be exposed as a principle feature of modern, conservative, nation-building ideology? The conflict for Dorfman will be most critical when he posits the notion that the children of today are the hope for the future and that this hope relies on the children of today learning from their parents' mistakes. Nevertheless, Dorfman's work consistently exposes the ways in which such a social structure is quite rigid and traditional and is easily co-opted by authoritarianism. His work focuses on the tension between patricide and family legacy, between community and anarchy. Whereas Goytisolo sought to create an alternative nation where he could belong, Dorfman desires the creation of an alternative family that can mimic an alternative social structure capable of challenging modern capitalism. Unlike in Goytisolo's work, betrayal of the nation is not the key to an alternative. Because Dorfman played a role in the success and demise of Allende, he focuses on the question of the individual's responsibility for the nation's future. As an author, and like a father, he hopes that his books, which he repeatedly refers to as children, will be able to create hope for the future.

In Dorfman's first novel written in exile, *Viudas*, the issue of the family and its connections to state power are central concerns of the narrative. In a Greek village where all of the men (all of the benevolent fathers) are missing, the only men present are those that represent an authoritarian state. As the novel opens, the village is being governed by a new captain, who is replacing Captain Gheorghakis: "Él le dejaba, en todo caso, al nuevo comandante, una región saneada de todo peligro armado, que se gobernaba con mano de hierro, bien patrullada, con una población sin otra alternativa que obedecer, eliminados los focos potenciales y virtuales de rebeldía" (26) ["In any case, he had left the new commander a region secure from all armed terrorism, a region governed with an iron hand, well patrolled, a population with no alternative but to obey, actual and potential centers of rebellion eliminated, the military situation under control"; 13]. The populace of the village had no alternative but to obey because Gheorghakis had treated them like naughty children whom he needed to control. Now the new captain's job was to, "de acuerdo con el plan general del Supremo Gobierno—granjearse con los residentes, inaugurar una fase constructiva, de desarrollo económico y social, sólo posible ahora que los elementos desquiciadores habían sufrido la sangría de una y otra derrota" (26) ["in accordance with the general plan of the Supreme Government—to win the sympathies of the residents, begin a constructive phase of social and economic development, possible only now that the disruptive elements had been bled white by one defeat after another"; 14]. Now the villagers are to be taught how to behave according to the standards of Western civilization, i.e., to support the capitalist economy, obey the authorities, pledge allegiance to the state, etc.

The military, after forcibly removing the "real" fathers of the village, will now substitute for them, functioning as the patriarchy that rules the village as a large family. The case of the orderly who serves the Captain is the best example of the tension between the concept of a benevolent or a tyrannical father. *Viudas* presents the reader with two competing versions of the father's relationship to the family, one which is evil and one which is benevolent. The orderly (Emmanuel), a villager who works for the government and gives the captain inside information about the villagers, rejects his family's peasant background and decides to work for the landowner, Don Arturo. Emmanuel's father had forbidden him to work for Don Arturo, believing him to be responsible for the economic suffering of the peasants. His father told him that "La familia de don Arturo nos había quitado las tierras que eran nuestras, por fraude y por la fuerza" (141) ["Kastoria's family had taken away land that was ours, by fraud and by force"; 99]. Nevertheless, Emmanuel leaves home and Don Arturo becomes like a father to him. The Captain asks, significantly using his name for the first time: "¿De veras han sido como padres para ti?" (144) ["Were they really like parents to you?"; 101]. Emmanuel responds that he was treated like a son of the family, and the captain states: "A los padres les debemos todo. . . . Pero por ahí surgen conflictos. Pongamos por caso, es un decir, que de repente hubiera un conflicto, bueno, no necesariamente un conflicto, digamos más bien un desentendimiento, entre tu patrón y el Ejército, qué sé yo, una diferencia de opiniones" (146–47) ["We owe everything to our parents. . . . But that's where conflicts can arise. Suppose, let's say, there were suddenly a conflict. Well, not necessarily a conflict, let's call it a misunderstanding between your master and the army, who knows, a difference of opinion"; 103]. Although Don Arturo is behind the war that has led to authoritarianism, the captain wants to assure himself that he can count on Emmanuel's loyalty. Emmanuel must have allegiance first to the state as father. Emmanuel cannot have two fathers, and the captain wants to make sure that he has the ultimate authority over him.

In contrast with Emmanuel's disappointing choice to leave his father and become a child of the state, Alexis, the grandson of Sofía (the leader of the women's rebellion), will remain faithful to his family despite his father's absence. The importance of the family is emphasized when the mothers of the village begin their rebellion motivated by the belief that they have the right to bury their loved ones with their family. In the absence of benevolent fathers, it is the mothers who are forced to resist the domination and repression of the state. Alexis, a child, is forced to act like a man and to remain faithful to his family. Contrasting these two young men, Alexis and Emmanuel, Dorfman's novel reflects the role of the family as capable of producing two contradictory nations: one evil and the other benevolent. In one case the father is threatening and must be in control: in the other, the father is loving and cares for his family. In this way, the novel poses the question of whether fathers or family structure can be trusted. The family serves as the base for community as well as for rebellion, but it is also the cause of repression and authoritarianism.

In Dorfman's second novel of exile, the debate over the role of the family as representative of the nation is further fragmented and problematized. For example, Pamela, the lover of the son of Sendero, is an orphan, but she is not alone: "she had made the whole world her family" (51). For her the nation is the family: "Pamela might not know the names and biographies of the man and woman that cast her adrift in this world, but, on the other hand, she had a country where she was nourished and grew strong" (51). As the son of Sendero returns to his native land he looks to Pamela for a sense of family and community.

> During all his half-life in the saddle, an immobile emigrant, like a child born on a ship that will never reach land, Grandfather had appeased his sense of foreignness by the certainty that in some hemisphere, maybe on the other side of the world or on the other side of Doralisa's wondrous foliage, awaiting him were familiar avenues, intonations of a language that was a remembrance, a way of smelling the sun and inheriting grapes and other foods that were, would be, completely his own. He tried not to remember that the only experience he had of such a promised banquet was borrowed, just hearsay, secondhand. Even though Eduardo had excluded him, not only in the present, but also in advance from the future, denying him the right to return, making everything ominous and threatening, even in those moments when everything was alien and lacked a name, it was enough to close his eyes in that open darkness inside Pamela, next to Pamela, and to let her lead him by the hand like a little child being taught to walk; Pamela was enough to make everything familiar again, to make everything family. (161)

Pamela's body becomes the way to find a home; her body acts as a surrogate motherland and he is a child by her side. The son of Sendero seeks a cultural community, through language, food, familiar places, and Pamela's body.

During the time when both the son of Sendero and Pamela were in the womb as part of the fetal rebellion, they had a great sense of community and family. All of the unborn felt like part of a great family, which, hopefully, would be able to create a great nation. On the outside of the womb, however, Manuel Sendero significantly loses his voice precisely when he is forced to take off his wedding band (45). The unborn's visions of a nation are exposed as illusory when contrasted with the harsh realities Manuel must face as a father being dominated by an authoritarian state. The rebellion of the unborn, unwilling to leave their wombs, is referred to by the Caballero as "fetal terrorism" and he further equates state power with traditional family structure when he states that the rebellion is an effort to "discredit the nation's most sacred institution, marriage" (191). In the contrast between the ideals of the unborn and the realities of life under the Caballero, Dorfman points to the deep crisis that connects family and state power.

In the part of the narrative referring to the "Outside," many of the same conflicts are repeated. David tells of the night when Allende won the presidency, and he was overcome with a sense of belonging. Walking the streets with other citizens of Santiago he thinks: "After so many centuries, at last her favorite children, her true native sons, her heirs, among whom I included myself had reached her borders" (148). The nation is like a mother welcoming home her children. Here the nation as a symbolic family is a positive and reassuring metaphor. Yet, once in exile, David is alienated from his nation as well as from his family and the nation represents a tyrannical and oppressive family. His ex-wife, Cecilia, returns to Chile and takes David's son, Alejandro. In a telling account of David's agony as an impotent father figure he explains that his son had recently received a medal and, when he had accepted it, he had neglected to mention his father. Instead he thanks his grandfather (Cecilia's father), who is a colonel in the army. David is frustrated that he is unable to be a father to his son and that the military is substituting for him. "And with that grandfather; they're really impressionable, easily taken in. The fatherland, the little soldier, the military band, the Medal of Honor, the big he-man" (214). David, exiled from fatherhood, is panicked that Alejandro's grandfather will have a greater effect on him than David does, now that they have been separated. As the novel ends, David's fears of parental impotence are validated when the novel suggests that Alejandro has committed suicide.

Once in exile, the national problems associated with Allende's death can no longer be strictly relegated to state politics for David and his comrades. David explains how a friend had told him "that exploitation starts in everyday life, in the family, in sexual relationships, in emotional happiness, in the authority of the father over the child and the husband over the wife. That while that wasn't changed, revolutions would go on reproducing the same old structures of domination" (264). The problem, then, is how to construct a family structure that does not imply domination. What the novel reveals is that the issue of domination is omnipresent and that the connection between family and oppression cannot be separated. How, then, can we find a way of creating a community that is not dictatorial? Is such a notion possible?

In David's comic strip, which Felipe has asked him to develop, he fantasizes about the extremely damaging ties between identity and power structures. In the strip, Carl Barks, a cartoonist from Walt Disney, has been commissioned by the leaders of a country named "Chilex" to help them create the perfect "nation." The leaders firmly believe that it is paramount to their success that they develop an appropriate ideology to support their political goals. Barks is given a description of his project: "We need a virile friendship, like a father's; and we need a forgiving love like a mother's. There's only one country in the world that can be a father and a mother at the same time. That country is yours, Mr. Barks" (106). The United States serves as the role model for capitalist modernization and family values as they had been espoused through the works of such cultural producers as Walt Disney, and Carl Barks, as one of the cartoonists for Disney, is the perfect source of ideas for the creation of Chilex.

This segment of the narrative also represents the problems between family structure and state oppression. Barks's wife, Sarah (note the biblical reference), has never been able to conceive, but she learns that part of the tourist business that the leaders of Chilex hope to create involves bringing sterile women to Chilex, where they will become miraculously pregnant. Furthermore, Barks's mind will become the symbolic father of the national ideology, which relies on controlling the "X-Factor" within all citizens. The "X-Factor" is described as that level of energy and determination, which, if present to a great degree, will lead people to be rebellious, but which, if completely absent, will not produce good workers. As Barks is dying and his mind is being sapped of all of its creative powers, he is told that he will never truly die: "we're going to embalm your dreams. . . . We'll find the X-Factor you'll see . . . give us your mind, Mr. Parks, my son, give us your virtue" (421). Like Jesus, Barks is the son who will die but will leave behind a powerful ideology capable of controlling the masses. In contrast with *Viudas,* where the dilemma of the family's ties to the state appeared to be primarily connected to the power of a military government, *The Last Song of Manuel Sendero* places great emphasis on the cultural constructs that affect the role of the family within national ideology. The symbolic child must grapple with both national genealogy and cultural inheritance.

As in *Viudas, The Last Song of Manuel Sendero* is a novel full of evil figures of male authority that are counterbalanced by benevolent ones. Nevertheless, what is most significant is that in both novels it is the evil fathers who clearly have greater powers of persuasion. The benevolent fathers, because they resist using oppressive tactics, lose to the more overtly aggressive leaders. Moreover these novels continue to maintain hope that the family and its love are important sources of a sense of community and collective. Dorfman's narrative reveals the impossible desire for a family that can guide its children without oppressing them. In the last lines of *The Last Song of Manuel Sendero* Eduardo is speaking to a blind woman, who tells him that the son of Sendero has asked that he care for his children as if they were his own. But Eduardo refuses to promise and the reader is once more reminded of how fragile the child is in the father's hands, just as a nation is vulnerable when caught in the hold of a dictator. And yet, Dorfman's novel does not end with despair, and the narrative closes: "Let's wait and let's hope, we'll keep on hoping that that's the way it is" (453).

These lines of hope are absent from Dorfman's third novel, *Máscaras*. It is important to note that *Máscaras* was finished after Dorfman had been "re-exiled," having been given a brief chance to reenter the country. It was also published fifteen years after the death of Allende and the beginning of Pinochet's rule. Like Goytisolo's later work, with its angry tone, Dorfman's narrative seems to see many of his previous ideals as foolish and embarks on one of his most bitter narratives to date. It is interesting to note that Dorfman refers to this text as less political than his prior works. In an interview he states: "It's not an overtly political novel. It doesn't deal with events in Chile or Latin America. There are no human rights violations" (qtd. in Incledon 103; Dorfman seems to disregard the treatment of Oriana by the faceless man as his sexual toy or the murders, which she witnesses, when he states that there are no human rights violations in this novel. Moreover the practices of the doctor seem to function as metaphors for torture and human rights violations). In the same interview, Dorfman goes on to remark that "A lot of my political obsessions are present in *Mascara*, for instance, alienation; the use of deception in relation to the public and the private world; memory, the need for memory; the erasure of memory as a form of control; and the idea of a hidden structure that acts like a vampire in our lives" (103). To a certain degree, the hidden structure to which he refers here is precisely the connections between family structure and state power. What is most interesting to note from this quotation is that, as Dorfman moved his critique of power to a more universal scale, he considered that the critique was not as overtly political. Nevertheless, this novel may be the most political of his three works written in exile, specifically because it constructs a metaphor for the social organization of the nation that exposes the nation to be necessarily repressive and that calls for its political challenge.

In *Máscaras,* the obsession with medical technology's ability to alter the human soul, as demonstrated in the segments referring to the cartoon from *The Last Song of Manuel Sendero,* is replaced by a different obsession with medical technology. In *Máscaras,* medical technology is capable of altering people's appearance, consequently affecting their memory and actions. The plastic surgeon of *Máscaras* is able to erase his patients' history through his surgical manipulation, and he is also capable of achieving the dreams of the scientists in *The Last Song of Manuel Sendero* who desired control over people's emotions.

There are three main characters in this novel, each of whom narrates a section. The first is the nameless and faceless man who speaks to the doctor. The second section is narrated by Oriana, a constant amnesiac, who relays her traumatic story of watching her family's torture by the secret police only to be raped afterward. She is unable to remember who she is, and yet the only thing she remains constantly aware of is the fact that she is being followed by the secret police. They follow her because she has been removing the hands of their victims. She rescues their hands because they hold their histories. The doctor narrates the last section. He speaks to the faceless man and explains that he, in fact, has greater power precisely because he is responsible for the alienation and suffering that the faceless man has endured. Having seen him as a patient when he was a child, the doctor, instead of helping the man to have a face, saw his deformity as something which he would later use to his benefit.

All three characters, then, are society's outsiders. These characters may be interpreted in many ways: as three components of the same identity, as the holy trinity, or as a dysfunctional micro-family where the doctor is the father, the faceless man is the son, and Oriana is his mother/sister/daughter/lover. It is significant to note that in this bizarre triangle the two men struggle for power, using Oriana as the prize, while she remains disconnected from the macho battleground, suggesting that the quest for power is male-gendered, while women are the welcoming mothers and the faithful guardians (repositories?) of memories and history.

The faceless man is angry at society and, in particular, at the way in which family structure regulates the behavior of children. In *Máscaras,* the hopeful and insightful children of *The Last Song of Manuel Sendero* are gone. They have been replaced by submissive and disgruntled children who either replicate the tyranny practiced on them by their parents or suffer and learn obedience. The exceptions, of course, are the faceless man, who is never really "part" of his family, and Oriana, who loves her parents but has been so deeply traumatized by her experiences that she is incapable of mentally maturing. The faceless man believes that children have their faces superimposed on them: "son las caras de los padres—o alguien que sustituye a ellos—las que se superponen sobre el pizarrón en blanco que traen los niños . . . ese adulto tiene que seguir interfiriendo entre el recién nacido y el mundo. El niño paga el resto de su vida esa protección contra las miradas ajenas" (39) ["what is superimposed upon the blank blackboard children bring with them is the parent's face . . . the adult must keep on interposing himself between the just-born baby and the world. For the rest of its life the child will pay for that protection against alien eyes"; 32]. Children, then, are not born to freely choose their identity: they are stuck into a prefabricated parental mold. They are taught that they should adopt "la cáscara de su padre contra el mundo invasor. Era así como los seres humanos quedan atrapados en las caras muertas de sus lejanos antecesores, repetidas de generación en generación" (39) ["his father's shell. Human beings are trapped inside the dead faces of their remote ancestors repeated from generation to generation"; 32]. Children are stripped of subjective agency by their parents and they are trapped into a family legacy. Yet the faceless man has not been sucked into this social structure because his mother, a make-up artist, was too busy with other faces to worry about him, and his father, who sells medical equipment to hospitals, was too busy to spend time with his son or even notice him. Criticizing his father's job, he states: "Agujas hipodérmicas, estetoscopios, cosas que penetran el cuerpo e intentan rescatar un simulacro de lo que está pasando allá adentro" (41) ["hypodermic needles, stethoscopes, things that penetrate the body and try to emerge with a representation of what is happening inside"; 34]. In these lines, the faceless man reveals his disgust at the way in which society demands the manipulation of the body at the expense of the "soul."

The disturbing way in which this novel critiques the notion of a modern "civil" society is best exemplified by the relationships between the faceless man and Oriana and the faceless man and the doctor. In the first relationship, the faceless man uses Oriana's amnesia to force her to play the roles of his sister, his ex-lover—essentially, any woman he desires: "Que ella no sepa quién es, que incluso haya traspapelado la experiencia del día anterior, me permite elegirle, para cada jornada, un rol original" (84) ["That she should not have the slightest idea of who she is, that she has even lost the previous day's experience, lets me choose for her, upon our awakening, an original role"; 78]. Like a god he can create her daily according to his wishes, each day placing a mask on her that allows him to fantasize revenge on the women who have hurt him. No matter what face he chooses for her, she ends each day at his mercy (85). His greatest fear, though, is that her recurring amnesia will not remain. He states, "Supe que para que fuéramos felices era absolutamente indispensable destruir toda posibilidad de que viniera a perturbarnos la mujer que alguna vez ocupó su cuerpo" (83) ["I knew that if we were to stay together, it was absolutely essential to destroy any chance that the woman who had once occupied this body should come to disturb us"; 78]. It is important to note that he uses the first person plural to refer to "their" happiness. He merely assumes that his happiness implies hers as well, but isn't a woman without a past nothing but a toy, an object for him? Interestingly, he believes that his acts are in her best interest: "Lo único que me importaba era la salvación de la mujer que tiene la única cara que no está a la venta en este mundo" (88) ["The only thing I cared about was to save the woman who had the only face in this world that was not for sale"; 83]. But isn't she the ultimate product for him? He dreams that his ideal woman would have a face free from commodification, and yet, to achieve this, he reifies her. He seeks to control her identity absolutely and totally much in the same way that the doctor seeks to control the identity of the citizens of his country so that the government will remain in power.

The doctor represents the evil and ubiquitous father figure responsible for the oppression of all of his patients/children. As he proposes to the faceless man that they switch their faces, giving the faceless man a recognizable and constant identity and giving himself ultimate power in anonymity, he refers to the faceless man as "his son" (145). The ultimate source of social power, the doctor is the father to all. In Dorfman's last exile novel, the father and the family are no longer possible sources of a collective and benevolent nation: they are the social structure at the root of all suffering. The characters in this novel no longer have the "free will" to choose a benevolent over a tyrannical social system because there is no social system that is not implicitly repressive and controlling. All identity is a mask because all identity is a performance orchestrated by those in power.

Dorfman investigates the connections between family structure and nation and each of his exile novels reveals increasingly complex and irresolvable issues. Each novel is less hopeful and is less able to describe the family as a source for positive national values. Nevertheless, Dorfman continues to equate the relationships between family members and between lovers with larger systems of social organization. Unlike Goytisolo, who is obsessed with narrating a space for a community, Dorfman constantly returns to the problems of friendship, love, and family ties insofar as they reflect the possibilities of creating an alternative nation.

CRISTINA PERI ROSSI AND THE CITY

Unlike the work of Goytisolo and Dorfman, Peri Rossi's exile literature does not use the same metaphor as both a positive and negative reflection of the nation. In her work, the city is the repressive source of national identity and cultural communities, while the sea and its islands are spaces of communal isolation that bring freedom from the constraints of modern civilization. The first lines of *La nave de los locos* emphasize the ties between the city and the exile when Equis hears in a dream: "La ciudad a la que llegues descríbela" (9) ["You will come to a city—describe it"; 1]. But when the voice ordering Equis to describe the city is gone, he becomes confused: "La duda me ganó" ["Doubt overwhelmed me"]. He can no longer tell the significant from the insignificant. Such a request, to describe the city he has arrived in, is impossible because the exile's complex relationship to cities destroys the exile's ties to territory in such a way that knowledge of what is important becomes impossible. Each city, like the floors of the tower of Babel, is organized differently, leaving the exile as a constant foreigner: "cada planta tenía sus horarios, su rutina, sus leyes, su código" (60) ["each storey with its timetable, routine, laws, codes"; 56]. The city is the source of systematicity and individual restraint, while the sea and its forgotten islands are the open spaces facilitating utopian fantasies about unrestricted life. Yet those who inhabit the sea and its islands are also outcasts who suffer and often die because they have been expelled without means of survival. So even in the spaces providing possible alternatives to the pain of the city, the exile finds further alienation of the self.

David Harvey contrasts the modern city with the postmodern city. "To the [modern] ideology of the city as some lost but longed-for community, Raban responded with a picture of the city as a labyrinth" (5). He explains that the modern image of the city is a center for discipline. Peri Rossi, in an article describing the genesis of her collection of poems *Europa después de la lluvia,* mentions "la alienación de la sociedad de consumo" ["the alienation of consumer society"] as a central theme of the poem "Nocturno pluvioso en la ciudad" (Rainy Evening in the City), which "procura imitar al ritmo de la vida moderna, su alienación, su confusión de señales, todo eso que por despersonalizado y enajenante llamamos alienado" ("Génesis" 75) ["manages to imitate the rhythm of modern life, its alienation, its confusing signs, all of that which because it depersonalizes and distances we call alienating"]. For Peri Rossi, it is this modernist version of the city and its containment of all of the repressive apparatuses of the nation that she critiques through her writing. Peri Rossi's cities contrast with Goytisolo's postmodern cities like Barcelona, Tangiers, and New York, which are represented as labyrinthine and full of potential for marginalized existence. In a self-referential poem Peri Rossi refers to the textual significance of cities in her work: "apoyado sobre la metáfora del viaje y la transparencia de ciudades-símbolo, a la deriva del tiempo, aparezcan textos" (*Europa* 66) ["supported by the metaphor of the journey and the transparency of city-symbols, adrift from time, appear texts"].

Europa después de la lluvia, written in Berlin and Barcelona, depicts the city as the site of social repression. In her first collection of poetry written in exile, Peri Rossi explains the way in which her condition of exile informs her vision of Europe:

> Le debo al exilio la posibilidad de mirar, aún con ojos de extranjera, la realidad europea sin el velo de los mitos ni la miopía de quienes nunca han salido de ella. . . . Si en mi libro hay una visión melancólica, casi decadente de Europa es porque el ángulo de mi observación del no integrado, del extranjero (el ángulo del excluido) me permite desarrollar algunos temas, sentimientos y sensaciones por las que experimento atracción: la agonía, el contraste, el paisaje natural degradado, el paisaje urbano y su alineación. ("Génesis" 71)
>
> I owe to exile the possibility of seeing, albeit with the eyes of a foreigner, European reality without the veil of myths or the myopia of those who have never left her. . . . If in my book there is a melancholic, almost decadent, vision of Europe it is because my angle of observation, non-integrated, foreign (the angle of the excluded) allowed me to develop certain themes, feelings and sensations that attract me: agony, contrast, the degraded environment, the urban landscape and its alienation.

The spaces of these poems are islands and cities connected by the flux of the sea, where the sea constantly reappears in the poems as the means for transporting the unwanted from the cities. In the poem "La nave" (The Ship) the passengers are sent adrift so that they will no longer threaten the progress of the city.

In her second collection of short stories written in exile, *El museo de los esfuerzos inútiles,* a constant theme is the modern city as a metaphor for the repressive nation. All of the stories deal with systems and institutions which attempt to control identity and the ways in which people resist or are subjugated by these systems. Those who do not fit into the goals of the modern nation must be extinguished or forgotten as in, for instance, the stories "La grieta" ("The Crack") and "El viaje inconcluso" ("The Inconclusive Journey"). The best example of Peri Rossi's association of the city with the alienation of modern society and, in particular, exile, can be seen in "La ciudad" ("The City"). "La ciudad" begins as a recurring dream where "*alguien* de sexo impreciso" (160) ["*someone* of indeterminate sex"; 137] is present. The dreamer is perplexed by the presence of this person of uncertain sex as well as by the fact that the city of his dreams is a city he simultaneously recognizes and is unfamiliar with. "[E]n el sueño *sabía* que se trataba de su ciudad de sus orígenes, muchas cosas habían cambiado en ella, hasta volverla irreconocible, aunque en el sueño, supo que se trataba de su ciudad natal" (160–61) ["[I]n the dream he *knew* that that was the city he was from, so many things had changed there that it had become unrecognizable. Yet still, in his dream, he knew it was the city where he had been born"; 137].

This recurring dream reminds the exile of the symbolic role the city of his dreams plays in his condition as an exile: "su presencia en ella no tenía más justificación que provocar ese sentimiento de extrañeza y de reconocimiento, al mismo tiempo, similar a lo que experimentamos delante de una vieja fotografía" (161) ["his presence there only served to bring about a feeling of strangeness and, at the same time, of recognition, not unlike what happens when one looks at an old photograph"; 138]. Because the exile cannot return to his city as it was when he left, it becomes, by definition, both familiar and unfamiliar. In an attempt to understand the meaning of this recurring dream the narrator speaks to his ex-wife, who has never experienced exile. He tries to explain to her that the city of his dreams functions metaphorically, not literally: "No es ésa ciudad, Luisa, ¿entiéndelo? No se trata de volver a ninguna parte. Ni de ir a otra. Quizás, los que no son extranjeros no llevan una ciudad adentro—reflexionó en voz alta—. No sueñan con mapas desconocidos" (170) ["No, Luisa, I'm not talking about *that* city, don't you understand? It's not a matter of returning anywhere. Or of going anywhere. Maybe people who aren't foreigners don't carry a city inside them, he thought aloud. They don't dream about unfamiliar maps"; 146]. This description of the city as metaphor coincides with the strategies used by Goytisolo and Dorfman in their metaphorical nations; Peri Rossi is articulating the city as a symbolic place of belonging, which is a necessary notion for the outsider (i.e., exile) who has suffered a sensation of lost identity and dissociation from society. This alienation, arguably, is representative of the modern condition and is not typically a narrative practice indicative of postmodernism. As the story demonstrates, the metaphorical and ambiguous nature of the city in the narrator's dream and the irresolvable enigma it poses for him are signs that the city is a contained space of progress and the basis of Western civilization. This ambiguous city suggests, perhaps, an intersection of modern notions of the city as the cultural center and postmodern notions of the city as a deterritorialized symbol.

The narrator then asks a fellow countryman to help him understand his dream. Juan, the narrator's friend, has just returned from the city of their birth. After his trip,

Juan does not remember that the street corners of his exiled land are different from those of his native land and he is almost run over. He ponders the thought of his death: "Extranjero muerto en la avenida. Morirse en un lugar que no es el tuyo tiene algo de impúdico. Sólo deberían morir los nativos" (171–72) ["Foreigner dead in the middle of the street. There's something indecent about dying in a place that isn't one's own. Only natives should die"; 147]. They speak about statues (symbols of national identity): Juan says that during his trip he saw statues that he had never seen before and the narrator explains that in his dreams he can never see the faces of the statues, only their backs, and that he is incapable of determining the identity of the statues. Like the problem of identity for the exile, the statues are present but anonymous. Juan tells the narrator that the city of his dreams has no relationship whatsoever with the city in which he was born: "no me cabe ninguna duda que la ciudad con la que sueñas no tiene nada que ver con la que te vio nacer. Lo he comprobado" (173) ["I have no doubt that the city you dream about has no connection with the one where you were born. I know this for a fact"; 149]. Once again the text emphasizes the difference between the external geographic realities in which the exile lives and the fantasy visions of national spaces.

As the narrator leaves Juan, the city in which he is walking transforms into the city of his dreams. "Ésa era una ciudad sin gatos, pero cuando atravesó la calzada, un par de gatos negros, de gran tamaño, cruzaron por encima casi de sus pies. . . . Pero lo más extraño era la ausencia de autos. Sin duda estaba perdido" (176) ["It was a city without cats, but when he crossed the street a couple of huge black felines almost scampered across his feet. . . . Strangest of all was the absence of autos. . . . He must be lost"; 151]. He is lost in space between the reality of the foreign city in which he lives and the dream city, which he has fantasized. The bank has become a run-down provincial home. He gets caught in mud, becoming increasingly distressed and confused. He is immobilized and feels an androgynous presence, which is the force keeping him stuck in the dirt, tied to the land. Androgyny, like exile, in contrast with clearly defined gender roles and a clearly defined place in the nation, is a condition that leaves one stuck and isolated.

The exile is cast off from the nation, as the sexually ambiguous person is cut off from the dominant mode of sexual relations. This creates both a loss and a gain. As Peri Rossi explains in an interview: "a causa del exilio, se vuelven más claras las raíces culturales" (qtd. in Golano 48) ["cultural roots become clearer as a result of exile"]. So the exile, an outcast from the nation, cannot avoid ties to nationalism while simultaneously dreaming of the advantages of transnational existence and alternative communities. While traveling by boat, Equis in *La nave de los locos* speaks to a little boy who tells him: "Quiero ir a la calle" (17) ["I want to go out in the streets"; 10]. So Equis describes for him an underwater city where the streets the boy yearns for exist without the repression of the streets from which they where exiled. In their former city the streets were spaces of fear: "El auto se deslizaba a gran velocidad por las calles de una ciudad que quedaba súbitamente vacía como bajo una alarma nuclear y los escasos transeúntes corrían a guarecerse debajo de los portales o detrás de las esquinas" (57) ["As the car sped through the streets, the few pedestrians went running to hide under archways or behind corners: soon the town was as empty as under a nuclear alarm"; 54]. Fantasizing, Equis tells the boy: "Hay una ciudad llena de calles con árboles en forma de pez y pulpos que giran como tiovivos" (17) ["Down there is a city full of streets with trees shaped like fishes, and the octopus turn like carousels"; 11]. Yet this alternative city, like the concentration camp inhabited by Vercingétorix, remains outside the official city—a modern city governed by an oppressive system that remains oblivious to the pain such a system causes: "Nadie conocía, tampoco, la existencia de los desaparecidos, en ese lugar, atrapados entre el polvo del olvido y el polvo de la muerte, como una legión de hormigas que trabajaba en las cañerías mientras la ciudad, ajena, duerme" (58) ["Nobody knew of the disappeared either, trapped in the sands of oblivion and death, like a column of ants working their tunnels while the distant city slept"; 55]. The concentration camp, like the ship transporting Equis, "era un lugar de paso" (58) ["was a place of passage"; 55]. These outcasts "no eran sacados para ser devueltos a la ciudad" (58–59) ["weren't taken away to be returned to the city"]. What is most difficult for these outcasts, as exemplified by the child's desire to return to the streets, is that they are unable to resist the desire to find a place where they belong. Despite himself, Equis continues to look for "la ciudad para la residencia" ["a city to reside in"].

The city in Peri Rossi's exile writing, then, is a place distinct from other spaces, like the sea or islands, which hold the possibility of an alternative to the official nation. Yet such a vision is utopian because it ignores the reality that all spaces face heightened urbanization. Even the provinces, or Peri Rossi's symbolic islands and seas, in the "real" world are increasingly influenced by the urban sprawl of global capitalism. Consequently, even if those spaces remain unevenly modern, they no longer remain isolated from the reach of capitalist ideology. Fredric Jameson argues that the concept of the city has been transformed from the modern contained city to the postmodern global city (see *Seeds*). But the notion that the social organization of the city is no longer confined to the modern great cities described in Peri Rossi's writing does not change the fact that Peri Rossi considers the city to be one of the primary sources of social oppression. Lucia Guerra Cunningham points out that the modern city, as a symbol of western civilization, functions as the source for alienation (66). This persistent construction of the city as the symbolic container of modernization leads Peri Rossi to construct a somewhat utopian vision of the relationship between the city and the provinces/non-urban spaces. Jameson explains:

> modern technologies are everywhere, there are no longer any provinces, and even the past comes to seek an alternate world, rather than an imperfect, privative stage of this one. Meanwhile, those 'modern' city dwellers or metropolitans of earlier decades themselves came from the country or at least could still register the coexistence of uneven worlds; they could measure change in ways that become impossible once modernization is even relatively completed (and no longer some isolated, unnatural, and unnerving process that stands out to the naked eye). (*Seeds* 11–12)

To Peri Rossi's narrative eye, these differences still remain, perhaps because they are necessary for an imaginary utopic space the exile can occupy.

The best example of this contrast in *La nave de los locos* is the juxtaposition of the city, Gran Ombligo (Great Navel), and the island, Pueblo de Dios (Town of God). The positive vision of an alternative nation is the island, Pueblo de Dios, where *different* people coexist. The negative version of the nation is the Gran Ombligo, where all of the inhabitants have assimilated to the national ideology. When Morris, the exiled writer hoping to publish his book, receives a letter that he must visit a publishing house in the city, the contrast between life on the island and in the metropolis is made clear. The description of the Gran Ombligo, provided to the reader through Morris's observations, presents the metropolis as a metaphor for the authoritarian state (117). Morris is terrified of traveling to the city and yet his desire to publish his text forces him to overcome his fears and embark on the trip. Whereas the inhabitants of Pueblo de Dios occupy themselves with a variety of activities (Equis fishes, Graciela researches the deflowering of girls, Stanley—the dog—chases cats and other animals, etc.), Morris explains that in the Gran Ombligo "La principal ocupación de los habitantes de la ciudad consiste en mirarse el ombligo" (119) ["The principal occupation of the city's inhabitants is staring at their navels"; 121]. This act of navel gazing hinders the city dwellers' ability to recognize the oppressive nature of the metropolis, but the exile, or outcast, is able to see the pitfalls of such behavior. "La operación de contemplarse el ombligo requiere estar adentro, y no afuera, por lo tanto, sólo quien no se mira el ombligo puede ver quien lo hace, principio de toda soledad" (120) ["The navel-gazing operation implies being inside and not outside the navel, with the result that only those who do not contemplate their navel can see those who do, which leads to a complete state of isolation"; 121]. So the exile, by being an outsider, is in a unique position to comment on the problems of the nation-state and its center of ideological power—the city. Only the outsider is aware of the pain caused by the condition of exile, because those inside remain unaware that an "outside" even exists.

The central ideology of the city is totalitarian; everything must be in order and controlled. For the citizens of the city, the world is "un todo circular, cerrado, siendo ellos los principales habitantes, los investigadores, los dueños y los señores del ombligo" (120) ["a circular enclosure, of which they are the main inhabitants, as students and masters of the umbilical"; 122]. Because the inhabitants are self-satisfied, they are incapable of political action. They are only interested in economic success: "El tráfico de ombligos ocupa gran parte de la vida de los ciudadanos de B, quienes han constituido una fuerte industria y un activo comercio, próspero" (121) ["The navel industry occupies a large part of the life of the citizens of B, creating active and prosperous businesses"; 122]. Morris explains that the city is based on patriarchal order and that in this city the order is centered on the fetish of the belly button, which provides the ideological source of faith in the system: "Cada ombligo es una fábrica como cada familia es una industria" (121) ["Each navel is a factory, just as each family is an industry"; 123]. The city is the site of production of material products, social ideology, and personal identities.

Nevertheless life in the city/modern nation is full of contradictions, and, despite its totalizing ideological ground, there remain cracks in the system: "dentro del ombligo se vive mal" (122) ["But life is not pleasant here"; 124]. The streets smell. Beggars, children, and the elderly suffer. The air is contaminated. What the city dwellers consider to be progress is only "convulsion." The noise of the city is extraordinary and it makes communication difficult. "Entonces los ombliguistas enferman de incomunicación y deben ir al psicoanalista" (123) ["This leads to a lack of communication and the need for psychoanalysis"; 125]. The favorite animal is a car. Morris enters a department store and becomes delirious from the consumerism (125). The city, then, is the receptacle for all of the evils of Western civilization. All cities referred to in the novel are similar in their restriction of inhabitants' actions and in the way they force their citizens to conform to capitalist, patriarchal ideology.

The city poses a great dilemma for the exile, because it is from this system that he has been expelled. A non-conformist, the exile must remain on the margins and the margins always imply the center from which one has been cast away. Interestingly, as Equis contemplates the answer to the enigma of his dreams he wonders if the solution lies in the city: "¿La ciudad de sus recuerdos o de sus sueños, la ciudad imaginada?" (183) ["The city of his memories or of his dreams, the imagined city?"; 188]. Could the answer to the King's question of how to pay tribute to a loved woman lie in the concept of the city? But which city? Can he imagine a city that is free of repression? Could he build a utopian city? After considering the notion, Equis concludes that the answer does not lie in the city, and finally determines that the answer is to offer the woman his virility, thereby subverting patriarchal order.

The closest approximation to Equis's vision of an alternative nation is Pueblo de Dios, where all of its inhabitants are outcasts, social misfits, and even criminals (one of whom is a rapist) (105). This utopic place is exemplified by its emphasis on difference, which is precisely the bond uniting the inhabitants. Each person, even each animal, is able to act in any way desired with no repression. Moreover, the inhabitants have cut themselves off from the repressive "cities" which expelled them. They are free-floating and not tied down by the pain and determination of history. "Los alucinados que llegan a Pueblo de Dios parecen brotar de algún lejano confín, o haber nacido de sí mismos: no reconocen procedencia, no portan equipaje, ni arrastran compañía" (97) ["The deluded ones who come to Pueblo de Dios seem to have sprung up from beyond the far horizon, without origins: they acknowledge no country of provenance, carry no luggage, have no friends"; 97]. Or, at least, that is the utopic vision of the island. Yet, as we know from Morris's foray into the city, such existence is illusory because the inhabitants remain tied to the city, despite their desires to be free from such restrictions. Even Pueblo de Dios is incapable of truly providing an alternative nation free from the limitations and constrictions of nation-states. Just as Goytisolo could not construct the concept of "home" and Dorfman could not construct the concept of "family" in a way that did not restrict individual self expression, Peri Rossi does not effectively construct an alternative nation which can liberate the exile from the pain of expulsion and nostalgic nationalism. Even on the island the outcasts are not free from the power of the city. The city and the island remain in a dialectic, center versus margin, never one without the other, with no possibility of synthesis nor of isolated existence, but in perpetual, shifting tension.

In sum, the most interesting connection between Goytisolo's, Dorfman's, and Peri Rossi's attempts at defining alternative nations is that, in each case, they focus their narrative on structures integral to modern society and modern notions of progress. The home, the family, and the city are considered, in their work, to be the building blocks of pro-capitalist, modernist ideology. Moreover, in their critiques of these structures, these writers tend to resort to literary strategies more commonly associated with modernist writing: they attempt to counter the official meta-narratives of dominant culture with equally powerful counter-narratives. They struggle with the notion of oppressive nationalism and attempt to challenge it by substituting another, liberating vision of nationalism or communal living. Moreover, all three writers rely on traditional definitions of these terms, where "home," "family," and "city" are symbolic referents clearly associated with modern notions of nation-building. These terms of reference and their meanings are locked in a binary struggle between the way in which official culture describes them and the way in which marginalized culture challenges this description. The "home" for Goytisolo is either oppressive or liberating. For Dorfman, the "family" is either a source of solidarity or of authoritarianism. These writers deal with the internal ambiguities of these concepts. Peri Rossi, on the other hand, presents polar opposites, where the "city" is the ideological source of individual oppression and "seas" and "islands" are spaces for unhindered, free existence.

Perhaps what makes each of these literary efforts at countering the official nation so complex is the way that these writers also combine modernist efforts with an attempt to use postmodern strategies of fragmentation and skepticism to undermine social organization. So while they use the modern notion of straightforward dialectical challenge, they also question whether such approaches are meaningful or hold any hope of being transgressive because, as is the case with each writer's work, the official dominating version of nationalism responsible for restricting identity prevails. It is clear in each of the texts studied here that the authors are keenly aware of the pitfalls in their efforts to reconstitute the nation along non-oppressive lines. Yet, they still find it necessary to make such narrative efforts. I would argue that it is the importance of the concept of nationalism for the exile that serves as the backdrop to such literary endeavors. As exiled writers, the only way for them to combat official versions of the nation is to write a counter to that definition, even if that means resorting to some of the same tactics used by those in power. In the end, the question remains whether these works of literature are capable of challenging the power structures that forced the condition of exile on these writers. It is a question these writers confront directly but are unable to answer. Their only response is to keep writing and to continue challenging the social systems they are at one and the same time expelled from and contained within.

THERE'S NO PLACE LIKE HOME:
THE TENSION BETWEEN UTOPIA AND DYSTOPIA

Tengo nostalgia de un país que no existe todavía
en el mapa.—Eduardo Galeano

Borders and the borderlands, like Victor Turner's concept of liminality, are terms that have been removed in some examples of recent scholarship from their original context, where they originally described cultures literally on the edge. They are now often used as a metaphor for a cultural identity that flows across spatial relations and which is in constant flux. If, in my discussion of "space" and its connections to the exile's cultural identity, I have shied away from the term "border," it is precisely because of the way in which the notion of the border has been altered in much recent scholarship. D. Emily Hicks's *Border Writing*, which argues for the value of a "deterritorialized" writing, analyzes Gabriel García Márquez, Julio Cortázar, and Luisa Valenzuela. Yet, never in her exaltation of the "border" does she discuss her authors' existence as exiles. It is just this type of separation between theoretical analysis and attention to historical particularity and circumstance that I have tried to avoid in my critique of the work of Goytisolo, Dorfman, and Peri Rossi.

Borders are real concerns for the exile, even in the postmodern age of advanced hypercapitalism. The exile does not float free, but must worry about such practical things as visas and prohibited reentry into his or her nation. In the literature of Goytisolo, Dorfman, and Peri Rossi, the border becomes both a real limit of confinement and an abstract metaphorical symbol of space—a space to occupy. In this sense the literature of exiles always includes some utopic vision of existence. This utopic impulse in their narratives is also driven by their fears and experiences of dystopia. The nation, which was meant to be a welcoming home, has become a place of torture and violence—a hell. Moreover, this same dystopic nation has expelled the exile and has condemned him or her to exist in heterotopia, a place for those who do not conform to the system. Indeed, often in the case of exile literature, heterotopias are described as utopic borderlands occupied by social outcasts. But these heterotopias are false utopias, because, as far as these authors are concerned, ultimately, there is no place like home: that is, there is no place that can be home for the exile who refuses to be subsumed by the traditional and conservative ideology of "home" as a symbolic monad for the state. In this way, the literature of Goytisolo, Dorfman, and Peri Rossi demonstrates their complicated connections to spatial existence. They narrate fantasy, utopic worlds, and exaggerated, dystopic worlds. They alternate between the desire to imagine a place, a space, which would welcome them, and the need to represent their fears that such a place is pure illusion. In addition, they are constantly aware of the fact that the work of the exiled writer is in an extraordinarily tenuous relation to discourses of power.

The most salient example of the way in which these writers waver between literary fantasy and political frustration is their use of the womb as an idyllic utopia, an idyllic home, while contrasting such a pedantic and common stereotype of the womb with visions of the world where heterosexual reproduction is tied to capitalist production. Interestingly, in all three authors' works, the womb is a fantasy utopic space. But this vision is accompanied by a rejection of heterosexual reproduction that, for these writers, poses problems for the creation of utopia. Paradoxically, the womb is both the site of potential utopic existence and the source of capitalist ideology.

Narrating these problems with procreation is a way of rejecting capitalist production. In Goytisolo's and Peri Rossi's utopias there is no reproduction. For Dorfman, birth requires the establishment of a benevolent, socialist state. So these writers narrate the resistance of the "unborn," the "impotent," and "homosexuals" as threats to the "survival" of capitalist reproduction. Moreover, in each case, women's bodies are the battlegrounds for these issues: Goytisolo narrates Spain as the body of the Virgin which must be raped, Dorfman describes eternal pregnancy for women, and Peri Rossi describes women who suffer abortion and genital mutilation. Klaus Theweleit discusses the male fantasies of fascist soldiers in which the image of woman was created to satisfy their desires. But he also points out that a constant theme in much non-fascist cultural production is the connection between women and water. He considers this practice to be an obvious allusion to the use of the woman's body in the fantasy of return to the womb.

> A river without an end, enormous and wide, flows through the world's literatures. Over and over again: the women-in-the-water; woman as water, ... as a limitless body of water that ships pass through... woman as the enticing (or perilous) deep, as a cup of bubbling body fluids; the vagina as wave... as a sea voyage; ... where we are part of every ocean, which is part of every vagina. To enter these portals is to begin a global journey, a flowing around the world. He who has been inside the right woman, the ultimate *cunt*—knows every place in the world that is worth knowing.... It is oppression through exaltation, through a lifting of boundaries, an "irrealization" and reduction to principle—the principle of flowing of distance, of vague, endless enticement. (283–84)

There is no doubt that Goytisolo, Dorfman, and Peri Rossi have all been enticed by this vision of the woman's body and the possibilities it offers to cross social and geographical boundaries.

In *Señas de identidad* Alvaro has sex with Dolores and fantasizes: "Ojalá, te decías, no hubieras salido nunca" (158) ["Oh, you said to yourself, if only you had never come out"; 132]. In *Reivindicación del conde don Julián* the narrator wanders the streets of Tangiers trying to lose the restricting aspects of his Spanish cultural heritage, repeating the words, "hacia dentro, hacia dentro" (89) ["penetrating deeper and deeper"; 73]. Going back inside the womb will enable him to begin again and recreate himself. Paul Julian Smith has commented on Goytisolo's misogynistic use of the female body where the womb, vagina, and the entire female body are all used without any critical reflection (70–71).

In Dorfman's *The Last Song of Manuel Sendero,* Manuel Sendero's brother, Juan, takes refuge inside Doralisa's womb from the authorities who are looking for him

(56–57). The womb is a utopian space: "The dark refuge of a woman is the safest place in the world" (442). Doralisa's womb becomes the home of her unwilling-to-be born son as well as a home for those hiding from the military police. Importantly, in Dorfman's novel women are active participants in this use of their body. The son of Sendero is told by a woman's voice of unclear identity in the narrative: "You'll have to hide yourself here deep inside my sexual waters, so they won't find you and, from inside there, keep on making them, keep on birthing them... wandering in pilgrimage from womb to womb until the end of time, helping us to be born, telling each one about your father's song" (448–49). The voice of the son of Sendero as he resides in his mother's womb comes "from an unconquered faraway place, from an island in time, where the verb *to fear* couldn't be conjugated" (26). In these lines Dorfman treats the female body in traditional stereotypical ways that are similar to Goytisolo, but Dorfman's work lacks the anger and desire for violence against women found in Goytisolo's writing.

In Peri Rossi's *La nave de los locos* Equis recalls: "siempre partimos del lugar donde hubiéramos sido eternos y felices" (109) ["we always leave the place where we could be forever happy"; 109]. In this way the womb functions as a Paradise Lost and a utopic space to which the exile yearns to return. The second chapter of the novel begins quoting Exodus: "Y no angustiarás al extranjero" (10) ["And thou shall not oppress a stranger"; 2]. The words of the Bible tell humanity not to suffer the experience of forced travel to new lands, but Peri Rossi's characters suffer anyway. After quoting the Bible the narrative begins: "Extranjero. Ex. Extrañamiento. Fuera de las entrañas de la tierra. Desentrañado: vuelto a parir" (10) ["A stranger. Ecks. Estranged. Expelled from the womb of earth. Eviscerated: once more to give birth"; 2]. The passengers on the ship carrying Equis away from his home have been metaphorically expelled from the national, territorial womb. Peri Rossi connects the ideology of Judeo-Christianity with the alienation of exiles who suffer but are taught that their suffering is a result of Original Sin, because it originated in humanity's expulsion from Paradise (the symbolic womb). Lucía Guerra Cunningham explains: "La expulsión del Paraíso, luego de desobedecer el mandato divino, postula el exilio como signo primordial en la representación y simbolización de la naturaleza humana, la cual paradójicamente posee, como núcleo esencial, la pérdida del espacio original" (63) ["The expulsion from paradise, after disobeying the divine mandate, postulates exile as a primordial sign of the representation and symbolization of human nature, which paradoxically possesses, as essential nucleus, the loss of the original space"]. Although Peri Rossi criticizes this ideology in her novel, she continues to postulate the womb as a referent for a utopic space that the exile seeks and from which he or she has been expelled.

Theweleit analyzes this use of the woman's womb and explains that "the depersonalization of women, ... the dissolving of their boundaries, is a consequence of the extreme abstractness of a desire that lacks adequate objects. And the only things preventing desires having adequate objects are the barriers of domination" (286). The symbolic woman/womb becomes in the literature of Goytisolo, Dorfman, and Peri Rossi a fantasy space for these exiles as it has also been for many other writers. Given that these exiles have been denied access to their nations, they respond to this denial and rejection by fantasizing about returning to the symbolic, welcoming home of the womb. It is quite interesting to note that despite the differences among these writers' narratives, they continue to incorporate this traditional metaphor. It is also interesting that all three writers practice this type of female objectification of the womb despite their distinct sexual identities as a bisexual male, a heterosexual male, and a lesbian.

Contrasting this traditional trope of the womb as utopia, these writers also incorporate a contrary picture that challenges the norms of heterosexual reproduction and which connects heterosexual reproduction with capitalism. In this alternative utopia, the womb is no longer the source of perfect existence. Smith explains the ties between theories of sexuality and state power as they relate to the three stages of Guy Hocquenghem's theory: "first, the analysis of paranoid hostility to homosexuality; second, the relation of that hostility to the Oedipal family and reproductive sexuality; third, the attempt to resist familial sexuality through anti-capitalist and anti-Oedipal struggles" (56). For Goytisolo, heterosexual sex comes to epitomize the ties between cultural identity and nation formation. In *Juan sin tierra* he parodies the "parejita reproductora" ["reproductive couple"] who marry and reproduce so that Western capitalism will have a source of workers and consumers for the system. As Smith explains: "Heterosexuality is thus inextricable from consumerism and the universal expansion of capital.... The acedia or aboulia of reproductive heterosexuality is the nausea of consumerism: no space is uncolonized by the same, no relation free from consumerism" (81). In *Juan sin tierra* Goytisolo contrasts the "parejita reproductora" ["reproductive couple"], with its lack of sensuality and its rigid support of the system, with a utopian vision of a sexual world full of promiscuity and without any sexual taboos. He seeks a world with no repressions: "represiones? : ninguna : estimamos a la colectividad directamente responsable de los actos delictivos del individuo, y, en vez de sancionar a éste según el esquema antiguo, juzgamos más lógico enmendar la sociedad" (232) ["repression?: none: we hold the collectivity directly responsible for the delinquent acts of the individual, and instead of punishing the latter according to the old scheme of things, we consider it more logical to reform society"; 204]. The narrator hopes to create a narrative world where individual desire is boundary-free. Nevertheless, in his contrast between the "cara" (face) and the "culo" (ass) Goytisolo privileges the sexuality of the gay male by focusing sexual liberation on a valorization of the anus. Goytisolo's obsession with the anus in *Juan sin tierra* is, according to Smith, "not merely a gratuitous shock tactic. It is also a pointer to the interdependence of capitalism and heterosexuality, both of which sublimate the anal" (80). In this way, Goytisolo utilizes contrasting utopic visions, one that seeks return to the womb, similar to the "myth of eternal return," and another that is non-traditional and threatens the reproduction of human beings as a way to threaten state power.

Like Goytisolo, Peri Rossi also posits an alternative utopian vision that relies on the destruction of capitalist ideology's valorization of heterosexual sex. This utopia requires that the phallus no longer be the central sexual signifier. These words from Smith's analysis of Goytisolo might also apply to the work of Peri Rossi in *La nave de los locos:* "Goytisolo's destabilizing anal utopia dramatizes both the infinity of desiring relations and the collapse of the phallic hierarchy" (83). For Goytisolo, the anus is just as important as the penis, whereas for Peri Rossi the "collapse of the phallic hierarchy" implies an end to genital hierarchy. Peri Rossi sees male-biased heterosexism as the basis for dominant power structures and she narrates ambiguous gendered identities. Modern society causes the suffering of men, women, and nature: "Delicado sistema.... Autobuses de embarazadas, niñas infibuladas y el suicidio de las ballenas en las costas del Atlántico, donde no deberían ir, porque los peces están envenenados" (171) ["A delicate business.... Coach-loads of pregnant women, infibulated girls, and whales committing suicide on the Atlantic shores where they should know the fish are all poisoned"; 175]. Lucía (after her abortion) will never sleep with another man, Morris is in love with a young boy, and Equis is impotent. Speaking to an old prostitute Equis reveals: "Hace mucho tiempo que no tengo una erección.... Y no me importa" (188) ["I haven't had an erection in a long time.... And I don't mind"; 194]. She responds: "Por si te importa, te diré que encuentro en la impotencia una clase de armonía" (188) ["If you want to know, I find that there is a kind of harmony in impotence"; 194]. Most significantly Equis does not *care* that he is impotent, and, for the prostitute, impotence implies utopic harmony. If all men were impotent, then she would no longer have to use her body as a commodity. Such a restructuring of gendered power relations would subvert the capitalist system, which dominates, according to the logic of the novel, almost all facets of modern life.

The connections between the family and the state are also integral components of Dorfman's literature. As discussed above in his use of the family as a metaphor for the nation, Dorfman narrates the family as both the source of authoritarian/patriarchal systems and as the necessary birthing ground for an egalitarian collective. In *The Last Song of Manuel Sendero,* David's live-in girlfriend in exile, Gringa, goes to have an abortion, which then causes David to have a vasectomy (219). He will not father any more children if they have to live in the oppressive world in which he lives, and which he doubts will ever change. Interestingly, abortion appears in the work of all three authors. In *Señas de identidad,* Dolores has an abortion after Alvaro insists that she do so. In *La nave de los locos,* Equis works for a company that organizes trips out of the country for women seeking abortions, where he meets Lucía. Even the son of Sendero is told that he was never born but was aborted from Doralisa's womb by the Caballero. Abortion symbolizes the complex ties between birth and death for exiles. The authoritarian state threatens to control both birth and death as a means of creating an ideal, subservient population.

Dorfman also deals with reproduction and state power in the comic strip that David works on with Felipe about Chilex. A fantastic exaggeration of the effects of hypercapitalism on Chile, Chilex develops a tourist industry that provides sterile women with a cure to their infertility. Sarah, Carl Barks's wife, tells him that she has learned that the new technology of Chilex would enable her to have a baby after years of being barren. Reproduction in Chilex is equivalent to capitalist production, where the state is able to control who gives birth. David's comic strip, contrasting his experience of abortion, vasectomy, and the (probable) suicide of his son, is a further critique of the relationship between human reproduction and authoritarian state power. Dorfman's narrative suggests that utopia, i.e., an egalitarian collective existence, requires that authoritarian control of human reproduction be destroyed. Nevertheless, Salvador Oropesa states that

Dorfman locates his utopic impulse in a shift in the power relations between men and women. He suggests that Dorfman narrates a world where both revolutionary machos and fascist machos have failed to construct a better world, leaving women to be the modern heroes that will construct utopia (16). While Dorfman does explore the pitfalls of the fascist and revolutionary aspects of masculine identity as a hindrance to the creation of an alternative social construction, Dorfman's utopic imaginary goes beyond a shift in power relations among the sexes. Women must be part of history and active participants in a utopic social configuration, but it is not the job of women to construct utopia. For Dorfman, the process must be unisex, because it must destroy the concept of authoritarian patriarchy. *The Last Song of Manuel Sendero* in its description of the fetal rebellion clearly argues that, until patriarchy and capitalism are destroyed, no one should be born.

The conflicting literary gestures of narrating utopias and dystopias in these writers' work are directly connected to their fear that utopia is purely fantasy, a place that is no place, and that hypercapitalism has successfully created all nations and their inhabitants as commodities: the world is a dystopic system of oppression and omnipotent ideological social control. Agnes Heller explains: "The demise of class-related cultures can be explained in terms of the increase in consumerism" (505). This leads to a lack of a foundation for political resistance (507). For writers who have experienced exile at a time of ever-increasing commodification of the spaces in which people live, political resistance appears to be extremely fragile and class-based politics seem to be useless strategies for upsetting the globalized power of capitalist ideology. For these reasons, space, geography, territory, and the concept of "home" are difficult notions for these writers. They exist in a transnational world and also within the confines of national laws. Harvey argues that "in money economies in general, and in capitalist society in particular, the intersecting command of money, time, and space forms a substantial nexus of social power that we cannot afford to ignore" (226). Goytisolo's, Dorfman's, and Peri Rossi's conditions of exile from nations that replaced the threat of socialism with dictatorial authoritarianism and that embraced capitalist modes of production cause them to associate the problem of space with the problem of possibilities of political change.

Space in these writers' work is often equated with containment and confinement. The exile has become the victim of a system of social containers—systems of spatial organization—that place their ability to interact with the world on the margins. As these writers confront the complex intersections between modernism and postmodernism, they address the way in which such intersections and changes affect the spatial basis of economic and political control. Harvey suggests: "If space is indeed to be thought of as a system of 'containers' of social power (to use the imagery of Foucault), then it follows that the accumulation of capital is perpetually deconstructing that social power by re-shaping its geographical bases" (238). How can the exile confront the system that has caused displacement when the system itself is constantly being reconstructed along different territorial lines? These exiles cannot merely deal with the concept of one's space of existence as a national issue, nor can they argue that human existence is disconnected from territory and is transnational. Harvey explains the intricacies of resistance during an era of shifting theories about the way in which individuals relate to the spaces in which they live:

> Movements of opposition to the disruptions of home, community, territory, and nation by the restless flow of capital are legion. But then so too are movements against the tight constraints of a purely monetary expression of value and the systemitized organization of space and time. What is more, such movements spread far beyond the realms of class struggle in any narrowly defined sense. (238)

Most importantly, Harvey identifies distinct forms of opposition. These competing forms exist simultaneously in the literary works of Goytisolo, Dorfman, and Peri Rossi: they oppose the effects of transnationalism on their nations, they critique the way in which such changes are tied to capitalism, and they seek critiques that are multifocal and not only class-based.

A significant way in which the work of these writers poses a substantial challenge to literary criticism is the refusal of their texts to be confined by traditional categories of literary genre. Fredric Jameson argues that, in large part, literature has been either utopian or dystopian, but not both simultaneously (*Seeds* 55–56). Even though these texts are not, strictly speaking, utopian or dystopian narratives, they do include a combination of utopic and dystopic narrative. At the same time, they desire the representation of an alternative social system to that which has forced them into exile and they fear that the system itself is ever expanding and increasingly unstoppable. This dialectic is an important facet of their work and one that relates directly to their concept of the spaces of human existence.

That exile literature fears dystopia and seeks utopia is not a new observation. Edward Said explains that "much of the exile's life is taken up with compensating for disorienting loss by creating a new world to rule" ("Reflections" 363). What is distinct, though, in the work of these writers is that their literature refuses to choose between narrating utopia or dystopia. Instead, their work presents the reader with both visions of the future as the most potentially "shocking" way to demonstrate the crisis of cultural identity. Moreover, the descriptions of utopia and dystopia are multiple and extend beyond the use of the womb as a utopic space and the description of heterosexual reproduction as a dystopic necessity of hypercapitalism.

For instance, beyond the exaltation of the womb and the destruction of heterosexual reproduction, Goytisolo's work displays further utopic images meant to counteract the effects of Franco's control of Spain and its ideological base in the doctrines of the Catholic Kings. In *Señas de identidad,* Alvaro dreams of an alternative to his oppressed existence: "Soñabas despierto de una España real, . . . en una existencia humana impuesta frente a los voraces enemigos de la vida. . . . La muerte no importa. Unos instantes—unos breves instantes—de libertad valen—lo sabemos ahora—toda una eternidad de siglos" (138) ["You were daydreaming about a real Spain, . . . with a human existence maintained in the face of the voracious enemies of life. . . . Death does not matter. A few seconds—a few brief seconds—of freedom are worth—we know now—a whole eternity of centuries"; 114–15]. Alvaro dreams of successful resistance to Spanish authoritarianism, even if it lasts for only a brief moment, because the feeling of freedom, while fleeting, is valuable and will remain important for centuries. Yet, it is *Juan sin tierra* that best exemplifies Goytisolo's multiple imaginary utopias. In the desert, he narrates an oasis where his narrator can be "entre los tuyos al fin" (87) ["amid those of your kind at last"; 72]. Utopia, then, while rejecting reproduction, does not reject the notion of community. Most importantly, this community is boundary-free, spatially indefinite: "nosotros creemos en un mundo sin fronteras" (89) ["we believe in a world without borders"; 74]. Rejecting the national image of Spain as Catholic and capitalist, the narrator offers an alternative "cara y culo parejos, libres y descubiertos, utopía de un mundo completo, sin asepsia ni ocultación" (218) ["the face and the ass equals, free and bare, the utopia of a complex world, without asepsis or concealment"; 192]. Even though this utopia implies a complete/complex world, it is a world which rejects the institution of the nation that forces assimilation and implies repression: "otra particularidad : ni bandera ni himno nacional : oposición radical a tajante a todo lo que institucionalice, momifique, enmascare" (224) ["another feature: neither a flag nor a national anthem: a radical incisive opposition to everything which institutionalizes, mummifies, disguises"; 198]. Nevertheless, the narrator recognizes these utopian visions as limited to the realm of fantasy. Reinforcing his fear that literature is incapable of changing the force of history, the narrator exclaims: "todo es posible en la página" (110) ["everything is possible on the written page"; 96].

In Dorfman's case, utopia refers to both the past and the future. The Allende years are remembered as utopic. Under Allende, Chile was like a Socialist Eden (Howard 31). The utopia of Allende is a powerful experience that continues to affect Dorfman's characters even after the coup. Manuel, like David, "believed in paradise, in the Promised Land, in the Golden Age. With no modesty whatsoever he presented himself as an outrageous example of the existence of utopias, where there were no conflicts, where nothing could be criticized, where failures are only symptoms of an illness that's rapidly being cured" (74). When Manuel sang, people formed a harmonious group that felt empowered to control their own destiny: "Because those bridges in his voice pointed the way toward another future, another crossroads: history could be, would be made by our very selves" (29). Yet these feelings are just dreams because, despite the power of Manuel's voice, he becomes mute and the people only have the memory of his song to give them hope. Dreams and fantasies are the mental spaces for utopia when living in exile or under dictatorship: "Dreams are the hardest thing to exile" (292). Like Goytisolo, Dorfman is quick to highlight the limitations of his literature as a force for political change. Yet, also, like Goytisolo, he believes that it is in literature that hope and utopia can continue to exist and possibly reach the reader.

Cristina Peri Rossi also describes the utopian possibilities of literature. In *La nave de los locos* the reader is told that every text "por el mero hecho de existir" ["by the mere fact of existing"] is optimistic and a sign that the social system has not (yet) controlled every space of human imagination. Beyond Peri Rossi's reference to the utopic space of the womb, Pueblo de Dios functions as a utopic community where difference is not repressed and heterosexual reproduction is absent. This utopic space is a fantasy island that is supposedly separate from the limitations and control of identity found in the city. Elia Kantaris explains that the suffering caused by sexually driven power complexes and stereotypes of modern Western society, like the rape of Christie's character and the case of the Jewish women used for experiments, is the focus of Peri Rossi's utopic vision. Her narrative endeavors to conceive of a world without such "power complexes." "In the light of these and subsequent events, the whole novel becomes an attempt to undo the *cultural* bond between sexuality and power" (261). Equis is a utopic male who stands as an exemplary man, capable of subverting the ideology of masculine virility and power. Utopia is androgyny, contrasting the rigid gendered identities of Western society. In "La historia como metáfora" (History as Metaphor), Hugo J. Verani describes the way in which Peri Rossi's fusion of the sexes is utopic (in particular in the scene where Equis watches Lucía dressed as Marlene Dietrich act out a lesbian scene with another woman dressed as Dolores del Río). "Esta utópica fusión de los sexos le permite a Equis entrever la armonía nunca alcanzada" (86) ["This utopic fusion of the sexes permits Equis to glimpse a harmony never reached"]. Equis loves Lucía because of her ambiguity. Equis is an impotent male who is willing to give his virility to a woman, or to renounce virility altogether, because he considers this to be the only way to create a society free of patriarchy and phalologocentrism. Yet these images of a genderless society are fiction: the exaggerated description of the way in which Equis's answer to the enigma destroys the King, who turns into a toy and then "gime antes de morir" (197) ["dies with a whimper"; 204], is a clear example of Peri Rossi's use of literature as a space for utopic fantasy.

Contrary to using literature as a site for the exploration of a utopic imaginary, these writers also use literature as a vehicle for representing the dystopic extremes of hypercapitalism and its effects on the possibilities of cultural free will. It is significant that all of these writers are concerned with the way in which the mass media affect the construction of cultural identity and increasingly diminish the power of the written word. Fernando Calderón asks: "Why do most Latin Americans watch North American television programs, which, most of the time, implant in us the new values of market and atomic violence?" (55). The transnational existence of North American cultural production increasingly threatens the possibilities of locating, maintaining, or creating an alternative autochthonous culture in Latin America or in Spain. This effect of mass media and mass dissemination of North American cultural production directly threatens the cultural clout of exiled writers. (Both Dorfman and Goytisolo have narrators who fancy themselves movie directors in their novels; *Máscaras* 16, *Juan sin tierra* 44; Peri Rossi's Equis is obsessed with the film *Demon Seed*.) Calderón describes this dystopic cultural landscape as "a world that simultaneously tends to a greater production of wealth and to a growing social marginalization, a terrifying cultural homogeneity... which tends to completely negate the search for liberating identities" (60).

In Goytisolo's narrative, popular culture has both the liberating possibility of destroying Catholic values and the dystopian effect of destroying literature. *Reivindicación del conde don Julián* makes countless references to popular culture: the Rolling Stones, James Bond's *Thunderball*, Little Red Riding Hood, etc. (28, 163, 13). The mass media are an aspect of cultural identity that cannot be avoided in social critique. When the narrator fantasizes that Isabel la Católica listens to the Rolling Stones, she becomes sensual and susceptible to rape. In this way, mass culture can be the tool for subverting Francoist ideology. (See Sieburth, chapter 4, on Goytisolo's use of mass media as a way to destroy Spanish culture.) Elsewhere, though, mass media are seen as a threat to literature. In *Juan sin tierra* the narrator appears on a television program and is interrogated about his novel. He must defend the "point" of his writing and explain why he has deviated from "realism" to a "mystifying subjectivism" (266). He is asked, "Por qué manifiesta usted en su obra tanta amargura, pesimismo y resentimiento?" (268) ["Why do you manifest so much bitterness, pessimism, and resentment in your work?"; 237]. Vosk, the ultimate voice of official culture, is on the show as a critic and exclaims that the narrator must be censored (269). In the same way that tourism is both a tool for destroying Sacred Spain and a source of national commodification, the mass media hold both the possibility of destroying rigid Catholic values and threatening the value of literature.

Dorfman's approach to the role of the mass media in cultural identity is much more straightforward. He sees it as a threat to the power of literature and also as a powerful means for disseminating authoritarian ideology. For instance, Carl Barks is asked to come to Chilex precisely because the leaders believe that their nation's power must be maintained through the controlled use of the media. Yet, given that mass media are the central site for cultural production, Dorfman argues that the media must be used as a possible forum for subversive information. Battles must be fought on television and in literature or else there will be no chance of gaining control of the system. The son of Sendero goes on the television program *Search, Search* because he knows that the Caballero will see him and that they will then have the chance to meet. *Search, Search* is a program that advertises that it can solve all problems (296). As the son of Sendero gets up to speak he exclaims: "If all of you, . . . would follow me, life wouldn't be a search, my friends. Life would be an endless encounter" (304). Just as his father sang to create collective harmony, the son recognizes that, in his era, television was his only chance to reach the people. Yet, after his speech, the police quickly remove him from the stage, similar to the way that his father went mute and died.

In *Máscaras* there is an important emphasis on the power of the image over the word. The gaze and photographs of the faceless man have extraordinary power. The faceless man states: "Lamenté tener un solo televisor. Los dos noticieros se dan en forma simultánea, así que esa noche tuve que ir cambiando de un canal a otro, ida y vuelta" (20) ["Too bad I had only one television set. The two newscasts are transmitted at the same time, so that evening I had to switch from one channel to the other, back and forth"; 12]. He channel surfs hoping to get the news but finally exasperatedly recognizes that the news is censored and that he has no control over the images the screen shows him. In an act of rebellion he watches a channel that is only a gray screen, because the news is "[m]entiras, sólo mentiras" (20) ["Lies, only lies"; 13]. In the dystopic world of the novel *Máscaras,* culture is flat and meaningless. Society receives an endless repetition of useless and inaccurate information: "Los telespectadores no se daban cuenta de que la clínica que ella inauguraba, o la escuela, o el parque, o la avenida, era la misma de la semana anterior y que sólo le habían cambiado el nombre" (102) ["The viewers seemed not to understand that the clinic she was opening, or the school, or the park, or the avenue, were the same ones that had been on last week and that only the name had changed"; 99]. The transnational experience of globalized information control creates a dystopic image of the world that leaves little room for the space of literary resistance.

Like Goytisolo, Cristina Peri Rossi also refers to myriad images from popular culture, including Little Red Riding Hood and Snow White (119). Yet, it is the scenes from the novel dealing with the film *Demon Seed* that best demonstrate her depiction of the ties between mass media and cultural authoritarianism. The film is a powerful representation of the monster of technology, able to rape and control anyone who threatens its hegemony. The monster is invisible but omnipotent, "como las dictaduras" (23) ["like dictatorships"]. Dictatorships require such films. They rely on mass media to project their ideology to the population and they choose which films can be seen. For the exiled writer whose work is banned from his or her country, such a practice is terrifyingly dystopic and undermines the idyllic possibility that his or her writing will be able to threaten the system. The interaction between utopia and dystopia in these writers' work is a necessary consequence of their concern for the spaces of human existence and for cultural production. Return to the womb, for instance, is an impossible, yet central, part of the exile's utopian imaginary (as in the desire for the lost object). The literature of exile reveals a need to be associated with a territory and yet these writers' work demonstrates that such an association will never bring the gratification of unification. Therefore the notion of the nation is utopic when it functions as a place for community and it is dystopic insofar as it requires that difference be repressed. Exile literature confronts the importance of space at a time when cultural and economic borders are in flux. As a counter to transnational capitalism and to the sweeping instability of cultural identity, the reaction of these exiled writers tends to be a search for some ground. Harvey explains:

> it is exactly at this point that we encounter the opposite reaction that can best be summed up as the search for personal or collective identity, the search for secure moorings in a shifting world. Place-identity, in this collage of superimposed spatial images that implode upon us, becomes an important issue, because everyone occupies a space of individuation (a body, a room, a home, a shaping community, a nation).... Furthermore if no one 'knows their place' in this shifting collage world, then how can a secure social order be fashioned or sustained? (302)

Although these writers desire a "secure" place of existence, they also reject nationalism's confining qualities by analyzing the role of transnationalism on cultural identity. Transnationalism is utopic because of its borderless, free-floating possibilities for existence, but it is also dystopic because of its association with multinational capitalism and the globalization of mass media. These writers expose the dialectic of transnational capitalism—which is at one and the same time capable of standardization (through transnational capitalism) and change (through a de-centering of traditional values). According to Jameson, "In this form, the paradox from which we must set forth is the equivalence between an unparalleled rate of change on all levels of social life and an unparalleled standardization of everything . . . that would seem incompatible with just such mutability" (*Seeds* 15). In this way the conflict between the cultural ideals of difference and identity politics—where one argues for the endless changeability of individual identity and the other argues for the standardization of cultural communities—becomes irresolvable.

Aijaz Ahmad argues that the postmodern age has brought with it a notion of *an excess of belonging:* "not only does the writer have all cultures available to him or her as a resource, for consumption, but he or she actually belongs in all of them, by virtue of being properly in none" (130). Ahmad's description of transnational culture implies a utopic vision of the effects of transculturation—a concept these authors question. Therefore, their representation of multiple means of social control and of social subversion does not imply that they are disconnected from the problems implicit in both the notion of belonging and that of alienation. Ahmad goes on to argue that those theorists and writers who take their lead from Derrida and Foucault and see existence as "cage-like" and victimized by an "all-encompassing Power" are left to see the course of history as beyond change: "Resistance can only be provisional, personal, local, micro, and pessimistic in advance" (131). But these authors vacillate between believing that forces of power fundamentally hinder their resistance and demonstrating utopic desires, which indicate their hope that narrative still has the power to sway the reader to perceive the world differently. The representation of this conflict as a crisis without a clear solution is not an apolitical narrative gesture for these writers: it is the only means by which they can describe the complexities of cultural identity. Cultural identity occupies a battleground that is not won or lost by advocating nationalism or transnationalism. Harvey explains that these battles over space are always political: "A number of general conclusions can now be ventured. Spatial and temporal practices are never neutral in social affairs. They always express some kind of class or other social content, and are more often than not the focus of intense social struggle" (239).

Hopenhayn explains in "Postmodernism and Neoliberalism": "If the 'postmodern narrative' declares the obsolescence of the idea of progress, historical reason, vanguards, integrating modernization, and ideologies and utopias, what is it that it proclaims in exchange? Basically, the exaltation of diversity, aesthetic and cultural individualism, multiplicity of languages, forms of expression and life-projects, and axiological relativism" (97). This analysis has shown, however, that these writers are caught in a historical moment that is simultaneously pre-modern, modern, and postmodern. Separating these ways of perceiving the world is not so straightforward, since the need for literature to construct utopic visions is not necessarily a pre-modern, modern, or postmodern project. Utopia falls into the realm of imagination and is a necessary aspect of the human condition, particularly for the exiled writer who is "lost in space" and located in a complex relation to territories of existence. Perhaps, for the exiled writer, an attack on the system can only be enacted symbolically. Yet, such mental games seem by definition destined to failure—or are they? These writers' only way of narrating the connection between individual existence and spatial relations is to imagine both the utopic and the dystopic possibilities of their historical experience. Simon Wiesenthal has said, "Hope lives when someone remembers." These exiles have suffered the pain of expulsion from their nations and through their writing they display both frustration and the hope that their history will be not be forgotten.

CHAPTER SEVEN
Culture Shock

Goytisolo's, Dorfman's, and Peri Rossi's dialectical descriptions of nation, time, language, and space lead them to create complex theories of cultural identity. Their intricate relationship to many of the terms commonly applied to questions of cultural identity allows for insight into some of the most pressing issues concerning cultural politics. Much cultural theory rests on a series of binary oppositions—assimilation versus dissimilation, identity politics versus multiculturalism, essentialism versus free will, etc. Exile literature tests the limits of these binaries and reveals that they operate in society according to dialectic tensions rather than mutually exclusive categories of cultural existence. For instance, the work of the writers studied here presents contrasting positions on the issues of assimilation and dissimilation: if the exile's cultural identity is caught between two cultures and two, if not more, nations, to which aspects of dominant cultural paradigms does the exile assimilate and to which does he or she dissimilate? The concept of cultural dissimilation implies the ability to rebel against pre-conceived versions of identity. Yet, exiled writers are also trapped between contrasting visions of cultural essentialism. Cultural essentialism describes the notion of a pre-determined cultural inheritance. Such a concept contrasts with that of cultural free will, whereby cultural identity is a consequence of choice and experience. The case of these writers, then, allows for a test of theories of assimilation, dissimilation, and essentialism.

The exiled writer also represents a dialectical relationship to identity politics versus multiculturalism. Identity politics has been a cultural strategy used by minority cultural groups politically interested in challenging the dominant cultural system that has marginalized them. The cultural identity implied by identity politics is that the group it represents, for instance Chicanos or Native Americans, has a common cultural bond that is undeniable and unchangeable. Therefore the group must attempt to reverse the way in which society has used this cultural difference to marginalize and disempower them. Such a practice might be considered a "strategic territorialization" insofar as the strategy implies claiming a legitimate territory, i.e., space, for such cultural existence to survive apart from the control of the dominant cultural paradigm, which has historically displaced the group and denied it access to discourses of power. On the other hand, multiculturalism, based on a notion of cultural difference and incongruity, is a position that argues that group identity, by necessity, implies conformity to a systematic way of defining cultural identity. Multiculturalism argues for diversity with no privilege accorded to a specific group and with no recourse to a clear political agenda aimed at helping a group that has been marginalized. Multicultural politics revolves around fighting for acceptance of difference, as opposed to identity politics' valorization of uniqueness. Identity politics requires that cultural groups form common and coherent political projects based on shared cultural traits. Multiculturalism, then, questions such practices and names them as oppressive in much the same way that dominant culture defines and controls identity. Multiculturalism, as it is centered on rejecting a "basis for identity," may be seen as a "strategic deterritorialization," because it argues that identity should not be fixed or localizeable. So, technically, identity politics and multiculturalism present two distinct strategies for challenging dominant discourse.

The condition of exile tests the relationship between these two positions because the exile often fights for identity politics but subscribes to the arguments of difference and multiculturalism as well. Interestingly, exiles tend to organize their identity politics along national lines, as in the case of Cuban-Americans, and do not consider fellow exiles from other nations to be part of their "group." In the cases of Goytisolo, Dorfman, and Peri Rossi, though, their work takes up both identity politics and multiculturalism. Moreover, their arguments in favor of identity politics are based on broader terms and include a group identity that is not merely made up by Spanish, Chilean, or Uruguayan exiles but refers to the group with which the author identifies, i.e., social pariahs, outcasts, the politically powerless, etc. This is quite significant, because, unlike proponents of identity politics, these authors suggest that the common cultural bond that must be defended is not simply defined by gender, race, class, nationality, or ethnicity, but rather by the way in which all of these factors play a role in cultural marginalization.

These texts do not solve dilemmas about cultural identity: they exemplify the most pressing crises of community linked with recent historical events resulting in mass emigration and exile and they pose important dilemmas for the categories of analysis often used in the field of cultural studies. The protagonists of these texts are concerned with cultural essentialism, cultural nationalism, and cultural experience. They try to make sense of these different ways of describing identity and they consistently contrast the predominant tactics used for cultural self-definition with those of cultural domination. Since they employ dialectical strategies of defining cultural identity, they argue that cultural identity is always formed by multiple competing factors. The following analysis will examine the distinct ways that Goytisolo, Dorfman, and Peri Rossi represent cultural identity.

In Goytisolo's case, an allegiance to Official Spain is false cultural nationalism, which fabricates a masked version of cultural essentialism for the Spanish people. Goytisolo's texts try to counter this version by offering a replacement, and they also argue for experience over inheritance. Furthermore, at other times, they see cultural ties as constitutive of repressive restrictions to individual self-formation. The argument for experience over inheritance, free will over predetermination, takes place through the repeated efforts of the narrators to create their own cultural community, or individual self, by forsaking the cultural traditions associated with Official Spain. But, as we have seen, these efforts are constantly denied fruition.

There are a variety of theories about national identity put forth in Goytisolo's trilogy. Using the example of *Reivindicación del conde don Julián* as representative of the myriad positions described in these novels, it becomes clear why Goytisolo creates a confusing cultural context. First, the narrator rejoices in his willful ability to assimilate: "libre de la presencia de los tuyos y de su condensada necedad : árabe, árabe puro: amigo y cómplice del robusto Tariq" (41) ["free of the presence of your compatriots: an Arab, a pure Arab: friend and crony of good old dependable Tariq"; 30]. As we have now become accustomed to these exclamations of certainty, it should be no surprise that irony undercuts these dreams of assimilation. As the narrator relates the sights and sounds of the Tangiers market, he speaks of his cultural dissimilation: "inmerso en la multitud, pero sin integrarte a ella... captando sutilmente la presencia (irrupción) de signos que interfieren (violan) el orden aparente de las cosas" (39–40) ["immersed in the crowd, yet not a part of it... subtly capturing the presence (the inrush) of signs that disturb (violate) the apparent order of things"; 28–29]. He hears the Rolling Stones, sees signs for the film *Thunderball*, and takes in the chaos of the market. This mix of cultural markers constructs, for him, a transnational space where culture does not have a clear connection to national origin. On the other hand, though, he does not integrate and remains an outsider. So examples of transnational spaces do not necessarily lead to transnational identity. Moreover, this view of the cultural environment may merely be the product of an outsider's gaze, since we learn of this cultural space from a "foreign" narrator.

Later he goes to a teahouse and begins to feel like part of a collective, but the television program on in the background reminds him of Spain and arouses his anger at the effects of modernization: "estudios hollywoodenses de Almería y hoteles Hilton en Motilla del Palancar! : transformaciones espectaculares, sí, pero que no alteran en absoluto las esencias perennes de vuestra alma : enjundia de estoicismo senequista metido en la cañada de los huesos" (90) ["Hollywood studios at Almería and Hilton hotels at Motilla de Palancar!: transformations that are admittedly spectacular, but which in no way alter the eternal essences of your country's soul: the quintessential spirit of Seneca that is a part of your very bones"; 74]. Eternal essences? The narrator now represents—with irony—Francoist cultural essentialism. Seneca's stoicism is infused in Spanish identity upon birth. We must remember that significant passages of *Reivindicación del conde don Julián* are dedicated to undoing the theory that Seneca is part of a Spanish cultural essence. Elsewhere the text pokes fun at the concept that there are national essences. There is an entire section on the role of the garbanzo and "las esencias hispánicas del garbanzo" (151) ["the Hispanic essence of the garbanzo"]. As he continues, he associates the garbanzo with other so-called national essences, like the Quijote and Seneca: "y vuestro símbolo, héroe de honda raigambre ibera, de añeja, ranciosa cepa senequista, Garbanzote de la Mancha" (151) ["and your national symbol, the hero with the profoundest of Iberian roots, of the finest Senecan stock, Don Chichote de la Mancha"; 127]. His utopian dream is that culture can be created or at least willfully remembered differently: "prehistoria española, hontanar de vuestras más limpias y claras esencias" (190) ["Spanish prehistory, the source of your purest and brightest essences"; 161]. From Spain's pre-history of multicultural chaos, he posits, the clearest national essences emanate. But if this is true, then Seneca is part of that same Spanish pre-history. So the conundrum remains. His worst fear is that cultural identity is based on pre-determined national essences that leave his project in the margin. His texts leave us somewhere between the narrator's dream and his worst nightmare.

The countless references in these novels to the question of culture espouse a variety of explanations on the nature of cultural identity. Consequently, Goytisolo does not have a single, unified theory about cultural identity. He has a variety of opinions and his protagonists act out an assortment of options in the hope that one of his strategies will be capable of shocking the system. One of the weakest elements of his attack, though, is that in his novels, culture is organized from an official Western perspective. Many scholars have criticized Goytisolo for his Orientalism in reference to Muslim society (see, in particular, Schaefer-Rodriguez, chapter two). Even Goytisolo himself tries to defend his use of Arab culture, but he must admit that in *Reivindicación del conde don Julián* "the Spain-Islam dialectic retains its Manichean and irreducible opposition: values are changed to anti-values and vice versa.... Although the Moroccan reality of today seeps in through a few interstices, the Morocco and Islam of the book are not the Morocco and the Islam of reality" ("Orientalism" 116). Goytisolo explains his Orientalism as necessary, for the fictive Moorish invaders had to be phantoms to spark fear in Catholic Spain. Since the point of the novel was to attack the basis of cultural identity in Catholic Spain, he felt it best to recuperate the most frightening image of Islamic identity, even if that meant providing a Western-biased perspective. He fights essentialism with essentialism, substituting Spanish, Catholic essentialism with an essentialist vision of Muslim identity.

In other areas Goytisolo's cultural containment is also drawn along Western lines. The notion of the pariah is not altered from its traditional use. The female body is also appropriated by him in order to do damage to the sacred Virgin and the materialist tourist, critiques meant to attack Western values but that do so at the expense of turning these figures into whores or victims and defiling their bodies—strategies which hardly challenge official Western culture. In *Juan sin tierra* he opposes white versus black, preferring black. He favors the "culo" over the "cara" per the influence of the Mexican Octavio Paz, but the binary remains. Most importantly, at the end of *Juan sin tierra*, he is on the *other* side. There are still two sides and the Manichean division continues its hold: he has just reversed the charge. It is important to question whether these novels successfully advocate an alternative to dominant culture, or whether they perpetuate the rigid social divisions of Third Worldist ideology and Western values. Is it necessary to dominate others in order to liberate the self?

These problems of representation lead us to the central concern of these texts: the possibility of liberation, transformation, and change. In each novel the main question revolves around such desires. The trilogy focuses on the use of memory to combat the past (*Señas de identidad*), on betrayal to destroy official culture (*Reivindicación del conde don Julián*), and on writing as a key to utopic fantasy (*Juan sin tierra*) as ways to understand identity, but each narrator is never certain that he has arrived at a solution. The problem of free will persists and phrases like "No me hagas reír" ["Don't make me laugh"], "Tu pasión fue un error" ["Your passion was an error"], and "Pero no su victoria no es tal" ["But no, such is not your victory"], contribute to these doubts. There is a discrepancy between affirmative enunciations, where he has managed to achieve his dreams, and other phrases (like those above), which express doubt at his ability to liberate himself or make a difference. As Sieburth points out, the narrator of *Reivindicación del conde don Julián* does not become free by merely becoming a negative (150). This predicament follows the narrators throughout the trilogy. In *Señas de identidad* the narrator demonstrates his frustration: "tu casta (sí, la tuya) pese a tus esfuerzos por zafarte de ella, a menos que (¿o era otra rebeldía inútil?) afrontases con resolución el destino y acortaras voluntariamente el plazo" (67) ["your caste (yes, yours) in spite of your efforts to get away, unless (or was it just another useless rebellion?) you stood up to fate with resolution and voluntarily cut off the allotted time"; 54]. In *Reivindicación del conde don Julián* the narrator also shows distress at not being able to access the truth: "sin saber dónde está la verdad : en la impresión sensorial o la memoria del verso" (39) ["not knowing where the truth lies: in your sensory impressions or in the memories of the Poetic Word"; 28]. He mumbles these words to himself as he leaves the library of Tangiers and encounters the labyrinthine streets surrounding the market. He seeks stability and reality: "al acecho de la realidad oculta... mensaje cifrado cuyas señas llegan con intermitencia hasta ti" (42) ["lying in ambush for the reality hidden... a message in code, intermittent signals that come your way"; 30–31]. He has doubts, but he has not resigned himself to losing contact with history. Even in *Juan sin tierra*, the novel many critics hail as Goytisolo's exaltation of free-floating identity, the doubts persist and the quandary of cultural transformation is not resolved. While the narrator questions the ability of literature to alter cultural identity he complains:

> pero no, tú deliras, y el poeta alejandrino lo sabe la ciudad / en donde has gastado tus días subsiste y a ella estás condenado / en sus mismas callejas errarás / en sus mismos suburbios llegará tu vejez / bajo sus mismos techos encanecerás / inútilmente, esperarás a los bárbaros. (104)

> no, you are spouting delirious nonsense, and the Alexandrian poet knows it / the town where you have wasted your days continues to exist and you are condemned to living in it / you will wander endlessly down its back streets / old age will overtake you in its suburbs / your hair will turn white beneath its rooftops / you will await the barbarians in vain. (90)

He wants to destroy civilization, but he is awaiting the barbarians in vain, using biblical rhetoric which is itself a cornerstone of Western civilization. He is, once again, in Spain, alone. His community is a fantasy. His betrayal is illusion. His distance from Spain is a dream.

Another relevant issue is that Goytisolo constantly relies on the narrative trick of having his narrator be in an altered state, i.e., drunk, drugged, fantasizing, or mad. His narrators' observations and conclusions often cannot be trusted. Nevertheless, like Don Quijote's madness, Buñuel's dreams, and Sade's fantasies, these images are powerful weapons of transgression. Goytisolo forces the reader to see these texts as fiction and repeatedly stresses that what appears in these novels pertains to the world of literature while simultaneously hoping to affect our understanding of society.

The trilogy is full of contradictions and contrasting impulses: create/destroy, remember/forget, assimilate/dissimilate, access reality/fabricate utopia, etc. I believe that these contrasting impulses should not be overlooked and that these dialectical tensions can be explained, in part, by the historical circumstances that affected Goytisolo. His association of cultural identity with the nation and of exile with orphanhood explains some of the textual paradoxes in his work. Perhaps it is through his writing on another exiled outcast who fit uneasily into a generation of exiles that we can best uncover his complex and contradictory theory of national identity. In his introduction to the translation of a selection of the writings of José María Blanco White, a Spanish exile in England at the turn of the nineteenth century, Goytisolo considers the fellow exile as part of his "family," a resident of his symbolic home.

Writing the introduction after the completion of *Juan sin tierra,* Goytisolo was able to synthesize some of his opinions about cultural identity. He tells us that culture travels, and that the nation is not fixed to geographic territory: "la patria no es un trozo de tierra ni el hombre un árbol condenada a la inmovilidad" (96) ["the homeland is not a piece of land and man is not a tree condemned to immobility"]. But the political question of cultural nationalism is a different story. For Goytisolo, patriotism requires different responses on the part of the intellectual according to the situation. One must uphold the concept of nation for a colonized country in order to facilitate independence and liberation: "Fuera de eso no puede haber otra patria para el escritor (si dejamos al lado el lenguaje) que la sociedad libre y justa, y, como ésta no se encuentra por ahora en ningún lugar de la tierra, su deber es contribuir a su advenimiento, denunciando los defectos y taras que obstaculizan el proyecto en un país del orbe en que le tocó nacer" (96n) ["Outside of this there can be no other homeland for the writer (if we leave out the issue of language) than a free and just society, and, since this is not found currently in any place on the earth, his duty is to contribute to its advent, denouncing the defects and blemishes that obstruct the project in the country in which he was born"]. As we can see, Goytisolo's predicament as an exile from Spain led to both reactions to patriotism: he tried to fight Franco and he tried to dismantle the repressive features of civilized society. As Goytisolo puts it, first Marx criticized capitalism, now we must critique the State itself (96).

As is typically the case with his writing, Goytisolo uses his discourse on Blanco White as a springboard for his thoughts on exile, culture, and Spain. Once again, he seeks a new nation to symbolize home: "Llamémosle mejor fraternidad de *outsiders,* parias y marginales—de meteoritos cuya fuerza centrífuga venció el atractivo de nuestra ley nacional de gravedad" (97) ["Let's call it a fraternity of *outsiders,* pariahs and marginalized—of meteorites whose centrifugal force conquered the attraction of our national law of gravity"]. Even after the completion of *Juan sin tierra,* Goytisolo had not forgotten Spain. He was not landless and he remained in search of an alternative to Official Spain. While many of his strategies for transformation are problematic, his attack on Spain is effective. The mythology of the nation is exposed and deflated. As Goytisolo closes his introduction to the work of Blanco White, an exile whose texts did not reach Spain during his own lifetime, Goytisolo sums up his theory of the Spanish nation: "España, el nombre de 'España', cubre difícilmente la proteica realidad peninsular. Es un mito también, un nombre que ha envejecido y contra el que el escritor parte en guerra: guerra fantasmal, desproporcionada" (98) ["Spain, the name 'Spain,' covers only with difficulty the protean peninsular reality. It is a myth also, a name that has aged and against which, the author launches war: phantasmal, disproportionate war"]. The trilogy has shown us heroic acts of memory, betrayal, and imagination. The exile never returns home. He is a product of history and will carve out his place. He waits, sharpening his knife, for the next assault. The war of the words is not over.

The exile's recourse to language as his primary weapon of attack is also evident in the work of Ariel Dorfman. His work, like that of Goytisolo, battles the competing notions of cultural assimilation and dissimilation. For instance, speaking about his post-exilic relationship to Chile, he states that during a visit to Santiago, "Yo era una especie de resabio del pasado y me sentía muy extraño. Mira, yo creo que no encajo totalmente en Chile, nunca he encajado, nunca he encajado. Pero, por otra parte, ¿Dónde encaja uno de verdad?" (qtd. in Angel 125) ["I was some sort of bad habit from the past and I felt very strange. Look, I think that I don't totally fit in in Chile, I have never fit in, I have never fit in. But, on the other hand, where does one really fit in?"]. The notion that the individual cannot "fit in," or really assimilate to the dominant cultural paradigm, and that dissimilation is, to a certain extent, the "norm" is an interesting concept belying the contradictory way in which exiled writers experience complex relationships to cultural identity. The contradiction revolves around the assumption that dissimilation requires an act of free will and resistance and that the individual's fragmented subjectivity tends to create a susceptibility to the power of assimilation.

The struggle between dissimilation versus assimilation appears in the novel *Viudas* when the captain, frustrated by the resistance of the village, posits that the nation requires a new populace. "No hay caso con este país. Habría que despoblarlo y traer a otra gente, gente de afuera, gente con otra mentalidad. Con esta raza, no hay cómo, no hay por dónde" (180) ["This country's hopeless. They'll have to depopulate it and bring in other people, people from outside, people with some other kind of mind. With this race, there's no way, there's no place"; 129]. The resistance (dissimilation from the social demands of the dictatorship) makes the populace undesirable. Yet the dictatorship exists precisely because these individuals were not "willing" to follow the modernizing goals of the government. In this case, then, dissimilation represents a collective effort capable of threatening the system. In contrast to the prior quotation from Dorfman's interview, the cultural resistance in *Viudas* goes beyond musing about the overall inability of the individual to truly be a part of a group.

In this sense, Dorfman's work also demonstrates the conflict between modern and postmodern versions of the subject. Modernity allows for the notion of a Marxist collective as well as cultural nationalism, both of which are elements present in the novel *Viudas*. Yet, in the women's struggle to provide a collective challenge to the system, the text questions whether the self is actually capable of such acts, or rather, whether the self is identifiable and therefore able to participate in history. The captain asks, pointing to a dead man's body at the riverside, "¿Y cuál de ustedes lo encontró?—Hicieron un gesto envolvente, total, múltiple, algo que articularon todas y ninguna.... Todas, lo habían encontrado todas juntas esta mañana" (36) ["And which one of you found it?—There was an inclusive, total, multiple gesture indicating all and none.... All, they'd all found it together this morning"; 22]. The women are a mass without individual identity. As they turn over the body that has been found, the women look, but say nothing: "cuando le vieron lo que alguna vez había sido su cara. Estaba hecha una sola pulpa, carcomida y malograda por los golpes y la inmersión" (36) ["when they saw the face, when they saw the pulp that had been its face, decayed and wasted by the pounding and soaking"; 22]. As with the faceless man in *Máscaras*, an authoritarian society has annihilated the identity of the dead man's body. With this absence of identity he loses any possibility of being a historical agent. He is only a subject of the system and no longer an active subject capable of resistance to the powers of the government's modernizing goals.

This description of identity is also found in *The Last Song of Manuel Sendero* when the son of Sendero returns to his land and is not recognized by anyone. As he crosses the border of the unnamed country, which symbolically represents both the national experience of Chile and the transnational experience of advanced capitalism, he crosses more than a territorial border but a cultural one as well. Within this space, he is powerless, owing to his anonymity and his absence from history. We are told that it was "as if Grandfather were not crossing the official boundary of a nation but rather the tenuous barrier of regulations that separates dream from reality, the living from the dead, the future from the past" (175). All of these distinctions have become very tenuous during the narrative of the novel and have a great impact on the frustrated vision of the subject as either a historical agent or a social/political construct.

Dorfman continues to struggle with the notion of the subject as either an agent or a subject when he contrasts Karl Marx and Carl Barks using each figure as symbolic of the shift in the notion of the individual subject from the nineteenth to the twentieth century, or rather, from modernity to postmodernity. Barks is told:

> the Communists have a hero from the 19th century, and they're always showing him off. His ideas stir up crises, his prophecies go unfulfilled, and his disciples fight among themselves. But we haven't succeeded in banishing his confused rhetoric from our world. Confronting that man whose name was Karl Marx, we celebrate you, a man of the twentieth century, the twenty-first century, a man of the future, Carl Barks. We're determined that history will preserve your name and not your adversary's. He had his model for society: totalitarian, obscure, oppressive, and impoverished. In the face of that model, we, you and all of us, seek a world full of joy, order, healthy leisure and ennobling labor, satisfied faces and sunlight. Which is going to be mankind's future? (109)

Marx is the past and Barks is the utopic future of hyper-capitalism. Yet both of these figures act as sources of power that control and shape the identities of those affected by their ideology, leading Dorfman's text to further question the notion of the subject's agency.

What is most important in this radical questioning of the conditions of possibility for historical agency is that, regardless of whether identity is stable or in flux, the subject may be incapable of affecting these conditions. For instance, as a consequence of the disappearance of many Chileans, those that disappeared, like the men found in the river in *Viudas,* have both a fixed and an absent place in the nation's culture. As one's name appears on a list and is fixed into history as an enemy of the state, one is simultaneously removed from history without a trace. The debate over whether the subject is capable of carving an individual identity or is merely a product of social and historical constructions can be seen in the conversation between David, Felipe, and Paula when they discuss the comic strip they are working on in *The Last Song of Manuel Sendero.* Felipe believes that there are elements of Chile that will never be changed: there are endemic qualities of the nation: "Chile's something permanent ... it's not just mountains and grapes and folk dances, it's people" (132). Felipe wants to believe that the Chilean people are not merely controlled by Pinochet's ideology, that the people have certain qualities. Felipe believes that the Chileans have essential qualities that allow them to resist the domination of Pinochet's state. This paradoxical description of the self as both pre-constructed and resistant to dominant ideology is an interesting facet of Dorfman's investigation into the ways in which dictatorship and national identity interact.

David is forced into exile because he is incapable of assimilating to the resistance movement's rules of behavior. Despite feeling like he had belonged and had assimilated after Allende's election, once in exile, David is forced to see that he was always an outsider even though he desired a place in the resistance movement. His personality (or fixed cultural identity) hinders his desire to change himself, "as though he'd always considered his personality an obstacle and saw the coup as a chance to change himself, to finally become someone else: taciturn, reserved, introverted, trustworthy. He wanted to kill his old personality, to start over again, from scratch. In a word: to be reborn" (330). But rebirth is a fantasy and such fantasies are not capable of changing the course of history and the condition of David's exile.

The three exiles continue to debate the question of whether Pinochet is a product of Chilean culture or an aberration. Paula says that Pinochet is part of Chile, but Felipe says that he is "an aberration, just a parenthesis" (132). David believes that the Chile of Allende has been overshadowed by the "Chilex" of Pinochet: "Chilex, Felipe, Chilex is the real country. Everything is exportable, everything's for sale, even the people" (133). For David, Pinochet is merely symbolic of the globalization of capitalism, which is not only a Chilean phenomenon. By contrasting the opinions of Felipe, Paula, and David, Dorfman highlights the way in which Chilean cultural identity is not fixed, precisely because Chileans conceive of the nation and their ties to it in many distinct ways. It is impossible to understand the cultural identity of those exiled from Chile, if these competing versions of the experience are not taken into consideration.

The comic strip created by David represents his paranoia about the implications of postmodern fragmentation of the subject and its ability for cultural determination. In a scene where Carl Barks watches television, Dorfman's novel ties pre-modern religious ideology to modern imperialism and postmodern hypercapitalism:

> God, announced Rev. Rex, is like a giant computer, a screen filling infinity, a videocassette recording every one of our thoughts, retaining in its memory everything we do or tried to do. The faithful have to facilitate God's labor, so that His work will be advanced. That's why His ideal man is being fashioned in this exceptional country.... What better imagination for that man than your own? What greater contribution could you hope to make, Mr. Parks? To live forever, Mr. Parks, is an assurance that your dreams will enrich paradise, will bring smiles to the lips of the archangels, will move the saints to compassion. To live forever, my dear friend, is to colonize the Great Beyond. (369)

The movement from the colonization of territory to the colonization of thought is a sign of Dorfman's depiction of cultural imperialism in the postmodern era. Despite the fact that the dominant ideologies of the pre-modern and modern eras also implied and relied on "the colonization of thought," what is distinct in postmodernism, as Dorfman's novel describes it, is that such a practice is highlighted as the primary goal of social control and is no longer hidden behind "benevolent" notions of human salvation or modern progress. Even though Reverend Rex uses the same rhetoric of pre-modern religion, the novel exposes this rhetoric as a blatant act of aggression, where rhetoric serves no other function than to hide its enunciator's desire for total control over cultural identity.

It is in *Máscaras* where Dorfman suggests most clearly an unstable, yet powerless, version of cultural identity, where the individual is a victim of postmodern social constructions, and where fragmentation does not imply subversion of the dominant cultural paradigm. The doctor, as he speaks to the faceless man, reveals that he had seen him as a baby and was fascinated by the baby's ability to metamorphose. "Un camaleón, después de todo, una mariposa que cambia de color, un conejo que transforma su pelambre según sus estaciones.... Pero un ser humano que pudiera entremezclarse hasta fusionarse con un telón de fondo siempre cambiante" (130–31) ["A chameleon, after all, a butterfly altering its colors, a rabbit shedding its fur according to the seasons.... But that a human being would be able to fuse with his ever-changing backgrounds, could mix in to the point of invisibility"; 127]. With his unstable identity the baby is able to blend into any cultural context, but the experience of the faceless man is that such ability leaves him, like an exile, always outside and never a member of a group. This description of cultural identity under postmodern social constructions is significant insofar as it challenges those theories of cultural identity that herald fragmentation of the self as the only means to challenge the social system. Against theories proposed by Derrida, Deleuze and Guattari, and Bhabha, who see fragmentation, dissemination, plurality, and schizoanalysis as potentially subversive tactics, Dorfman suggests that the fragmentation of identity under postmodernism is the most total destruction of the individual's free will.

Nevertheless, in addition to this pessimistic and hopeless description of the possibility for individual self-formation, Dorfman's work also posits the notion that there may be a viable alternative to cultural essentialism and social determination. Early in the novel *The Last Song of Manuel Sendero*, Dorfman suggests that cultural identity cannot be simply categorized as either a process of individual choice or external definition. As the Son of Sendero retraces his father's footsteps, he speaks to Croupy, a fellow member of the fetal rebellion, and recalls an incident where a sergeant shot a bakery deliveryman who failed to obey him and stop pedaling his bicycle. The Son of Sendero tells Croupy, "someday we could end up growing up and becoming the sergeant himself, pulling the trigger against one of our own. Is that what you want, Croupy? Is that the set of alternatives you want to be left with—pull the trigger or get the bullet? Is that what you want?" (15). This quotation suggests that cultural identity is not merely a question of being the good guy or the bad, the source of power or the one who resists. There may be an alternative to the binary.

This alternative, while not clearly articulated, is one of the hopes that drives the narrative of *The Last Song of Manuel Sendero*. The problem is quite simple: Chileans voted for Allende, an act which seemed to reveal the power of choice, and then they were punished by the forces of international capitalism, an act which seems to reveal that such choices are illusory. David, once in exile, is obsessed with the way in which Pinochet's regime has affected Chile and he is frustrated by the feeling that after a brief moment of self-determination the Chilean populace was placed under strict authoritarian rule and cultural control. These issues are the focus of his comic strip project, yet, Felipe admonishes him: "Foreign readers won't understand what you're talking about.... Get rid of all of this obsessive shit" (131). Felipe believes that David's project is an act of nostalgia: "Why force everything that makes you homesick down our readers' throats?" (132). But Felipe misses the point, which is part of the reason that their friendship has become so strained. David feels that his national concerns have broader international ramifications. Chile was "sold out" and became nothing more than a country entirely commodified. "Ex-Chile: it was, but is no more. A trademark, a copyright, a department store more than a country. Like a supermarket of underdevelopment... Third World Shopping Center, continuous show.... Who will buy the first Chil-child?" (92–93). This is David's vision of Chile under Pinochet, where people have become commodities and do not have any rights. So while the exiles are unable to return—i.e., borders persist—national borders do not impede the surge of capitalism. In David's description of Chilex, a fictional exaggeration of Chile, he endeavors, through his extremely distressing description of cultural control, to affect his readers, who he hopes have the power to resist. Herein lies the supposed contradiction: how can a text be both nationalist and transnationalist? How can a description of the absolute powerlessness of the Chileans to control their identity lead others to learn from this and gain control? David explains his desires: "Your poor readers should realize, while there's still time, that what happened to us can happen to them too. They can lose their country, not know how to get it back, search for it forever" (132). If such realizations are possible within the already grim world of international capitalism and, if they are capable of inspiring people to resist the horrors of military coups, then David is suggesting that cultural identity lies somewhere between individual choice and social control. At least, that is his hope.

In contrast with the hope of Dorfman's second novel, the possibilities for self-formation in *Máscaras* are absent. Even though the faceless man is like a chameleon, this does not give him the freedom of self-definition. Instead, in order to ameliorate his frustration at being cast out of society, he uses Oriana to fulfill his desire for control and power. He has no face and she has no past. A perfect subject of male fantasy, the faceless man explains: "Pensará como una niña chica, pero hace el amor como una mujer adulta" (81) ["She may talk like a small girl, but she makes love like an adult woman"; 76]. Seeking power over her in return for the oppression he has suffered, he fancies himself her God and believes that she can experience "las más grandes perversidades...y emerger sin lesiones" (85) ["the most perverse of aberrations...and emerge without a scratch"; 80]. He makes her into Eve and he becomes both God and the serpent: "con la posibilidad de recomenzar al otro día una nueva historia, una nueva galaxia, otro Jardín y otra Expulsión,...y siempre seré yo el que la ha de narrar, mil y unas veces si hace falta" (86) ["with the chance to begin the next day another story, a new galaxy, another Garden and another Exile,...and it will always be my narrating her, a thousand and one times if that is necessary"; 80–81]. He loves the control and does not care that it is all fantasy, like the narrator of Goytisolo's *Juan sin tierra*. But what kind of identity are these writers describing? As they both refer to the fantasy of re-writing history, and as they are both exiled writers cut off from official power structures, it appears that through narrating sadistic characters they are deeply questioning their own interests regarding the issue of power and cultural identity. It is significant that the only moments when their characters appear to have any cultural control are perverse abuses of power that are always contingent on the oppression of another.

This radical questioning of the motivations behind an interest in the future of cultural identity reveals Dorfman's concern that such a project relies on the desire for power. Even David, who retains extraordinary hope, reminds himself in *The Last Song of Manuel Sendero* that he should have learned as a student that cultural identity and the society that it forms are about power: "To screw the owner of the cage...you have to have power at least equal to, and, it is hoped, superior to, his own" (122). He states further, as he muses on his frustrating position as an exile, that "According to the second axiom of that famous law, precisely the one we would ignore years later, when your hands are empty and the enemy is on the brink of declaring total war and of annihilating you, the only option is to withdraw from the field of battle" (123). The question of power, then, is tantamount to the question of the relationship between the self and its cultural definition. History repeats itself, and David is angry that he and the other members of the Unidad Popular were oblivious to the issue of power. Dorfman states in the introduction to his collection of essays *The Empire's Old Clothes*: "I have also been discovering and exploring, through my poetry and fiction, that jungle which each of us can become.... These internal contradictions will not disappear with a simple change in the ownership of the means of production" (12). Dorfman suggests that Marxism is no longer sufficient as the central answer to liberation from cultural oppression, because the dialectical conflicts are not only present in the external world, but also within the self. His work in exile revolves around a deep concern for the possibilities of reversing the forces of power that determine history and control cultural identity.

Cristina Peri Rossi's exile writing is also obsessed with the possibility of self-formation, but unlike Dorfman and Goytisolo, her concerns focus more explicitly on the issues of gender and sexuality. In an interview with Eileen Zeitz, Peri Rossi presents her view that the female condition is inextricably linked to political power: "En cuanto a la condición femenina, estoy convencida de que se trata de una suerte de esclavitud ligada al sistema de producción económica mundial" (82) ["In terms of the female condition, I am convinced that it is a question of some sort of slavery linked to the global economic system"]. Although both Dorfman and Goytisolo explore the ways in which gender is an important aspect of social control, Peri Rossi's investigations into the crisis of cultural identity for the exile directly connect to the way that society controls desire in order to maintain patriarchal order. For example, the outcasts Equis and Morris are sexually attracted to old women and young boys, respectively. As exiles they are also sexually outcast from the norms of society. Unlike Dorfman and Goytisolo, Peri Rossi grapples with the relationship between desire and power versus desire and liberation, and she includes a far greater variety of permutations of these relationships. Her description of the tapestry of Creation in *La nave de los locos* and its connections to the enigma of Equis's dreams reveal her interest in the relationship between exile and patriarchy. Furthermore, her description of the role of Adam and Eve as symbolic Western ideals for the distinction between the sexes is counterbalanced by her alternative suggestions for these stereotypes: the relationships between Morris and Percival and between Equis and the women he encounters illustrate her narrative impulse to depict the outcast as a function of the strict and fixed gender definitions required by the goals of Western modernization. Mabel Moraña in "*La nave de los locos* de Cristina Peri Rossi" points out that Peri Rossi uses a complex strategy to both represent and dismantle the role of women in society (208). Her description of Julie Christie's role in *Demon Seed* is an example of the conventional treatment of women, which is later contrasted by another performance where two women on stage represent a lesbian sex scene while acting out the roles of Marlene Dietrich and Dolores del Río. As was seen in the writings of Goytisolo and Dorfman, Peri Rossi writes about fantasy worlds, where difference and dissimilation are choices, while also narrating the opposite possibility, where the self is powerless and a subject of social construction.

Similar to Dorfman and Goytisolo, Peri Rossi also questions whether one can escape from the conditions of cultural experience that bind the self to national identity and a specific place in the social order. The crisis over the contrasting notions of assimilation and dissimilation is never answered in her work. Literature, for her, depends on a particular historical moment: "Tengo que interpretar el rol del individuo en la historia, en su momento, en su época... la política entra en mi propia obra literaria por el mero hecho de que soy víctima de la política desde el momento en que nací" (qtd. in Zietz 83) ["I have to interpret the role of the individual in history, in its moment, in its epoch.... Politics enters into my own literary work by the mere fact that I have been a victim of politics from the moment I was born"]. National identity indelibly marks one's past: "Estoy agravada por el hecho de que uno no es lo que quiere ser, sino lo que lo dejan ser" (qtd. in Zietz 83) ["I am aggravated by the fact that one is not what one wants to be, but rather what they let you be"]. Therefore, she describes the condition of the exile, the woman, the madman, the homosexual, and the outcast as one of forced dissimilation. Like Dorfman's notion of dissimilation as the "norm" for the exile or the socially powerless, dissimilation no longer refers to individual choice. Society determines the criterion for judging those who do not "fit in," i.e., those who threaten its political goals of modernization and control of the populace. Those who rebel against the "order of things" must be eradicated from the system and they are not described as triumphant rebels but as lonely and troubled outsiders.

For instance, the protagonist of "La ciudad" ("The City") is haunted by his recurring dream of a city. This short story from *El museo de los esfuerzos inútiles* focuses on the problem of cultural identity as it relates specifically to a lost space within the nation. Unlike *La nave de los locos*, the story, despite the troubling presence of an androgynous figure in the dreams, focuses more directly on the issue of national identity and less on the connections between national identity and gender/sexual relations. In this way, "La ciudad" is one of Peri Rossi's most explicit investigations into the dilemma of nationalism versus transnationalism as they relate to notions of assimilation versus dissimilation. The city of the protagonist's dreams seems to float in an imprecise temporality with a shifting array of cultural referents: "Él no podía asegurar que la ciudad que veía en sus sueños formara parte del pasado, ni del presente, ni del futuro: era otra sin duda, pero flotaba en un espacio sin tiempo, sin precisiones geográficas o cronométricas, flotaba en el espacio, increada todavía" (161) ["he couldn't be certain whether the city he saw in his dreams was part of the past, the present, or the future: it was a different city, to be sure, and it floated in a space detached from time, from chronometric exactitude, in a space yet to be created"; 138]. What is most crucial to note from this description of the exile's nightmare vision of the lost nation is that the city, which floats in a timeless, deterritorialized space, produces an unstable cultural identity, which causes anguish, not liberation. Moreover, the dreamer knows that the city of his dreams is *not* the same as the "real" city in which he was born, but he nevertheless is haunted by this ambiguous city, which is is at one and the same time his lost home and an unfamiliar, distant place. "Con seguridad la ciudad de sus orígenes no era así, no lo había sido, ni lo sería; pero en el sueño, correspondía a su ciudad" (161) ["Surely, the city where he was born was not like that, hadn't been like that, nor would it be like that; but in the dream it was his city"; 138]. The implication is that the exile, once expelled from his birthplace, can no longer connect to his nation. It becomes something foreign and at the same time remains important for his identity. So Peri Rossi contrasts the certainty of the dreamer who knows that his dream represents something unreal with the uncertainty of his ability to ascertain how the dream symbolizes his identity. His cultural identity is at one and the same time fixed—he is exiled and not in his native city—and unfixed—he does not understand the spatial effects of exile on his identity.

It is significant that in the dream he is the architect of an urban site he does not want to build. His position as an architect is a symbolic reference to the way in which his dreaming mind continues to be obsessed with his lost nation and cannot avoid imagining the ways in which dictatorship has altered the national space. He sees a deserted plaza covered with statues, the symmetrical windows of homes positioned to receive the afternoon light, a clock that has fallen down and which tells an impossible time (161). The androgynous figure "dominates" his dream and forces him to question whether the figure existed before he left the country or was created as a result of his emigration/imagination. This figure is an important ambiguity for the dreamer, because it is not clear whether the figure represents the authoritarian control of his nation (and his dream) or his own madness. He considers this recurring dream as a sign of his own sickness: "Su amigo Juan lo llamaba el vértigo de la aniquilación. Lo padecían algunos seres en el mundo, y parecía incurable" (168) ["His friend Juan called it annihilation vertigo. The condition afflicted some members of the world and was apparently incurable"; 144]. The significance of this ambiguity is that Peri Rossi suggests that the instability of cultural identity in exile may be a direct result of the authoritarian regime that required the exile to depart. Yet it may also be the case that the instability of the exile's cultural identity is the result of the exile's own inability to "fit in," i.e., it is a problem created by the exile and not by the regime.

In the dream the protagonist is both an outsider and a member of society: he simultaneously assimilates and dissimilates. Like the Son of Sendero or the faceless man, he suffers from not being recognized by his countrymen. "Tan raro . . . era su sentimiento de pertenecer y no pertenecer, al mismo tiempo, al extraño lugar. Nadie lo reconocía, lo cual lo asombraba, a pesar de que él tampoco reconocía a nadie; a veces, lo tomaban por forastero, a veces, lo trataban como si siempre hubiera vivido allí" (163–64) ["As strange . . . was his simultaneous feeling of belonging and not belonging to the place. No one recognized him, which surprised him, even though he himself recognized no one. Sometimes they took him for a foreigner, other times for someone who had always lived there"; 140]. This contrasting sense of assimilation and dissimilation also occurs in his waking life and is exemplified by the conversation he has with his ex-wife, Luisa. She is European and eurocentric and he is from the "Third World," which creates an unbridgeable distance between them, constituting their identities as fixedly different: "ese océano vanidoso que los separaba, porque la función del océano siempre fue la misma: diferenciarlos" (169) ["that vainglorious ocean that separated them, because the function of the ocean was always the same—to differentiate them"; 145]. Contrasting Derrida's valorization of "difference" as a liberating notion, Peri Rossi's story describes difference as a condition which alienates the self and which does not give the self a source of power or control. The ex-wife does not understand why he has not yet assimilated to "her nation" and why he continues to suffer when thinking of this city from his past. Like the typical Western-minded provincial who considers her nation to be the center of the universe, she is incapable of understanding why assimilation is a problem and is perhaps impossible for the narrator. "Has vivido los suficientes años en ésta como para haberte adaptado ya—la contestó ella, severa. También se sentía vagamente herida y pensó que esas cosas eran las que terminaban por separar a la gente: heridas imprecisas, escoriaciones, rivalidades" (170) ["'You've lived in this city for long enough to have adapted by now,' she said harshly. She too felt vaguely hurt and thought to herself that those were the things that in the end distanced people from one another: vague wounds, sores, rivalries"; 146]. The protagonist and his ex-wife, then, cannot understand one another. The question is whether Peri Rossi is suggesting that there is an irresolvable difference between those who suffer social marginalization and those who do not. Although Luisa is a woman who has trouble making eye contact and appears depressed (i.e., she seems to have difficulty assimilating to mainstream society), she does not connect to her ex-husband's emotional problems. Their understanding of their place in the world is entirely distinct; their cultural identities are at odds.

This same notion continues to be an important part of Peri Rossi's theory of the exile's cultural identity in *La nave de los locos*. Yet, as mentioned, she broadens her definition of those that are included in the system and those that are excluded: exiles relate to women, the elderly, homosexuals, and all other members of society who have been forced to remain on the margins. In each tale of the conflict between individual desire for self-formation and a system intolerant of such behavior, the novel suggests the metaphor of the ship of fools as a means of describing the way in which marginalization is both confining and liberating. Unlike "La ciudad," where the protagonist suffers alone, *La nave de los locos* explores the ways in which outsiders construct alternative nations and cultural identities and thereby form communities of social pariahs, like that found on the island Pueblo de Dios. Lucia Invernizzi explains that in each case of marginalization the ship of fools refers to an act of brutal violence exercised against a defenseless humanity that is expelled because it is inconvenient, dangerous, or threatening (35). Even though the characters of *La nave de los locos* suffer expulsion from the system, they do not, ever, desire the chance to return. They do not want to be part of the rigid social restrictions required by modernity. There is an important loss of self-determination in a transnational capitalist society, but it is a loss of self which is inevitable if one is incapable of conforming. Recall these lines from Equis: "Me llamo Equis.... Por circunstancias especiales, que tienen más que ver con la marcha del mundo que con mis propios deseos, desde hace años viajo de un lugar a otro, sin rumbo fijo" (78) ["Ecks is my name.... For the past few years, due to special circumstances having more to do with the way the world turns than with my personal wishes, I have traveled from one place to another without any firm direction"; 76]. Once again, there is an interesting contrast between Equis's assertion that his peripatetic state is not a function of his own will, and that his position as an outsider allows him to "know" the system of power which forced his exile and which he "chose" to reject.

Nevertheless, as has been the case with analyses of the work of Goytisolo and Dorfman, scholars tend to focus on only one of these competing descriptions of cultural identity in Peri Rossi's work. Jorgelina Corbatta states: "Esa superación de las fronteras impuestas por la existencia de razas, límites nacionales, ideologías, religiones, lenguas, costumbres—si se logra—le concede al escritor una mayor universalización" (168) ["This surpassing of the borders imposed by the existence of races, national limits, ideologies, religions, languages, customs—if achieved—gives to the writer greater universality"]. In this quotation Corbatta emphasizes the positive effects of transnational existence for the exile and neglects to recognize that Peri Rossi's writing, while referring to an issue with a wide (universal?) application, does not disconnect from the historical and social determinants that motivate her literary interests.

In *La nave de los locos,* the question of who has the power to control cultural identity, the individual or the dominant social system, is also, as mentioned, represented by Peri Rossi's interest in the issue of women's identity. Like Dorfman and Goytisolo, Peri Rossi sees the condition of exile as only one of many social conditions that demand an analysis. She begins by exposing the way in which women's identity has been determined by society: she deals with abortion, the abuse of Jewish women by the Nazis, prostitution, and popular culture's use of the female body as an object of macho manipulation. For example, in the description of the film *Demon Seed,* the character played by Julie Christie is raped by an omnipotent machine symbolic of a patriarchal, capitalist society (24). Nevertheless, the machine, while representative of the power of patriarchy over women, does not imply that all men oppress women. Even though Equis's fascination with the film and his repeated visits to see it may suggest that he finds the rape of Christie erotic, it is also possible that his attraction to the film is based on his interest in the connections between the role played by Christie and his own fragile role in society.

Women have inherited a subjugated position in society; yet the chapter "El hombre es el pasado de la mujer" ("Man Is Woman's Past") suggests that a brighter future for gender relations requires that the "macho" man become part of the past. This theory is also consistent with the enigma that haunts Equis, where the King is destroyed by the notion that a man who loves a woman will give her his virility. In this dream, as in the fantasies of Dorfman's and Goytisolo's characters, cultural identity can resist domination and the imbalances of power can be altered. At the end of the novel, Equis dreams that he has subverted patriarchy with his answer and he imagines that such an answer is capable of destabilizing gendered identities. Yet this is only a dream, and it is a dream that does not solve the problem of how such a de-gendered society would necessarily imply the end of subjugation.

Even though the novel ends with the destruction of patriarchy—through the symbol of the King—throughout the novel patriarchy has been repeatedly revealed as a powerful mode of social domination. Apart from the inclusion of Vercingétorix's time in prison and the terrible events in the Southern Cone, the novel also refers to the medieval expulsion of the insane, thereby revealing the patriarchal system to have been responsible for the suffering of those that threatened its control dating back to the Middle Ages. Recall the scene where a girl from the Midwest commits suicide in New York City after spending eight hours wandering the streets carrying a sign reading: "Me siento muy sola, por favor, hable usted conmigo" (70) ["I'm very lonely. Please, someone talk to me"; 67]. As in the epigraph from George Steiner ("Nada nos destruye más certeramente que el silencio de otro ser humano") ["Nothing destroys us more surely than the silence of another human being"], Peri Rossi returns again and again to the notion that the transnational existence of the outsider is painful and that "silence" and solitude are the consequences of Western capitalist society, where the marginalized do not actually form a collective powerful enough to challenge the system. Therefore, as was the case with Goytisolo's and Dorfman's characters, Equis is victorious through delusion; he fantasizes in his dream that he destroys phalologocentrism and its corresponding social power. These limited rebellions can be understood through the social context of these literary works. The fact remains that all three writers are still outcast from their nations, desperately trying to imagine the possibility of cultural free will and yet incapable of avoiding the representation of their experience that cultural identity is primarily determined by the requirements of social order and Western progress.

How do these complex definitions of cultural identity relate to the issues of nationalism and transnationalism for these writers? Because these writers are both part of their nation's history and cast out of it, their theories about cultural and national identity suggest that nationalism and transnationalism are not mutually exclusive means of defining cultural identity. These complex descriptions of the role of the individual in social formation are necessary features of their literary strategies, which investigate through literary means the ways in which cultural identity is shaped by exile. Does exile free the self from the nation or bind the self to it? The answer is neither and both. Exiled subjects are national, tied to their nation's history and their experience in the nation prior to exile, and transnational, linked to other exiles and social outsiders by the cultural connection of being an outcast. In their texts, dissimilation is not a choice and is a solitary condition. It cannot be the basis of an identity politics capable of resisting the dominant cultural paradigm. Nor is dissimilation based on the values of difference and multiculturalism because the condition is not liberating but forced on the self. This position contrasts theories of cultural identity that assume that the self must be either/or—assimilated or dissimilated, national or transnational, essential or different, inherited or chosen. Moreover, these authors' works, through their description of this crisis and their self-reflexive concern for the possibility of communicating a story which itself has not already been determined by the power structures of society, are the best example of the crisis of the exiled subject. These texts try to jolt the reader by revealing the culture shocks—contradictions and complexities—which are inevitable aspects of the crisis of the self in the postmodern era. Certain theories of postmodernism at one and the same time theorize the end of the subject and the potential subversion of the system by the fragmented and "different" self (Baudrillard, Derrida, Bhabha). Nevertheless, the texts analyzed in this study challenge these assumptions by demonstrating that such contradictions do not necessarily lead to to cultural liberation. Fragmentation as liberation is unthinkable for the exile who has suffered one of the most extreme forms of social control. In those brief moments where their texts narrate liberated, free-floating identities, these authors reveal their desire to maintain faith in the possibility of social resistance. Yet their characters are always thrust back into the social cage and must begin, again, to find a key to the way out of its confining power.

Conclusion

The literature of exiles is vast and varied. Yet, despite differences in historical period and geographical context, certain tropes and literary motifs reappear throughout these texts. The central conflicts in exile writing are never resolved: they persist throughout this literature in varying forms and in varying degrees. The tendency to parse these tensions into binaries has led many scholars to emphasize one element of a multifaceted dialectic. However, this book has shown that a dialectical approach allows one to identify and analyze all of the various forces in tension in a given work. In this way, the analysis of exile writing begins from the premise that each text contains a number of contradictory and competing ways of presenting cultural identity. The strategy, then, is to identify all of these distinct elements and to study the ways in which they interact, interpenetrate, and contradict.

In this study I have focused on three writers: Juan Goytisolo, Ariel Dorfman, and Cristina Peri Rossi. Although these writers' experiences of exile were quite different, their writing shares many common features that are elucidated by employing a dialectical method of analysis. Such a strategy could productively be applied to other cases of exile writing. In addition to approaching exile literature dialectically, this book has highlighted a number of key concepts that are central to exile writing. Whereas it has often been argued that exile literature is either nostalgic, regional, and mournful, or creative, cosmopolitan, and celebratory, this study has demonstrated that exile literature often displays all of these tendencies. In terms of the nation or the homeland, the literature of exile revolves around the exile's sense of loss after being cast out of his or her homeland and the exile's feeling of freedom once the bonds of the nation are loosened. The exile often attempts to rewrite national history and also often attempts to create wholly alternative notions of community that are not predicated on the nation. These conflicting views and their challenge to contemporary theories of cultural identity were analyzed in the chapter "Alien Nation."

"Exile's Time" argued that contemporary exile literature depicts time in premodern, modern, and postmodern modes. Since fascist-oriented authoritarian regimes often revert to pre-modern notions of time and existence, describing their control of the country as a return to the normal course of history, exile writers respond to the authoritarian use of myth by providing counter-myths. They also describe the exile's time in pre-modern ways in response to their sense that their experience is timeless and eternal, linking them to exiles across the ages. Regarding the exile's sense of history and time, exile literature is modern, representing time as linear and progressive. In this way, exile literature is able to recount the specific events that led up to the moment of exile, countering the official version of history offered by the authoritarian regime. Yet exile literature also challenges the notion of modern, linear time because exiles are sensitive to the ways that history has been manipulated by dictatorship. Exiles often sense that linear time is a patriarchal, authoritarian notion that confines and restricts identity. In addition to pre-modern and modern notions of time, exile literature from the latter part of the twentieth century describes time as postmodern. When the exile narrates time as neither circular nor linear but absent and meaningless, then time is narrated as postmodern. Recognizing the complex ways these notions of time intersect and contradict each other reveals exile literature's dialectic of time.

It might be said that all literature deals with the problem of language. Language becomes an even greater area of focus when the exile is forced to live in a new land where a foreign language is spoken. "To Be Is Not to Be" surveyed and analyzed exile literature's complex relationship to language. For instance, exiles seek to turn experience into language and to use language to record the past. In these moments, exiles have great faith in language's power and its ability to shape human understanding and memory. Exiles also attempt to destroy language due to their experience that language can be traitorous and can be manipulated by official discourse. In these moments, language is ruptured and disconnected from meaning and reality. Exile writers also have a very complex relationship with issues of authorship and authority as a consequence of their experience of censorship and authoritarian ideology.

"Lost in Space" evaluated the multiple ways that exile writing depicts the geography of exile. The nation continues to be a main part of the exile's landscape, but this chapter explored the ways that the space of exile often combines the nation with alternative communities and social formations. Exile texts might describe the space of existence as confined, cramped, and limiting. It might also be open, vast, and fluid. The geography of exile is both utopic and dystopic and what constitutes utopia and dsytopia for a given writer will also fluctuate and shift. Often the space of exile corresponds to the community of exile. Furthering my examination of the social context of exile, "Culture Shock" tested the limits of many binary oppositions used in describing cultural identity.

The authors discussed in this study, while different in many respects, shared a common historical moment of exile. The advent of postmodern theory coincided with their experience of forced social dislocation. At a time when the exile was often heralded as a metaphor for a free-floating, deterritorialized, unfettered existence, these exiles wrote texts that challenged the notion that writers working on the margins can ever be free of social constraints, exposing such critical positions as naïve and untenable. The literature of exile is a practical denial of ludic postmodern theories, which are founded on an extreme doubt of all methodological descriptions of cultural identity—nationalism, history, language, gender, class, ethnicity, etc. These exiles live in a world where being a "postmodern nomad" is impossible. For these writers, free-floating transnational existence is illusory, because the exile, by definition, is grounded in a historical, political world that caused the conditions of his or her exile. What makes the case of exile literature such a poignant site for investigating the ramifications of postmodern theories of the end of the self, history, politics, etc. is that the condition of exiles in the latter part of the twentieth century may be the best practical example of a subjectivity free of boundaries. Nevertheless, these writers cannot narrate worlds that are free of outside constraints and political concerns. Their literature highlights the conflicts between practical and symbolic modes of describing the condition of exile.

In much contemporary criticism it has been argued that a binary opposition exists between, on the one hand, modern notions of being grounded in a totalizing, dogmatic view of society and, on the other hand, ludic postmodern notions of being free of rational, historical, territorial, and cultural categorizations. For certain theorists of the postmodern, modernist theory is described as a commitment to a grounded world view, while postmodern theory is unconnected to an outside reality and free of the oppressive valorizations of modernity. The work of these writers epitomizes the shortcomings of certain postmodern positions by revealing their practical failures. In the literary works that have been analyzed in this study, these writers have been unable either to float freely or to remain grounded in reason and reality. Their work, consequently, is a challenge to the supposed dichotomy between modernity and postmodernity. Instead, these writers' literature demonstrates that one cannot narrate the experience of exile without both questioning the premises upon which cultural control is based and also fighting to regain cultural control and the possibility of self-definition. The work of Juan Goytisolo, Ariel Dorfman, and Cristina Peri Rossi demonstrates the way in which these writers are caught in a bind between the binary where the modern and the postmodern intersect dialectically.

Goytisolo, Dorfman, and Peri Rossi demonstrate a self-reflexive concern for the crisis that literature faced after 1960. They also openly admit that, despite the crisis of representation, they remained committed to telling stories about the social problems of transnational capitalism, authoritarian governments, and the marginalization of the "other"—problems which were, for them, exacerbated by the condition of exile. In this way their dialectical writing challenges the dichotomy between the modern and the postmodern. Moreover, these writers' work is difficult to place within traditional literary genres because these authors found it necessary to use multiple, and often contradictory, strategies of representation within their writing. As I have argued, these multiple strategies are a result of the historical circumstances of exiled writers in the latter part of the twentieth century: these authors remain committed to challenging authoritarianism and, simultaneously, uncertain of their role in history and of the possibilities of narrating for change.

Works Cited

Ahmad, Aijaz. *In Theory: Literatures, Classes, Nations*. London: Verso, 1992.
Albó, Xavier. "Our Identity Starting from Pluralism at the Base." *Boundary 2: The Postmodernism Debate in Latin America* 20.3 (1993): 18–33.
Althusser, Louis. "Ideology and Ideological State Apparatuses (Notes Towards an Investigation)." *Lenin and Philosophy and Other Essays*. By Louis Althusser. Trans. Ben Brewster. New York: Monthly Review P, 1972. 127–86.
Alcalay, Ammiel. *After Jews and Arabs: Remaking Levantine Culture*. Minneapolis: U of Minnesota P, 1993.
Anderson, Benedict. *Imagined Communities: Reflections on the Origin and Spread of Nationalism*. New York: Verso, 1991.
Angel, Raquel. "Interview with Ariel Dorfman." *Rebeldes y domésticados: Los intelectuales frente al poder*. Buenos Aires: Ediciones el Cielo por Asalto, 1987. 123–29.
Aronna, Michael, John Beverley, and José Oviedo, eds. *The Postmodernism Debate in Latin America*. Durham: Duke UP, 1995.
Ashcroft, Bill, Gareth Griffiths, and Helen Tiffin. *The Empire Writes Back: Theory and Practice in Post-Colonial Literatures*. London: Routledge, 1989.
Aub, Max. *Jusep Torres Campalans*. Barcelona: Plaza y Janés, 1985.
Baker, Graham, dir. *Alien Nation*. 20th Century Fox, 1988.
Balibrea, Mari-Paz. *En la tierra baldía: Manuel Vázquez Montalbán y la izquierda española en la postmodernidad*. Barcelona: El Viejo Topo, 1999.
Bammer, Angelika, ed. *Displacements: Cultural Identities in Question*. Bloomington: Indiana UP, 1994.
Barea, Arturo. *La forja de un rebelde*. Vol. 1, *La forja*. Vol. 2, *La ruta*. Vol. 3, *La llama*. Buenos Aires: Losada, 1958.
Barran, José Pedro. "El nacimiento del Uruguay moderno en la segunda mitad del siglo XIX." *Red Académica uruguaya* (2002): <http://www.rau.edu.uy/uruguay/historia/Uy.hist3.htm>.
Barthes, Roland. *The Pleasure of the Text*. Trans. Richard Miller. 1973. New York: The Noonday P, 1989.
Basualdo, Ana. "Cristina Peri Rossi: Apocalipsis y paraíso." *El viejo topo* 56 (1981): 47–49.
Baudrillard, Jean. "The Year 2000 Has Already Happened." *Body Invaders: Panic Sex in America*. Ed. Arthur Kroker and Marilouise Kroker. Montreal: The New World Perspectives, 1988. 35–44.
Benveniste, Emile. *Problems in General Linguistics*. Coral Gables: U of Miami P, 1971.
Bertrand de Muñoz, Mayrse. "Fascism in the Spanish Novel." *Fascism and European Literature*. Ed. Stein Ugelvik Larsen, Beatrice Sandberg, and Ronald Speirs. Bern: Peter Lang, 1991. 215–37.

Best, Steven, and Douglas Kellner. *Postmodern Theory: Critical Interrogations.* New York: The Guilford P, 1991.
Beverley, John. *Against Literature.* Minneapolis: U of Minnesota P, 1993.
Bhabha, Homi K. *The Location of Culture.* London: Routledge, 1994.
Bhabha, Homi K. "DissemiNation." *The Location of Culture.* London: Routledge, 1994. 139–70.
Bhabha, Homi, ed. "Introduction: Narrating the Nation." *Nation and Narration.* Ed. Homi Bhabha. London: Routledge, 1990. 1–7.
Boyers, Peggy, and Juan Carlos Lertora. "Ideology, Exile, Language: An Interview with Ariel Dorfman." *Salmagundi* 82–83 (1989): 142–63.
Brennan, Timothy. "The National Longing for Form." *Nation and Narration.* Ed. Homi Bhabha. London: Routledge, 1990. 44–70.
Cabrera Infante, Guillermo. "The Invisible Exile." *Literature in Exile.* Ed. John Glad. Durham: Duke UP, 1990. 34–40.
Calderón, Fernando. "Latin American Identity and Mixed Temporalities; or, How to be Postmodern and Indian at the Same Time." *Boundary 2: The Postmodernism Debate in Latin America* 20.3 (1993): 55–64.
Callinicos, Alex. *Against Postmodernism: A Marxist Critique.* Cambridge: Polity P, 1989.
Calvino, Italo. *Invisible Cities.* Trans. William Weaver. San Diego: Harcourt, Brace & Co., 1974.
Campra, Rosalba. *América Latina: La identidad y la máscara.* Mexico: Siglo Veintiuno, 1987.
Cantar de mío Cid. 7th ed. Madrid: Espasa-Calpe, 1955.
Carr, Raymond. *Spain: 1808–1975.* 2nd ed. Oxford: Clarendon P, 1982.
Castro, Américo. *La realidad histórica de España.* 1954. Mexico: Editorial Porrua, 1962.
Caudet, Francisco, and Maryse Bertrand de Muñoz. "History and Literature in the Fascist Period in Spain: An Outline." *Fascism and European Literature.* Ed. Stein Ugelvik Larsen, Beatrice Sandberg, and Ronald Speirs. Bern: Peter Lang, 1991. 191–97.
Chacel, Rosa. *Desde el amanecer: autobiografía de mis primeros años.* Madrid: Revista de Occidente, 1972.
Chacel, Rosa. *Teresa.* 1941. Madrid: Mandadori España, 1991.
Colás, Santiago. *Postmodernity in Latin America: The Argentine Paradigm.* Durham: Duke UP, 1994.
Connor, Steven. *Postmodernist Culture: An Introduction to Theories of the Contemporary.* Oxford: Basil Blackwell, 1989.
Constable, Pamela, and Arturo Valenzuela. *A Nation of Enemies: Chile under Pinochet.* New York: Norton, 1991.
Corbatta, Jorgelina. "Metáforas del exilio e intertextualidad en *La nave de los locos* de Cristina Peri Rossi y *Novela negra con dos argentinos* de Luisa Valenzuela." *Revista Hispánica moderna* 157.1 (1994): 167–83.
Cortázar, Julio. "The Fellowship of Exile." *Review* 30 (1981): 14–16.
Cowley, Malcolm. *Exile's Return: A Literary Odyssey of the 1920s.* 1962. New York: Viking P, 1974.

Da Cunha-Giabbai, Gloria. *El exilio: realidad y ficción*. Montevideo: ARCA Editorial, 1992.
"Definitions of Dialectics." *Marxists Internet Archive* (2002): < http://www.marxists.org/reference/archive/hegel/help/sampler.htm#dialectics>.
Dejbord, Parizad Tamara. *Cristina Peri Rossi: Escritora del exilio*. Buenos Aires: Editorial Galerna, 1998.
Deleuze, Gilles, and Félix Guattari. *Anti-Oedipus*. Trans. Mark Hurley, Mark Seem, and Helen R. Lane. New York: Viking P, 1977.
Deleuze, Gilles, and Félix Guattari. *Kafka: Toward a Minor Literature*. Trans. Dona Polan. Minneapolis: U of Minnesota P, 1986.
Deleuze, Gilles, and Félix Guattari. *Nomadology: The War Machine*. Trans. Brian Massumi. New York: Semiotext(e), 1986.
Deleuze, Gilles, and Félix Guattari. *A Thousand Plateaus*. Trans. Brian Massumi. Minneapolis: U of Minnesota P, 1987.
Derrida, Jacques. "Edmond Jabès and the Writing of the Book." *Writing and Difference*. By Jacques Derrida. Trans. Alan Bass. Chicago: U of Chicago P, 1978. 64–78.
Derrida, Jacques. "Structure, Sign, and Play." *Writing and Difference*. By Jacques Derrida. Trans. Alan Bass. Chicago: U of Chicago P, 1978. 278–94.
Derrida, Jacques. *Writing and Difference*. Trans. Alan Bass. Chicago: U of Chicago P, 1978.
Doblado, Gloria. *España en tres novelas de Juan Goytisolo*. Madrid: Editorial Playor, 1988.
Dorfman, Ariel. "Adiós General." *Harper's* (Dec. 1989): 72–76.
Dorfman, Ariel. *Death and the Maiden*. Trans. Ariel Dorfman. London: Nick Hern Books, 1991.
Dorfman, Ariel. *The Empire's Old Clothes: What the Lone Ranger, Babar and other Innocent Heroes Do to Our Minds*. Trans. Clark Hansen. New York: Pantheon Books, 1983.
Dorfman, Ariel. "El fuego purificador de Augusto Pinochet." *Araucaria de Chile* 35 (1986): 15–20.
Dorfman, Ariel. *Heading South, Looking North: A Bilingual Journey*. New York: Farrar, Straus, Giroux, 1998.
Dorfman, Ariel. *Konfidenz*. Buenos Aires: Grupo Editorial Planeta, 1994.
Dorfman, Ariel. *The Last Song of Manuel Sendero*. Trans. George Shivers and Ariel Dorfman. New York: Viking, 1987.
Dorfman, Ariel. *Last Waltz in Santiago and Other Poems of Exile and Disappearance*. Trans. Edith Grossman. New York: Penguin Books, 1988
Dorfman, Ariel. *Mascara*. New York: Penguin, 1988.
Dorfman, Ariel. *Máscaras*. Buenos Aires: Editorial Sudamericana, 1988.
Dorfman, Ariel. *Moros en la costa*. Buenos Aires: Editorial Sudamericana, 1973.
Dorfman, Ariel. *Pastel de choclo*. Santiago: Editorial Sinfronteras, 1986.
Dorfman, Ariel. *Some Write to the Future: Essays on Contemporary Latin American Fiction*. Trans. George Shivers and Ariel Dorfman. Durham: Duke UP, 1991.
Dorfman, Ariel. *La última canción de Manuel Sendero*. Mexico: Siglo XXI, 1982.

Dorfman, Ariel. *Viudas*. Mexico: Siglo XXI Editores, 1981.
Dorfman, Ariel. *Widows*. Trans. Stephen Kessler. New York: Penguin Books, 1983.
Dreyfus, Hubert L., and Paul Rabinow. *Michel Foucault: Beyond Structuralism and Hermeneutics*. Chicago: U of Chicago P, 1982.
Eagleton, Terry. *The Illusions of Postmodernism*. Cambridge: Blackwell Publishers, 1997.
Ebert, Teresa L. *Ludic Feminism and After: Postmodernism, Desire, and Labor in Late Capitalism*. Ann Arbor: U of Michigan P, 1996.
Edwards, Jorge. "Discussion." *Literature in Exile*. Ed. John Glad. Durham: Duke UP, 1990. 5–7.
Eliade, Mircea. *Myth and Reality*. 1963. New York: Harper and Row, 1975.
Ellwood, Sheelagh M. *Franco*. New York: Longman, 1994.
Engels, Frederick. *Herr Eugen Dühring's Revolution in Science (Anti-Dühring)*. Trans. Emile Burns. London: Lawrence & Wishart, 1936.
Engels, Frederick. "The Science of Dialectics." *Socialism: Utopian and Scientific*. By Frederick Engels. Trans. Paul Lafargue. *Marx/Engels Selected Works*, Volume 3, Moscow: Progress Publishers, 1970. Vol. 3, 95–151. Available online at *Marx/Engels Internet Archive* (1999): <http://www.marxists.org/archive/marx/works/1880/soc-utop/ch02.htm>.
Fernandez Retamar, Roberto. *Calibán: apuntes sobre la cultura en nuestra América*. 1972. Mexico: Editorial Diógenes, 1974.
Ferrés, Antonio, and José Ortega. *Literatura española del último exilio*. New York: Gordian P, 1975.
Fitz, Earl E. *Sexuality and Being in the Poststructuralist Universe of Clarice Lispector*. Austin: U of Texas P, 2001.
Foucault, Michel. *The Birth of the Clinic: An Archaeology of Medical Perception*. Trans. A. M. Sheridan Smith. New York: Vintage Books, 1975.
Foucault, Michel. *Discipline and Punish: The Birth of the Prison*. Trans. Alan Sheridan. New York: Vintage Books, 1979.
Foucault, Michel. *The History of Sexuality*. Trans. Robert Hurley. New York: Vintage Books, 1980.
Foucault, Michel. *Madness and Civilization*. Trans. Richard Howard. New York: Vintage Books, 1973.
Foucault, Michel. *The Order of Things: An Archaeology of the Human Sciences*. New York: Vintage Books, 1973.
Franco, Francisco, and Augustin del Rio Cisneros. *Pensamiento político de Franco: Antología*. Madrid: Servicio Informativo Español, 1964.
Freud, Sigmund. *The Interpretation of Dreams*. Trans. A. A. Brill. New York: Avon, 1971.
Fuentes, Carlos. "Juan Goytisolo or the Novel of Exile." *Review of Contemporary Fiction* 4.2 (1984): 72–75.
Ganivet, Angel. *Idearium Español*. Madrid: Espasa-Calpe, 1970.
García Canclini, Néstor. *Culturas híbridas: Estrategias para entrar y salir de la modernidad*. Buenos Aires: Editorial Sudamericana, 1992.

García Canclini, Néstor. "Cultural Reconversion." *On Edge: The Crisis of Contemporary Latin American Literature.* Ed. George Yúdice, Jean Franco, and Juan Flores. Minneapolis: U of Minnesota P, 1992. 29–44.

García Canclini, Néstor. "The Hybrid: A Conversation with Margarita Zires, Raymundo Mier, and Mabel Piccini." *Boundary 2: The Postmodernism Debate in Latin America* 20.3 (1993): 77–92.

Garretón, Manuel Antonio. "Fear in Military Regimes." *Fear at the Edge: State Terror and Resistance in Latin America.* Ed. Juan E. Corradi, Patricia Weiss Fagen, and Manuel A. Garretón Merino. Berkeley: U of California P, 1992. 13–25.

Gellner, Ernest. *Nations and Nationalism.* 1983. Ithaca: Cornell UP, 1991.

Gillespie, Michael Allen. "The Question of History." *Hegel, Heidegger and the Ground of History.* Chicago: U of Chicago P, 1984. 1–23.

Giroux, Henry. "Postmodernism as Border Pedagogy: Redefining the Boundaries of Race and Ethnicity." *A Postmodern Reader.* Ed. Joseph Natoli and Linda Hutcheon. Albany: State U of New York P, 1993. 452–96.

Golano, Elena. "Soñar para seducir: Entrevista con Cristina Peri Rossi." *Quimera* 25.47 (1982): 47–50.

González, Marcial. "Jameson's 'Arrested Dialectic': From Structuralism to Postmodernism." *Cultural Logic* 2.2 (1999). <http://eserver.org/clogic/2-2/gonzalez.html>.

González Echevarría, Roberto. *Isla a su vuelo fugitiva. Ensayos críticos sobre literatura hispanoamericana.* Madrid: J. P. Turanzas, 1983.

Gould Levine, Linda. *Juan Goytisolo: La destrucción creadora.* Mexico: Joaquín Mortiz, 1976.

Germani, Gino. *Authoritarianism, Fascism, and National Populism.* New Brunswick: Transaction Books, 1978.

Godoy Urzúa, Hernán. *El carácter chileno.* Santiago de Chile: Editorial Universitaria, 1981.

Goytisolo, Juan. *Campos de Níjar.* Barcelona: Seix Barral, 1959.

Goytisolo, Juan. *Count Julian.* Trans. Helen R. Lane. New York: Viking P, 1974.

Goytisolo, Juan. *España y los españoles.* Barcelona: Editorial Lumen, 1979.

Goytisolo, Juan. *En los reinos de Taifa.* Barcelona: Seix Barral, 1986.

Goytisolo, Juan. *El furgón de cola.* Barcelona: Seix Barral, 1976.

Goytisolo, Juan. "From *Count Julián* to *Makbara:* A Possible Orientalist Reading." *Review of Contemporary Fiction* 4.2 (1984): 109–19.

Goytisolo, Juan. *Juan the Landless.* Trans. Helen R. Lane. New York: Viking P, 1977.

Goytisolo, Juan. *Obra inglesa de José María Blanco White.* Buenos Aires: Ed. Fomentor, 1972.

Goytisolo, Juan. *Juan sin tierra.* Barcelona: Editorial Seix Barral, 1975.

Goytisolo, Juan. *Libertad, libertad, libertad.* Barcelona: Editorial Anagrama, 1978.

Goytisolo, Juan. *Marks of Identity.* Trans. José Rabassa. London: Serpent's Tail, 1988.

Goytisolo, Juan. *Para vivir aquí.* Buenos Aires: Sur, 1960.

Goytisolo, Juan. *Pueblo en marcha. Obras completas.* By Juan Goytisolo. *Relatos y ensayos.* Madrid: Aguilar, 1977. Vol. 2, 717–803.

Goytisolo, Juan. *Realms of Strife: The Memoirs of Juan Goytisolo, 1957–1982*. Trans. Peter Bush. San Francisco: North Point P, 1990.
Goytisolo, Juan. *Reivindicación del conde don Julián*. Mexico: J. Mortiz, 1970.
Goytisolo, Juan. *Señas de identidad*. Mexico: J. Mortiz, 1966.
Graham-Yooll, Andrew. "The Wild Oats They Sowed: Latin American Exiles in Europe." *Third World Quarterly* 9.1 (1987): 246–53.
Griffith, Roger. *The Nature of Fascism*. New York: St. Martin's, 1991.
Grinberg, Leon, and Rebeca Grinberg. *Psychoanalytic Perspectives on Migration and Exile*. Trans. Nancy Festinger. New Haven: Yale UP, 1989.
Guerra Cunningham, Lucía. "La referencialidad como negación del paraíso: Exilio y excentrismo en *La nave de los locos* de Cristina Peri Rossi." *Revista de Estudios Hispánicos* 23.2 (1989): 63–74.
Guillén, Claudio. *Múltiples moradas: Ensayo de literatura comparada*. Barcelona: Tusquets Editores, 1998.
Guillén, Claudio. "On the Literature of Exile and Counter Exile." *Books Abroad* 50 (1976): 271–80.
Guillén, Claudio. "El sol de los desterrados: literatura y exilio." *Múltiples moradas: Ensayo de literature comparada*. By Claudio Guillén. Barcelona: Tusquets Editores, 1998. 29–97.
Gurr, Andrew. *Writers in Exile: The Identity of Home in Modern Literature*. Brighton: Harvester P, 1981.
Hardt, Michael, and Antonio Negri. *Empire*. Cambridge: Harvard UP, 2000.
Harvey, David. *The Condition of Postmodernity: An Enquiry into the Origins of Cultural Change*. Cambridge: Basil Blackwell, 1989.
Hegel, G. W. F. *The Logic*. Trans. William Wallace. London: Clarendon, 1975. Available online at *Marx/Engels Internet Archive* (1999): <http://www.marxists.org/reference/archive/hegel/works/sl/slappear.htm>.
Hegel, G. W. F. *Hegel's Science of Logic*. Trans. A. V. Miller. Atlantic Highlands: Humanities Press International, 1989.
Heller, Agnes. "Existentialism, Alienation, Postmodernism: Cultural Movements as Vehicles of Changes in the Patterns of Everyday Life." *A Postmodern Reader*. Ed. Joseph Natoli and Linda Hutcheon. Albany: State U of New York P, 1993. 497–509.
Hicks, D. Emily. *Border Writing: The Multidimensional Text*. Minneapolis: U of Minnesota P, 1991.
Hobsbawm, E. J. *Nations and Nationalism since 1780: Programme, Myth, Reality*. New York: Cambridge UP, 1990.
hooks, bell. "Postmodern Blackness." *A Postmodern Reader*. Ed. Joseph Natoli and Linda Hutcheon. Albany: State U of New York P, 1993. 510–18.
Hopenhayn, Martín. "Postmodernism and Neoliberalism." *Boundary 2: The Postmodernism Debate in Latin America*. 20.3 (1993): 93–109.
Howard, John. *Writing from the Left: New Critical Analysis and Interpretation of the Works of Ariel Dorfman*. B.A. Research Essay. Fayetteville: U of Arkansas, Department of Spanish, 1993.
Hutcheon, Linda. *A Poetics of Postmodernism: History, Theory, Fiction*. New York: Routledge, 1988.

Hutcheon, Linda. *The Politics of Postmodernism*. New York: Routledge, 1989.
Ilie, Paul. "Exolalia and Dictatorship: The Tongues of Hispanic Exile." *Fascismo y experiencia literaria: Reflexiones para una recanonización*. Ed. Hernán Vidal. Minneapolis: Institute for the Study of Ideologies and Literature, U of Minnesota, 1985. 222–54.
Ilie, Paul. *Literature and Inner Exile*. Baltimore: Johns Hopkins UP, 1980.
Incledon, John. "Liberating the Reader: A Conversation with Ariel Dorfman." *Chasqui: Revista de literatura latinoamericana*. 20. (1991): 95–107.
Invernizzi, Lucía. "Entre el tapiz de la expulsión del paraíso y el tapiz de la creación: Múltiples sentidos del viaje a bordo de *La nave de los locos* de Cristina Peri Rossi." *Revista Chilena de Literatura* 30 (1987): 29–53.
Jameson, Fredric. *Postmodernism; or, The Cultural Logic of Late Capitalism*. Durham: Duke UP 1991.
Jameson, Fredric. "On 'Cultural Studies'." *Social Text* 34 (1993): 17–52.
Jameson, Fredric. *The Political Unconscious: Narrative as a Socially Symbolic Act*. Ithaca: Cornell UP, 1981.
Jameson, Fredric. *The Seeds of Time*. New York: Columbia UP, 1994.
Jameson, Fredric. "Third World Literature in the Era of Multinational Capitalism." *Social Text* 15 (1986): 65–88.
Kaminsky, Amy K. *After Exile: Writing the Latin American Diaspora*. Minneapolis: U of Minnesota P, 1999.
Kaminsky, Amy K. *Reading the Body Politic: Feminist Criticism and Latin American Women Writers*. Minneapolis: U of Minnesota P, 1993.
Kantaris, Elia. "The Politics of Desire: Alienation and Identity in the Work of Marta Traba and Cristina Peri Rossi." *Forum for Modern Language Studies* 25.3 (1989): 248–64.
Kristeva, Julia. "About Chinese Women." *The Kristeva Reader*. Ed. Toril Moi. New York: Columbia UP, 1986. 138–59.
Kristeva, Julia. "Women's Time." *The Kristeva Reader*. Ed. Toril Moi. New York: Columbia UP, 1986. 187–213.
Labanyi, Jo. *Myth and History in the Contemporary Spanish Novel*. Cambridge: Cambridge UP, 1989.
Labanyi, Jo. "Postmodernism and the Problem of Cultural Identity." *Spanish Cultural Studies: An Introduction*. Ed. Helen Graham and Jo Labanyi. New York: Oxford UP, 1995. 396–406.
Lacan, Jacques. *Ecrits*. Alan Sheridan. New York: Norton, 1977.
Larsen, Neil. Foreword in D. Emily Hicks, *Border Writing: The Multidimensional Text*. Minneapolis: U of Minnesota P, 1991. xi–xxi.
Larsen, Neil. *Determinations: Essays on Theory, Narrative, and Nation in the Americas*. London: Verso, 2001.
Larsen, Neil. *Reading North by South: On Latin American Literature, Culture, and Politics*. Minneapolis: U of Minnesota P, 1995.
Lázaro, Jesús. *La novelística de Juan Goytisolo*. Madrid: Alhambra, 1984.
Lee Six, Abigail. *Juan Goytisolo: The Case for Chaos*. New Haven: Yale UP, 1990.
Lenin, Vladimir Il'ich. *Collected Works*. 4th enlarged ed. Moscow: Progress Publishers, 1977.

Lerin, François, and Cristina Torres. *Historia política de la dictadura uruguaya (1973–1980)*. Montevideo: Ediciones del Nuevo Mundo, 1987.
Lindstrom, Naomi. *The Social Conscience of Latin American Writing*. Austin: U of Texas P, 1998.
Lyotard, Jean François. *The Postmodern Condition: A Report on Knowledge*. Trans. Geoff Bennington and Brian Massumi. Minneapolis: U of Minnesota P, 1984.
Mantarás Loedel, Graciela. "Historia contemporánea de la literatura uruguaya: Cristina Peri Rossi." Unpublished Manuscript.
Martí, Jose. *Nuestra América*. Barcelona: Editorial Ariel, 1970. Available online at *BitBiblioteca*: <http://www.analitica.com/bitblioteca/jmarti/nuestra_america.asp>.
Marx, Karl. *Capital*. Trans. Samuel Moore and Edward Aveling. Moscow: Progress Publishers, 1965.
Marx, Karl. *Grundrisse*. Trans. Martin Liclaus. Baltimore: Penguin Books, 1973.
Marx, Karl. "Economic and Philosophic Manuscripts of 1844." *The Marx-Engels Reader*. Ed. Robert C. Tucker. 2nd ed. New York: Norton, 1978. 70–93.
Massey, Doreen. "A Place Called Home." *New Formations* 17 (1992): 3–15.
McClennen, Sophia A. "Comparative Literature and Latin American Studies: From Disarticulation to Dialogue." *Comparative Cultural Studies and Latin America*. Ed. Sophia A. McClennen and Earl E. Fitz. Thematic Issue of *CLCWeb: Comparative Literature and Culture: A WWWeb Journal* 4.2 (2002): <http://clcwebjournal.lib.purdue.edu/clcweb02-2/mcclennen02.html>.
McClennen, Sophia A. "A Critical Overview of Ariel Dorfman." *The Review of Contemporary Fiction* 21.3 (2000): 81–132.
Mirkovic, Damir, and Arthur Kent Davis. *Dialectic and Sociological Thought*. St. Catharine's: Dilton Publications, 1980.
Moeller, Hans-Bernhard, ed. *Latin America and the Literature of Exile: A Comparative View of the 20th Century Refugee Writers in the New World*. Heidelberg: Carl Winter, 1983.
Moi, Toril, ed., and Julia Kristeva. *The Kristeva Reader*. New York: Columbia UP, 1986. 1–22.
Moi, Toril. *Sexual/Textual Politics: Feminist Literary Theory*. London: Methuen, 1985.
Mora, Gabriela. "Peri Rossi: *La nave de los locos* y la búsqueda de la armonía." *Nuevo Texto Crítico* 2 (1988): 343–52.
Moraña, Mabel. "*La nave de los locos* de Cristina Peri Rossi." *Texto Crítico* 12.34–35 (1986): 204–13.
Nelson, Alice. *The Body Politic: Gender and the Struggle for Narrative Power in Chilean Literature of the Pinochet Years*. Diss. Durham: Romance Studies, Duke University, 1994.
Olivera-Williams, Maria Rosa. "*La nave de los locos* de Cristina Peri Rossi." *Revista de crítica literaria latinoamericana* 11.23 (1986): 81–89.
Ortega, Julio. "An Interview with Juan Goytisolo." *Review of Contemporary Fiction* 4.2 (1984): 4–19.
Ortega, Julio. "Towards a Map of the Current Critical Debate about Latin American Cultural Studies." *Comparative Cultural Studies and Latin America*. Ed. Sophia A. McClennen and Earl E. Fitz. Thematic Issue of *CLCWeb: Comparative Lit-*

erature and Culture: A WWWeb Journal 4.2 (2002): <http://clcwebjournal.lib.purdue.edu/clcweb02-2/ortega02.html>.

Oropesa, Salvador. *La obra de Ariel Dorfman: Ficción y crítica.* Madrid: Editorial Pliegos, 1992.

Ortiz, Fernando. *Contrapunteo cubano del tabaco y azúcar.* Caracas: Biblioteca Ayacucho, 1987.

Ortiz, Fernando. *Cuban Counterpoint, Tobacco and Sugar.* Trans. Harriet de Onís. Durham: Duke UP, 1995.

Ovid. *Metamorphoses.* Trans. Arthur Golding. London: Penguin, 1967.

Peri Rossi, Cristina. "A los amigos que me recomiendan viajes." *Europa después de la lluvia.* Madrid: Fundación Banco Exterior de España, 1987. 96–97.

Peri Rossi, Cristina. "Aeropuertos." *El museo de esfuerzos inútiles.* Madrid: Seix Barral, 1983. 103–07.

Peri Rossi, Cristina. "Las avenidas de la lengua." *El museo de los esfuerzos inútiles.* Madrid: Seix Barral, 1983. 92–95.

Peri Rossi, Cristina. "La ciudad." *El museo de los esfuerzos inútiles.* Madrid: Seix Barral, 1983. 160–77.

Peri Rossi, Cristina. *Descripción de un naufragio.* Barcelona: Editorial Lumen, 1975.

Peri Rossi, Cristina. "Diálogo de exiliados." *Europa después de la lluvia.* Madrid: Fundación Banco Exterior de España, 1987. 42–44.

Peri Rossi, Cristina. "En la playa." *La tarde del dinosaurio.* Barcelona: Plaza y Janés, 1980. 27–42.

Peri Rossi, Cristina. *Europa después de la lluvia.* Madrid: Fundación Banco Exterior de España, 1987.

Peri Rossi, Cristina. "An Exercise in Return—Thirteen Years Later." *Another Chicago Magazine* 18 (1988): 222–25.

Peri Rossi, Cristina. "Génesis de *Europa después de la lluvia.*" *Studi di letteratura ispano-americano* 13–14 (1988): 63–78.

Peri Rossi, Cristina. *Indicios pánicos.* Montevideo: Nuestra América, 1970.

Peri Rossi, Cristina. "La influencia de Edgar Allen Poe en la poesía de Raimundo Arias." *La tarde del dinosaurio.* Barcelona: Plaza y Janés, 1980. 43–60.

Peri Rossi, Cristina. *Lingüística General.* Valencia: Editorial Promoteo, 1979.

Peri Rossi, Cristina. *El museo de los esfuerzos inútiles.* Barcelona: Seix Barral, 1983.

Peri Rossi, Cristina. *The Museum of Useless Efforts.* Trans. Tobias Hecht. Lincoln: U of Nebraska P, 2001.

Peri Rossi, Cristina. "Naufragio." *Europa después de la lluvia.* Madrid: Fundación Banco Exterior de España, 1987. 37.

Peri Rossi, Cristina. *La nave de los locos.* Barcelona: Seix Barral, 1984.

Peri Rossi, Cristina. *Panic Signs.* Trans. Mercedes Rowinsky-Geurts and Angelo A Borrás. Waterloo: Wilfrid Laurier UP, 2002

Peri Rossi, Cristina. "Relación de tripulantes que participaron en el naufragio." *Descripción de un naufragio.* Barcelona: Lumen, 1975. 96 99.

Peri Rossi, Cristina. *The Ship of Fools.* Trans. Psiche Hughes. Columbia: Reader's International, 2000.

Peri Rossi, Cristina. *Solitario de amor*. Barcelona: Grijalbo, 1988.
Peri Rossi, Cristina. "La tarde del dinosaurio." *La tarde del dinosaurio*. Barcelona: Plaza y Janés, 1980. 81–112.
Peri Rossi, Cristina. *La tarde del dinosaurio*. Barcelona: Plaza y Janés, 1985.
Peri Rossi, Cristina. "El tiempo." *Europa después de la lluvia*. Madrid: Fundación Banco Exterior de España, 1987. 17.
Pfaff, William. *The Wrath of Nations: Civilization and the Furies of Nationalism*. New York: Simon & Schuster, 1993.
Pinochet Ugarte, Augusto. *Camino Recorrido: Memorias de un soldado, Tomo II*. Santiago: Zig-Zag, 1991.
Poem of the Cid: A Modern Translation with Notes. Trans. Paul Blackburn and George Economou. Norman: U of Oklahoma P, 1998.
Pope, Randolph D. *Understanding Juan Goytisolo*. Columbia: U of South Carolina P, 1995.
Pope, Randolph D. "Writing after the Battle: Juan Goytisolo's Renewal." *Literature, the Arts and Democracy*. Ed. Samuel Amell. Cranbury: Associated UP, 1990. 58–66.
Pratt, Mary Louise. *Imperial Eyes: Travel Writing and Transculturation*. London: Routledge, 1992.
Rama, Angel. "Founding the Latin American Literary Community." *Review* 30 (1981): 8–13.
Rama, Angel. *Transculturación narrativa en América Latina*. Montevideo: Fundación Angel Rama, 1989.
Ramos, Julio. *Desencuentros de la modernidad en América Latina*. Mexico: Fondo de Cultura Económica, 1989.
Renan, Ernest. "What Is a Nation?" (1882). *Becoming National: A Reader*. Ed. Geoff Eley and Ronald Grigor Suny. New York: Oxford UP, 1996. 41–55.
Rial, Juan. "The Social Imaginary: Utopian Political Myths in Uruguay (Change and Permanence during and after the Dictatorship)." *Repression, Exile, and Democracy: Uruguayan Culture*. Ed. Saúl Sosnowski and Louise B. Popkin. Durham: Duke UP, 1990. 59–82.
Richard, Nelly. *Masculino/Femenino: Prácticas de la diferencia y cultura democrática*. Santiago: Francisco Zegers Editor, 1993.
Rodó, Jose Enrique. *Ariel y Motivos de Proteo*. Ed. Carlos Real de Azúa and Angel Rama. Caracas: Biblioteca Ayacucho, 1983.
Rowe, William, and Teresa Whtifield. "Thresholds of Identity: Literature and Exile in Latin America." *Third World Quarterly* 9.1 (1987): 229–45.
Said, Edward. *Orientalism*. New York: Vintage Books, 1978.
Said, Edward. "Reflections on Exile." *Out There: Marginalization and Contemporary Cultures*. Ed. Russell Ferguson, Martha Gever, Trinh T. Minh-ha, and Cornel West. Cambridge: MIT P, 1990. 357–66.
Saldívar, José David. *The Dialectics of Our America: Genealogy, Cultural Critique, and Literary History*. Durham: Duke UP, 1991.
Sanz, Santos. *Lectura de Juan Goytisolo*. Barcelona: V. Pozanco, 1977.
Sarduy, Severo. "Deterritorialization." *Review of Contemporary Fiction* 4.2 (1984): 104–08.

Schaefer-Rodríguez, Claudia. *Juan Goytisolo: del "Realismo Crítico" a la utopía*. Madrid: J. Porrúa Turanzas, 1984.

Schmidt, Cynthia A. "A Satiric Perspective on the Experience of Exile in the Short Fiction of Cristina Peri Rossi." *The Americas Review* 18.3–4 (1990): 218–26.

Schwartz, Kessel. *Studies on Twentieth Century Spanish and Spanish-American Literature*. Lanham: UP of America, 1983.

Seidel, Michael. *Exile and the Narrative Imagination*. New Haven: Yale UP, 1986.

Sender, Ramón. *Crónica del alba*. Barcelona: Destino, 1977.

Shaw, Donald L. *The Post-Boom in Latin American Fiction*. Albany: State U of New York P, 1998.

Sieburth, Stephanie Anne. *Inventing High and Low*. Durham: Duke UP, 1994.

Smith, Paul Julian. *Laws of Desire: Questions of Homosexuality in Spanish Writing and Film 1960–1990*. Oxford: Clarendon P, 1992.

Sosnowski, Saúl, and Louise B. Popkin. "As Seen from Another Shore: Uruguayan Culture." *Repression, Exile, and Democracy: Uruguayan Culture*. Ed. Saul Sosnowski and Louise B. Popkin. Durham: Duke UP, 1993. 1–16.

Sosnowski, Saúl, and Louise B. Popkin, eds. *Repression, Exile, and Democracy: Uruguayan Culture*. Durham: Duke UP, 1993.

Tabori, Paul. *The Anatomy of Exile*. London: Harrap, 1972.

Theweleit, Klaus. *Male Fantasies*. Minneapolis: U of Minnesota P, 1987.

Tötösy de Zepetnek, Steven. "From Comparative Literature Today toward Comparative Cultural Studies." *Comparative Literature and Comparative Cultural Studies*. Ed. Steven Tötösy de Zepetnek. West Lafayette: Purdue UP, 2003. 235–67.

Tötösy de Zepetnek, Steven. "From Comparative Literature Today toward Comparative Cultural Studies." *CLCWeb: Comparative Literature and Culture: A WWWeb Journal* 1.3 (1999): <http://clcwebjournal.lib.purdue.edu/clcweb99-3/totosy99.html>.

Tötösy de Zepetnek, Steven. *Comparative Literature: Theory, Method, Application*. Amsterdam: Rodopi, 1998.

Traba, Marta. *Conversación al sur*. Mexico: Siglo XXI Editores, 1996.

Turner, Victor Witter. *The Ritual Process: Structure and Anti-Structure*. Chicago: Aldine Pub. Co., 1969.

Ugarte, Michael. *Shifting Ground: Spanish Civil War Exile Literature*. Durham: Duke UP, 1989.

Ugarte, Michael. *Trilogy of Treason: An Intertextual Study of Juan Goytisolo*. Columbia: U of Missouri P, 1982.

Uslar Pietri, Arturo. "¿Existe la América Latina?: Una reflexión en dos tiempos." *Perfiles de América Latina: Ocho visiones venezolanas*. Ed. Arturo Uslar Pietri et al. Caracas: Monte Avila, 1992.

Veciana, Cira. *Censorship and the Maintenance of Power in Dictatorships: A Comparison of the Franco and Castro Regimes*. Undergraduate Thesis. Durham: Comparative Area Studies, Duke University, 1995.

Verani, Hugo J. "La Historia como metáfora: *La nave de los locos* de Cristina Peri Rossi." *La Torre: Revista general de la Universidad de Puerto Rico* 13 (1990): 79–92.

Vidal, Hernán. *Cultura nacional chilena, crítica literaria, y derechos humanos.* Minneapolis: Institute for the Study of Ideologies & Literatures, 1989.
Weinstein, Martin. *Uruguay: Democracy at the Crossroads.* Boulder: Westview P, 1988.
Weiss Fagen, Patricia. "Repression and State Security." *Fear at the Edge: State Terror and Resistance in Latin America.* Ed. Juan E. Corradi, Patricia Weiss Fagen, and Manuel A. Garretón Merino. Berkeley: U of California P, 1992. 26–35.
Williams, Raymond L. *The Postmodern Novel in Latin America: Politics, Culture, and the Crisis of Truth.* New York: St. Martin's P, 1995.
Wisenberg, S. L. "Ariel Dorfman: A Conversation." *Another Chicago Magazine* 18 (1988): 196–210.
Yañez, Rubén. "The Repression of Uruguayan Culture: A Response to the People's Response to Crisis." *Repression, Exile, and Democracy: Uruguayan Culture.* Ed. Saul Sosnowski and Louise B. Popkin. Durham: Duke UP, 1993. 133–46.
Yúdice, George. "Postmodernity and Transnational Capitalism in Latin America." *On Edge: The Crisis of Contemporary Latin American Literature.* Ed. George Yúdice, Jean Franco, and Juan Flores. Minneapolis: U of Minnesota P, 1992. 1–28.
Zavarzadeh, Mas'ud. *Seeing Films Politically.* Albany: State U of New York P, 1991.
Zeitz, Eileen. "Cristina Peri Rossi: El desafío de la alegoría" (Interview.) *Chasqui* 9.1 (1979): 79–101.
Žižek, Slavoj. *The Sublime Object of Ideology.* London: Verso, 1989.

Index

alienation, 37–40, 47, 51, 58, 70, 85, 98–99, 107, 113–14, 118, 144, 149, 162, 174, 180–81, 183–85, 187, 193, 202
Allende, Salvador, 9, 11–12, 23, 41, 66, 81, 93–95, 97–98, 115, 136, 176, 178–80, 198, 212
Anderson, Benedict, 3, 22–23, 79
Armand, Octavio, 119
assimilation, 26, 28, 173–74, 198, 204, 210, 216–18
authoritarianism, 2, 4, 12–13, 21, 35, 37, 55–56, 69–70, 72, 74, 81–82, 92, 101–03, 105, 109, 112, 114, 116–17, 121, 130–32, 148, 150, 152, 157, 169–70, 176–77, 190, 196, 201, 224

Bammer, Angelika, 1, 3, 20, 122
Barthes, Roland, 83, 136, 145
Baudrillard, Jean, 72–73
Benveniste, Emile, 119, 148
Best, Steven, and Douglas Kellner, 17, 19, 39, 47–48, 72–73, 112, 131, 165
Beverley, John, 115
Bhabha, Homi, 1, 27, 36, 46, 51–53, 165, 213, 221
Blanco White, José María, 209
boom literature, 14, 43–44, 117, 125, 152
Bordaberry, Juan María, 81
borders, 191

Cabrera Infante, Guillermo, 16–17, 121
Callinicos, Alex, 18
Castro, Américo, 89
colonialism, 5–6
colonization, 7, 213
Companys, Luis, 77
Cortázar, Julio, 15, 43, 67, 125, 128, 161, 191
Cuban Revolution, 9, 44, 169
cultural essentialism, 21, 28, 204–07, 214
cultural identity, 1–5, 8, 14, 21–29, 35–37, 42–43, 45, 51, 53–54, 97–98, 113, 116–17, 160, 164–68, 170–71, 191, 194, 197, 199–202, 204–05, 207–10, 212–19, 220–23
cultural nationalism, 42
definition, 21–24

Deleuze, Gilles, and Félix Guattari, 1, 16, 40, 48, 53, 88, 112, 151, 165, 213
Derrida, Jacques, 1, 17, 25, 49, 52–53, 73, 131, 135–36, 157–58, 202, 213, 218, 221
destiempo, 58, 60, 61–64, 91
deterritorialization, 48, 54, 167, 205
dialectics of exile, 3, 5, 28–35, 37, 56, 58
diaspora, 1, 6, 15, 124, 127
dissimilation, 204, 210, 216–18, 221
Dorfman, Ariel
  circumstances of exile, 11–12
  connections to Europe and Latin America, 7–8
  Empire's Old Clothes, The, 127, 215
  Heading South, Looking North, 7, 11
  How to Read Donald Duck, 11
  Konfidenz, 68
  Last Song of Manuel Sendero, The, 12, 44, 61, 67–68, 93–98, 100, 103, 109, 114, 123, 127, 129, 132, 135, 137, 146–48, 153, 155, 157–58, 164, 166, 180–81, 192, 195–96, 211, 212, 214, 215
  Máscaras, 12, 68, 148, 153, 155, 180–81, 199–200, 211, 213, 215
  Moros en la costa, 38, 81
  muerte y la doncella, La, 128
  Pastel de choclo, 12, 53
  Some Write to the Future, 126
  treatment of cultural identity, 210–16, 221
  treatment of fascism, 80
  treatment of language, 119–20, 122–23, 126–29, 132–38, 146–48, 152–55, 158–59, 160
  treatment of nationalism, 41, 54–57
  treatment of sexuality, 195–96

237

treatment of space, 164–67, 175–83
treatment of time, 60–61, 66–68, 71, 92–100, 113–18
treatment of utopia and dystopia, 198, 200–01
Viudas, 12, 40, 45, 60, 61, 66, 108, 122, 127, 132, 134, 135, 147, 148, 152, 155, 176, 177, 180, 210, 212

Edwards, Jorge, 125
Eliade, Mircea, 72, 83
Engels, Frederick, 30, 31
Epps, Bradley, 55, 86
exile and sexuality, 68–70
definition, 14–17

fascism, 9, 74–75, 79–81, 101
Fernández Retamar, Roberto, 22, 43, 152
Fitz, Earl E., 18
Foucault, Michel, 4, 88, 95, 103, 109, 111–12, 131, 145, 196, 202
Franco, Francisco, 4, 9, 14, 18, 22, 44, 68, 76–77, 79, 81, 83–84, 86–87, 91–92, 94, 100, 126, 138, 151, 169, 170, 209
Fuentes, Carlos, 128

García Canclini, Nestor, 113, 115–16
Garretón, Manuel Antonio, 80
Gellner, Ernest, 20, 21
globalization, 1–3, 36–37, 167, 201, 212
Goytisolo, Juan
  circumstances of exile, 10–11
  connections to Europe and Latin America, 6–7
  En los reinos de Taifa, 10, 68
  España y los españoles, 76–77, 84, 87, 90, 126
  furgón de cola, El, 128
  Juan sin tierra, 11, 49, 60, 63, 65–69, 76, 114, 130, 138–39, 148, 151, 155, 157–58, 160, 164, 167, 170–74, 194, 198–200, 207–09, 215
  Para vivir aquí, 11, 38
  Reivindicación del conde don Julián, 11, 49, 54, 60, 69, 76, 83,
  85–87, 89, 91, 109, 128, 138, 139, 146, 148, 151, 154–55, 157–58, 166–71, 173–74, 192, 199, 206–08
  Señas de identidad, 11, 45, 59, 63, 65, 75–77, 85, 90, 115, 123, 138–39, 148–49, 151, 154, 166–68, 170, 171, 173–74, 192, 195, 197, 207–08
  treatment of cultural identity, 205–10, 221
  treatment of language, 119–20, 122–23, 126–28, 138–41, 146, 148–49, 150–52, 154, 157–60
  treatment of national myths, 75–79, 83–92
  treatment of nationalism, 44–46, 54–57
  treatment of sexuality, 68–69, 171, 194
  treatment of space, 164–75
  treatment of time, 59–60, 63, 65–66, 71, 83–92, 113–18
  treatment of utopia and dystopia, 197–98, 199–200
Guillén, Claudio, 2, 5, 16, 31–32, 48, 58–59, 120
Gurr, Andrew, 121

Hardt, Michael, and Antonio Negri, 3, 24–25
Harvey, David, 17–18, 184, 196–97, 201–202
Hegel, G.W.F., 30, 34
Heraclitus, 29, 106
Hobsbawn, Eric, 36
hooks, bell, 150

identity politics, 28, 159, 202, 204–05, 221
Ilie, Paul, 37–38, 45, 50, 53, 59, 122, 124, 128, 141
Invernizzi, Lucía, 111

Jameson, Fredric, 17, 24, 51, 57, 63–64, 73, 117, 187, 197, 202

Kaminsky, Amy, 1, 6, 15, 17, 33, 52, 58, 64, 70
Kantaris, Elia, 104, 112–13, 115, 144, 146, 199
Kristeva, Julia, 64, 71–72, 114, 121, 132, 150, 157

Index

Labanyi, Jo, 18–20, 72, 75, 83–84, 86, 117, 169
Lacan, Jacques, 109, 131, 143
Larsen, Neil, 19, 22, 25, 27, 48, 51–52

marginalization, 2, 14, 29, 103, 199, 205, 219, 224
Martí, José, 22–23, 36, 40, 43
Marx, Karl, 30, 38
Massey, Doreen, 164, 167
modernism, 11, 18, 24, 39, 41, 43, 92, 94, 108, 113, 196
Moraña, Mabel, 103, 111, 129
multiculturalism, 26, 28, 84, 85, 204–05, 221

national identity, 1, 8, 21, 23, 25, 28, 36, 43–44, 46, 49, 50–53, 66, 74, 76, 80, 90, 94, 170, 172, 176, 183, 186, 206, 209, 212, 217, 221
nationalism, 1–2, 4, 21–25, 28, 30–31, 35–37, 40–42, 44–46, 53, 55–57, 71, 75–78, 95, 113, 164–66, 175, 186, 189, 190, 201–02, 217, 221
  definition, 20–21
Neruda, Pablo, 125
nomad, 40, 48, 53

O'Higgins, Bernardo, 79, 92
Ortega, Julio, 6, 117
Ortiz, Fernando, 26, 43, 125
Ovid, 2, 31, 34, 174

Peri Rossi, Cristina
  circumstances of exile, 12–13
  connections to Europe and Latin America, 8
  Descripción de un naufragio, 13, 54, 56, 156
  Europa después de la lluvia, 13, 50, 62, 129, 184
  Indicios pánicos, 12, 38, 81, 142, 146
  Lingüística General, 13, 70, 120
  museo de los esfuerzos inútiles, El, 13, 124, 166, 184, 217
  nave de los locos, La, 13, 63, 65, 69, 70, 82, 101–03, 108, 111, 114, 120, 127, 129, 130, 144, 149, 155, 157, 159, 161, 164, 183, 186, 188, 193, 194–95, 198, 216–17, 219, 220
  Solitario de amor, 109, 143
  tarde del dinosaurio, La, 13, 45, 61–62, 123, 131, 142–44
  treatment of cultural identity, 216–21
  treatment of fascism, 80–82
  treatment of language, 119–27, 129–30, 142–46, 149–50, 153–61
  treatment of nationalism, 42–46, 54–57
  treatment of sexuality, 68–69, 186, 194–95
  treatment of space, 164–67, 183–90
  treatment of time, 61–63, 68–71, 100–118
  treatment of utopia and dystopia, 198–99, 201
Pinochet, Augusto, 4, 8, 9, 61, 66, 74, 78–81, 92–98, 100, 135–36, 175–76, 212
Pope, Randolph, 7, 10, 18–19, 50
post-boom literature, 14, 44, 117, 126
postcolonialism, 5–7, 27, 51, 53, 152
postmodernism, 4, 13, 38, 40–41, 46–47, 50–51, 58, 64, 71–74, 83–84, 88–89, 91–92, 94–97, 100, 108–10, 113, 116–17, 120, 130–31, 143, 152, 157, 165, 184–85, 187, 190–91, 196, 202, 210, 213–14, 221–24
  definition, 17–20
poststructuralism, 120–21, 126, 131, 159
  definition, 17–20

Rama, Angel, 26, 43, 125, 127, 152
Ramos, Julio, 116

Said, Edward, 1, 33, 53, 122, 138, 164–65, 197
Sarduy, Severo, 128
Seidel, Michael, 2, 23, 33, 40, 174
Sieburth, Stephanie, 69, 116
Smith, Paul Julian, 69, 194
Spanish Civil War, 9–10, 14, 45, 77, 115, 150

Tabori, Paul, 58–59, 65–66, 71
Theweleit, Klaus, 192–93

Tötösy de Zepetnek, Steven, 28
transculturation, 125–26, 202
  definition, 26–27
transnationalism, 2, 8, 25–27, 31, 35–37, 41–42, 50–51, 57, 71, 94–97, 113, 164–66, 167, 172–73, 186, 196–97, 199, 201–02, 206, 211, 217, 219, 220–21, 223, 224
  definition, 24–26
Turner, Victor, 191

Ugarte, Michael, 30, 45, 49, 76, 83, 151, 167, 173, 174
utopia and sexuality/reproduction, 191–96

Verani, Hugo J., 107
Vidal, Hernán, 79, 175

Yúdice, George, 117

Zavarzadeh, Masu'd, 143
Žižek, Slavoj, 44, 143, 161

Index